MW01031146

EDGES OF SCIENCE

Thom Powell

Willamette City Press, LLC

Edges of Science

Cover design by Guy Edwards, Brainjar Media. www.brainjarmedia.com
Artwork by Alicia Bateman
Copy Editing by Molly Hart Lebherz and Jack Powell

Published by Willamette City Press, LLC. www.willamettecitypress.com

for Jane

Contents

Introduction: The Big Tent

This book is about the *edges* of science, those enigmatic mysteries that cannot be unequivocally proven, but really do happen. These topics fall into the category of 'paranormal.' They defy scientific understanding; that is, they are outside the boundaries of science.

However, the strict rules of science can and do change. Historically, at least a few topics that were once dismissed as 'paranormal' were eventually invited into The Big Tent of mainstream science. Astrophysics, for example, was the original paranormal pseudo-science. As recently as the mid-1800's astrophysics, then known as astronomy, was said to be utterly unverifiable, owing to the inaccessibility of the phenomena being studied. Without doubt, that thinking has changed. Astrophysics is now seen as one of the purest of the 'hard sciences.'

More recently, psychology and sociology were dismissed as 'soft sciences.' Reductionist thinkers in 'The Big Tent' dismissed these unverifiable areas of study as pseudo-science. With the explosion of applied statistics, psychological and sociological experiments could finally be verified. Reductionist thinking was replaced with *holism*, also known as 'emergent' thinking. Equipped with the new shield of holistic thinking and statistical analysis, the social sciences muscled their way into 'The Big Tent.'

The topics that are now excluded from 'The Big Tent' are the ones that are still stigmatized with the scarlet letter 'P' for paranormal: Mima mounds, alien abductions, crop circles, vanished peoples, worm holes and portals, UFOs, and of course, bigfoot. Without doubt, these topics baffle all attempts to reduce them to physical and mathematical definition. Yet, as with astronomy and psychology, this will someday change. It has to. Within the realm of the paranormal exists some enormously unanswered questions that people really want answered.

Even while public interest in these topics is steadily increasing, acknowledging the reality of paranormal events is still taboo for the mainstream scientist. This conflict creates the oxymoron of 'paranormal science.' It may be impossible to scientifically investigate paranormal events, but that does not mean paranormal events cannot or should not be scientifically investigated.

Science vs. Intel

Paranormal events occur too randomly to study, even in places where they are known to occur. Scientific investigation, on the other hand, requires not only a controlled experiment, but one that can be replicated by other scientists in similarly controlled circumstances. Thus, scientific investigation of paranormal phenomena is almost a contradiction. To the mainstream scientist, 'paranormal' is anti-science.

If paranormal events cannot be scientifically verified, how *can* paranormal mysteries be better understood? The answer is a process that is a lot closer to intelligence-gathering than science, so we might look to the CIA for an answer. As it turns out, CIA doesn't really do science most of the time, but the information they gather is hardly worthless. The difference is that almost nothing in the intelligence gathering arena is utterly verifiable. Controlled experiments cannot be performed upon rogue entities that are being intelligently directed. This statement is the crux of this book, so it bears repetition: ***controlled experiments cannot be performed upon rogue entities that are intelligently directed.***

Paranormal researchers *can* do much of what spies do: gather and evaluate data from admittedly uncertain sources. Much of this data is anecdotal. It's stories, really. However uncertain, anecdotal data can be analyzed by keen minds to suggest patterns that have definite predictive value.

In the initial stages, *intel* may not rise to the level of a scientific inquiry, but it can also lead to verifiable scientific testing at a later date. But, in the pre-science stages, intel is about the best we can do with the mysterious category of events that are currently dismissed as 'paranormal.'

This idea renders those who study the paranormal as essentially pioneers. They are modern-day explorers. They are probing the scientific frontiers that will someday be mapped, like shorelines of a newly discovered continent. This book is an early map; a map without all the shorelines drawn in; a map that presents paranormal origins, threads, and possible connections to other mysterious events.

Alfred Wegener was ***the*** pioneer in probing the once-baffling mystery of drifting continents. In his fifty-year lifetime, he never could resolve the question of how and why continents move. He did accurately describe the means by which the mystery would eventually be resolved. His words about the earth sciences ring equally true when trying to understand paranormal mysteries:

> "Scientists still do not appear to understand sufficiently that all earth sciences must contribute evidence toward unveiling the state of our planet in earlier times, and that the truth of the matter can only be reached by combing all this evidence. It is only by combing the information furnished by all the earth sciences that we can hope to determine 'truth' here, that is to say, to find the picture that sets out all the known facts in the best arrangement and that therefore has the highest degree of probability. Further, we have to be prepared always for the possibility that each new discovery, no matter what science furnishes it, may modify the conclusions we draw." Alfred Wegener, 1880-1930.

In his day, Wegener endured perpetual indignities in response to his efforts to verify his theory of continental drift. Wegener postulated that the surface of the Earth was in slow but constant motion, but he could not prove it. His fellow scientists reacted with derision to his bold suggestion that huge landmasses were somehow on the move. Wegener was admirably undaunted, but he died an accidental death in Greenland before the definitive evidence he sought was ever accumulated.

Hopefully Wegener's example inspires paranormal researchers to be similarly undaunted by the dismissiveness of mainstream scientists. It was no consolation for Wegener, but it is worth noting that Wegener's once-radical ideas were verified fifty years after his death.

The People Factor

Science is neutral and indifferent, but scientists are not. Science, as an institution, is devoid of personality or prejudice. Scientists, (the people) *do* have personalities that often display prejudice and ego. Properly done science is never wrong, but scientists are often wrong.

Science is indifferent to media attention. But, scientists sometimes succumb to ego-gratification born of media attention. Media attention, in and of itself, is not a bad thing. It becomes unproductive when scientists are invited to make publicized pronouncements that they are not qualified to make, or when they are qualified, and just happen to be wrong. There is an utterly human tendency to hold strong opinions on matters that are outside one's area of expertise. That tendency is alive and well under The Big Tent of science.

Perhaps the most important point here is that, even though paranormal research is not a truly scientific endeavor, it has validity, and it is certain to gain greater traction in the future. With each new generation of scientific progress, the frontier of knowledge moves further and further out. We are now in an age in which the frontier of science lies at the very edge of what science is even capable of verifying.

Paranormal research represents a valid set of questions that can only be resolved with some new kind of science. Instead of reductionist scientific thinking, which breaks every problem down until it is ultimately expressed by mathematical formula, we need a type of science that is expansionist, holistic, and big-picture oriented. We also need a kind of science which shares information and makes connections between disparate fields; one that somehow incorporates information from science, history, and even religion, spirituality, and metaphysics. Empowering science to investigate paranormal matters may even provide a more precise definition of the entity or entities that we now know only as 'God.'

Whether paranormal research will ever uncover better answers to such profound mysteries is still uncertain. What seems much more certain, when one looks over the horizon of present human knowledge, is that the paranormal topics of today will not remain paranormal forever. History certainly tells us that one day, at least some of the stuff that is now dismissed as 'paranormal' will reside inside The Big Tent.

Chapter One: The Coconut Telegraph

I didn't plan to become a 'paranormal researcher.' As a science teacher who obligates kids to do science projects every year, it seemed only fair to assign myself a science project when a scientific mystery confronted me in my own back yard.

I had an interest in the bigfoot subject since the mid-1980s. My interest consisted of reading an occasional book on the subject, and devouring any newspaper or magazine articles that I came across. Things got more personal in 1996. While perusing the community bulletin board at the nearby Barton country store, my eyes landed upon a business card for Frank Kaneaster, who described himself as a local bigfoot researcher. He was looking for sasquatch sightings to investigate. This was the first time it dawned upon me that such things actually happened in my immediate area. I rang him up the next day and learned that he lived outside the nearby community of Estacada, on the edge of 'the Hood,' (the Mt. Hood National Forest.) I was intensely skeptical, but Frank assured me that sightings did occur in the unincorporated part of Clackamas County in which I lived.

Frank's interest in the subject began with a sighting he had while growing up near Colton, Oregon. In his late twenties, Frank actively investigated any sighting reports that came his way, marking them with pins on a map, and casting the footprints with plaster whenever he found them.

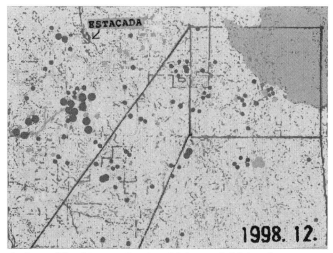

A photo of Frank's map, showing sightings and sighting clusters, most notably the sighting cluster just south of Estacada where Clear Creek crosses under Hwy 211 between Estacada and Colton.

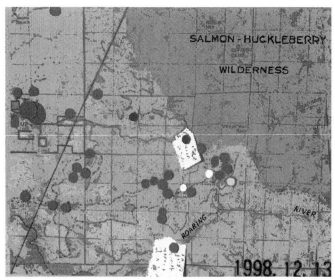

An enlargement of a portion of Frank's map: The large green push pin at left denotes a sighting cluster around Squaw Mountain, which has been renamed the more politically correct Tumala Mountain (see essay, Appendix 1.)

I always supposed that, if bigfoot creatures did exist, they would reside in remote, forbidding places like the Salmon Huckleberry Wilderness, as suggested by the clusters of pins on Frank's map (above). Not necessarily.

Frank speculated that the sasquatch were sometimes opportunistic scavengers that operated on the very margins of civilization in various places throughout rural America. In such surroundings, they were essentially nocturnal operators, casing farms and rural homesteads under cover of darkness. "You control your property only in the daytime," Frank told me.

"Why don't I see any evidence of their passing?" I inquired.

"Grover Krantz, one of America's academic pioneers of the bigfoot subject, used to say that you have to *believe* to *see*. By that he meant that evidence of bigfoots' presence may be more abundant than most people realize, but folks just don't grasp the significance of the subtle evidence they stumble across. They dismiss the evidence because they don't 'believe in bigfoot' in the first place. You have to believe to see."

It took a couple years, but darned if I didn't find an example of this very idea right on my own property. I now see that Frank was correct.

Just after I bought land in Clackamas County in 1985, my next-door neighbor, a curmudgeonly dentist, fisherman, and long-time resident, marched over to my side of the fence and accused me of stealing apples from his orchard. I was quite flummoxed by this point-blank accusation. He didn't want to hear my unpersuasive denials, for Doc Carter was already sure that I stole his apples. We didn't interact much after that awkward encounter. Two years later he sold his place and moved to the coast where the fishing was better.

Another few years passed. One day, I was making photocopies in the office of the school where I worked. A charming teacher, Dianne George, happened to mention that she knew my former neighbor, Doc Carter. She was one of his dental patients. As I waited for the copies to accumulate, Dianne confided that Carter once told her I stole his apples. I laughed. For Dianne's benefit, I recollected the whole strange incident that rendered me a suspect in the theft of Doc Carter's produce. I confessed to Dianne that I was baffled by the whole matter but I shrugged it off as the slightly paranoid ponderings of an eccentric Clackamas County resident. "Why would I want to risk my reputation," I asked Diane rhetorically, "or even risk getting shot, just to steal an apple that was worth less than a dime?"

"No, no," Dianne said smiling, "He thinks you stole *all* his apples."

"He *what?*"

"Oh, I dunno," she replied, "He said you stole *all* the apples from one of his apple trees. They all disappeared in a single night, right before he was about to pick them. It was right after you bought the place next door. He felt it *had* to be you."

That conversation with Dianne left me even more baffled than before. What did Carter think I would have done with several bushels of apples? Open a produce stand? I didn't give the matter anymore thought until about seven years later when another interesting encounter took place.

By the late 1990s, I was following in the footsteps of Frank Kaneaster, investigating bigfoot sighting reports in my local area. The internet was in its infancy but websites were beginning to proliferate like dandelions on a spring lawn. Whatever websites did exist were accessed with dialup modems connected to (ironically) Apple MacIntosh computers. Netscape Navigator was the browser of choice. Google did not yet exist. I used the search engine to find information on the bigfoot phenomenon. It led me to a very primitive version of "Matt Moneymaker's Bigfoot Field Research Organization" website. It was about the only prominent bigfoot-oriented website to be found in cyberspace in 1996. As a Frank Kaneaster protégé, I ingratiated myself with the mercurial Moneymaker and before long he was routing me all the sighting reports region-wide for follow-up investigation.

In those days, when it rained bigfoot sighting reports, it poured. The downpour would begin with an interview of a bigfoot eyewitness on late-night talk radio; typically Art Bell's 'Coast to Coast.' Such an interview would typically include the emerging data base of sighting reports on Moneymaker's fledgling BFRO website. The consequence of this publicity became very predictable. In the ensuing hours or days, the BFRO website would be inundated with comments and sighting reports, some dating back more than a decade.

Clearly, such radio interviews were touching a nerve of pent-up bigfoot encounters continent-wide. It appeared that the opportunity to finally report a fairly traumatic encounter, and even speak with a serious investigator, provided a certain catharsis for these conflicted witnesses. They were getting a troubling experience off their chest, and getting a certain validation by finding that others had nearly identical experiences. Indeed, sprinkled in the mix of serious reports were a host of crank reports and profane insults directed at those of us who took the subject seriously. As early as the late 1990s, the anonymous 'haters' were a dark and emerging internet phenomenon.

Amidst these occasional cascades of on-line sighting reports were dozens of reports that referred to places in the Pacific Northwest. As the sole arbiter of which regional reports would be investigated, I would cherry pick the most recent, the closest, and the most vivid reports to investigate. It was a heady time, studying tiny lines of print on the screen of my MacIntosh Classic late into the night. Cathode ray computer screens being what they were, it was far easier on the eyes to print out the reports and study the hard copies. I still have the big stacks of printed sighting reports in a box in my garage.

I should offer that, by this time, it was as plain as the nose on my face that this phenomenon was very real. The statistics were just impossible to deny. Anyone who took the time, as I did, to contact the witnesses, listen to their descriptions, and then overlay them against the backdrop of other reports could see that the similarities and the patterns were compelling. Prior to this, I was much less sure of what to make of the bigfoot phenomenon. But once I had the opportunity to use the internet to sample rural populations continent-wide, there could be no doubt.

It was still troubling to face the irrefutable logic of statistics. An imposing group of human-*ish* beings had somehow gone scientifically unverified right into the present. Yet, this simple statistical conclusion was completely undeniable to anyone who had access to the whole body of emerging data. The descriptions were remarkably consistent, and the integrity of many of the witnesses was beyond reproach. I spoke with doctors, cops, teachers, scientists, engineers, and even a priest. All reports emanated from rural or wilderness locations. At the time, the information I was in possession of was too new and the idea was also too radical to share with others, including my wife, but the reality of the situation was beyond question: sasquatches were real.

Almost all witnesses shared my reluctance to share everything they knew *publicly*. Witnesses were typically willing to allow their experiences to be electronically published as long as their name and contact information was withheld. They had already experienced the ridicule that results from sharing with friends and family one's encounter with a real-life monster. The main reason witnesses took the risk of contacting a bigfoot website was the need for answers to the lingering questions that haunted them in the wake of their unexpected encounter. When speaking with witnesses over the phone, the same questions surfaced over and over: *Are there other sightings in my area? How many of **them** are there? Are they dangerous? Are they intelligent?*

Sometimes a hunter (like Richard Ritchie or Robert Anderson) or motorist (like Terry Reams) would have a sighting at such close range that they actually looked into the eyes of one of these mysterious creatures. What they uniformly described was a penetrating stare that spoke of great intelligence and sensitivity. While such observations may not be the utterly scientific, they were some of the most fascinating observations that I was collecting. The frequency and the consistency with which I was hearing this impression gave me pause. I had the definite feeling that I was personally experiencing a scientific frontier.

It became increasingly clear that I was in over my head. There were just too many reports to manage for a solitary person with a marriage, two kids, and a job. Eventually, I was able to add other willing volunteers to the local stable of 'field researchers.' It was a relief to farm out the reports that I could not handle.

The most local sighting reports were always the highest priority. One such sighting report came from a rural couple on Bauer Road right outside Frank Kaneaster's old stomping ground of Colton, Oregon. These particular residents informed me that they looked out their window one morning, just after dawn, and observed a tall, dark, hair covered form standing beneath one of their apple trees. An instant later, the whole apple tree violently shook and every apple fell off the tree at once. The creature then set about picking up as many apples as it could carry. A smaller version of the hirsute creature emerged from the woods and assisted in the surreptitious harvest.

This sighting was only twelve miles from my home, so I visited the property at my first opportunity. The residents showed me a big pile of feces that consisted entirely of half-digested apples. I asked them if it might have been a bear. They said they had seen a bear eating the apples on the ground the next day, but the things that shook the tree at sunrise then gathered up the apples was definitely moving on two legs the whole time they watched it.

Suddenly, as I stood in that pasture on Bauer Road, a light bulb went on in my head. I felt a sudden chill. The unsolved mystery of Doc Carter and his missing apples came flooding back! It seemed that Krantz and Kaneaster were correct! You *do* have to *believe* to *see*! Like almost everything else surrounding the 'bigfoot hypothesis' it could never be proved, but there I was on Bauer Road with a completely analogous situation that seemed to offer an explanation for Carter's missing apples.

Even if he *had* still been living next door, I would not have wasted my breath trying to convince the curmudgeonly dentist that I may have stumbled upon an explanation for his missing fruit. His orchard was situated on the edge of a mature forest, along a major waterway, and I had personally documented multiple creature sightings in the immediate area. Still, I think every reader of this passage would agree that, under the circumstances, trying to convince Doc Carter that a bigfoot bagged his produce would have been a 'fool's errand.'

What was even more interesting was that this seemed like yet another indication that Frank Kaneaster was correct: Carter's missing apples were an indication of possible bigfoot activity right there in my rural Clackamas County neighborhood. At least a dozen other reports exist continent-wide of sasquatches raiding orchards. A few even include the vivid observation of the violent shaking, followed by the fruit dropping to the ground all at once. Since then, enough other orchard-related reports have surfaced that orchards are now seen as logical feeding spots for the sasquatch. According to seasoned researcher Paul Graves, the large commercial orchards around his home near Wenatchee, Washington get raided by the local sasquatches much more frequently than anyone realizes.

Meanwhile, Frank Kaneaster's 'take' on the bigfoot phenomenon had new credibility in my own mind. Frank, like most other sasquatch researchers at the time, advocated the view that the sasquatch represented a population of wild apes roaming the forests of the Pacific Northwest. While this seemed like the most plausible interpretation in the early days when the flow of information was limited, it was not consistent with many of the claims when the pool of sighting reports really got huge. I interviewed witnesses who described staring into a pair of eyes that bespoke of intelligence in the brain behind them. Other people were describing childhood experiences that included friendly, even on-going interaction with the local wildmen. Nothing scientifically verifiable; just more intelligence gathering, but such observations began to show a definite pattern behind them.

Meanwhile, he was collecting track casts, but what Frank wasn't doing was pursuing the problem photographically. This was still the day of the film camera, but that was about to change. Remotely-triggered trail cameras were available, but they were expensive. I learned that there were a couple of commercial designs that were being used by wildlife professionals. U.S. Forest Service researchers Thomas Kucera and William Zielinski were using these older, film-loaded trail cameras, also known as 'camera traps,' to verify the presence of wolverines and other rare members of the *Mustelid* (weasel) Family.

Digital cameras were about to hit the market in a big way. Professional digital cameras had been on the market since 1988. They recorded image data using high resolution charged-coupled devices (CCDs) that cost many thousands of dollars. With the development of Complementary Metal Oxide Semiconductors (CMOS), in the late 1990s, this cheaper data storage system made the digital camera truly affordable.

By 2000, small, film-free digital cameras were widely available for the first time. The digital camera revolution was soon applied to trail cameras and the market for those devices exploded. Single sensor systems that emitted an infrared beam were being challenged in the marketplace by dual sensor 'Manley' systems that triggered by detecting changes to microwave and passive infrared radiation. The devotees of the bigfoot subject who were watching this market explosion quickly applied the new technology to our favorite scientific question. This was the real attraction of the bigfoot phenomenon for me and many others at the time. It was the opportunity to apply our interest in traditional photography, and newer electronic imaging systems, to the open question of bigfoots' existence. Like others, I surmised that, if bigfoots were the wild apes that everyone including Dr. Krantz was saying, it shouldn't be too difficult to trick one into getting its picture taken with a motion-activated wildlife camera.

I got busy. My goal was to get my hands on a couple of those camera traps and place them in a bigfoot hotspot. My own neighborhood seemed like a possibility, but by this time I had processed enough regional sighting reports to see that the Mt. Rainier area had a greater concentration of sighting reports than almost anywhere else in the nation. Mt. Rainier was a hundred miles distant, but the sightings were so concentrated in that area that it seemed like the best place to start.

I laid low and watched waves of sighting reports inundate the BFRO website after each tremblor of talk-radio publicity. After one such event, I spotted exactly the kind of report I was looking for. A rural-living couple in a remote homestead near Mt. Rainier had submitted an intriguing report to the BFRO website. In the report, one of the residents stated something that was pretty radical, even to us 'bigfoot believers' at BFRO. Allen Hoyt, and members of his family, were claiming multiple encounters with sasquatches around their rural acreage. It was their opinion that there were resident sasquatches living in their immediate vicinity.

I was on the phone to Allen the next day. He was polite and soft-spoken. He described a few encounters and shared that his wife and daughter had seen the creatures more often. At first they were frightened by the realization that these mysterious beings were hanging around, but they eventually decided that they meant no harm. I asked Allen why he was sharing this information with the BFRO. He responded that he heard an interview with Moneymaker on Art Bell's Coast to Coast. The forest adjacent to his property was about to be logged. He was concerned for the well-being of the creatures. He doubted he could stop the logging, but he thought it was time to raise the awareness of these creatures.

A year earlier, an interesting report came out of Honobia, Oklahoma. Some rural residents in southeast Oklahoma were being somewhat terrorized by the aggressive overtures of a couple of sasquatches. It was their considered opinion that creatures were opportunistically preying upon the deer that proliferated in the area. Not only were the live deer being picked off, but these rural residents observed that large pieces of deer meat had disappeared from an outdoor freezer. The idea that sasquatches would raid an outdoor freezer was as logical as it was unprecedented. I kept that idea in the back of my head, and when I had Allen on the line, I matter-of-factly inquired whether he had an outdoor freezer. He did. Had he ever lost anything from the freezer? Yes, a side of pig that was intended for a pit-barbecue party had once disappeared. On other occasions, the freezer door was found wide open in the morning. Allen reflected that, at the time, he blamed the kids, who denied responsibility for leaving the freezer door open. Allen never made the connection between the freezer tampering and the sasquatch activity until that moment I had him on the phone. I was in my car and motoring toward Mt. Rainier the next day.

In retrospect, I committed just about every blunder possible. The freezer tampering completely stopped as soon as we put the trail camera on the freezer. Later, we moved the trail camera to other locations of the property. Then, the freezer raids resumed. Could the creatures be averse to cameras? That obvious thought was a bit too much to accept at the time. After all, we were still of the view that we were chasing wild apes.

Eventually, through BFRO sponsorship and technical assistance from brilliant tekkies like Intel engineer Vaughn Hughes, we were able to upgrade to video surveillance of the Hoyt's forest. With Vaughn's knowledge and a generous donation from Richard Hucklebridge, by 1999 we accomplished motion-sensor-activated recording, streaming video, and 24/7 on-site recording onto VHS tapes.

At the time, we thought this was a pioneering innovation in sasquatch research. I later learned from Henry Franzoni that this was not the case. Another very determined camera project had been tried in the beginning internet years between 1993 and 1996. In that effort, computer and electronics expert Jeff Glickman, with assistance from Henry, deployed a very elaborate camera system in a remote corner of the Bull Run Watershed in the Mt. Hood National Forest. This project was part of the Bigfoot Research Project (BRP) led by Peter Byrne. Funding for this effort came from anonymous sources via Robert Rhines and the Academy of Applied Science in Boston. In those pre-internet days, Jeff Glickman's technical team achieved streaming video using a much more complicated and expensive 2.5Ghz microwave relay, achieving the 15 mile range required to reach a VHS recorder in Hood River in two line-of-sight segments. This was all done in an ideal location: a vast and restricted parcel of U.S. Forest Service wilderness that provided drinking water for the nearby city of Portland, Oregon.

The BRP team deployed powerful microwave antennas and early solar cell technology that recharged the battery of a complicated and expensive camera system. The essential element of the system was a pair of $30,000 cameras, one normal, one infrared, and a circuit which switched between them each daylight and darkness period. They buried recently-declassified troop movement sensors to trigger the camera.

One day after their system was up and running, it was disabled by a mysterious blast of electricity. All the circuits were fused into a smoking lump, but the cameras still functioned. Lightning was the official explanation. Henry had reasons to doubt this explanation. It took six months to rebuild the system and deploy it again, and it was then deployed for a two year period, during which elk, bear, deer, hikers, ATVs, and motorcycles were seen and recorded, but no sasquatch. The Forest Service allowed the experiment to continue as long as it was suitably scientific, with all observations properly recorded and shared with U.S.F.S. personnel so they could be used as population estimate data.

At the time, the Forest Service personnel advised the group that they were wasting their time and money since the sasquatch did not exist. Twelve years later, one of the same Forest Service employees he dealt with at the time told

Henry that if they were looking for the sasquatch, they looked in the wrong part of the Bull Run.

In 1999, our system near Mt. Rainer enjoyed the benefits of being on private land, and being much closer to electric power and telephone lines. It quickly emerged that the real problem was screening all the video tapes that we were accumulating. Allen Hoyt was very conscientious about keeping the tape player rolling and swapping tapes on a daily basis, but I just could not keep up with the screening process. Even today, fifteen years later, I still have a stack of video tapes from the project that I never got around to screening.

It was now summer of 2001. I was spending as much time as I could monitoring the equipment and trying everything I could think of to entice the mysterious creatures to step in front of the cameras. Various food items were put in front of the cameras. At one point we, like Henry did seven years earlier, were collecting road kills and used them to bait the camera sets.

Sasquatch activity around the Hoyts' homestead continued. A few eye-ball sightings occurred on the property but our cameras were never in the right place. As often as possible, I would drive my little blue Toyota Tercel up to Allen and April's place, move the cameras to new locations, and leave more food. We would use meat, candy, graham crackers, peanut butter, and anything else that came to mind.

Sometimes, Allen would phone me when a sighting or another kind of activity occurred somewhere nearby. I would head up there and stake out their woods for several hours. The joke between Allen and me was that, as soon as I showed up, the activity would cease. As soon as I left, the suspected sasquatch activity would resume.

At first, this was just something to tease me about, but eventually it began to take on the appearance of a definite pattern. On one summer evening, not long after I left the property to head home, Allen and April happened upon a juvenile sasquatch cowering beside a large fern right next to the trail. My 1990s-era cell phone, which was the size of a brick, rang as I motored south on I-5. The Hoyts gave me the news of this latest sighting. The next weekend, I returned to continue my vigil. The Hoyts dutifully showed me the location of their most recent sighting and described the encounter in vivid detail.

I decided to spend the night, or at least most of it, staking out that particular location. Early in the evening, Allen joined me. We sat, listening and talking softly, as the sun set. As darkness closed in on us, there was a lot of faint snapping of twigs encircling our location.

17

Allen calmly stated, "That's them."

I didn't dispute his claim. He was the more experienced woodsman. Yet, inwardly, it really was a very difficult claim to accept. It sounded like chipmunks or bunnies travelling in the underbrush, although I must admit that it did, strangely, encircle our location, always just beyond sight. By this time, Allen's sincerity and reliability were, in my mind, beyond question. He was calmly dedicated to the project, not just for months but years. He never exaggerated or sensationalized his observations. As the 'brush popping' took place all around our position, I strained to see, or at least hear more. This went on for a couple of hours.

One idea that gets a lot of discussion, even today, is that the sasquatch will knock on trees as some sort of signal to each other. I had heard this from Frank Kaneaster in the mid-1990s. It continued to get mention on the BFRO sighting reports.

After Allen left, I started a regular ritual of tree-knocking using a wooden bat. Every fifteen minutes, I would get up and whack a nearby tree three times, with my Louisville Slugger. I discovered that there was a definite technique to producing nice, loud, resonating whacks. There was one particular spot on the bat that made the best noise, and finding just the right tree also made a big difference. Small diameter cedar trees seemed to produce the most resonating whacks.

As the night wore on, the summer air took on a crisp coolness. By midnight, I swaddled myself in a sleeping bag for warmth as I maintained my vigil. I centered my noise-making efforts on one particular tree, moving my chair next to it, and whacking it every fifteen minutes without getting up. I dozed from time to time but kept up my tree-knocking vigil into the wee hours. Never once did I hear any kind of answer. Save for my regular tree-whacking, the woods remained silent all night.

It was summer but I had a mid-day commitment the next day, so at 3:30 a.m. I gathered my belongings and headed for the trusty Tercel. In retrospect, that was a mistake. I was in no real shape to make the two hour drive home. It was a drive I'll never forget; probably the most difficult drive of my life. Fortunately, the freeway traffic was sparse. Solitary tractor-trailers blew by as I conservatively confined myself to the right lane. I opened the window to let in more fresh air. I turned the stereo louder. Still, my eyelids were anvils. I squeezed the steering wheel to boost the blood circulation through my tired arms. At one point, my eyes involuntarily slammed shut.

I regained consciousness an instant later. Mercifully, I was still with the boundaries of the same two white lines, but clearly, my level of fatigue had become dangerous. Fortunately, a lonely off-ramp beckoned on my right. I rolled to a stop at the top of the off-ramp. I let my eye lids fall and took my hands off the steering wheel. The echo of tree-knocks resonated in my head as I drifted off into unconsciousness. Fifteen minutes later, my eyes snapped open and I felt momentary panic before I registered the fact that the car was not moving. I was still sitting on the shoulder at the top of the off-ramp.

I restarted the car, feeling slightly refreshed. It was 4:15 a.m. and I was still an hour from home. Eventually, the blear returned to my eyes and my eyelids again grew heavy. I choked the steering wheel so hard I might have bent it. The lane lines steadily slid past and it became tougher and tougher to hold my eyes open. More fresh air…more isometrics on the steering wheel…more loud music on the stereo…and eventually another unscheduled stop to let my eyelids fall. I was never so pleased to finally cross the Columbia River and enter into Oregon. I still had another ½ hour of driving, but I was invigorated by my progress. I knew I would make it. I rubbed my eyes, and I sang aloud. At 5:05 a.m., as the tiniest hint of daylight illuminated the eastern horizon, I rolled into my driveway in a zombie-like state.

I shut off the engine, let my heavy eyelids fall, and said a prayer of thanks. I almost slept right there, but a cozy bed beckoned only a few steps away. I peeled my weary bones from the seat of the Tercel. Stumbling to my feet, I took in a deep breath of the cold pre-dawn air.

I softly shut the car door, took my first step toward the house, and at that exact moment I got one of the biggest surprises of my life. From the woods at the back of my rural property, six hundred feet from where I had just parked the car, came three, loud, crisp, resounding knocks!

Despite my intense fatigue, the irony of the situation was abundantly clear. I had been whacking trees all night, always in triplets, only to be greeted with the identical triplet of tree knocks upon my arrival home. And, the responding knocks that I'd been trying to coax from the woods all night finally came at the precise moment when I was absolutely too exhausted to walk any further than the bedroom. Even if I did have the stamina to detour in the direction of the woods, I knew what I would see back there: NOTHING. It may have been the ultimate failure of my bigfoot researching career, but I just could not bring myself to walk a few hundred yards to check out the situation in that forest on my own property. The only thing I felt was that I was lucky to be alive. I did about the only thing I had the energy left to do: I smiled and raised my arm and extended a middle finger toward the sky, or whoever might be watching. Then I stumbled inside and collapsed on the bed. My wife never stirred.

I've had a lot of time to ponder what happened on that summer night in 2000. More than any other event, it forced a paradigm shift in my view of the sasquatch phenomenon. It was the first time I felt compelled to admit that the sasquatch did have some paranormal powers. Even if the tree knocks I heard on my own property were attributable to coincidence, it would have to be the most remarkable coincidence of my life. But I have never heard three sharp knocks emanate from my woods before or since. I've discussed the other possible explanations with sasquatch researchers many times. Could a sasquatch have followed me home from Allen and April's? Doubtful. It's a one hundred mile trip. I averaged fifty-five miles an hour, not including my rest stops.

A more reasonable possibility may be that a sasquatch at Allen and April's place somehow communicated my tree-knocking antics to another sasquatch that was nearer to my house. However it was done, the whole event seems to bear the unmistakable appearance of a perfectly timed practical joke. Sense of humor is, of course, the hallmark of higher intellect and the tree-knocks that welcomed me home when I was a sleep-deprived zombie positively reeked of a keen sense of humor. Whatever the sasquatch is we still do not know, but the events of that night certainly showed me very plainly what the sasquatch was *not*, and that was a wild ape. Whatever they are, they are smart, powerful, and not above perpetrating a mildly elaborate prank at the expense of a clumsy sasquatch researcher like me.

Jimmy Buffett released an album in 1981 entitled "Coconut Telegraph," but he didn't invent the phrase. It is a nautical term that refers to the 'rumor mill.' This reference is derived from a form of Morse code drumming that is used to communicate between adjacent Caribbean islands. Coconuts, of course, are the percussion instruments of choice.

It is obviously not a very secure type of communication. Everyone within earshot can learn whatever is being conveyed, as long as they know the code. The coconut telegraph, then, references the rumor mill. The coconut telegraph also references another mysterious phenomenon that is well-known in the Australian Outback. Suitably empowered aboriginal hunters have the ability to mentally telegraph, almost to the hour, the time of their anticipated return to the village. This telepathic communication is accomplished over distances of a hundred miles or more. Science has absolutely no explanation for how it is done, but it is very real to the aboriginals who practice it. Clearly, if there is any fact to the matter, then the human brain has powers that extend beyond the confines of the body it lives within.

If the sasquatch are indeed sentient beings that are uniquely attuned to their natural surroundings, then they ought to have the same arsenal of tricks as the aboriginal humans who inhabit the Australian Outback. In that case, one sasquatch ought to be able to alert another one who is a hundred miles away that a certain buffoon of a researcher who needs a mental smack-down, is heading their way. If the sasquatch do have the 'coconut telegraph' at their disposal, then I am pretty sure that, on that particular night in August of 2000, I got coconut telegraph-ed. It's a bit ego-centric, but every time I reflect on that weird event, I am inwardly amused by the idea that it was all a joke at my expense. A more troubling conclusion is also implied: the sasquatch do indeed possess at least some capabilities that are so scientifically un-provable that we must label them "paranormal."

It doesn't end there. Later that same year, I found myself on the Skookum Expedition with a dozen or so distinguished researchers who felt the pressure to deliver some compelling evidence for the benefit of an Aussie TV crew that was following our efforts. We had generated some pretty good 'call backs' in response to broadcasting taped calls into the Gifford Pinchot National Forest with a loudspeaker. Despite our best efforts, nothing of substance was successfully recorded for the benefit of the planned TV show. One of the team members, Rick Noll did find a pretty good sasquatch footprint in a bed of moss. That was about our best piece of evidence as the week drew to a close.

At that point, the Aussie TV crew was feeling a bit unfulfilled. The fall weather had taken a turn for the worse and we were almost out of food. At this critical juncture, the rain stopped, the night sky cleared, and the team extemporaneously assembled around a campfire. We were all silently trying to figure out what to do next. Time was running out.

Up until that point, I had not said anything about any of my recent paranormal experiences at the Hoyt's place. With so much ego-driven testosterone in one place, my emerging paranormal orientation seemed too controversial to bring up with so little to substantiate it. The TV show, and the individuals behind it, had a very flesh-and-blood orientation. My main role that week was keeping the woefully under-equipped Aussies from starving or freezing to death. Everyone else in the group was surprisingly indifferent to

21

the plight of the film crew from down under. They clearly had not seen the memo that they were going to spend a week in the wilderness with snow in the forecast. Their sleeping bags were inadequate and they had no food. They expected they would be able to dine at restaurants. No one told them they were bound for the wilderness. Fortunately, I had packed plenty of extra food and even a couple of spare sleeping bags.

On the final night of my stay, I decided to take a chance and open my big mouth. I wasn't trying to tell anyone else what to think, I explained, but my work at Allen and April's place seemed to suggest that the creatures were very much smarter than *I* ever supposed. My own experiences had really set my own thinking right on its ear. Rather than spend another night sneaking and stalking around, maybe we should try a gesture of friendliness or accommodation. Let's consider the possibility that the creatures are able to observe us at close range without being detected. "It may even be possible," I submitted, "that they are listening to our conversation at this very moment."

Nobody spoke. If it was any lighter around that campfire, I'm sure I would have seen some pretty skeptical looks from the assembled expedition members. Moneymaker was already in his tent for the night, so at least he wasn't there to restate the BFRO company line. Even without Matt's input, this was definitely a "flesh and blood" camp, in more ways than one. We had a wildlife biologist, a trapper, a few seasoned hunters, and a whole bunch of card-carrying BFRO members. More importantly, they were all trying to portray bigfoot research in the most saleable, scientific light possible for the anticipated television audience.

In the general sphere of 'bigfoot research,' there are two diametrically opposed camps. The 'flesh and blood' camp sees the sasquatch as a population of wild apes. The opposing 'paranormal' camp attributes any manner of higher powers to the sasquatch, including the ability to disappear, shape shift, and communicate telepathically. The ideas I was expressing at the campfire that night were a bit too paranormal for this particular crowd. Still, their own validity as cutting-edge bigfoot researchers was 'on the ropes.' They had little to show for their week of 'flesh and blood' bigfoot research and they knew it.

I jumped in with both feet. I related the story of the tree knocking incident that began at Allen and April's house and followed me home. I also described how the sasquatch activity seemed to pick up whenever I wasn't there, and drop off whenever I arrived. In my limited experience, the sasquatch seemed to know precisely when we are setting traps or tricks for them. They know when I'm visiting the Hoyts and they lay low when I'm there.

"I think they know we are looking for tracks, and they know to avoid leaving them," I dared to suggest. "We should use our limited remaining time to try some other approaches. Let's put out food and make some other gestures of accommodation and respect. The tricks and traps haven't worked."

The team reacted with a deafening silence. To their credit, a few saw the value in trying some new approaches. Derek Randles spoke up first. "Rick and I are going out to try the thermal camera along the roads. We'll take some of your fruit and look for some good places to leave it."

The tide just shifted. The rest was history. The next day, Rick, Derek, and LeRoy left a frost-covered camp to check the bait stations they set up only a few hours earlier. At one roadside bait station, the fruit had been substantially disturbed. Some fruit was partially eaten. Some of it was gone. There were not any of the anticipated big footprints, but the mud around the fruit showed definite signs of fresh disturbance. Upon carful study, Rick was able to discern the impression of an arm, a leg, a heel, and maybe even buttocks. The trio stood and studied it more. The closer they looked, the more certain they were that they were seeing signs that something laid down in the mud to reach the fruit. Word was sent back to camp and we all came running.

LeRoy, Alan, and Derek await the return of the group to begin casting.

Fortunately, the means and the know-how to preserve the impression was present in the group. A full day was spent preserving the three foot by four foot impression in plaster. Whatever it is, the cast is now known as the 'Skookum Cast,' in honor of the Skookum Meadow area where it was obtained. Perhaps the cast is nothing more than some weird impression made by an elk.

The Skookum impression before casting with possible body part indentations highlighted. Photograph courtesy Rick Noll.

Experienced elk hunters, of which Derek Randles is certainly one, mostly concur that the wet but firm mud beside the road is *not* an elk wallow. In the heat of summer, elk will wallow in deep puddles to cool off and shake fleas, Derek agreed, but this was fresh but firm mud. This was no elk wallow.

In any case, the resulting impression seemed to suggest the passing of a creature that sat down in the mud in a most unexpected manner. Rather that walk up to the fruit pile, whatever made the impression lay down next to it, and then disturbed the fruit while maintaining a certain distance from it. It is as though the creature, whatever it was, wanted the fresh fruit but it didn't want to leave footprints. Instead, it is speculated, it sat down in the mud and reached for the produce from a distance. Maybe, it was all a random accident. Maybe, it knew exactly what it was doing, in which case it deliberately left a different sort of impression than the familiar footprints we were expecting.

Skookum cast and expedition members (from left) R. Noll, G. Bambanek, Ian (sound man from Australia), A. Terry, J. & E. Lemley.

If this is true, then our powers of observation were being tested. Call me 'paranormal' but this does not seem particularly paranormal to me. It does smack of an intelligence that most are unwilling to attribute to the sasquatch. Strangely, the manner in which the fruit was disturbed was somehow consistent with my suggestion that the sasquatch are trying to out-trick our attempts to be tricky. This was even the conclusion of others who were much more 'flesh and blood' in their orientation than I; and people who steadfastly rejected my view that the sasquatch are anywhere near our intellectual equals.

In the ensuing months, the cast was dutifully put before a parade of experts. Impressions of a heel, a forearm, fingers, a thigh, and buttocks were resolved by Dr. Grover Krantz from Washington State and Dr. Meldrum, of Idaho State University. Primate expert Dr. Esteban Saramiento was also consulted. His considered opinion was that the pattern of hair striation imprinted in the cast was clearly *primate* in origin. Dr. George Schaller, a primate expert and mentor of Jane Goodall, eventually viewed the cast. He was *inclined* to agree.

Dr. Grover Krantz examines the Skookum Cast in Edmonds, Washington

It was a rare moment of vindication for some unconventional thinking. I didn't really force a paranormal point of view upon my fellow 'flesh and blood' researchers, I only suggested that the creatures, or beings, or whatever they are, are smarter than we are giving them credit for.

Once the publicity from the Skookum Cast hit the media, my world went a little crazy. I was asked to make a presentation of our 'big find' at one of Ray Crowe's Western Bigfoot Society meetings in Portland. A local TV station showed up to cover the event. That evening I appeared briefly on the eleven o'clock news, showing pictures of the Skookum Cast and explaining how we came to obtain it. A day later, a morning radio show called my house and requested an on-air interview.

As is the case with most morning radio shows, comedy is all they are after, so any discussion of bigfoot or bigfoot's butt is going to be tongue-in-cheek at the very least, if not fuel for a constant stream of wisecracks. The on-air personalities led with the obvious jokes, starting with questions about the size of bigfoot's butt. What they weren't expecting was that my bigfoot jokes would be better than theirs. No useful information about cryptozoology was conveyed. The whole interview was just a steady stream of one-liners.

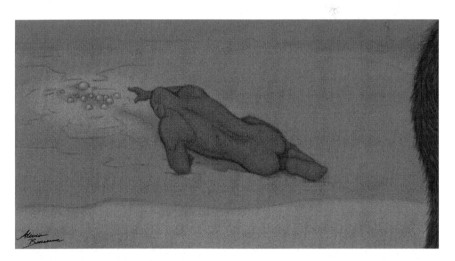

There is a service that radio stations have which rates and recommends interviewees based on previous interviews. If one radio station finds a live wire of a guest, the word spreads to virtually every other radio station before nightfall. Radio stations have a coconut telegraph, too. I found this out when my telephone began ringing off the hook. I asked one of the DJ's how they got my number. The 'coconut telegraph,' of course. The next thing I knew, I was doing four or five live interviews a day, and I wasn't even calling back the folks that left messages on my answering machine. No one wanted the real story of the Skookum Expedition. They just wanted jokes. I got really good at making jokes about bigfoot, the Skookum Cast, bigfoot researchers, you name it. This went on for at least a week, maybe ten days. Then, life returned to normal.

Things Get Paranormal

Following the discovery and ensuing publicity given to the Skookum Cast, Ray Crowe was experiencing a big increase in the interest in his monthly bigfoot meetings. He was hearing from eyewitnesses with new and old sightings to report. While the majority of these sightings begin with some variation of, "I saw bigfoot dash across the road," a small percentage of the reports were very different. One unusual report came from a very serious person named Rick Snyder, who lived at a remote Job Corps site in the Mt. Hood National Forest. At this facility just down the road from the Ripplebrook Ranger Station, Rick taught professional painting to young men who were trying to rehabilitate their lives.

On the telephone, Rick Snyder informed Ray that, in and around his remote cabin, he was actually *interacting* with the local sasquatch on a fairly regular basis. Rick even felt that the sasquatch seemed to be able to interfere with his dreams, to wake him up in the middle of the night, and to cajole him into coming outside. Rick was more than a little bit troubled by all of this. What Rick really wanted to know from Ray was whether, in his vast experience with the sasquatch phenomenon, was he aware of anyone else who was reporting similar experiences.

Ray had no such previous reports, but since Rick seemed sober and serious, Ray was kind enough to refer Rick to local author and bigfoot researcher, Joe Beelart.

Concentrating his research on the Clackamas River basin, Joe Beelart was in the process of compiling a book about sasquatch activity in the Clackamas River basin: *The Oregon Bigfoot Highway*. Joe gave Rick Snyder a listen and even ventured up to Ripplebrook to meet with Rick in person. Once Joe was satisfied that Rick was on the level, he suggested to Rick that he might want to talk to this Thom Powell fellow whom he knew to be accumulating a pretty big file of bigfoot reports that bordered on the paranormal. On Joe's encouragement, Rick Snyder phoned me to share his unusual experiences. He explained that he lived in a Forest Service cabin behind the old Ripplebrook Ranger Station, deep in the southern end of the Mount Hood National Forest, which, of course, is prime sasquatch habitat.

As he explained, it was too much for him to accept at first, but ultimately, Rick was forced to conclude that there was at least one sasquatch that inhabited the vast forests surrounding his remote residence. More incredibly, the sasquatches seemed to be making overtures toward him. His curiosity was much stronger than his fear, so Rick decided to see whether he could interact with the mysterious beings.

After dark, Rick would get on his scooter and haul a Coleman camp stove and some canned chili up a primitive forest road behind his cabin. He would set up the stove and heat the chili. When the chili was warm, Rick would shut off the stove, get on his scooter, and leave. Sometimes he would move a short distance away, other times he would just go home. When he returned, the chili would always be gone, the pot licked perfectly clean. Everything else was still sitting neatly on the collapsible table just as he had left it. Such tidiness is certainly not the hallmark of bear visitation. Black bears always make a complete mess of any camp they visit.

And that's not all. Rick was certain that the creatures of interest knew where he lived, and that they would sometimes come to his cabin looking for him. If he was asleep when they came by, the creatures would wake him up by interrupting his dreams. Rick even felt that they were somehow communicating with him in his sleep. When they did communicate, the message Rick most often received was something along the lines of, "Wake up! Come out," or, more bluntly, "We're hungry!"

Rick's big question for me was whether other folks were having similar experiences. Clearly, he was searching for other reports that might serve to validate his most extraordinary experiences. About this same time, Ray Crowe was also approached by a local TV station in connection with a bigfoot story they were doing. Ray took them to the 54 Road and did his 'talking head' spiel with the Mt. Hood National Forest as a backdrop, a short distance down the 46 road from the Ripplebrook Ranger Station and Rick's cabin.

Rick was a little annoyed to learn that Ray Crowe brought a TV crew almost to his front door. Rick had no interest in appearing in the TV spot. He was a house painter and teacher of troubled youths at the Job Corps site in Ripplebrook. He was living on Forest Service property and working with the

29

Forest Service, although he was not a USFS employee. Still, Rick knew that the Forest Service would not be pleased to know that the Ripplebrook Ranger Station was being used as a backdrop for a TV news spot about bigfoot. Meanwhile, he kept up his informal feeding experiments and had some very close encounters with these mysterious nocturnal beings as a consequence.

By the time he found me, Rick was pretty sure that he had a family of sasquatches in the vicinity of his cabin. Incredibly, Rick also felt that he had acquired some form of telepathic communication with the neighborhood sasquatches. He patiently explained all this to me in a couple of late night phone calls. I had waded through enough paranormal waters by then that I was no longer shocked by such claims. I had already encountered other such examples of people living in remote situations that were habituating the sasquatches to their presence, or vice versa. I was still a bit skeptical of Rick's most extraordinary claims, especially the claims of communication, but I also knew that I had the ability to actually check Rick's claims against the experiences of at least one other family of sasquatch habituators. If there was any truth to the suggestion that the sasquatch can telepathically communicate with people, I reasoned, the Hoyts should know about it.

A week later, I was up at the Hoyt's place collecting tapes and putting more food in front of the cameras. We sat down for a beer at their kitchen table.

"So, guys," I began, "I spoke with this fellow the other day who said that he's been feeding the bigfoots that live in the woods near his mountain cabin. Better yet, he thinks they communicate with him, in his sleep, no less. When he told me this, I immediately thought of you guys. It all seemed a bit far-fetched to say the least, but I figured that if there *was* any truth to his story, you would know. I mean, you live as close to the sasquatches as anyone, so I thought I'd put it to you directly. Does any of this make any sense to you?"

Long pause. Allen looked at April. Neither one spoke. The stared at each other. Then Allen turned to me.

"Yes," was Allen's sober reply, "We've had that, too."

I looked over at April. She was nodding in agreement. I almost fell off my chair.

"We've been working this project together for about two years, now! Why didn't you tell me this before?" I implored.

The answer was so predictable I probably didn't need to ask the question in the first place.

"We didn't want you to think we were crazy."

I thought for a moment. "OK," I said, "you're not crazy. So, would you mind telling me exactly what you know about this communication?"

"Well, several things," April began. "It happens to Nina the most."

Nina is their high-school aged daughter who always exhibited a strong empathy for all kinds of animals. Nina was also very aware of the local 'forest people'.

"One night," Allen explained, "Nina was awakened by a loud voice that almost commanded her to, 'Get up! Come out and play!' Everyone in the house was asleep, but she heard the voice so plainly that she assumed it was us calling to her. She came into our bedroom and asked what we wanted. When she said, 'Why are you calling me?' I woke up. I sat up in bed as she repeated the question. I told her we didn't call her. She said she heard someone calling her to come out and play. I repeated that it wasn't us."

April jumped in. "If that had been the last of it, I don't think we would have ever thought anything about it. We assumed she was dreaming it, until it happened to me."

"Go on," I encouraged.

"A few weeks ago, just after we moved your camera from the outdoor freezer to the edge of the clear cut, I was out taking a walk and smoking a cigarette. I had a lot on my mind. Nathan [their son] was in some trouble at school and I was trying to sort things out. I was walking along the edge of the woods when I heard a very distinct voice. It sounded like someone was right behind me. I spun around expecting to see someone, but there was no one there."

"What did the voice say?"

"It said, 'Quit trying to trick us.' Then a second later, it added, 'And don't smoke those cigarettes. They're bad for you!'"

"So wait a minute. Are you saying the voice you heard was in English?"

"That's the only language I speak."

"Naturally." Since I was asking stupid questions, I thought I'd ask one more question that I already knew the answer to. "So what do you make of it? What do you think was meant by, "Quit trying to trick us?"

"Oh, I think they're talking about the cameras. I think they don't like what we're doing with the cameras."

That much I had already guessed. I wasn't sure that this new revelation was reason enough to abandon the project, but it certainly made me suspect that it might be time for a change in tactics.

While we were sharing paranormal experiences, the Hoyts had a few other unusual events to report. One day Nina returned from school and found her bedroom window was open, the curtains and the curtain rod were pulled down, and the items on her night stand, which was beneath the window, were scattered. In other instances, the window would be opened and earrings would be missing from the night stand. By now, Nina had a pretty good guess as to who or what was to blame for messing up her nightstand. Still, they hadn't mentioned any of this to me until I brought up Rick Snyder's experiences.

All of the new revelations forced me to reconsider my approach to the cameras. We had two cameras on the property that were yielding a whole bunch of nothing. The cameras were covering places in the woods. Meanwhile, the activity seemed to be occurring right around the house. With Nina's permission, we put a video camera in Nina's window, facing outside. The other camera was moved to a tree at a corner of the house, aimed so that it covered the woods just outside Nina's window.

Around this time, during the summer of 2001, I got a call from a local bigfoot researcher who had heard about my involvement in the acquisition of the Skookum Cast. His name was Steve Frederick. Steve explained to me that, for the past eight years, he had been spending his spare time following up on sighting reports and looking for indication of bigfoot activity in Oregon's thickly-forested Coast Range Mountains. Sometimes he would silently observe forest activity from a commanding vantage point, other times he would casually walk the trails while practicing his harmonica playing.

Steve explained that one of his favorite spots was Jordan Creek, where he recently had a bigfoot sighting of his own. By way of following up on that sighting, Steve spent the night in a make-shift blind.

Steve had hollowed out a comfortable observation point in a large pile of creek-side driftwood. As he maintained his all-night vigil, he experienced a very strange sensation. It seemed to Steve as though he was getting some sort of communications that he could not explain. It was a very distinct message, and it said quite plainly, "This is not going to work."

The way Steve described it to me over the telephone, it was a message that he felt, more than he heard. At first, he supposed that he was just imagining it, but it was just too vivid to ignore.

"Why not?" Steve wondered, as he sat, wrapped in a sleeping bag inside his blind along Jordan Creek.

"Because the game is 'hide and seek' not 'hide and hide'!"

The words seemed to emanate from the woods, loud and clear, and Steve was a little worried. He knew that hearing voices is one of the symptoms of schizophrenia.

"Had you called me a few months ago, I would have said, 'No,' but in the past couple months, I've heard two such reports," I assured him. "It's not exactly proof, but such reports aren't unprecedented."

"There's more," Steve continued. "While I was in the blind and all this was happening. And when I reviewed the video tape,…"

"Let me guess, Steve." I interrupted. I don't know why I interrupted him, but I just felt that I knew where this was going. "When you reviewed the video tape, there was nothing there but rolling static," I blurted out.

"That's amazing! That's exactly right. How did you know that?" Steve demanded. "Have other people had such experiences?"

"It's really rare, but, yes, I think so. There's a guy in Ohio named Robert W. Morgan who's been researching bigfoot since the 1960's. He's been saying for quite a while that bigfoots have paranormal abilities like telepathy. He's also been saying they can interfere with electronics. There's another guy named Jim Brandon who says pretty much the same thing. His book is *The Rebirth of Pan*. I just read it."

Coincidentally, I had also just had the conversation with Rick Snyder only a few weeks ago. The details of Rick's experiences, and then Allen and April's, were still fresh in my mind. I was able to reassure Steve that I *had* encountered such reports before. I briefly recapped the Rick Snyder events. Steve was somewhat relieved that there was a precedent for his strange experiences. I qualified my remarks by reminding Steve that it was impossible to confirm Rick's claims of telepathic contact.

As I continued talking with Steve, it suddenly dawned on me that there just might be a way to test Steve's highly paranormal claims. With all this strangeness coming my way since the Skookum Expedition, Steve just might represent the perfect opportunity to attempt to verify Rick Snyder's extraordinary claims. Steve felt that he may be receiving telepathic messages, but it had not occurred to him that it might be possible to send some of that same communication back the other way.

"Let's try an experiment, Steve," I suggested.

Robert W. Morgan (right) and two associates visited
Skamania County, WA, conducting bigfoot field research
around Mt. Adams in Summer of 1969. (photo courtesy
of the Skamania County Pioneer.)

The Experiment

I told Steve of a conversation I had recently with Erik Beckjord, a
particularly eccentric and overbearing devotee of the bigfoot phenomenon. In
truth, you don't talk to Beckjord as much as you just *listen* while *he* talks. On
this particular evening, Beckjord lectured me on the fact that he was sure that
the sasquatch were essentially a species of extraterrestrials. In his view, the
sasquatch were genetic hybrids installed here on Earth thousands of years ago
by another, more powerful set of extraterrestrial entities. I wasn't sure I agreed
with his logic, but Erik's view did suggest a line of questioning that Steve
Frederick might pursue in his possible telepathic communication with the
sasquatch.

"Ask them where they are from, Steve," I encouraged. "Ask them if they
are ETs, like Beckjord says." Steve seemed a bit surprised by all of this.
Perhaps he was expecting something more scientific from a career science

The Coconut Telegraph

teacher. I didn't care. "We've got nothing to lose," I encouraged. "Also, Beckjord insisted that they can spy on us while we think we're being sneaky. You might also ask how they like your harmonica playing. I'm a harmonica player, too. Ask them how they like my harmonica playing." Steve seemed amused by my off-the-cuff suggestions but he was willing to give it a shot. My unconventional ideas were almost reassuring. This time, I was the crazy one. He may have heard voices, but I was suggesting he ask the voices what planet they were from, and while he's at it, ask them their opinion on our musical talent. He sheepishly confessed that he did what I suggested.

"And did you get an answer?" I asked.

"Well, yes. When I asked whether they were from someplace else in the galaxy, the answer I got was, "We live here with you, but *everything* on Earth was put here. If we're from outer space, so are you."

It was a much more profound answer than anything I expected. I was not sure that Steve was on the level with his claims of possible telepathic contact with the sasquatch, but I was impressed by this thought-provoking statement.

"Oh, and as far as the harmonica playing," Steve continued, "They said I need more practice. They said you are a lot better than I am."

I still wasn't sure how seriously to take this whole situation, but it certainly was amusing. Paranormal research may not be worth anything to mainstream science, but it was immensely interesting and it didn't cost anything. It may also be a scientific disaster, but nobody has to know.

At that point, the science teacher in me kicked in. The initial results were as interesting as they were unverifiable. Here was a perfect opportunity for me to conduct some 'citizen science.'

"I have another idea, Steve," I declared. "Let's try a little experiment of our own. You have some interesting but totally unverifiable results. Let's see if we can produce a tangible result...from telepathic contact.

"After thinking about the stuff, Steve, I have an idea. We're going to test the coconut telegraph, or whatever it is. I've got a camera site going up by Mt. Rainier in Washington. To make a long story short, the reports from the residents, and some of my own experiences, suggest that these beings, these 'forest people,' are a whole lot smarter than I ever expected. The residents are reluctantly admitting that there seems to be some telepathy coming from the sasquatches. Meanwhile, absolutely nothing is going on with the cameras. They're set up and they work, but they're not producing anything. We keep moving the cameras to the location of the last observed activity, but the signs of recent activity always shift. The residents think the creatures are wise to us. I'm inclined to agree. They describe at least one telepathic message that said, "Quit trying to trick us."

"You're saying that you think you may be having some kind of telepathic contact with the something out at Jordan Creek. Fine. Let's just see whether we can capitalize on that. Suppose it's a two way street and you can send messages as well as receive them. So let's try to submit a request. Up until now we've been trying to trick them into giving us physical evidence of their existence. Let's try just asking them for it. We're going to ask for three things. First, we want them to give us a footprint; a really good one. We also need to ask them to step in front of our cameras up at Allen and April's place. We need their picture. And finally, we want a bone."

"Jeez, is that *all?*" Steve replied sarcastically. "They're not going to like this."

"I guess not, but what's the harm in asking? Will you at least try?"

"I'll sure try. It would help if I could just drive the area near this camera site. Can you steer me toward the general area?"

"Sure, Steve, but you can't visit the camera site. It would contaminate any results we might get if you knew the exact location of the camera site. If we get anything by way of results, it will be assumed that *you* planted it. I'm not going to tell the residents about this telepathy part of the experiment. We don't want our results be attributable to a Rosenthal Effect."

"A *what?*" Steve inquired.

"A Rosenthal Effect. That's just psycho-babble for 'a self-fulfilling prophecy.' Basically, it means that, for this experiment to be official, you cannot know the location of the camera station, and the people who live at the camera station cannot be *expecting* anything to happen."

"I don't need to know exactly where the camera location is. I just need to visit the general area. As long as I'm within a couple miles, that's close enough."

I gave Steve directions to Middle Fork Road; two miles and a few unmarked turns from the Hoyts' place in the woods outside Onalaska. In order to be as scientific as possible, considering the screwy circumstances, I said nothing to Allen and April. If anything were to happen, it wasn't going to be on account of any self-fulfilling prophecies.

In a properly designed medical or psychological experiment, neither the experimenter, nor the experimentee, is supposed to know which of the competing treatments are being administered to specific subjects. This is what's known as a 'double blind' experiment. By comparison, the experiment I was proposing would be *single blind*. That is, I knew what Steve was going to ask for and I knew where it was supposed to happen. If Steve did not know the precise location, he could not be accused of planting evidence or otherwise rigging the outcome of the experiment. Likewise, if residents did not even know that there was a guy named Steve who was going to try and ask the 'the locals' for cooperation, they could not be accused of rigging the results. I could still be accused of rigging the results, but that could not be completely avoided. I was designing the experiment. Still, I was happy with the overall plan.

Naturally, I did not discuss my paranormal experiment with my quasi-scientific colleagues at the BFRO, or anyone else. They certainly knew all about the camera project since they found sponsors and provided so much technical assistance. They didn't know, however, that I was now going to tweak things. After two years of no significant results, I was going to attempt to use telepathic back-channels of communication to coax the results that we had not been able to achieve in two years of passive efforts.

Clearly, I was crossing over to 'the dark side' and I knew it. I also knew there was nothing to lose. The whole camera project was a bust so far. I was pretty confident that there were sasquatches in the vicinity but they just weren't playing ball. Why not try to shake things up a little? I didn't go looking for the whole telepathy angle. It more or less found me. I just decided to see if it could be put to the test. It probably wouldn't work but it seemed a shame not to give it a try. Even if we got some results, I didn't need to attribute it to anything but sheer luck. If I did tell the BFRO operatives that I met a guy who hears voices and he is submitting research requests directly to the bigfoots, on my behalf…,well,…at the very least, I would get kicked out of the BFRO, and at worst they'd have me hauled off in a straightjacket. I kept my plan to myself.

It took a few days for Steve to get the chance to drive the area and try to log on to the coconut telegraph. It was late October of 2001 when Steve called me to say that he finally made it up to Middle Fork Road. He had done his best to submit my request via the 'coconut telegraph.' Back in Portland, Steve submitted his telepathic requests for tangible evidence. The response from the other side seemed luke-warm, at best. It was as though they weren't listening.

"But I did my best," Steve insisted.

To be perfectly honest, I wasn't expecting anything to happen at all. I would even say that I put the whole matter out of my mind, beginning the day after Steve phoned to say that that he *tried* to submit my requests. Just the fact that Steve said "it didn't seem like they were listening" was reason enough not to get my hopes up.

Two weeks later, on a rainy night in early November, I got a call from Allen Hoyt. They had found a very strange impression in the mud inside one of his horse corrals. It was the impression of something that was very furry. The corral did not have a horse in it at the time, and the fur was too long to be the short, fine hair that covers a horse hide.

By now, it had been a little over a year since the Skookum Cast had been collected. Allen has seen photos but never viewed the cast in person, though it seemed to Allen that he was looking at a very similar Skookum Cast-style impression in his horse pasture. Whatever it was, Allen was very confident it had not been made by a horse.

It was a rainy weekend. The impression had already been rained on when Allen found it. He covered it with a piece of plywood just before he called. At first, I didn't really make any connection to Steve Fredericks and the telepathy experiment. I did grab a bunch of plaster at the local Home Depot before heading up there to try and cast at least some of this mysterious impression. With help from Allen and his son, we laid a four-foot-square frame and filled it with plaster. Two weeks later, the impression was dutifully delivered to my garage by the Hoyts. Meanwhile, I mentioned my newest and largest plaster cast to Matt Moneymaker at BFRO.

Matt could not have been more *unenthusiastic* about this latest find. The Skookum Cast was still embroiled in controversy. As with all things bigfoot, the community was divided and the battle lines were clearly drawn. Some felt it was the best piece of sasquatch evidence ever obtained since the acquisition of the Patterson-Gimlin footage in 1967. Others felt that it was the impression of an ordinary elk. Efforts were still underway to put the cast before qualified experts. What the world did *not* need, Matt emphatically declared, was another Skookum-style cast to distract and dilute the limited interest in scientific analysis of the original. Matt added that this second cast was also a little too convenient. He seemed to be inwardly wondering whether I might have concocted this second large cast because I was feeling left out of the attention and recognition that was being bestowed on those who were shuttling the Skookum Cast around the scientific community.

I could see his first point. The world didn't need two Skookum Casts. On the second point, I knew there were no subconscious motivations on my part.

I didn't even find the impression. I just agreed to try and preserve it before it washed away in the rain. I did however, take the hint. I stayed quiet on the matter of obtaining another big cast. It stayed in one piece in my garage for a couple years. In order to make it easier to store, I finally cut it into four smaller squares with a masonry saw. I still have the pieces, and I still scratch my head and wonder about the discovery, and the timing of the impression that we started calling the Newaukum Cast. (Allen lived along one of the forks of the Newaukum River.)

Throughout it all, I never mentioned to Allen the telepathy experiment, but I did feel obliged to call Steve Frederick and let him know that the mysterious impression had appeared in Allen's horse corral a little less than two weeks after he attempted his telepathic communication.

The cameras outside the Hoyt's home: IR illuminator is in the top bird box; lower box contains the video camera.

Another month passed. We came into the holiday season of 2001 and I was fully preoccupied with family and holiday matters. Bigfoot matters were on 'hold' for the holidays. Out of the blue, on New Year's Eve, as I was getting ready to go out on the town with my wife, the phone rang. It was Allen Hoyt. He wanted me to know that we just got the best camera images he's ever seen in the two years we'd been deploying cameras on his property! On the previous night (December 30th) something large had moved back and forth across the camera's field of view." At the time, one of our cameras was out of order. The only working camera was the one that was trained on the woods outside Nina's window.

Being New Year's Eve, I wasn't about to jump in my car and drive a hundred miles to see the images, but I would do my best to get up there the following day. I managed to make it up to Allen's place on Monday. Frankly, I was a little disappointed with the quality of the images. They were just moving shadows. There was no detail, just some outlines. Still, it was the first time that we got images on the camera after many months of trying.

This time, I was a little less willing to dismiss the timing of this event as mere coincidence. Like the so-called Newaukum Cast, the video evidence our devices had collected was not overly compelling. It was the best set of images we had ever collected in the two years of camera deployment at the

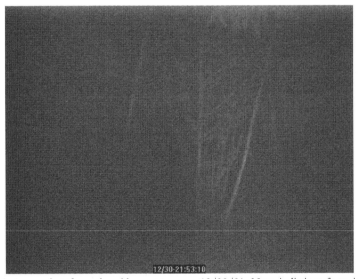

A screen shot from the video capture on 12/30/01. Note indistinct form in center of photo, just above the time-stamp.

site, but I could plainly see that there was no detail and no clear resolution of images; just vague, albeit moving images of what looked like a massive head and shoulders that moved back and forth across the camera's field of view.

I thought of Steve and the telepathy experiment, but I still did not tell him about the interesting images. Nor did I mention anything to Allen about Steve and the telepathy project. It just seemed too likely that mere coincidence had produced an interesting, but inconclusive set of camera images several weeks after Steve attempted a telepathic request. What was most intriguing was the fact that the camera system had gone on and off at fairly random intervals all during the night when the interesting images were obtained. As the power to the system cycled on and off, 'blue screen' images were recorded on the computer-driven image capture system. On and off power cycling had never happened before in the whole history of our efforts at the site, not to mention the shadowy images of something resembling a torso.

I shared the images with Vaughn Hughes and Matt Moneymaker at BFRO. Vaughn was the more intrigued of the two. He was also intrigued by the cycling of the computer and all the blue screens. He could not explain why the equipment would have done that on that particular night. The images from that night were dutifully posted on the BFRO website. They can still be viewed there. (If interested, try Googling: BFRO Wireless Wilderness Project.)

Naturally, we were encouraged by this interesting night of video results. On the one hand, we were now batting two-for-three on our requests for an impression, a photographic image, and a bone. On the other hand, the impression in the mud was huge but not real definitive, and the video images were numerous but also of dubious quality. Allen still didn't even know Steve Frederick existed. Nor did Steve know that I now had a second set of these curious results from the telepathy project. Inwardly I was vacillating between incredulous amazement and skeptical indifference. I kept reminding myself that I still had no definitive evidence to show the world.

Now, try to imagine my surprise when, two weeks later, my daughter hollered that Allen Hoyt was on the phone. I took the call. Allen greeted me warmly and informed me that he just found a very strange bone lying on the ground at the base of the camera tree outside Nina's window. I was thunderstruck. I felt chills run up my spine. I thought to myself, "Steve Frederick, you are a genius!" Then, I restrained myself with a second thought, "This cannot be. This isn't possible!"

I had to do my best to rule out tampering. I asked Allen, "Have you had any uninvited guests, that is, any strangers show up in the past few days?"

"Nope," was the immediate reply.

"Can you think of anyone who might have put a bone there for you to find as some kind of joke?"

"Nope."

"Okay, tell me about the bone."

Well, it's about the size and shape of a coffee saucer. It's circular and concave, and very thick. It looks like the top of someone's skull, but it is much too thick to be a human skull."

"Wow. I'll be up tomorrow, if that is OK with you."

"Sure. I'll see you then."

The next day, Allen showed me the bone. We looked all around the camera tree for tracks and clues, and looked through the computer memory for video images. There were some indistinct scuff marks around the camera tree, but that was about it. The ground near the house was so compacted that it was not surprising that footprint tracks could not be found. It was a strange looking bone indeed; ragged around the edges, like it had been out in the weather for quite some time, very thick (about ¾") and light, as if it were belonging to a bird. But what part of a bird could it be?

I knew just who to ask. LeRoy Fish held a doctorate in biology and his area of specialty was bird behavior. I phoned him in Triangle Lake, Oregon and arranged to meet. I wasn't about to explain the circumstances under which I came by this bone. I told him only that Allen had found it at his place. LeRoy had been to Allen and April's place. In fact, he spent the night there. It was on his way home from the Skookum expedition. I gave him directions and asked Allen and April if they would greet Dr. Fish and show him around the camera site. LeRoy ended up spending the night, sleeping outside in the woods near the house. For much of that night, LeRoy heard knocks, cooing noises, and even something that sounded like garbled speech. LeRoy left the place very impressed by what he experienced. After spending the night, LeRoy was not at all skeptical of Allen and April's claim that they had sasquatches inhabiting their woods. Even Allen was a bit surprised at how vocal the wildlife was on that night that LeRoy slept out. Usually, things were very quiet when visitors showed up, and I can attest to the fact that that was *especially* true when I visited the Hoyt homestead.

I met up with LeRoy at a Denny's Restaurant just off the freeway. I showed him the bone. He could not identify it, but he felt certain that it was from a bird of some kind. It was so thick yet so very light. He had absolutely no idea what kind of bird it could be, but it had to be a big one.

After pondering this new information, I began to develop a suspicion. At one point in the camera project, Allen placed a dead emu in the clearing that was being watched by the infrared camera about a quarter mile from the house. We logged video images of coyotes and dogs that were interested in the dead bird, but nothing more exotic ever showed up to feed on the emu. Allen obtained the carcass from his father, who raised the large ostrich-like birds on his property a few miles away.

Two views of the bone found at the base of the 'camera tree.'

As it turned out, a neighbor of mine also raised emus. One day, I invited myself over and introduced myself. The neighbor was cordial and also very knowledgeable about this new type of livestock that originated from in Australia. He produced a reference text and we found a page that depicted the emus' entire skeleton. After careful study, he and I both agreed that the bone I held bore a reasonable similarity to the breast bone of an emu. There was a ridge where wing muscles attached that seemed to be absent, but given the deteriorated condition of the bone, it seemed that it still was a pretty good match. At that point, one element of the mystery was tentatively solved. I had a match that seemed quite plausible. There was also a way that an emu bone could have ended up on the property. How it ended up at the base of that particular tree (the camera tree), on that particular evening, was a wide open question.

The most prosaic answer to that question rested with the Hoyts' dogs that freely roamed the property. Of course, there are other members of the local wildlife community that could be responsible for moving bones around on the property. That said, one point was still undeniable: it was the precise tree that I had specified when I asked Steve to request a bone at 'the camera tree' and no one at the property knew anything of the telepathic request!

I still have the bone and I would very much like to have a few other opinions about the origin of the bone. Still, I'm not holding out any hope that I'm in possession of a bigfoot bone. I keep the bone only as a reminder of the mighty strange set of circumstances that led to its discovery.

In my own mind, I guess I still tend to write off the whole matter as a really odd set of coincidences. I certainly pondered the possibility that it was something more deliberate. I wanted to try some more experiments at the Hoyts' place, but it was at this juncture that the Hoyts decided that they needed to take a break from the project. They had indications that their house had been searched. The phone company report of their phone line being tapped still bothered them. Having heard similar stories from other bigfoot researchers, I was not surprised. Truth be told, after more than two years of back and forth trips to west-central Washington state, I needed a break, as well. I had become increasingly convinced over the past year that they (the sasquatches) were wise to us. I was also pretty sure that our electronic monitoring efforts had lost the element of surprise, if we ever had it in the first place.

I took the cameras out the following weekend. Family matters kept me busy and I didn't speak to Steve for almost a year. One day, he called to tell me he was having a garage sale and I stopped by. I apologized for not getting back to him sooner about the outcome of the telepathy experiment. Steve was pleasantly surprised to hear that we had obtained some interesting results at the very least. Up until this time, he had assumed nothing interesting happened. He was eager to hear the details.

I told him about Allen finding the bone at the base of the camera tree. I related the efforts I made to identify the bone and the fact that it ended up being an emu bone.

Steve fell silent as he recollected some long-ignored memories.

"Those rascals…" he mumbled and his voice trailed off.

"Whaddaya mean, Steve?"

"I mean, they are either very literal thinkers, like Mr. Spock on *Star Trek*, or they are quite the comedians."

"I'm not following you."

"I asked for a bone, but you know what?" Steve offered, "I never specified. I never really said, 'Would you please give us a *sasquatch* bone?' I assumed that they understood that I was talking about one of *their* bones, but I never actually specified. Those rascals. I bet they knew exactly what we were after. They just had no intention whatsoever of giving it to us. Instead, they decided to have a little fun at our expense. Those rascals! Can't you just see them saying among themselves, 'Ha! They want a bone, eh? Let's see how long it takes 'em to figure this out! This'll keep them busy for a while!'"

"I have to admit, Steve, it does start to look like somebody is messing with us. It's just a question of who is doing the messing around. I guess if we're willing to consider the possibility that they have telepathic powers, we can also suppose that they have a sense of humor."

By this time, I had convinced myself that the appearance of the bone was just an extraordinary coincidence. Suddenly, I was less sure. If it was more than a coincidence, it was an extraordinary coincidence; a veritable synchronicity.

First the impression in the mud, then the shadowy video images, then the appearance of the bone; taken as a whole, it seemed to be something much stronger than matters of simple chance.

The conversation with Steve shifted to other matters. I asked him how his garage sale went. Steve confessed that it was disappointing. He had been laid off and if he didn't raise some money soon, he would have to find a less expensive apartment. By the way, Steve asked, would I like to buy some tools?

Steve lived only a mile from the school where I worked in southwest Portland. I stopped by, visited for a while and gave him a few bucks for a portable television.

He was very appreciative and I was happy to help him. It suddenly occurred to me that there might be a little more I can do for the guy.

I had been working in the neighborhood so long that former students had grown up and become employees at many of the neighborhood businesses. I could scarcely walk into a shop in the neighborhood without being recognized by a former student who was now an employee of that store.

A thought occurred to me. "Will you be here for the next half-hour or so? I think I might know where there's a job."

I had just filled my tank at a gas station about two miles from Steve's apartment. As usual, I chatted with a former student who told me that he had just quit his job at the gas station. He was going off to college in England. I returned to that gas station. The former student, Jim Thorson, was still there. I told Jim I had a friend who needed a job. He directed me to his boss: an Indian fellow named Raj. I found Raj counting cash. I told him I knew of a person who needed work and whom I could personally vouch for.

"Could he start tonight?" Raj asked.

Minutes later I was back at Steve's house and shortly after that I dropped him off at the gas station to chat it up with Raj. I wished him luck and drove off with the TV set Steve sold me. By the time I got home, Steve was on the phone.

"I haven't even been able to get an interview in a month of trying and you came over and found me a job in five minutes. I can't tell you how big a favor you just did for me."

"Don't mention it, Steve. It's not the greatest job in the world. In fact, it may be closer to being one of the worst jobs in the world. But at least you can pay the rent while you look for a better job, and when you find one, I sure hope to hear that you quit working at that gas station."

I couldn't help but feel good about doing my daily good deed. I distinctly remember also thinking, "Well, if there is any truth to Steve's connection to the sasquatch, I hope they're watching, or listening, or whatever they do. I just helped out their buddy. Maybe they'll quit giving me the brush-off."

As quick as I had the thought, I dismissed it. And that would have been the end of it, except, that very night, I had an uncommonly vivid dream. It was also the first time in my life that I ever had a dream in which a sasquatch made a personal appearance.

It began with a sasquatch running across an open, sagebrush covered hillside, in full view of a group of people, one of whom was me. It was my mind's recreation of what is known in sasquatch circles as "the Memorial Day footage," a short video clip made by some campers of what appears to be a sasquatch running across open terrain. In this dream, the creature didn't disappear behind a contour in the landscape as it does on the Memorial Day footage. Instead, it detoured and ran inside a nearby building that looked like the bathhouse of a public swimming pool. When I saw it enter the building, I turned to the other people who were watching in stunned disbelief. I insisted that we had to go in the building. They flatly refused. I ran over to the building and opened the door.

Once inside, I saw a hairy hominid sitting on the floor in a brightly lit and featureless corridor made of white sheetrock walls. I stopped and stared at the hirsute form and as soon as gazed I upon it, *poof*, it turned into a blonde haired surfer-dude in a Hawaiian shirt. He stayed sitting on the floor with one arm perched atop his bended knee, looking up at me. And, as if he were continuing a conversation we had started previously, he matter-of-factly uttered, "OK, so what do you want to know?"

I knew right away what he meant... I had a free question. I took the opportunity: "How many of you are there?"

"Thousands," was the immediate reply. "Not hundreds, not millions, but thousands."

"Where are you guys from? I mean, do you live here or do you come from someplace else?"

"Oh, no, we live here, just like you...mostly."

"Mostly?"

All of a sudden, my eyes popped open. The morning sun shone in the window. It felt so real, but clearly, it was all a dream. I wondered whether finding Steve a crummy job had any genuine connection to that particularly vivid and fascinating dream. If it did, then finding someone a gas station job earns you just two questions, and the answers you get will be pretty vague in any event. I humorously wondered if I would have gotten more questions if I had found Steve an accounting job.

As I said at the beginning of this chapter, I didn't set out to become a paranormal researcher. I pretty much backed into the whole subject by moving to the country. Then, I stumbled across some paranormal phenomena as an outgrowth of my pursuit of the sasquatch phenomenon. Specifically, I came across reports of telepathic contact with bigfoot that I never went looking for. Both Rick Snyder, and then Steve Frederick found me, mostly as a consequence of the publicity that came from the Skookum Cast.

The camera project that I always wanted to do was now officially over. That project started out as an attempt to quantify the sasquatch as scientifically as possible. Owing to a series of chance encounters, it morphed into a big pool of paranormal quicksand. I never did get any good pictures, but I *may* have earned the opportunity to ask a sasquatch a few off-the-cuff questions. I can't be sure. Maybe the dream was just another coincidence, an invention of my mind that was, by that time, mired in that same paranormal quicksand. I have no regrets. It was fun while it lasted. And now I have one completed, single-blind scientific telepathy/bigfoot experiment to put on my 'paranormal researcher' resume.

Gone Fishing

Just the other day, I was fishing with my pal Cliff Barackman. He was home between the long road trips that are required of him in his starring role of the TV show 'Finding Bigfoot.' As we floated down the Clackamas River on that cold and rainy Sunday, we talked of bigfoot, telepathy, and the chapter I was writing. Cliff expressed the honest opinion that he didn't think telepathic contact was anything more than one's own 'self-talk,' combined with a dose of wishful thinking.

I could certainly relate to that suggestion. My own self-talk is positively deafening. As a writer, I am constantly thinking and rethinking ways to express thoughts. My mind is constantly coming up with new ideas and reformulating old ones. My own 'self talk' is so loud I cannot imagine what it would be like to hear a voice that came from outside my own mind.

I did happen to once ask Steve how he knew that any voices he may have heard back then had not originated *within* his own mind.

By way of an answer, Steve recollected the days in the late 1990s when he was searching coastal drainages for bigfoot tracks. He had one long circuit that he covered repeatedly in remote parts of the Salmonberry River valley. In these travels, he discovered one particular sand bar composed of fine sediments. It seemed like an excellent place to watch for future tracks. One day, as he was trying to get to sleep, he heard a very clear voice say, "Come now!"

The statement had no connection to anything that was on his mind at the time, but the most significant point, Steve felt, was that if it had been his own mind trying to direct his actions, the statement would likely have been, "Go now." It wasn't. It was, "Come, now." This is a very significant difference, Steve felt, and I wholeheartedly agree. It seems reasonable to interpret the particular choice of verbs as an indication that the statement originated somewhere outside his mind. In fact, it could be argued that, by saying "Come," rather than "Go," the voice was beckoning Steve to return to a place where Steve had already been, as well as the place somewhere near the place where that voice presently was.

Granted, this is hardly strong evidence. While it is highly speculative, I think it is also astute of Steve to recognize that the choice of verbs indicates something significant. I'm reassured that Steve is at least trying to be objective and analytical when considering the possible origins of the telepathic messages he may or may not have been receiving.

There is one other reason why I doubt that all of the above examples of possible telepathy originate from within the minds of those who are claiming them. In the case of the Hoyts, two different members of the family, April and Nina, had these experiences, while other members of the family, namely their two sons, had no such experiences to relate. Also, Nina and April were not in any way expecting, thinking about, or even receptive to the idea of receiving telepathic messages. They had no previous experiences like that and they did not think such things were possible.

This is a common thread with the very few others I have spoken to over the years who were claiming similar experiences. It was completely unexpected. It was described as a very bewildering experience that was absolutely without precedent. Knowing the Hoyts, and Steve Frederick, as sober, level-headed individuals who were not at all inclined to make outrageous claims, I am willing to take the descriptions of their experiences at face value. I knew Rick Snyder much less well, but he was a little sheepish about sharing the details of his experience until I was able to reassure him that I was open-minded. Rick's main concern was whether I knew of other people who could corroborate his bewildering experiences. At the time, I could not validate those experiences citing other examples. I can now.

I asked Steve Frederick to proof-read this chapter before publication. He called me after he read it to offer a few thoughts:

"If you're trying to argue for the existence of telepathy, using examples from the dubious field of 'bigfoot research' probably won't work. But perhaps people can relate to a cell phone analogy. Cell phones work because of frequency matching. A specific frequency is generated that is matched to a specific receiver. Our brain works on ultra-low frequency signals. We can hear between 20 and 20,000 hertz. We cannot *hear* below 20 hertz, but our brains actually *work* at frequencies between 10 and 18 hertz. We cannot consciously hear at those frequencies but our brain can still receive them. A sasquatch can vocalize in the same ULF range of 4 to 18 hertz range and hear at that range as well. They're very good at what they do. Many other animals can hear at those same frequencies. Infrasound is well known in the animal kingdom."

"That said," Steve continued, "Since you're looking for patterns, here's one I think you missed. You mentioned that I experienced the statement, *"Come now,"* not *"Go* now." The specific words used suggests the statement originated outside my brain. I agree. Then you wrote of others experiencing the same thing but you didn't point it out to the readers. I think you might have missed the other examples."

"Let's hear it, Steve."

"April Hoyt's reported the message, "Quit trying to trick *us."* If the message had been her own self-talk, it should have been, "Quit trying to trick *them."* Her daughter Nina reported, *"Come* out and play," not *"Go* out and play." Rick Snyder reported, *"Come* out. *We're* hungry." not *"Go* out, *they're* hungry."

Further, Steve observed that the messages seem to happen during times of low brain activity, when one is awake but very idle, or when asleep. It happened for Steve during a lonely all-night vigil. April was walking in the woods, although it's hard to know how active her mind was. It happened for Nina when she was asleep, as it did for Rick Snyder.

"I think I see a pattern there, too," Steve observed. "We all have the potential for telepathy. Sleeping quiets the brain, making it more open to receiving an external signal. Most of the time, we're distracted by other inputs. With all our modern-world inputs, we are not as receptive to subtle mental inputs. They [the sasquatch] probably have an evolutionary advantage. They also live in a world with many fewer distracting inputs. Our brains emit a weak signal. Their brains can emit a much stronger signal which we can receive, but only when our guard is down; when our filters are off. "

I must commend Steve on his keen observations. I still expect that most readers will, like Cliff, remain strongly skeptical of the whole telepathy question, especially as it pertains to the sasquatch. I am perfectly fine with that. Science requires proof. All I have are a few reliable observers, a few patterns; but no particular *proof.*

Yet, I think there is validity in putting all of this into print. I offer it for the reader's consideration as the interesting results of admittedly paranormal investigations that really did happen. All one can do in paranormal investigations of this kind is to glean information from sources that seem credible, and identify the patterns. After that, if there is any validity to the whole uncertain matter, it should emerge at some point in the future if other investigators can corroborate these results with lots more experimental results of a similar kind.

Perhaps someday, more vivid or more telling examples will surface. Maybe not. If no future observations surface, I will retract my suggestion that at least some sasquatches are telepathic.

Time will tell.

Chapter Two: Hillbilly Hollow

This sign outside the little store in Honobia, Oklahoma may be accurate for more than one reason. There are the hillbillies known for wearing overalls and sleeveless flannel shirts, but few folks know that the original "hillbillies" were something else altogether.

According to Kentucky researcher and author Bart Nunelly, the term 'hillbilly' was originally coined in Appalachia to refer to ominous beings that confronted explorers of the remote, densely forested hills and steeply forbidding hollers in the mountainous terrain of the eastern U.S. "Hillbilly" was basically a bigfoot reference. Later, it became a derogatory term for the coarser and less-cultured human inhabitants of that same region who were also skilled hunters and savvy outdoorsmen. Still more recently, the term has been cheerfully co-opted as a badge of honor among the more modern rural folk who still eek out a living in the remote mountains of the Eastern U.S.

Honobia, Oklahoma is such a place. The folks who reside in this mountainous corner of the Sooner State are still skilled hunters, savvy outdoorsmen, and even moonshiners. They take pride in their close connection to their native landscape. Most outsiders do not realize that these forested mountains are also home to a population of wildmen or *sasquatch*, as they are known in the Pacific Northwest. According to Bart, they are the area's original hillbillies. One way or another, Honobia, Oklahoma is 'Hillbilly Hollow.'

I first learned of Oklahoma's original hillbillies while researching the bigfoot phenomenon in 2000. I wrote in *The Locals* about some interesting sasquatch related events in this area at a time when no other published references to sasquatch in this area existed. At the time, suggesting that there were sasquatches in Oklahoma was going way out on a limb. I knew I was sticking my literary neck out, especially since I had never been to the area to personally experience this phenomenon. I didn't give Honobia residents their connection to the bigfoot phenomenon, but I may have been the first to write about it.

Honobia (pronounced HO-nobby) is a tiny crossroad village nestled between forested ridges of the Kiamichi Mountains in the southeast corner of

Oklahoma. Honobia's sole commercial building is a metal-clad double-wide structure that serves as a restaurant/store/RV park office. Outside the store stands a stout iron hook that is attached to a scale. It is used to weigh and register hunting kills, specifically deer or bear, which are bagged in the surrounding mountains. On the other side of the store stands a piece of wrought-iron art-work that identifies the area as "Hillbilly Hollow."

Aside from their identity as a gateway to some fertile hunting ground, Hillbilly Hollow has a newer identity. Honobia has more recently become a nationally-known gathering place for researchers and enthusiasts of the bigfoot phenomenon. I might have had something to do with that.

In 2000, a series of bigfoot encounters took place at a homestead outside Honobia. A cadre of well-meaning BFRO investigators conducted a clumsy investigation, adding another amusing twist to this story, and I published a description of the whole affair in 2003. In October of 2009 I finally made it to Honobia to attend Darrin Lee and Mark Hall's Honobia Bigfoot Festival and Conference. I half-expected to be cursed and vilified by at least some of the locals for my role in associating this unsuspecting community with the much-ridiculed bigfoot phenomenon. I could not have been more wrong. Honobia loves Bigfoot. The store features an array of bigfoot t-shirts, souvenirs, and books, including *The Locals*. They now have two annual bigfoot conferences. Honobia is downright proud of their connection to bigfoot. What a relief.

Far from being vilified, I felt like the guest-of-honor. Darrin Lee, Mike Hall, and many others were downright pleased that I made the trip to their conference. I met the Humphreys brothers, Tim and Michael, who defended their homestead from the bigfoot incursion back in 2000. They could not have been friendlier.

When I arrived in October, the brisk, unsettled weather of fall had replaced the muggy-warm days of summer. The woods were damp from a strong fall rainstorm that had just passed through, but the surrounding woods was still full of campers who were there to attend the festival, enjoy the Kiamichi National Forest, and of course, find bigfoot. The festival organizers generously provided me with comfortable accommodation in an historic bed-and-breakfast in the nearby town of Tahlina, but the forest beckoned. I passed on the plush accommodations and instead joined the campers on 'the ridge above *Ho-nobby*.'

The thunderstorms of the previous day had moved on, but because of the recent rains, the well-watered forest was rowdy with the chirps, hoots, and croaks of a host of nocturnal critters. Cricket, frog, and owl noises positively abounded. A friendly Texan named Lem Weaver offered me the use of a tarp that he had stretched between sassafras trees at his outpost camp. This was exactly the experience I had hoped for. It was a chance to spend a few nights in the woods, in a part of the country I had never seen before, amidst other friendly campers and bigfoot devotees. Life was good.

When it came to preparedness, this group wasn't kidding around. Among the spirited and friendly campers that surrounded me was enough camping gear to fill a sporting goods store. They were supremely well equipped with stoves, chairs, tents, food, and beer. Transportation was also well-covered, right down to the fleet of 'quads' (four-wheel drive all-terrain vehicles). And when groups of bigfoot enthusiasts get together, one of the most interesting aspects is the array of technology that is brought to bear.

Bigfoot devotees prefer to call themselves 'researchers.' I think it helps justify the considerable sums of money they sometimes invest on surveillance electronics. I expected to see night vision and thermal scopes, but these guys took the surveillance gear to a level I had never seen before. One fellow had outfitted a small travel trailer with an array of battery-operated video cameras, TV monitors, and listening equipment. Using his quad vehicle, Randy Harrington, one of the event organizers, deployed and baited camera stations a few miles deeper into the woods. Meanwhile, groups of people travelled around on foot with walkie-talkies, conducting various noise-making and attraction strategies that might or might not produce some kind of interesting response from the nocturnal wildlife.

While it might seem like this much concentrated effort should produce some kind of interesting result if there really were such creatures as bigfoot inhabiting the surrounding forest, I didn't expect much. Truth be told, such well-attended weekend gatherings are really a chance for local 'researchers' to showcase their area and their techniques for the benefit of the out-of-town visitors like me.

Every so-called 'bigfoot researcher' endures at least occasional ridicule, perhaps rendering them even more eager to be taken seriously. Their best hope for achieving some degree of credibility comes only when other bigfoot researchers gather at events like this. Whether this event was a 'conference', a 'festival,' or an 'open house' it was a gathering of bigfoot enthusiasts from the southeast region of the U.S. and therefore a good chance to see what passed for amateur bigfoot research in this area of the country.

Only a few years ago, it was widely held that only the Pacific Northwest had enough unpopulated forest land to accommodate the needs of a population of sasquatches. If they existed anywhere at all, it could only be in the extensive forested mountains of the Pacific Northwest. Therefore, it used to be thought that only in the Pacific Northwest was real bigfoot research being done. After all, that's the only place where the creatures existed. We laugh at that idea now, and in fact, that's one of the myths I was attempting to explode in *The Locals*. Indeed, it was the events in Honobia in 2000 that I used to open people's eyes to the fact that the bigfoot phenomenon was alive and well in numerous dispersed locations throughout the continent. No region of the U.S. lacks reported sightings.

Since publication of *The Locals*, groups of semi-organized amateurs have proliferated and annual events like the Honobia Conference have proliferated as well. Virtually every region of the U.S. now has at least one annual conference or festival. And when the local researchers put on an event, they want to know how their techniques and organization stack up against those in other regions of the country. The Pacific Northwest may have the most storied connection to the whole bigfoot phenomenon, so local researchers from these other places are eager to know how their efforts compare to whatever is being done in 'bigfoot central,' that is the Pacific Northwest.

Looking at the concentrated activity that was going on around me in my visit to Honobia, I couldn't help but be impressed. If camera equipment, camping supplies, vehicles, and personnel were any indication, these guys and gals in the southeast U.S. were every bit as serious as anything I had seen in the PNW. At this point, about all that can be said for the Pacific Northwest is that this is the place where serious bigfoot research *started*. But, at this stage of the game, the research efforts in places like Honobia actually look stronger, more organized, and better funded than what's currently going on in the birthplace of bigfoot research.

Randy Harrington checks his trail cameras in the Kiamichi National Forest

Perhaps the biggest difference I was seeing in Oklahoma, other than the amount of stuff they had on hand, was the organization. They worked in groups. Everyone had walkie-talkies and they stayed in constant touch with other field teams. They had specific protocols. They would spread out their squads over large areas and either make purported bigfoot calls or just listen. There was lots of back-and-forth walkie-talkie communication. Squads were dispersed but close enough to sometimes accidentally encounter each other. Is this always considered the best approach? I don't know, but it was certainly worth a try. There are many who advocate smaller groups, fewer groups or even groups of one. Large groups are considered counterproductive by just as many field researchers, though it *is* a whole lot safer to work in larger teams.

It just becomes harder to accomplish any degree of stealth when the groups get larger and communication systems like walkie-talkies are used.

As the visitor to the Kiamichi area, one thing I wasn't about to do was point out how we do things up in the Northwest. I was attending an impressively organized open house put on by the local researcher/enthusiasts so I just kept my mouth shut and tagged along, observing and enjoying everything that was going on, and trying my best not to get lost in the completely unfamiliar terrain.

On the second night, my basic approach of being as non-judgmental and friendly as possible began to pay off. I was invited to take a nocturnal tour of the surroundings in Randy Harrington's 'quad.' Randy had a couple camera stations set up a good way up the mountain above camp. He offered to take me and another visiting bigfoot researcher on up the mountain for a look-see. I jumped at the opportunity. I didn't come half way across the continent to sit around a camp fire, even if it was a very nice campfire.

The night was rather chilly but I came prepared. I hate being cold. I had at least two layers of clothing on every part of my body. Randy's quad was so beefy that it actually had an enclosed cab that fit two, and an open pick-up style bed in back. Randy and the professor were in the cab. I rode in the open bed as we rumbled up a series of ever-steepening narrow tracks through the dark deciduous woods. Taking reassurance from Randy's generally cautious and conservative driving, I decided to throw caution to the wind. I stood up in the bed, leaning my arms and upper torso on the top of the cab that contained the other occupants of the ATV. I was well aware of the fact that if Randy rolled the quad, I would be lucky to escape with only a broken neck. Getting pitched from the open bed of a rolling ATV would quite possibly be fatal. But no one was drinking and everyone was being cautious and prudent. Standing in the back of the quad, facing forward as we climbed the mountain in the pitch dark was also exhilarating. The headlights stabbed the darkness ahead of our vehicle. The lush growth enveloped the narrow jeep trail, creating an illuminated green tunnel through the foliage. Other times, the overhead vegetation would part and the nearly-full moon would illuminate the distant hillsides with pale white light. We moved swiftly and effortlessly through miles of unfamiliar terrain and I loved every minute of it.

Then headlights caught on a brick-sized foreign object in the middle of the single lane track we were following up the mountain. The quad lurched to a stop and we piled out to investigate the unexpected object in our path. We gathered around what turned out to be a block of the native limestone sitting atop a plastic grocery sack.

"This wasn't here a couple days ago when we were up here last," Randy observed.

"Maybe Bigfoot wants us to pick up this litter," I kidded.

"Maybe so," Randy agreed and we all laughed. I picked up the plastic sack and threw it in the empty bed of the quad. Randy kicked the stone out of the way and we all piled back into the vehicle.

A few minutes later, the quad again lurched to a stop and Randy hopped out. "This is it. This is where I set up the cameras."

"Fantastic," I said as I followed Randy and company into the woods to the right of the ragged roadway.

A couple hundred yards into the thicket, the undergrowth thinned to reveal a clearing decorated with yard ornaments. Motion-activated cameras encircled the clearing. Randy had positioned three different units to monitor traffic through this patch of woods. Little, solar-powered, flower-shaped lights provided items of curiosity for whatever sort of forest-dweller might be lurking on this hillside.

Having set more than a few cameras in the woods myself, I thought it was a very creative attractant. Most people use some kind of food, and although that brings results, it is invariably the familiar birds, squirrels, and possums.

The debate rages in sasquatch research circles as to whether the creatures of interest are of the pongid (ape) or hominid (human) lineage. This becomes an especially important issue when considering attraction strategies. Food would be the only reliable attractant if the target was a mere animal, even a clever one such as an ape. If the target were something more human-ish, then food might still work but items of curiosity might be just as productive and they don't have to be replenished like food. The ideal attractant is one that appeals to the creature of interest, *and nothing else*, so that the bait would be left alone by all the non-target species. Randy's choice of attractants, illuminated yard ornaments, would certainly have me checking them out if I came across them in the middle of the woods. I may not have a lot in common with your typical sasquatch, but the illuminated lighted ornaments would certainly catch my eye. It seemed a lot more creative than putting peanut butter sandwiches around the woods.

As the thinking in bigfoot researcher circles gradually shifts, more and more folks come to favor the idea that we are studying an hominid, not a pongid. And, as a result of this change in thinking, folks increasingly frown on use of the word "bait" when referring to our attempts to attract the creatures closer to cameras and other traps. "Baiting" sounds a little crude and implies that the creatures we pursue are pretty stupid. Instead, the new breed of sasquatch researcher prefers to put out "offerings" or "gifts." And, they might refer to their "attraction strategy" as opposed to calling it "bait." I am generally in agreement with this point of view, but I still find it easier to just call it "bait."

Solar-powered yard lights serve as attractants at Randy Harrington's camera set.

Whether he was baiting, attracting, or gifting, we looked over Randy Harrington's set up and his cameras and I certainly did not open my mouth to say that I had all but given up on my hope of ever getting photographs of a sasquatch with remote camera traps. Time and time again, I have seen indications that the sasquatch know a set-up when they see one. I know other researchers who feel similarly, but I still support anyone who wants to set up camera traps in the woods. They're interesting and fun to tinker with. The technology is constantly improving and the price is going down. When I began using them in 1998, all cameras still recorded photographs on film, and, compared to digital photography, what a hassle it was. One had to swap out rolls of film and have the film processed at the drug store in order to view the results. When a camera was triggered, we usually swapped out the whole roll, even if only a few shots had been taken. Thank goodness those days are gone. Now, one simply removes the memory chip and looks at the photos on a card reader or computer. Microprocessors control the operation of all modern camera traps, even the inexpensive ones. Sensitivity, shutter speed, battery life, and data storage of the equipment is all vastly better than it used to be in the early days of camera traps that relied on film cameras.

Things are so much easier and less expensive that I can't blame anyone for wanting to try their hand at deploying a few camera traps in hopes of getting photos of a sasquatch. Perhaps the best thing that can be said for tending a string of camera traps is that it gets one out into the woods, if only to set up and maintain the trap line. I have my doubts about the likelihood of getting a good photo, but checking one's trap line every week or so certainly puts you in the right place to have a chance encounter with whatever cryptid that might be around. And, having set more than a few camera traps myself, I'm always eager to see how somebody else does it.

So, when Randy invited me to take a spin in his quad up to his camera stations, I jumped at the chance, if for no other reason than to see some more of the local forest. Just riding around in the back of a quad, peering into the night like a hound peering out from behind the cab of a pickup truck as it bumped down a country road, was worth the trip. After we toured the camera station, they turned to me and asked whether I wanted to head back to camp or keep going deeper up the mountain, eventually looping around and take the long way back. I didn't even have to think about it. I just smiled and thrust my finger ahead.

We clambered back into the quad and I resumed my station standing up in the bed, facing forward and leaning on the back of the cab. We journeyed only a short distance further up the road before we again lurched to a stop. Another foreign object lay before us in the center of the narrow, two-track jeep trail. We clambered out for a look. Not having a door to open, I was the first one to inspect the obstruction. The headlights of the quad illuminated a flattened plastic water bottle lying atop a small stack of rocks. The other occupants of the quad approached as I held up the piece of litter and jokingly announced, "Here's another piece of litter Mr. Squatch wants us to take away."

The empty water bottle lay atop a stack of three stones. As the others stood and looked on, I disassembled the small pile of stones that lay in our path. In the center of the pile of stones lay a walkie-talkie. I picked it up and examined it in the glare of the headlights. Visible on the walkie-talkie was dried mud that formed the outline of rain drops. It had been rained on, but it was dry. I handed the walkie-talkie to Randy who immediately recognized it. It belonged to a member of his field team. Randy recollected that one of the members of his team lost the radio while they were checking their camera stations earlier in the week. It was all a bit puzzling. Randy recollected that the two-way radio had been lost in the vicinity of another camera set over a mile away. Randy was absolutely certain of this. The radio had somehow been moved to the location where we now stood.

"How about other researchers?" I suggested. "There's a BFRO expedition in town for the conference. Do you think they've been up here poking around this week? They may have found the radio and left it where they thought we would find it."

"I don't think they were in this area and they never would have found the camera stations, anyway. This area's too big and they're too well hidden," Randy insisted. "I would also think that if they found it, they would have kept it. These models are expensive and they can be set to any frequency at all, so you can use this walkie-talkie with just about any other model. This would have been a valuable find and one that I don't think they would have parted with. Besides, there's no guarantee that we would find it, even here in the middle of the trail."

Randy paused, then looked back at me and added, "We weren't even planning to come by here tonight, Thom. The only reason we kept going this far is because you wanted to!"

He had a point there. The group was ready to turn around but I wanted to see a little more of the area. I made the decision to venture up this road. We all stared at each other in a moment of bewildered silence. It was one of those weird moments in bigfoot field research when everyone realized at the same moment that something utterly unexplainable had happened. Could we be staring at something that was done for our benefit *by the bigfooted creatures themselves?*

The idea that the bigfoot creatures carried the walkie-talkie here and left it for Randy's field team to find and reclaim was an idea that was too far-fetched to consider. But there it was, and no one had any way to explain how that expensive little two-way radio ended up in the center of a pile of stones that had a piece of litter carefully placed on top of it. Clearly, the radio was left there with the hope and intention of being found by the group who lost it. The only real question was who left it there. It could have been left there by a hunter or other recreational forest user. Then there's the possibility that other bigfoot enthusiasts are in the area, which seems especially likely on this weekend with the Honobia Bigfoot Festival and conference taking place. Then there was the final possibility that seemed too far-fetched to consider: that it was left there by the bigfoots themselves. That seemed ridiculous.

The rock stack found in the middle of the jeep path with the water bottle on top. Beneath the first layer of rocks was the walkie talkie (next photo)

We reassembled the pile of rocks and replaced the water bottle in its original position just as we found it. We took a picture of the whole arrangement. Then we took the walkie-talkie and left. Oh, we also took the trash. We climbed back into the quad and continued taking the long way around to get back to the group campsite on 'the ridge.' You better believe we also strained our eyes every inch of the way back to camp, watching for any other suspicious items in our path. Nothing else was found.

I did find myself reconsidering all the possibilities, even the more far-fetched ones. The thing that I kept coming back to was the litter. Both items of curiosity that brought us to a stop on our nocturnal forest tour were rock stacks that were decorated with items of human litter. Could that be the important element of the pattern? Does bigfoot want us to pick up the trash? Is bigfoot trying to reward us for picking up the trash? I hesitate to put such far-fetched ideas in print. They are seen by almost everyone as an example of the kind of delusional and even egocentric thinking that unscientific bigfoot devotees are inclined to concoct. It implies not only that a bigfoot is around, but that it also knows that we are around, that we are coming back, and that we can be counted on to stop and investigate curious items that are left in our path.

What is most interesting is that this is precisely what *we* are doing when we leave attractive things like the lawn ornaments in the woods for the bigfoots to find. Randy had positioned items of curiosity a short distance away in the hope that they would attract the attention of the mythical bigfoot creatures that we believed really did inhabit this woods. Then, we happen along items of curiosity that are almost certainly left for us to find. Might the bigfoots be deliberately turning the tables on us, or is this still more delusional thinking?

When we returned to camp we met up with the owner of the walkie-talkie. He agreed that he lost the thing over a mile from where it was found. He added that he lost it while tearing through brush and it was unlikely in the extreme that it could have been found by other recreational forest users, BFRO members or otherwise. He had no idea at all how the radio got to the place where we found it but he was absolutely certain that it was his walkie-talkie.

The next day, Randy Harrington informed me of an even stranger event. While gathering up the litter we accumulated in the back of his quad the night before, he picked up the plastic grocery sack that we found in the middle of the road at the first of our unexpected stops. He was still pondering the mystery of the two way radio and he noticed the sack contained something.

He opened up the wadded sack for a look. In it, he found a photograph. It was a photograph he had seen before. It was a picture that one of his team members had in his pocket and had somehow dropped as they travelled between camera trap locations.

How the photograph ended up in a plastic grocery sack, under a stone in the middle of the jeep trail was still another mystery. The implications of this mystery were troubling enough. Still worse was the question of what exactly was the connection between the two different items we found that evening in the center of the road.

Clearly, there was a connection between the photograph and the walkie-talkie. They were both conspicuously placed in the middle of the jeep trail we were following. They were both placed amidst small piles of rocks in the center of the trail. They both consisted of litter as well as items that were connected to this group of local researchers I was travelling with, and the same ones who are responsible for the camera sets.

Whoever left the items in the roadway seemed to be saying, "We know you're here and we know what you're doing."   I think it was also saying something to the effect of, "Did you fellas lose these?" Since one of the items was valuable, it was even thoughtful that an attempt was being made to return it to its rightful owner.

Randy explained to me that both items were lost in the vicinity of the camera stations and then somehow transported to the place where we found them. The photo was one of a few that fell out of someone's pocket. It was not in the plastic grocery sack when it was lost. It was put in the sack, presumably by whoever positioned it in the middle of the road.

Meanwhile, Randy's carefully concealed cameras were not messed with and the cameras had not been tripped. The stations were completely intact and some pretty expensive equipment was untouched. Randy felt that the photographic bait stations were too well hidden to have been stumbled across by hunters or hikers. Having seen the camera stations myself, I would certainly agree.

"You know what this means?" I said to Randy.

"Not really," he replied.

"They're saying they know about your cameras."

"Who's saying?" he asked.

"Them," I said with a penetrating stare.

I'm sure the thought had already occurred to Randy but he didn't really want to go there.

I would not describe myself as a person who always embraces the paranormal possibilities when trying to understand the more mysterious aspects of the bigfoot phenomenon. After all, I am also a science teacher and I am frequently in a position of having to explain to students the need for concrete, empirical data wherever possible. But I did open up a least a few cans of paranormal worms in my last book on the bigfoot subject. Randy, on the other hand, had no particular affinity for paranormal questions or paranormal answers. He was quite the opposite, being a definite "flesh and blood" bigfoot researcher. That is, it is Randy's view that bigfoot is simply a species of wood ape; an ice-age remnant, that still inhabits the forests of North America. Apes don't pick up after researchers who have holes in their pockets, and then make an effort to return the lost belongings to their rightful owners by leaving them in plain sight on the circuit that the researchers are known to travel.

On the other hand, another possible implication of the items we found and the way that we found them is that the creatures are not only aware of what Randy and his team are up to, but also that the creatures are intelligent enough to understand their comings and goings, the value of the items, how to protect the photo from the weather (by putting it in a plastic sack) and how to leave them where we would find them. What's funny to me, but spooky at the same time, is that Randy and his team was trying to get surreptitious photos of the creatures and instead the creatures ended up with at least one photo of the researcher, *and they seemed to be letting the researchers know about it!*

I could tell that Randy 'didn't want to go there' as we say nowadays, but it was also clear that he was fresh out of other possible explanations for this most perplexing set of circumstances. The reason I was a little more willing to embrace such far-fetched possibilities was that first of all, none of the other, more ordinary explanations seem to hold up. Arthur Conan Doyle, through the words of his Sherlock Holmes character, advises, "When you have excluded the impossible, whatever remains, however improbable, must be the truth." Aside from the advice of a nineteenth century author, I had another reason to consider the improbable explanation for our forest mystery: It fit a pattern. I had seen things like this happen before. More than once!

Both previous sets of puzzling events happened in the same remote watershed high in the Oregon Cascades. The Roaring River is an absolutely pristine tributary of the Clackamas River. It is a steep, thickly forested, high elevation drainage that would certainly be called a 'holler' or 'hollow' if it were located in the eastern U.S. Some of us have known for years that the Roaring River is a perfect refuge for a group of sasquatches. It is so steep and inaccessible that, even if one knew the sasquatches were there, it would be a hopeless endeavor to go in there and try to find them. In the Roaring River, the indigenous sasquatches hold all the cards. The Roaring River is basically another Hillbilly Hollow.

While exploring the Roaring River Wilderness in the Mount Hood National Forest, my buddy Jim Henick and I took a lunch break at a particularly scenic spot. It was a narrow spur ridge that ends on a bluff high above the aptly named waters of the Roaring River. On an idyllically warm, sunny day we bush-wacked our way out the spine of this steep, trail-less ridge to the point where it dropped steeply, almost vertically, into the depths of the Roaring River canyon. The only way out was to head back the way we came in. Ahead, lay impossible steep slopes that plunged thousands of feet to the river far below. The terrain fell away steeply in all directions, save for the narrow ridge we hiked to get to the point at the end of the ridge. The view was spectacular and our location was extremely isolated. We had not travelled on a trail all day. We saw no other hikers at all. At lunch, Jim pulled out an expensive and precise pocket altimeter to determine our elevation. He put the instrument down on the rocks of the wide open ridge.

Fifteen minutes after departing our lunch spot, Jim suddenly realized he did not have his altimeter. He had left it on the ground at the lunch spot. We immediately did an 'about face' and retraced our steps to the isolated and scenic lunch spot. The altimeter was nowhere to be found. We searched for half an hour. Our lunch spot was unmistakable. The possibility that another hiker ventured across the altimeter at such an isolated spot in such a short period of time is out of the question. Yet, without question, something or someone made off with that altimeter. We never saw it again. To this day, we refer to that scenic spine as Altimeter Ridge.

The very idea that a mythical cryptid is responsible for the disappearance of Jim's altimeter is venturesome at best and delusional at the least. Even though the mystery of the disappearing altimeter was never solved, the reason I still find myself suspecting a bigfoot connection to this particular mystery is that another similar event took place nearby.

Russ Taylor is a Portland resident, professional photographer, and avid hiker who also shared my affinity for the bigfoot mystery. He is one of many active amateur researchers in the Portland area and we often share notes and coordinate our efforts. He, too, had a keen interest in exploring the remote and challenging terrain of the Roaring River. Russ was intrepid enough to venture into this trail-less wilderness alone. He always carried a pistol on his hip in the event of a chance encounter with a mountain lion. A year after the disappearance of Jim's altimeter, Russ was tearing through thickets in the bottom of the Roaring River drainage, directly below Altimeter Ridge some two thousand feet lower in elevation. In the heavily forested bottomlands of the Roaring River drainage, the trees are enormous. Strong winter storms will topple these majestic old-growth giants, making over-land travel very difficult. One quickly learns that the easiest way to travel is to climb up on the immense downed timber and use them as travel routes. One often will take roundabout paths, jumping from one eight-foot diameter tree to the next, seldom, if ever, setting foot on the lush verdant layer of bright green wood sorrel that covers the forest soil. As he travelled, Russ climbed upon and travelled along the sky-bridge of fallen timber. We call it 'log walking.' It's the only way to get around in the bottom of the Roaring River.

The Roaring River: A Hillbilly Hollow in Oregon's Mt. Hood National Forest

As fate would have it, Russ lost his footing and fell off one of the logs upon which he was travelling. No big deal. The ground is soft. Russ landed with a thud in a tangle of huckleberry bushes and wood sorrel. None the worse for

69

wear and tear, Russ picked himself up, and continued on his way, now traveling on terra firma instead of the log bridges. Upon returning to his car more than an hour later, Russ discovered that his six-shooter was not in the holster. The fall off the log was the only bad spill that Russ had taken all day. Russ decided that must have been the moment when the gun was lost. Unfortunately, there was not enough daylight left to make his way back to the place where the gun was lost. There was no way Russ was going to give up on recovering his expensive pistol, but he would have to wait until the following weekend to undertake a search.

Old growth timber in the bottom of the Roaring River drainage. Note how horizontal blown- down timber provides the path of least resistance when travelling across the forest floor.

A week later, Russ returned to the Roaring River. It took some effort but Russ was able to find his way back to the exact spot where he fell off the log. When he got there, he did not have to spend any time at all searching through the huckleberries for his missing gun. He was stunned to discover that his pistol was lying in plain sight atop the very log he fell off of, but it was also a short distance away from the exact place where he fell off the log. It was easy to find the exact location of his fall. The shrubs were still flattened where he landed. Further, Russ was quite certain that the gun could not have fallen from the holster until he hit the ground. A three or four pound weapon is not going to fall from the holster unnoticed unless one is in the process of falling or landing after a fall. The gun, in Russ' view, just could not have ended up atop that log without help, and the Roaring River is far too remote to accommodate the suggestion that another hiker found the gun and placed it atop the log. It is Russ' considered opinion that some sort of forest creature with intelligence and ability witnessed Russ' fall and decided it (or they) had no use for Russ' pistol.

"Did you find an altimeter, by any chance?" I asked him.

He did not. I didn't expect him to, but I thought I'd ask him just the same. He was less than a mile as the crow flies from where Jim's altimeter disappeared, although there was also a fifteen hundred foot difference in elevation.

We talked for a while about other possibilities for how the pistol reappeared. Could the gun have landed on the log as Russ was walking or as he was in the process of falling off the log? Russ did not think that this was possible. If he was walking, he surely would have felt it leave the holster or heard it hit the log, even if he had somehow missed seeing it fall. If it left his holster as he was falling from the log, it seems equally unlikely that it would have landed atop the log. Also, the gun was not in the exact spot where Russ fell from the log. It was some twenty feet distant from where he fell. Obviously, Russ' estimation of where he fell must be taken as fact if paranormal circumstances can be invoked as an explanation for the gun's reappearance. Might someone have found the gun and put it atop the log, I asked. Equally unlikely, replied Russ, for several reasons. He was not on any kind of trail, or even near a trail when he lost the gun. He was deep in a trail-less drainage in the remotest part of the Mount Hood National Forest. He was sure that the gun was jarred loose from the holster when he landed in the brush beside the log, and this does seem to be the most logical point at which the gun would escape its holster unnoticed by Russ. He could not envision any circumstances under which another person would have found it in the brush in a single week's time. Also, why wouldn't a finder keep it? How would another human know that the person who lost it was planning to return?

I found myself wondering what I would do if I found a gun in the wilderness. It's not about selfishness. It's a question of how likely anyone is to return for the lost weapon before it rusted into a single piece of useless steel.

OK, so let's just say for a minute that some sasquatch did find it. How are they any more likely than a human hiker to locate the gun?

"They must have seen me fall. I can only assume that I was being tailed as I travelled through the forest."

"Did you feel like you were being followed," I asked.

"No, I really can't say I was."

I recounted the story of Jim's altimeter then asked Russ, "Why wouldn't a sasquatch keep the gun? He could keep it on the same shelf as Jim's altimeter in his cave, wherever that is."

This is nearly the identical scene as the previous photo. Note the mysterious blue "orb" that appears in the center left portion of the photo. Is it a lens flare, a drop of water in an otherwise dry forest, or, as some paranormal sasquatch researchers would say, a sasquatch manifesting itself in an 'orb phase.' Your call.

Again, Russ was fresh out of answers. And then there was the most troubling question of all: How is it possible that a sasquatch could make all the observations and decisions necessary to find the gun and leave it where the owner would find it upon his return?

"Do you really think a sasquatch is intelligent enough to do all that?" I wondered. I knew full well that Russ was not going to have an answer to that one. It would just have to go down as another unsolved mystery, in the same category as the disappearance of Jim's altimeter. Just a mystery, nothing more, nothing less.

Only when such mysteries form a pattern do they become important, and a pattern really did not begin to take place until I ended up in Oklahoma where I was, once again, confronted with the mysterious relocation of certain objects that were accidentally separated from their human owners in the midst of prime sasquatch habitat. Even though all these events could be said to have occurred in sasquatch habitat, it may be a bit presumptuous to lay the blame at the feet of the local wildmen. Maybe certain parts of the forest are haunted by ghosts. Then there is always the possibility that in all three occasions, the reporting party made a mistake. Jim could have dropped his altimeter somewhere else after we got up and started walking after lunch. Maybe Russ really did drop his gun on the log. But I really don't think the fellas in Oklahoma dropped the two way radio beneath a pile of rocks. Same with the photograph in the bag. Someone or something HAD to have put them there. There's no other reasonable possibility on that one.

If there is a pattern to these events, it does not end there. The most amazing of these examples of items mysteriously moved involves a cat. This cat, grotesquely enough, showed up in pieces on my homestead in rural Clackamas County. It might be worth mentioning that Clackamas County, Oregon has more reported bigfoot sightings than any other county in Oregon. There are places in Washington state with more sightings, but on the BFRO database, Clackamas County is in the top ten counties in the country for bigfoot sightings.

All I know is that in 2006, I returned home from a week away with the family to find the head and one front leg of a cat in the front pasture of our five-acre homestead. Also, along with these large bits of a cat was the collar, complete with name of the cat and contact info of the owner. Before I had a chance to telephone the owner, I came to find out that a neighbor who lives on the same street found the remaining pieces of the cat on her property about a quarter mile down the road. I called the number on the deceased feline's collar and got a fellow resident who lived about six miles downriver on the opposite side of the Clackamas River. When a gentleman answered the number I dialed, I asked him if he was missing a cat. He was. I regretted to inform him that I found some of the remains of his cat on my property and the rest showed up on a neighbors place. He was baffled. The cat was an indoor cat that somehow got out about a week ago and was not seen since. When I told him where I lived, he mentioned that he and his wife had recently moved from a rented house only a couple miles upriver of my homestead.

Might the cat have decided to make a "Homeward Bound" style journey back to more familiar surroundings in my area? The guy on the other end of the phone did not think that made good sense. The cat seldom went outside and had no particular familiarity with its surrounding when it did live out by me. The cat would have had to cross a river that was over a hundred feet wide and flowing swiftly. There was a bridge that could have been used. The most likely possibility seems to be that the cat managed to escape the house where it lived, then got picked off by some predator like a coyote, mountain lion, or great horned owl. But why would such a predator carry the cat up river and across the river some eight miles, then drop the cat in two different pieces left in two different places, and still more interestingly, within a mile of where the cat lived up until some eight weeks ago when the family moved? And, after all that carrying, that cat was then dismembered but not eaten. All the parts of the cat were accounted for.

My feeling is that a land-based predator like a coyote or cougar would not have carried the cat so far, especially without eating any of it. The way the two pieces were separated seemed to suggest the unfortunate kitty had been transported by air. The problem, of course, is that even the largest of local birds, a bald eagle, cannot fly with an eight or ten pound cat. Something just doesn't figure in the whole predator scenario, but that is the only reasonable scenario that does not involve the paranormal.

Criminally-minded humans do not square as a suitable explanation for several reasons: the part I found on my property was in the middle of the property behind a locked gate, on a dead-end one lane access road. No other sign of malicious behavior was found, and if malicious intent was at work, I should think the degree of mutilation and the conspicuousness of the carcass would have both been greater. The oddest thing of all, I think, is the fact that the collar, with identification and contact information, was next to the severed head. Why didn't the collar become separated when the cat was violently dismembered? The contact info on the collar led me right to the owners of the cat with only a single phone call.

Now let's consider the items found in Oklahoma. Again, it seemed like they had the look of a calling card. That is, they were meant to be found. Sometimes I even wonder if it was meant to be found by me. In my more egocentric moments, I even wonder whether something or someone is playing games that are directed at me. Never before had Randy's crew encountered items that were carefully and conspicuously placed for them to find. Then I show up, the visiting amateur researcher from Oregon, and this stuff is left in a path that was largely determined by my extemporaneous, on-the-spot choices as to our direction of travel. I think the thing that surprised them the most as we stood there struggling to understand the significance of the clues we found was that the decision to venture toward them was made by me, not them, and I had never been in that woods before. The pieces of the cat that were left on my property were placed where they were sure to be found. They were in the middle of the lawn and not far from the main driveway, as well as right out in the open. Far from being concealed, they certainly seemed to take on the appearance of a calling card. The collar added greatly to the perplexing element of the events in that it invited me to trace the cat back to the owners.

As previously stated, it is more than a bit egocentric to suppose that these puzzling events are being directed at me, personally. I will submit that I have long been an advocate of the unpopular view that the creatures we are studying are far more intelligent than most people realize. Still more fringe is my view that, as I endeavor to study these creatures, it begins to appear that we are not the only ones doing the studying. I often run across vague indications that they are studying us. I sometimes bring this up in discussion with other researchers and it is always met with a fair amount of eye-rolling. But I am not the first one to suggest this very far-fetched idea. One pioneer of paranormal research, John Keel of *Mothman Prophecies* fame, suggested this in his seminal volume. Keel's book attempted to make sense of a host of paranormal phenomena that were taking place in and around the town of Point Pleasant, West Virginia. Even though Keel was not particularly concerned with the bigfoot phenomenon as we know it today, he did incidentally describe large, hairy apparitions among other spooky manifestations that were being reported in the days and weeks prior to the collapse of the Silver Bridge over the Ohio River.

I am not at all eager to assume that strange events are even related, much less being directed at me. But, when trying to explain paranormal events, I think all that one can do is look for patterns in the events and then put them out there for other researchers to either verify or refute, based on their similar experiences.

Then there is one final interesting item that really had me wondering when I discovered the cat parts in my pasture. The name on the collar of the dismembered cat makes me wonder whether whatever paranormal entity is behind the appearance of the cat can read English. The cat's name, which was printed neatly on the collar and verified by the owner was, "Little Bits."

In August 2012, my family took a summer trip to Glacier National Park in northwest Montana. We stayed three nights at the incredibly scenic Many Glacier Hotel on the east side of the park. We arrived after dark and, as the rest of my family admired the room and the surroundings, I made several trips from the distant parking lot to our room with luggage. Somewhere between the parking lot and the distant hotel, my laptop computer disappeared. The same black leather case also contained my cell phone and a checkbook. With a flashlight, I searched our minivan, the parking lot, the stairwell, and our room, for hours. The next morning, by light of day, I searched everything again. No luck. By mid-morning, I had finally come to accept the inevitable: my electronics (and my checkbook) were gone. I had no way of knowing whether they were stolen, or I somehow lost them between the car and the long trip on foot to the hotel.

I went to the hotel manager's office and reported the loss. I was determined not to let the whole matter ruin my family vacation, but inwardly, I was devastated. It wasn't the computer itself that was the big deal, it was the loss of writing files on the computer that was painful to consider. All the files for this book were on the computer, and they were not backed up anywhere else. The book was about half finished at the time.

The manager and her assistant were very helpful and sympathetic. They confided that it somehow did not fit the pattern of a theft, but they could not be sure. They were also very surprised that I was taking the whole matter so well. I told them only that I wasn't going to let it ruin my vacation. I filled out a form that detailed the loss for insurance purposes and thanked them for their time.

For two days we hiked trails in the park, witnessed an amazing array of wildlife sightings, and had a generally wonderful time. We left the hotel three days after we arrived and checked into another hotel on the park grounds some fifty miles away. When we checked in, I was handed a note to call the Many Glacier Hotel about my missing property. When I called, the switchboard routed me to the manager and she informed me that my missing case had been found by a security guard in the bed of his pickup truck, at his home in Whitefish, Montana almost a hundred miles from the Many Glacier Hotel.

It was now the weekend and the guard was home for the next couple days. We planned to drive through Whitefish on our way back home on Monday.

The security person gave us directions to his home, which was only a mile and a half out of our way. We navigated our way up the dirt road off Highway 97 and found his driveway. I was driving and as I made the turn into his driveway, something caught my eye. I slammed on the brakes and jumped out. There, at the foot of his long driveway, was a neat pile of hawk feathers. They were the large primary feathers of the wings and tail. No hawk carcass, just a neat pile of feathers. I gathered them up, and proceeded up the drive. I met the security person and his wife who were very pleasant.

He told me a remarkable story. He had been at the Many Glacier Hotel on Friday night to refill their cash machine. He was not actually a security guard under the employment of the hotel; rather he worked for the company that owned the debit machines that people use to get cash. He drives all over the place to service the machines and the hotel allowed him to stay the night on Friday and leave early Saturday morning. He parked his truck in front of the hotel in a V.I.P. parking space, not in the distant lot where our family car was parked. He arose before dawn on Saturday and drove the hundred miles across the park to Whitefish. When he got home he went to bed. Around mid-day he arose and went outside to organize his truck and that is when he found my computer case in the bed of his pickup truck. I asked him how he happened to know whose case it was. He told me he saw the checkbook with addresses on the checks. He called the hotel to report the mysterious find and they immediately recognized the name and description of the missing stuff. The hotel manager looked on her computer and was able to determine that we had relocated to the Rising Sun Motor Inn in St. Mary's, which was also part of the Glacier National Park hotel complex. The manager immediately contacted our new destination with the directions to have me call when we showed up to check in.

The security person handed me the case. Everything was intact: the computer, the cell phone, and the checkbook. No checks were missing. The security person refused to accept a cash reward so I gave him a copy of my novel, *Shady Neighbors*, which delighted his wife who confessed she was an avid reader.

My computer case was somewhere for forty-eight hours before it landed in the bed of his pickup truck. Very early on Saturday morning, the driver left to drive about a hundred incredibly scenic miles across the national park on the Going-To-The-Sun Road to get home. The computer was never seen or found by the driver until mid-day Saturday in Whitefish, so there is also a very remote possibility that the computer case was not put into the bed of the pickup until he arrived home. I am inclined to doubt this. It certainly seems more likely that the case was put in the truck before it left the hotel early Saturday morning. Where was the case for the two days between its disappearance and its reappearance?

Then there is the interesting matter of the pile of hawk feathers I found at the foot of his driveway. I even made a point to ask the fellow if he was aware of the pile of hawk feathers at the foot of his long driveway. He said the feathers were not there yesterday when he checked his mail. Coincidence? Perhaps so.

If a Good Samaritan or park employee found my case in the parking lot, why wasn't it turned in to the front desk? Why did it take over forty-eight hours for the case to surface?

The truck was not marked in any way. Nothing indicated it belonged to a trustworthy member of the park's extended network of employees; although the guard did observe that his truck was pretty well known among the regular employees. Is any of this sasquatch-related? Perhaps not, but it definitely seems to have a paranormal element. I still cannot believe I got the case back. How I managed to lose track of it, where it was for forty eight hours, and how I ended up getting it back, I will never understand. I cannot help but wonder whether it had anything to do with the fact that the computer files for this book were on that computer. Maybe I should have had the computer dusted for sasquatch fingerprints.

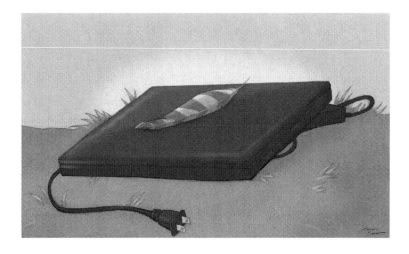

Chapter Three: Bigfoot Magnets

One of the earliest of the 'bigfoot book' genre is *Sasquatch: The Apes Among Us*, published in 1978 by journalist John Green. Among other original thoughts he expressed, Green made the point that sasquatch sightings were so rare that he was extremely suspicious of anyone who claimed more than a single sasquatch sighting in their entire lifetime. It was a thought that stayed with me as I, one of the new-breed of bigfoot researchers, followed in John Green's footsteps. On a few occasions, I met witnesses with multiple sightings. As I listened to the witness recall their remarkable tale, I would recollect Green's skeptical statement and wonder if I was too gullible.

Then, in the summer of 2013, I met what might be called an 'extreme bigfoot witness.' At the encouragement of veteran researcher Paul Graves, I journeyed up to the small beach town of Moclips, Washington to spend a weekend listening to the experiences and encounters of Jim Henry, an 82-year-old lifelong outdoorsman and retired mechanical engineer.

I gotta admit, in terms of gathering useful knowledge and information, it was one of the most interesting weekends of sasquatch research I've spent. This guy had more bigfoot sightings than I had baseball cards in my childhood collection. Jim describes something like 14 *sets* of sasquatch sightings. This had to be an all-time record. I could not help but wonder how a skeptical researcher like John Green would have reacted to hearing such a large set of sightings by a single soul.

Jim Henry

Among other things, Jim Henry was claiming to have seen a single, specific sasquatch multiple times. In fact, Jim Henry felt he had seen the same one so often that he had a name for it. Still others of Jim Henry's sighting collection involved multiple sasquatches. Not all of his sighting reports belonged to him directly. Some had actually happened to neighbors, but Jim felt they were important because he was the only living person who still had the memory of these important historical sightings from Washington's Olympic Peninsula.

Is Jim Henry a liar or even a man with an over-active imagination? I really don't think so. Statements like the one John Green has made in *The Apes Among Us* are probably a reflection of the limited perspective that existed in the minds of early sasquatch researchers. More than likely, a more sophisticated view exists today, as a result of a much greater body of available information.

Early researchers like John Green were a courageous bunch. They endured nearly constant ridicule for just writing and speaking the view that such a creature as the sasquatch actually existed. Of course, most skeptics misunderstood the claim that *bigfoots* existed for the more absurd idea that there was but a single creature, and his name was "Bigfoot." The critics seldom, if ever, got around to considering that these early researchers were speaking not of a single creature, but rather a *population* of bigfoot creatures.

I'm really not sure whether this is an easier idea to accept or a still more troubling one, but the early researchers were indeed advocating for the position that there was a reproductively viable population of sasquatches. John Green and others were of the view that the sasquatch were exceedingly rare, but they did insist that there would have to be a population of hundreds of such creatures continent-wide if there were any at all.

More recently, 'crackpot' researchers like me have found compelling reason to suppose that Green's estimates of continent-wide sasquatch population were way too low. That is, the sasquatch is not as rare as was once thought. Statistical analysis of sightings reports indicate that, because sasquatch sightings happen much more frequently than was originally supposed, the sasquatch population of North America must also be much higher. Current estimates now put the North American sasquatch population at thousands, not hundreds. The early population estimates were too low, not because the sasquatch were so rare, but because *eyewitnesses* who were willing to stand up and be counted were the rarer commodity.

Times have indeed changed. The stigma is largely gone. The ridicule associated with claiming to be a bigfoot eyewitness is tempered by a proliferation of serious TV treatments, radio shows, Internet websites, and published literature. Other big shifts in thinking have occurred since the days when John Green first published his bigfoot books. In the days of the "Four Horsemen" of sasquatch research, John Green, Rene Dahinden, Peter Byrne, and Grover Krantz, views of sasquatch population distribution were also rather provincial. It was generally felt that the sasquatch inhabited only the northwest corner of the North American continent. All of the 'Four Horsemen' regarded the sasquatch as physically massive, wild, and essentially stupid members of the *Pongidae* (ape) lineage, as opposed to the human or human derivative forms that are more often described by witnesses and researchers today. The title of Green's book says it all: *Sasquatch: The Apes Among Us.*

Three decades after Green's early work, the existence of the sasquatch is still hotly debated to be sure, but the evidence for existence is stronger than ever. And, along with the emergence of new and stronger lines of evidence, there also exists much more anecdotal evidence that the creatures are much more widespread, and more intelligent than was originally believed. It is also understood that the sasquatch are not always solitary. They may even be quite social. They *are* sometimes seen in groups. They reproduce. They raise sasquatch families. Credible sightings do include multiple bigfoot creatures and family groups that appear to span multiple bigfoot generations. Sighting reports include observations of bigfoot creatures interacting with other members of the animal kingdom, especially coyotes, and sometimes bigfoot creatures even interact with certain humans, particularly children.

Not everyone back in the 1980's was of the same mind. There were predictions, by dedicated researchers like Robert W. Morgan, that bigfoot activity would turn out to be much more widespread than most people realized. With so little acceptance of the simple idea of bigfoot existence, such views were roundly dismissed at the time, but they have steadily gained traction in the ensuing decades.

It also turns out that there were many more witnesses to bigfoot activity in the 1980's, but they kept their mouths shut, sometimes for their entire lives. Ridicule was the knee-jerk media treatment to any bigfoot sighting claims during this era.

When I was a BFRO investigator in the late 1990's and early 2000's, all it took was some publicity on a late night talk radio show like Art Bell's 'Coast to Coast,' initiating a flood of new sighting reports.

Ten years later, it's not just the BFRO who aggressively collects bigfoot sighting reports. There are more local groups investigating sightings than ever before. Even single individuals, who proudly portray themselves as 'bigfoot researchers,' can speak to local activity, local patterns, and local hot spots. One such researcher, Paul Graves of Wenatchee, Washington caught the attention of eyewitness Jim Henry. Impressed by Paul's knowledge and information, Jim Henry sought out and contacted Paul to share out his collection of sighting reports. Had he shared his entire array of sighting reports much sooner, Jim Henry's multiple encounters would have been seen as a wacky claim, even by serious bigfoot researchers, of which there were none.

In purely scientific terms, this is justified. Eye witness information *is* fallible. It may be admissible in court, but in the strictly scientific world of zoology, eyewitness testimony means nothing. Tangible proof, such as a live specimen or a carcass, is the *only* acceptable evidence of a previously undocumented species. Sometimes, even this is not sufficiently compelling.

For example, the duck-billed platypus was presented to English zoologists in 1799, and summarily dismissed as fake. It was alleged that the 'type specimen' had been created by an Asian taxidermist. Zoologist Robert Shaw even took a pair of scissors to the pelt that was presented, expecting to cut the threads that were used to sew a duck bill onto a beaver pelt. Similarly, meteorites were uniformly dismissed by scientists as recently as the mid-1800's. It was an unquestioned element of scientific dogma that the Earth's protective atmosphere, combined with the moon's gravity, kept all space rocks from making it to the Earth's surface. Today, astrophysicists laugh at how wrong-headed that thinking was.

Observations alone may not mean anything to scientists but they do hold sway in intelligence-gathering organizations such as the Central Intelligence Agency. The 'intel' gathered by CIA may not be utterly verifiable, but that doesn't mean it's worthless. It is understood that, however incomplete and unverifiable it may be, it still has great potential value. They would call it 'atmospherics' and while it may be a bit uncertain, it is still seen as useful and important. Even unreliable information can suggest patterns that have predictive value.

The intel community (spies), like researchers into the UFO phenomenon and other paranormal pursuits, know that eyewitness testimony from certain kinds of observers is much more credible than the rest. Trained personnel are much more reliable observers than untrained members of the public. Professional observers such as cops, airline pilots, and scientists are regarded more highly, as are engineers, doctors, and other members of professional and scientific fraternities who possess high degrees of technical training.

Jim Henry spent his career as a mechanical engineer. He designed and built complicated paper-making machinery. The largest part of his professional career was spent as an engineer for a major industrial design and manufacturing firm in Grays Harbor, Washington. This becomes important for two reasons: First, Jim is a man with a high degree of scientific education and technical training. Also, he was ideally located on the Olympic Peninsula of Washington State; a place with a well-known history of sasquatch encounters. Even the Four Horsemen, who didn't agree on much, would have agreed that Washington's Olympic Peninsula is 'bigfoot central.'

Nowadays, fringe researchers, like me, entertain other far-out possibilities that suddenly don't seem nearly as ridiculous as they once did. One such idea is that certain people constitute what might be described as 'bigfoot magnets.' Admittedly, such ideas are a real 'eye roller' in the minds of many, but, in trying to understand how certain credible and sincere witnesses can amass so many bigfoot encounters, I have become unafraid to entertain some unconventional possibilities.

So, as Jim Henry scrolled through his laundry list of sasquatch encounters, I interrupted him with a question that might just cut to the meat of the matter.

"Jim," I asked, "Do you by any chance have any Native American heritage?"

"Why, yes, I am part Cherokee Indian."

"Do you think your American Indian heritage has anything to do with your multiple sightings?"

"No," he replied. "It was more a matter of just being in the right place at the right time."

The Olympic Peninsula may be a 'right place,' but not every one of Jim Henry's sightings took place on the peninsula. He grew up in southeast Texas and, as a lad, Jim was particularly fond of a hundred mile float trip on the Brazos River. It's a long, slow, meandering river that traverses the sparse forests and rangelands of Texas. As a hardy retiree, Jim returned to the Brazos in 2000 with his son, Paul, to spend a couple weeks floating the same hundred miles section of the Brazos River he floated as a kid. They were floating a section of the river between Waco and Navasota. Traveling in separate motor-propelled canoes, Jim was in the lead and his son Paul was behind him and out of view.

As Jim recalls, he was floating through a large botanical preserve known as the Texas A&M University farm, just west of College Station, Texas. As he drifted along, waiting for his son to catch up, he slowly and silently rounded one of the river's countless looping meanders, and to his utter astonishment, happened upon two large bipedal creatures that were languishing in the warm water of the Brazos.

There before him was a pair of creatures, almost completely submerged, showing only their faces as they protruded above the surface of that southeast Texas waterway. The Brazos is not known for clear water, but the river water was just clear enough that Jim could discern the rest of their hairy bodies beneath the surface. The water was also full of yellow catfish fingerlings that schooled around the two submerged torsos.

The Brazos River, at 1,200 miles in length, is the longest river in Texas and the 11th longest river in the U.S.

The two creatures appeared to be bathing in the river until Jim's unexpected presence surprised them. The two startled creatures stood up in the shallow water near shore, giving Jim a pretty good look at their muscular forms as they moved hastily toward the brushy banks. He did his best to take in all the details he could retain. Jim describes the creatures as extremely physically fit and quite handsome to behold. The female was beautiful. As she strode toward shore, her muscles rippled beneath the thin covering of tan fur that fit like tight clothing. She had a tiny waist, small buttocks, huge shoulders, long legs, and obvious breasts. The male was extremely muscular and also covered in the same thin layer of tan fur. No genitals were visible on either creature. The male was holding onto what appeared to be a very supple, well-tanned cow hide. The male creature threw the wet cowhide over his shoulder and they both headed for shore. As they strode purposefully out of the water, the male glanced back toward Jim, giving him a very stern look that conveyed an unmistakable message: "You better not follow me." By his estimate, Jim Henry's sighting lasted slightly less than a minute.

By the time Jim had this sighting of multiple creatures on the Brazos, he had enough previous encounters that he knew what he was looking at. But the unexpectedness, and vividness, still left Jim in a state of absolute shock. Jim quickly looked around for his son's boat, but it was nowhere to be seen. When he was reunited with his son a half hour later, he could barely find the words to explain what he had seen. The fact that his son Paul was along on the trip but did not share in the sighting was enormously frustrating. He had seen a pair of apparitions that bordered on the miraculous yet he had no witnesses at all who could corroborate this sudden but astounding event.

In retrospect, Jim Henry offers three speculations about the sasquatch, based on the behaviors he witnessed on the Brazos:

1. The large piece of cowhide was a diaper that was being washed in the river.
2. There was a juvenile sasquatch nearby that was being attended to.
3. Juveniles are taught to remain still and quiet in the brush when parents leave to take care of business.

Interestingly, while investigating a habituation site near Chehalis, Washington between 1998 and 2000, I heard the very same suggestion from residents Allen and April Hoyt: Young sasquatch are left unattended while the adults go off to take care of sasquatch business. The Hoyts witnessed a juvenile waiting patiently and passively amidst a cluster of tall ferns. They were fearful of encountering a protective parent but they never saw one. The juvenile was, at least for the moment, all alone. It was their decided opinion that the whole reason for habituation on their property was so that the adult sasquatch could leave the juvenile in a place where it would not be harmed if the resident humans did happen across it.

While Jim Henry's sighting on the Brazos River is fairly spectacular even by today's standards, it is particularly interesting that it comes from a part of the continent where bigfoot sightings were not taken seriously until very recently. It is hard to find sighting reports from Texas that are more than fifteen years old. Had he submitted it in 2000, Jim's vivid account might not have gotten any serious consideration. Indeed, even Jim Henry couldn't quite believe what he was seeing. But, by the time Jim encountered the wading sasquatches, he already had several previous encounters. They all originated around his home on Washington's Olympic Peninsula but they provided some necessary context for his surprising encounter on the Brazos.

The first time Jim had a sasquatch sighting, it was the summer of 1972. Jim was a veteran of the military police, having been stationed in Korea right after the Korean War. Subsequent to his military service, Jim completed rigorous college coursework in engineering, then relocated to Seattle to take work as a mechanical engineer. Like a lot of folks living in the Pacific Northwest in the 1970's, Jim and his wife became avid backpackers. As a new arrival to the Northwest, he had no real awareness of the bigfoot phenomenon. Then one day, he and his wife hiked into a particularly remote alpine lake and witnessed a herd of twenty elk that were behaving in a very peculiar manner.

Between the two of them, Jim and his wife had but one pair of binoculars. From a distance, the couple spied on the herd through the shared binoculars. They saw the elk herd move in unison toward the lake. As they traded looks, Jim discerned six upright, two legged forms moving amidst the elk herd. It seemed like the upright creatures were even herding the elk in the direction of the alpine lake. At one point, one of the calves on the margins of the herd bolted in a different direction. To Jim's astonishment, one of the six two-legged creatures forcefully threw a rock, striking the hind quarters of the wayward calf and successfully redirecting it back toward the rest of the herd. The entire herd now swam or waded into the lake as Jim's wife watched intently through the binoculars. Jim recollects that his wife was astonished to see at least two forms in the lake, amidst the herd, that were moving through the water in a manner that was not at all elk-like.

"Look, honey," she observed while peering through the binoculars. "Two of the elk are swimming arm over arm, like people do!"

Jim grabbed the binoculars. He could indeed see that two forms in the mountain lake, amidst a calm elk herd, were swimming arm over arm, or, as swim teachers would say, doing the 'front crawl.' Even in the face of such an extraordinary observation, who can blame Jim and his wife for not being able to wrap their collective heads around the idea that they were witnessing six sasquatch that had first, herded the elk into the lake, and were now swimming in the mountain lake *with the elk*. Jim continued to study the situation through the binoculars. It was a coarse motion, with lots of splashing, but the things, whatever they were, swam all the way across the lake. Even while Jim knew elk were not capable of swimming in such a manner, he still had no real idea what he was seeing.

On yet another occasion, Jim and his wife were backpacking when they saw two very tall, very well-built forms swimming in another mountain lake. Still unaware of the possibility that they were witnessing swimming sasquatch, Jim's wife concluded that they were seeing two forest rangers swimming in a lake. When they emerged from the water, a covering of hair clung to the bodies of the tall, svelte creatures in such a way that it almost looked like clothing. Jim's wife concluded that they were seeing forest rangers swimming in the heavy canvas Filson uniforms that were worn at the time. From a distance, both Jim and his wife could discern a very muscular physique beneath the wet clothing (or whatever it was). Jim's wife, being an avid fitness buff herself, was particularly impressed by the physique of the individuals. Jim could not argue. Those 'forest rangers' were not only muscular, they looked huge!

"Look at the shape those guys are in!" she remarked. "You really ought to start exercising more."

What he saw bothered Jim more than a little. He dismissed the whole weird event but he didn't completely forget about it. Then, in the late 1980's, Jim finally became familiar with the 'sasquatch hypothesis.' That's when it all clicked. Those weren't 'forest rangers' they saw swimming in the lake and that wasn't wet clothing, either.

What probably troubles most sasquatch researchers about this sighting is how a person could see a sasquatch (or two) and not even realize what they were looking at. Jim addresses this issue by saying that, since he had no previous exposure to bigfoot lore, he never really made the connection between the mysterious creatures he saw and the whole bigfoot/sasquatch phenomenon.

I can relate to that. It's funny how the mind will sometimes not allow one to accept the reality of certain observations if they are well outside of one's realm of experience. I was very aware of the sasquatch hypothesis in the early 1970's even though I lived in northeast Ohio. Mind you, I certainly didn't take it seriously, but I was vaguely aware of the legends.

Had I seen a sasquatch in northeast Ohio, I'm pretty sure that I, too, would have found a way to mentally deny the veracity of that which I was seeing. There was no recognition, at the time, that there was even a *possibility* of sasquatch sightings, especially in that part of the continent. So, I can certainly understand how a scientifically minded engineer, even in the Pacific Northwest, might also have managed to keep his distance from any serious consideration of the 'sasquatch legend,' despite the fact that he had multiple sightings. I *am*, however, a bit surprised that Jim Henry had not heard serious discussion of the sasquatch phenomenon until the late 1980's.

Could Jim Henry really have had so many sightings during a time when it was thought that nobody could have more than a single one of these incredibly rare experiences? Multiple sightings by a single individual may have been doubted once, but not anymore. If there is still a researcher of the bigfoot phenomenon who has not met a witness with multiple sightings, then they haven't been researching very long. A better question to ask in light of the contemporary view would probably be, "How could the assumptions of early researchers like the Four Horsemen have been so wrong?"

The answer, I think, is that they just had a much smaller data set of sighting reports to draw from. There are now so many published volumes of sighting reports, so much on-line information, and so much more sharing of information, that many of the cherished assumptions of the early researchers have been exploded. Not to denigrate the efforts of these early researchers. They did the best they could. They were breaking new ground. Modern researchers with modern communications simply enjoy many advantages over our ground-breaking predecessors, and I for one, am nothing but grateful for these pioneering efforts, despite their inevitable mistakes. I find myself wondering only about what mistaken assumptions we may still be operating under.

The fact that Jim Henry didn't even know of, much less *believe in* the existence of the sasquatch actually strengthens his claims, in my view. In any case, that all changed around about 1982, when Jim took up residence in the Olympic Peninsula. That's when Jim took an engineering job at Lamb Grays Harbor, making equipment for the paper-making industry. He found that he liked the rural lifestyle, and the sense of rural community. Jim got involved in organizations like the local volunteer fire department. At the same time, he worked to clear the huge tangle of brush on the rural acreage he purchased in Copalis Crossing, near Humptulips, Washington. Part of the brush clearing process involves burning the big piles of branches and brush that are created as the forest is removed to create pastures, gardens, and yard. Jim torched a few huge burn piles which he tended each night after work. On one such evening, Jim drove the fire truck from the volunteer fire department down to his property to wet the area around the burn piles as a safety precaution.

Jim Henry and Paul Graves touring Jim's former homestead near Humptulips, WA.

That was the first night that Jim also noticed he was being watched. Over a series of nights, as Jim continued to tend his burn piles, he came to notice that the same mysterious creature was always right there, watching him as he worked. Gradually, the creature moved in closer and became more conspicuous. Jim and the creature became accustomed to each other. Jim never felt threatened by its presence. Rather, he felt a sense of companionship, albeit an uneasy one.

On one memorable evening, as it got late and Jim hurried to finish piling brush, Jim found himself stepping over a pair of very large feet that protruded from the thick foliage near a burn pile. The two feet were so big and so conspicuous as to be almost in his way. As he stepped over the feet, Jim lost his balance and fell directly backward, right into the lap of the large, hair-covered body in the bushes. As he tumbled into its lap, Jim let out a shrill squeal of such high pitch and volume that it surprised even himself. In a panic, Jim, jumped up and regained his footing. At the very same moment, the creature jumped as well. It emitted a grunt that Jim described as a gesture of disgust, after which it proceeded to stomp off into the thick tangle of salmonberry and alder saplings of the surrounding woods.

Having now been in such close proximity to a sasquatch, Jim certainly understood the notion of 'bigfoot' for the first time in his life. After all the encounters around the burn pile, there could be no doubt in Jim's mind that the sasquatch phenomenon was real, nor was there any doubt in his mind that a sasquatch resided in the woods around his property outside Humptulips. However, the thing didn't seem like it was any kind of ape. The creature that was hanging around Jim's property, observing him quietly and curiously from afar, was definitely way too smart to be some wild animal. Rather, it definitely seemed to be some sort of person. The physical features, the behaviors, and the whole passive, almost friendly demeanor just wasn't animalistic.

The scientific implications of this whole matter certainly were not lost on Jim, either. As a scientifically trained and scientifically-minded individual, Jim wanted to learn everything he could about these mysterious creatures. Jim found himself bringing up the subject with his friends at work. Most of his workmates did not take Jim's claims of sasquatch encounter seriously, and Jim endured a certain amount of ridicule.

Yet one co-worker, Roger Trotten, who had heard tell of Jim's repeated encounters, approached him discretely with words of reassurance.

"I know what you saw. I've seen him, too." Roger reassured him.

"Then you know who he looks like."

"Sure do."

"He looks just like Joe Louis," Jim asserted.

Roger smiled and agreed. From then on, it wasn't 'bigfoot' or even 'a sasquatch' that they talked about. It became, "Have you seen 'Joe Louis' lately?"

For those readers who are not students of boxing history, Joe Louis, also known as 'The Brown Bomber,' was the first African American athlete in any sport to rise to a level of national prominence. Joe Louis held the title of world heavy weight boxing champion from 1937 to 1949. He successfully defended his title in twenty-seven title bouts, making him the most accomplished heavyweight boxer in the history of the sport, even to this day. Interestingly, Joe Louis was also a serious devotee of golf. Joe Louis broke the color barrier in that sport as well, being the first black golfer to appear in any PGA-sponsored event (1952).

At 6'2" and 214 lbs., Joe Louis was extremely buff. By alluding to Joe Louis, Jim Henry was basically saying that the sasquatch he was repeatedly encountering was extremely muscular and reminded him of an iconic sports figure of that era. Additional, the being Jim Henry was seeing did not have a lot of facial hair. The hair that did cover the rest of the body was not very thick. Nor was its appearance ape-like in any other way.

The creature seemed very interested in Jim's large burn pile, and although it didn't step out into the open, it made its presence obvious to Jim. For a period of years, Jim saw 'Joe Louis' frequently. He became quite accustomed to his presence. He would leave food for Joe.

Jim had yet another sasquatch encounter while driving on the Olympic Peninsula. In what is surely the most common kind of sighting, Jim and his passenger saw a sasquatch dart across the road in front of his car outside Hoquiam, Washington, in the vicinity of the high school. As his familiarity with the creature grew, Jim became unafraid to talk about his encounters, and he began to gather accounts from others on the peninsula that had sasquatch encounters to share. Jim eventually came to understand that there were quite a number of other sightings on the Olympic Peninsula of Washington. He learned that 'Babe,' his elderly next-door neighbor, claimed to not only see the sasquatch, but she also felt that she had a sasquatch lair on her property. Still another neighbor saw one land atop a ten foot tall stump in a single, terrific leap. Some commercial cranberry farmers in the area told Jim that they would occasionally see a sasquatch eating their cranberries. Specifically, the sasquatch would hang around the corners of the cranberry rows, where their mechanical harvesters could not reach, and feed on the unharvested cranberries. Weird nocturnal screams were heard by numerous neighbors. Jim came to understand that the Native American tribes that inhabited the peninsula use the phrase 'Stick Indians' to refer to these elusive beings whom they consider to be members of another tribe.

Then one day, Jim got laid off from his position at Lamb. He loved the rural lifestyle, but like many rural-ites, economic necessity forced him to sell his place in the country and move back to the big city. Jim took an engineering job in Seattle, where he lived for the next fourteen years. By the time he sold his property in Copalis Crossing and moved back to Seattle, Jim had developed a fondness for 'Joe Louis.'

Habituation

Experienced researchers of the sasquatch phenomenon are increasingly embracing the once-wacky view that mutual trust *can* be built to the degree that the sasquatch will tolerate, even hang around specific homesteads. These days, we call these people 'habituators' although it is less clear who is habituating who. In either case, Jim Henry, would qualify as that which we now call a sasquatch 'habituator.'

Jim Henry himself is the first to question his role as a sasquatch habituator. He feels that one does not habituate the sasquatch, but rather, *they* habituate *you*. They select an accessible person in the rural landscape who seems trustworthy. Then, the sasquatch gradually accustoms that person to *their* presence. They know who they can trust and once they trust you, they gradually become more conspicuous, working their way up to the point where you are no longer frightened or surprised by their presence.

It's a real stretch for most to accept the view that the sasquatch are *that* intelligent and patient, but this is pretty much the same scenario that Allen and April Hoyt related to me back in 1999 when I was looking into the creature activity they were reporting around their rural homestead near Onalaska, Washington. And, an important conclusion that occurred to me at that time was that if Allen and April Hoyt's claim of regular sasquatch encounters was true, then there must be others. If one rural family was reporting regular encounters with the 'forest people' (as the more New Age sasquatch researchers like to call them), then there must be many other such families elsewhere on this vast continent with the same experience. If there is one, there must be more.

A decade later, I think we are seeing that this is precisely the case. A number of habituation cases have been identified and there are very definitely underlying patterns that unify these claims. Jim Henry is but one example of a person who was in the right place, and also of the right disposition, to notice the presence of the 'forest people' and to develop a certain rapport with them. Indeed, it took Jim a long time to just grasp the fact of the matter. Jim had encounters during his backpacking adventures in the seventies and eighties, yet it was only in the 1990's that Jim finally began to grasp the true nature of the phenomenon he was periodically encountering. Then, in his native state of Texas, he had the most unlikely of encounters with a *pair* of sasquatches. I suspect that there is something about his persona that resonates with the sasquatch beings.

Allen and April Hoyt's daughter, Nina, seemed to be of particular interest to the sasquatch that were hanging around their homestead. Nina was also a person with a great deal of empathy and affection for animals of all types. The very first time I ever visited the Hoyts, Nina showed me an injured crow that she found alongside the highway. She brought it home, bandaged its injured wing, and tried to nurse it back to health. Nina cared for many other animals as well and I could not help but notice that it was this big-hearted person who seemed to have the strongest bond with the sasquatches. More recently, I met a woman named Kathleen Odom who grew up in a remote part of northern California near Mount Lassen, who also had a lot of contact with the local sasquatches in her youth. It is Kathleen's firm opinion that it is one's innate kindness, compassion, and empathy, that enable one to get on the good side of the ordinarily cautious and secretive 'sasquatch people.'

My impression of Jim Henry is that he is exactly this kind of big-hearted person who empathizes with all creatures big and small. Jim was never interested in trapping or photographing the sasquatch that was hanging around his property. He seems to be a gentle soul in all ways, and if there is anything to the idea that a good-hearted person would resonate with the sasquatch, Jim seemed like a perfect candidate. Exactly how the sasquatch are able to assess a person's big-heartedness I do not know, but I am told by Kathleen and others that the sasquatch are extremely keen judges of human nature.

Even at his advanced age, John Green is still involved in the world of sasquatch research as of this writing. He did me the favor of reading this chapter and offering this feedback:

> "I admit to being very skeptical of the numerous habituators, particularly since none ever seem to challenge the ridiculous claims of some others who are fabulous liars. I am always hoping that one of them will come up with proof that will settle the matter without a dead type specimen being required, but at the moment none has so much as submitted hair for DNA analysis."

As far as my suggestion that John was suspicious of anyone who claimed multiple sightings, he offers this correction:

> "It was certainly cause for caution, but by the time I wrote that book I was seriously involved with Glen Thomas, who told of four sightings. He didn't want his name used but you will find him, among other places, on page 447, paragraph 3, line 8. There were also several double sighting stories I took seriously, in one case by a woman on the Olympic Peninsula. And with regard to reports from other parts of North America, the book contains a great deal of such information, including entire chapters."

It is particularly interesting that John brought up Glen Thomas, who famously saw a pair of sasquatches on Burnt Granite Ridge, in Oregon's remote Clackamas River drainage. Recently, friend and fellow researcher Joe Beelart did some follow-up on that sighting. While researching *The Oregon Bigfoot Highway*, his recent book about the long sighting history of the Clackamas River drainage, Joe interviewed Millie Kiggins, lifelong resident of the area. Millie knew Glen Thomas, and she happened to mention to Joe that Glen Thomas was full-blooded Cherokee Indian. Once again, the Native American connection resurfaces when looking at witnesses with multiple sasquatch sightings. As patterns go, I think the Native American connection to multiple sasquatch encounters is an important one. Those who bear Native American heritage, for whatever reason, do, at least sometimes, seem to be 'bigfoot magnets.' I have bumped into this pattern so often that I do have a piece of advice to other sasquatch researchers present and future: if you meet a witness who is claiming multiple sasquatch sightings, be sure to inquire about any Native American heritage.

Finding Bigfoot Researchers

For all his exposure to the sasquatch over the years, it was a couple more decades before Jim Henry decided to look up researcher Paul Graves and share his lifetime list of sasquatch encounters. Paul, being a musician as well, was so impressed with Jim's story that he wrote a pretty cool song about Jim and his litany of sasquatch encounters, which he sometimes performs at sasquatch research conferences. Through Paul's persistence, I was given opportunity to meet the man who inspired Paul's song, so I headed up to Moclips, on the southern edge of the Quinault Indian Reservation.

On a drizzly August Saturday, Paul and I spent the entire day talking of sasquatch matters with the Henrys. Jim certainly did not present himself as a person with all the answers. Rather he had as many questions for me as I did for him. He was still struggling to understand the whole phenomenon and he very much wanted to know what was being discussed in the contemporary research community. I made copious notes as we talked and when I was saturated with new material, I put aside the notepad and we just talked. At about 11 p.m., Paul and I decided to excuse ourselves and take a walk in the nearby woods along the Moclips River while Jim and his wife got ready for bed.

Paul and I headed for a wooded trail in the dark cedar grove along the estuary, just a few hundred yards from the point where the river meets the Pacific Ocean surf. The last thing I noticed before we ducked into the woods was two boys tending a campfire in the yard of the neighboring beach cabin.

I had no flashlight but I didn't feel I needed one. Paul was packing his high-tech starlight scope. It enabled us to see not just the trail, but pretty much everything else in woods, even on a completely moonless and foggy night. We walked along the Moclips River, looking through the scope, talking, and basically making no attempt at all to be silent or stealthy. We joked and laughed as we reminisced about the outings and conferences we'd attended.

We found a nice beach along the river beneath a particularly large cedar tree, so, we sat and reflected on the bewildering array of encounters that Jim Henry had shared with us that day. As we talked, we could also hear soft noises coming from the other side of the river. We both noted the sound of snapping twigs and rustling of leaves coming from the Quinault Indian Reservation just across the river from our location.

We got silent and strained to hear more. We wondered what kind of creature might be moving through the nocturnal forest on the reservation lands across the river. I inwardly supposed it was just wishful thinking on our parts, precipitated in part by the fact that we had just spent the entire day discussing the subject of sasquatch with our host. A sasquatch seemed to be way too much to hope for. Coincidences like that just don't happen.

We hadn't been sitting there for more than five minutes when we both noticed the flickering of flashlights in the woods on our side of the river. The flashlights gradually got brighter and closer.

"Now, what?"

"Uh, oh," I replied. "I think some hikers are coming our way."

I watched the motion of the lights intently for a few more moments then concluded, "They're coming right toward us. We might have to turn on a flashlight so we don't frighten them when they get close enough to see us." We both got to our feet.

I didn't have a flashlight but Paul did. He handed it to me. I turned it on and walked toward the lights, which were by now just yards away. "Hello," I said loudly while waving my light. The approaching flashlights halted.

"What are you doing out here?" A voice demanded.

I didn't answer.

"Bigfooting," Paul called back.

The flashlight snapped off and the human forms retreated in the direction from which they came. Now, Paul and I were once again standing in the pitch black forest, alone.

"What do you make of that?" Paul asked me as we stood there, slightly confused, in the middle of the trail.

"Not sure," I replied, "but I think I saw a badge on the shirt of one of those people."

"I saw two kids," Paul reflected, "but I didn't see a badge."

"Well, I'm pretty sure I saw a badge, and if I'm right, they'll be back."

Sure enough, a few moments later, more lights were approaching our position, but this time the lights were really big and really bright. We stood our ground and waited. Next thing we knew, Paul and I were bathed in a flood of illumination from a two foot square array of LED's.

"Keep your hands in the open where we can see them," ordered the voice from behind the LED lighting panel. And then, "I'm a Grays Harbor County Sheriff deputy. Can I see some I.D.?"

Turns out we were both correct about our initial observations. Two cops and two kids faced us in the darkened forest. I handed my driver's license to one of the deputies. They kept their eyes, and their lights, trained on us. I leaned against a tree and tried my best to look unthreatening. Paul and I waited while the deputies talked into their walkie-talkies. After ten minutes of this, the deputy handed me my driver's license.

"OK, you guys aren't suspects in a murder or anything, but do you mind telling us what you *are* doing out here.

"I already told you," Paul replied. We're bigfooting."

"Why here?" the deputy asked.

"We're guests of a local resident, Jim Henry." I offered. "We decided to take a walk. And, as you probably know," I added, gesturing across the river, "That's Indian reservation over there. Things are a little different over there. We're just checkin' things out. Is there a problem?"

"Well, we're not sure. These two fellas here heard a woman screaming," answered the deputy, gesturing toward two teen-agers who were keeping to the shadows. "They thought maybe someone was in trouble. Were you doing any calls?"

"Nope," Paul replied.

I was inwardly surprised that this cop was aware that people did such things as 'calls' in the name of sasquatch research. He must have seen our buddies Cliff and Bobo on their "Finding Bigfoot" cable TV show. Or, maybe we weren't the first 'bigfoot researchers' to cross the path of these two deputies.

"Did you guys hear any strange noises?" the deputy asked us.

"We were hearing lots of strange noises," I replied. "That is, until you guys showed up."

"OK, we're outta here," the deputy declared impatiently. And with that, he turned on his heels and strode off, followed by the other deputy and the two silent teen-agers.

Paul was indignant about the whole intrusion. "We have every right to be here. It's public property. We weren't breaking any laws."

I was a bit more circumspect. "Those were the same two kids who I saw tending a campfire as we headed into the woods," I recollected.

"Why would they call the cops on us?" I wondered. "We weren't being loud, were we?"

"The cop said they heard screams," Paul shrugged. "I wonder what those kids heard." We looked at each other and wondered again about the noises we ourselves had heard just before the posse showed up. It seemed like there must be something more to the story.

"One thing's for sure, after the flood light and all that commotion, our chances of bumping into Mr. Squatch are about zilch." We laughed and talked a bit more before heading back to crash at Jim's place. As we walked past the teenagers' cabin on the way to Jim's place, we checked things out. No one was outside, the fire was now a pile of glowing embers, and the cabin was dark.

The next morning, we got a few answers. We saw the same two boys packing their pickup truck. Paul drifted over and introduced himself. In a heartbeat, both boys, who turned out to be brothers, offered their sincerest apologies. They confessed that, after the cops checked us out, they felt badly about summoning the authorities. They were indeed fans of Cliff and Bobo's TV show on Animal Planet. They were also very surprised to learn that we were *bona fide* bigfoot researchers. They had absolutely no idea that the sasquatch phenomenon could manifest itself so close to home.

Paul explained that the immediate area did indeed have quite a history of sasquatch reports. It was then that the boys shared their most interesting news. Last night, as they sat around their campfire, they had been hearing very strange noises, even slightly alarming sounds coming from the reservation side of the river all evening long! First they heard what sounded like a baby crying. Then, a little later they heard a woman screaming, or at least, what *sounded* like a woman screaming. (Rule number one of sasquatch field research: never assume you know what sort of creature made a noise unless you saw the creature as it was making the noise.) The brothers eventually became so concerned by the noises that they were hearing that they awoke their father. The dad suggested that they just go ahead and call 911, which they did. Forty-five minutes later, a pair of county sheriff deputies finally showed up.

We reconstructed the time frame of the night before and concluded that the alarming sounds the boys heard occurred while Paul and I were still inside talking with Jim and his wife. When Jim decided it was bedtime, the cops had already been called. They took their time getting to the scene. Meanwhile, Paul and I headed for our nocturnal stroll along the Moclips River, unaware that the cops were already on the way.

Suddenly, all that 'brush-popping' that Paul and I heard seemed like it may have been just the tip of the iceberg. Quite possibly, it was the aftermath of the more frightening noises the teenagers reported. Perhaps Paul's and my presence even prompted the mysterious noise-makers to retreat toward the safe haven of the reservation lands. Like so much of sasquatch research, the whole story will never be known.

Once it was established that there were no hard feelings, the two boys, who were exceedingly personable and polite, had a couple more questions they wanted answers to.

"I always thought there was just one creature. You mean there's more than one?"

"That's what everybody thinks," Paul replied. "Yep, there's definitely more than one. Lots more."

"You mean there could be bigfoots right around here?"

"No reason why not. The Olympic Peninsula is one solid forest. They can hide anywhere. They probably lay low right over there on reservation land during the daytime. After dark, they can go just about anywhere they want. Who's gonna stop them?"

The irony of the second question was enormous. The kids hailed from nearby Olympia: 'Gateway to the Olympic Peninsula.' These kids were also interested in the sasquatch subject, yet they never knew that their vacation cabin was right next to Jim Henry, a sasquatch habituator and veritable fountain of local lore. Their beach cabin was also only yards away from a reservation where whites were not welcome and sasquatches probably enjoyed safe haven. They were just ten miles from Humptulips, or as the local researchers call it, 'Bigfoot Central.'

The dad came out of the cabin and joined our conversation. He too was polite and friendly. He had stories of his own to share about growing up in rural Washington. As a boy, he recollected finding sasquatch tracks and hearing strange creature calls coming from the forests he explored outside Olympia. Naturally, the dad never brought it up, out of fear of ridicule, of course.

Here we go again: Long-suppressed stories of sasquatch encounters getting told for the first time. Maybe all you have to do is follow a guy like Paul Graves around and the stories of sasquatch encounters will just *find* you. If Jim Henry is a bigfoot magnet, Paul Graves is a bigfoot *story* magnet.

And while we're at it, would someone please explain to me how it happens that, while we're in Jim Henry's beach cabin discussing the details of his life-long intersections with the bigfoot phenomenon, his next-door neighbors are having an experience that fits the profile of a fairly standard 'Class-B' sasquatch encounter? Coincidence? Someone once said to me, "Coincidences are just God's way of remaining anonymous."

That morning, after the neighbors packed up and headed back to Olympia, Jim Henry escorted Paul and me up to his old homestead near Humptulips. We toured the property where he, and 'Joe Louis' once eyed each other suspiciously. Jim showed us where the much-discussed burn pile had been. Everything was overgrown and the dense forest had reclaimed

Jim Henry points out the location of the burn pile.

the property that Jim had so painstakingly cleared all those years ago. Jim showed us the exact place where he stumbled backward and fell into Joe Louis' lap. He pointed out Babe's property that had the 'bigfoot lair.' We met the current owners who kindly allowed us to wander the property all the way down to the Humptulips River, where still other sightings had once taken place. At last, it was time for the three of us to part ways. Our respective towns, jobs, and families awaited our return.

We exchanged contact information. As I said good-bye to the fellow bigfoot researcher and the octogenarian engineer, Jim offered me the only piece of advice he'd given me all weekend.

As he shook my hand, Jim Henry looked me in the eye and said, "Thom, no matter what anyone says to you, don't ever doubt that the sasquatch really exists. I've seen them more times than I can count."

Thom Powell and Jim Henry

Lyrics to "Jim Henry"

by Paul Graves

Well I met a man, his name was Jim, who had a story, no one would believe in...
While camping out, his wife and he
Saw a heard of elk swimming in a lake, among a dark covered thing...
It pushed them along, had arms like an oar,
walked around on its tiptoes, looked like a hair covered man on the shore...
Didn't know what it was, 'till many years gone by,
But now he knows it's the creature, they say started back when the world was five...

CHORUS

> Oh Jim Henry's got a new friend,
> Walkin' with Jim Henry,
> There he goes again,
> With his hair covered friend...

It started to rain, and then a flood began,
On the back of Jim's place, where the water really started coming in...
There was a lair, where the creature stayed,
But even he had to get himself back and up and out of the way...
Jim felt his presence, right by his side,
But it was so pitch black and dark and cold and wet outside...
He gave a shout, more for Jim than he,
To try and scare his fright and all his misery...

CHORUS

Then one day while driving through the edge of town,
Something caught his attention in the ditch that made him really frown...
This thing was crouched, then bounded out,
And shot like an arrow, so fast across the street before he could shout...
Oh my what's that, looks like a hair covered man,
Running faster than a deer being chased by a bear through the bottom land...
One thing's for sure, Jim knows they're real,
And he hope's some day we can all get together and make a deal...
Just to live together, for ever more,
Because he knows this world's big enough for both, from shore to shore...

CHORUS, *Outro*...

Link to the song "Jim Henry" by Paul Graves:

https://www.youtube.com/watch?v=L_JXZ1o2b1I

103

Chapter Four: London Calling

I was setting up the school science fair when London called: Bigfoot tracks were found. Lots of 'em. It was Toby Johnson on the other end of the phone. Or was it bigfoot calling? Either way, that which ensued is the most convoluted, mind-boggling bigfoot investigation in which I have ever been involved.

London Calling is the name of a highly acclaimed 1979 musical release by an English punk band, The Clash. The varied musical tapestry of this double album often elevates it to lists of top ten long-playing musical releases of all time. The Clash's *London Calling* has also been one of my favorite records for a long time, but I never even knew that the state of Oregon had a village named London until the day that London called.

It all began when a retired car salesman, impulsively stopped his car near the London country store. London is an unincorporated village south of Eugene, Oregon. Besides being a retired car dealer, Max Roy is also an antique car buff. He sometimes drives the rural roads around Eugene, looking for old cars that he might be able to restore. On Sunday, February 12th, 2012, Max cruised the Weyerhaeuser-London Road with his dog, looking for a junker that he could acquire for parts. He never found the car but on his way home, Max decided to make a stop at a scenic pullout alongside a reservoir to walk the dog.

Synchronicity *(def.): The coincidental occurrence of events that seem related but are not explained by conventional mechanisms of causality.*

Max and his dog headed for a trail along the lake shore. Shortly after beginning his stroll, Max encountered another pet owner who was heading in the opposite direction. This anonymous fellow cheerfully informed Max that he should keep an eye out for some bigfoot tracks just a short distance up ahead. Max knew a little bit about bigfoot. He had seen cable TV shows on the subject, and his interest was piqued by this unexpected invitation to personally inspect some fresh bigfoot evidence. The unidentified dog owner even pulled out his cell phone and showed Max a picture of the track that he'd found. Now Max knew exactly what he was looking for. He watched intently as he walked and sure enough, he happened across three plainly visible barefoot tracks in the wet mud. Max studied the imprints with interest, and then continued his walk. The tracks impressed Max enough that, later in that day, he mentioned them at a meeting with his insurance agent.

The insurance agent, who was also a good friend of Max's, was even more interested in the tracks than Max expected. He told Max, in no uncertain terms, that the tracks were, potentially, a big deal. He suggested that Max ought to return to the site with a camera and a ruler and get some proper photographs.

It was this unexpected conversation that initiated a course of action that would go much further than Max ever expected. On his friend's advice, Max went back to the Cottage Grove Reservoir and took a photo (see below). Then, he took his insurance agent's advice and made an effort to share his photo with someone who might know what to do about Max's 'track find.' It didn't take long for Max to formulate a plan. He already had a pretty good idea where he could find a serious bigfoot enthusiast.

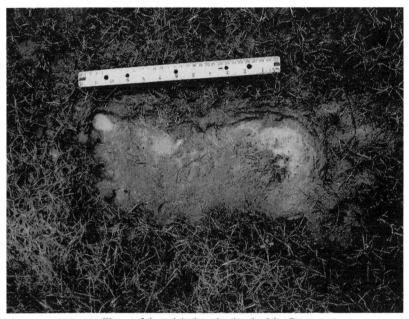

Photo of the original track taken by Max Roy

Being a career car salesman, Max always noticed people's cars. One particular car Max had seen around his neighborhood told Max he had a neighbor who was seriously into bigfoot. More than once, Max had seen a black SUV in his Eugene neighborhood that was decorated with stickers of sasquatch footprints. Surely, a person with bigfoot tracks all over his car would be interested in Max's track find. On his way home, Max detoured down the street where he'd seen the bigfoot car sitting in a driveway, but the car wasn't there. Later, he drove by again and saw the car, but the bigfoot tracks were gone. Still, being a 'car guy,' Max was certain it was the same car.

He knocked on the door. A woman answered and Max explained the reason for his interruption. The woman explained that the car *used to* belong to her ex-husband, Toby Johnson, but now it was hers. She didn't care much about bigfoot evidence herself, but this polite woman assured Max that her 'ex,' Toby, would be *very* interested. She gave Max Toby's cell phone number. Being a determined soul, Max rang up Toby. Now, ya gotta be impressed by any individual who would keep going so far out of his way for a situation with no obvious personal benefit, all because his insurance agent said he should. Eugene, Oregon, as it turns out, is full of people like that, and Max fits right in: he's determined, community-oriented, alternative-minded, and open to fringe ideas like 'bigfoot evidence.'

Max later confessed to me that it was indeed his insurance agent (and friend) who had impressed upon him the importance of this serendipitous discovery. Max wasn't going to let his insurance agent down. At last, Max had a bigfoot expert on the phone. Soon after being alerted, Toby Johnson and expert tracker Todd Bailey were making their way south out of town, heading for the Weyerhaeuser-London Road.

Sure enough, there were three exquisite fourteen-inch tracks waiting for them right where Max said they would be. They had no previous experience with casting bigfoot tracks, but Toby and Todd were determined to preserve the evidence of a bigfoot's passing.

My cell phone rang as I was setting up tables for our annual school science fair. Toby wanted some pointers on how to cast the tracks with plaster. It was one of the few days of the year in which my presence was absolutely necessary. I could not break free to motor south and give Toby a hand. I briefed him on how to mix plaster and make good casts then wished him luck.

As Toby dealt with the plaster, Todd decided to do what he does best. He set about surveying the surroundings and looking for clues. Todd Bailey is absolutely the perfect member of any advance team that is given to the task of investigating an incipient track find. He has the tracking experience that can potentially resolve the question of exactly what this creature might have been doing when it left the tracks near the Cottage Grove Reservoir.

What Todd found next was a game-changer of almost historic proportions. The three tracks next to the walking path were only the beginning. While searching the surrounding area, Todd stumbled across over a hundred bare-footed tracks that spoke of a creature parading through the mud flat along the shore of the reservoir. At first, the tracks appeared to be smaller than the three tracks Max reported to Toby. But, after some careful measurements, it emerged that Todd's newly discovered line of tracks was, in fact, a continuation of the first three tracks.

It was Todd's considered opinion that the creature that left the first three tracks was on its way to the lake. After leaving tracks by the walking path, the creature headed down to the fine-grained mud flat of the lake bed. For most of the year, the mud would be on the bottom of a shallow lake. In the winter, the reservoir is drawn down to prepare for possible winter floods, exposing the lakebed sediments. The scope of Max Roy's track find suddenly went from interesting to epic. Todd dashed back to inform Toby, who called me back and repeated his request for help. I suggested he call Cliff Barackman, who was in town on hiatus from filming his TV show.

It was now Thursday, February 16th. Oddly, Cliff was also at a school science fair. He cleared his schedule and headed 130 miles up the Willamette Valley toward Eugene and Cottage Grove. Toby also alerted other local researchers including Chris Minnear in Cheshire and John Bull of Eugene. Cliff called Autumn Williams. I sent an e-mail to Jeff Meldrum in Idaho. Chris left Newport, purchased 200 pounds of Hydrocal-white at a landscape supply place, and headed for the scene. John, Chris, and Cliff converged on the scene and spent the entire night casting seventy prints. Autumn Williams showed up and cast a few. The team pulled a total of seventy tracks from the scene before they ran out of plaster. At least thirty more tracks remained uncast in the exposed mud. My school science fair now over, I made a plan to get a bunch more plaster and head down to Eugene on Friday night with Guy Edwards and Beth Heikkenen, to finish the job.

It was dark, windy, and raining when we got to the reservoir. Toby and Todd were there to show us the track way. The wind was blowing so hard that the covers Toby had made to preserve the tracks had blown away. Sticky mud caked thicker and thicker onto our shoes with every step. There was no easy source of water for mixing plaster. My flashlight batteries were weak. Clearly, this was going to be an ordeal.

Ordinarily, when confronting a new track find, we would examine the tracks carefully and attempt to verify that they were authentic. With the wind, rain, cold, and darkness complicating our task, there just wasn't the time to stand there and debate the quality of this evidence. We just had to preserve it before it washed away. I had spoken with Cliff after he returned home from his track casting all-nighter. He was confident that the tracks were, in fact, the real deal. That was all I needed to know. Without further discussion, we got busy. We didn't get excited, or even try to grasp the enormity of the situation. There wasn't time for that. We just worked until the job was done, at which time we were soaked to the bone, and covered in mud. There was no jubilation, just exhaustion.

Beth, Toby, and Guy casting tracks at night in a rainstorm

Around midnight we left the plaster in the ground to cure and headed back to a motel by the freeway to get some rest. We returned to the scene the next morning before dawn to take measurements, make photographs, and extract the now-cured casts from the sticky mud.

By noon on Saturday, we had lifted all the tracks from the mud and loaded up the trucks. The casts were still in a very fragile state and needed proper storage. Before we parted ways, Toby suggested that this would be a good time to do some nighttime exploring of the local woods. We all agreed. Whether it was a solitary individual or part of a group, past experience suggests that a sasquatch will circulate in an area for a while before moving on. If anyone was going to hit the woods, then the sooner they went, the better.

As I drove north toward Portland with Guy Edwards and our load of track casts, we tried to grasp all that had taken place. We had collected about one fifth of the track way that would be described as the largest track find ever gathered. The rest of the casts were already safe in the possession of Cliff and a few other folks like Autumn Williams, Toby, and Beth. Guy and I couldn't help but wonder how it all happened.

Part of the London Trackway curing at sunrise

Knowing how experienced a tracker Todd is, I asked him to speculate as to why the London tracks were so numerous and conspicuous. Historically, it was assumed that the only explanations for track ways lay in the realm of survival. Tracks were left as a creature attempted to fulfill basic animalistic needs: food, water, shelter, and available mates. Yet, the London trackway did not seem to suggest a search for any of these basic animal needs. The tracks didn't go all the way to the lake shore, there did not seem to be any sources of food that were exploited, and the lakebed was so open and exposed. There was just one long set of tracks, all of them clearly belonging to a single individual with 14-inch long feet.

When I first arrived at the scene of the London track way, it was dark, windy, and raining, but I took a quick look around and tried to get an immediate sense of the situation. The immediate impression I got from the track way was that it was *so* conspicuous that it seemed like it was meant to be found. This could mean that the trackway was faked, as were the tracks that were found outside of Elbe, Washington on the Nisqually River later in 2012.

111

There were some very distinct differences between the Elbe and the London track finds. Perhaps most importantly, the London tracks were found by word of mouth. No on-line reporting of the tracks ever happened. On the other hand, the bogus Elbe tracks were reported to the BFRO website *and* they were anonymously reported to Cliff Barackman's website and blog. Cliff was either out of town or just plain busy at the time, so when there was no response from Cliff, the hoaxer sent another message reporting the same track find to the more prominent BFRO website. It was that message, and the accompanying IP address that left BFRO investigators Matt Pruitt and Cliff Barackman wondering. They astutely contacted Daniel Perez, long-time editor and publisher of the *Bigfoot Times*, and asked him if the IP address attached to the messages matched anything in his extensive file of addresses. It did. The IP address matched one Aaron Swepston, who had contacted Daniel back in 2009. That same year, Daniel had encouraged Aaron to attend a bigfoot conference that was being held that year in Natchez, Washington. This person was also a frequent contributor to a prominent bigfoot-oriented chat room called Bigfoot Forums.

Meanwhile, field investigators, including myself, descended upon the scene of the tracks in Elbe, all the while wondering how we could be so impossibly lucky as to happen across a second long trackway in the same year. The casting at Elbe went a good deal more smoothly than the London tracks, owing to the fact that it was a balmy late-summer day in September, instead of a cold, rainy night in February. Like the London tracks, the Elbe tracks were conspicuously placed, and it was noticed by Joe Beelart and me that the Elbe tracks even seemed to avoid the more stone-covered areas on that beach, where footprints would not have been very well preserved.

More significantly, there was no variation in the depth of penetration of the Elbe tracks, nor were there any changes to the splay of the toes from one track to the next. The stride of the Elbe trackway was easily matched by my own stride, and I'm six feet tall. The fifteen-inch footprints we cast at Elbe were consistent with a sasquatch of at least seven feet, according to Henner Farehnebach's published footprint-to-stride ratios. Yet, the measured strides of the Elbe tracks indicated a creature height of slightly less than six feet. It all seemed to perfectly fit the scenario of a regular-sized human wearing big, fake feet. Conversely, the London tracks showed feet that were only fourteen inches long, yet the stride on those tracks exceeded anything I could match, implying a creature a good bit taller than six feet.

Toby Johnson, 6'1" shows his stride to be considerably less than the average stride of the London track way.

The London tracks were also an absolute study in variation of toe-splay from track to track. In most of the tracks, only four toes were evident. In many of the tracks, only three toes were distinguishable. Only rarely were all five toes evident in the London tracks. Also, from track to track, the depth of penetration of the toes varied markedly. The toes penetrated the soft, sticky mud much more deeply than the heels in the London tracks. In order to hoax such a complex trackway, one would have to use multiple prosthetic feet or have some kind of extremely flexible set of fake feet. By comparison, the Elbe tracks were suspiciously uniform in their depth of penetration from heel to toe. In short, it was the experience and knowledge gained from studying the detail of the London tracks that enabled us to see the Elbe tracks as the counterfeits that they truly were.

Even as we had reasons to wonder about the Elbe tracks, we abided by the central rule of evidence collection: collect the evidence first; evaluate its authenticity later. In Elbe, Joe Beelart, Rick Noll, Derek Randles, and I wasted a lot of plaster and time casting the tracks that would ultimately prove to be fakes. As we cast the tracks, we could not help but notice that the beach on the Nisqually River was festooned with other barefoot tracks that were very clearly human. Clearly this beach, on the outskirts of the village of Elbe, was a popular spot for bathers and partiers. By comparison, the vast exposed lakebed of the Cottage Grove Reservoir was absolutely free of other human tracks when it was first inspected by tracker Todd Bailey.

For all of the above reasons, the evidence indicated that the Elbe tracks were fake, even before the original report was finally traced to a computer that belonged to the girlfriend of bigfoot gadfly Aaron Swepston. One has to wonder why it was so important to Mr. Swepston and his associates to prank his fellow cryptozoology enthusiasts. To me, it all seems very mean. No explanation or apology was ever offered.

In the end, the most damning element of the Elbe tracks was the same element that validated the London tracks: The Elbe tracks, on the one hand, were officially reported multiple times. Clearly the perpetrator of the Elbe tracks feared that his attempt at fakery might never be found and therefore wasted. The London tracks, on the other hand, were never reported to any website or on-line group of bigfoot researchers. Indeed, it was only through the most remarkable set of circumstances that the London tracks were even brought to the attention of anyone who even cared. The chain of communication was so serendipitous, so accidental, as to fall squarely into the realm of synchronicity.

The means by which the London tracks came to be known by the local community of bigfoot researchers borders on the spooky. The number of people, the number of accidental encounters, the unplanned randomness of Max Roy's decision to stop and walk his dog, the conversation between Max and his insurance agent, the way by which Max ultimately found Toby's car, the stickers, and his ex-wife, the chance venture by Todd Bailey down onto the lakebed in search of a few more tracks…there can be no more compelling scenario that speaks to the authenticity of the London track find than the series of events that unfolded around the discovery of the London tracks.

Had tracker Todd Bailey not ventured down to the lakebed, the long trackway that became the London tracks would never have been found. Toby would have cast a track or two. He would have gone home feeling pretty pleased with himself for successfully casting his first bigfoot track. The whole story would have ended right there.

Instead, Todd's secondary discovery brought the track find to the attention of a much larger group of researchers who then descended upon the scene. As we surveyed the situation during our visits there, the researchers all took time to assess the scene, and everyone seemed to pick up on the same unique aspect of the whole scene. There was a huge and raucous flock of geese that were wintering on the reservoir. The problem was that they seemed to be contentedly hanging out on the opposite side of the lake, at least a quarter-mile distant. A hungry sasquatch could have been stalking the goose flock from a distance.

The lake and the distant mountains made a very attractive landscape. The huge flock of geese that was roosting across the lake added lots of visual interest as well as a great deal of interesting sound. I wondered whether the sasquatch may have wandered out on the lakebed just to take in the view. At one point in the morning, as we dug the track casts out of the mud, the flock of geese was suddenly spooked and they took to the air in one huge 'whoosh' of pattering geese feet, thundering wings, and deafening honking. The spectacle of thousands of geese taking to the air at once is a memorable nature moment and I wondered whether that would be a reason in itself for a sasquatch to mosey out onto the lakebed. Any creature that was out there to appreciate the glorious mobilization of a huge flock of birds would have to possess a well developed sense of aesthetics.

When trying to understand the motivation of the bigfoot creature, it seemed only natural to ask the guy who found them, especially since Todd Bailey is such a good tracker.

I had previously mentioned to Todd my thought that the London tracks seemed like a 'throw down,' that is, a deliberate display of bigfoot presence for some unknown reason. Bear in mind that, since my work at the Hoyt's, I viewed bigfoot creatures not only as intelligent, but also aware that a community of researchers were actively collecting their foot prints. Why would they suddenly break from an enduring pattern of *avoiding* leaving obvious footprints?

Todd responded with the wisdom of a person who knows the training of Green Berets and Navy SEALs. "Sometimes," Todd said, "you deliberately expose yourself, just to see what the enemy does."

Well, in our case, 'the enemy' (namely 'us') came running right toward the scene, with ten pound bags of Home Depot plaster under each arm. To follow this line of reasoning to its logical conclusion then, that was just what the sasquatch perpetrators *expected* us to do: to expose ourselves, our numbers, and our tactics for its scrutiny. We must have given it an eyeful, out there on that lakebed swarming over the tracks with tape measures and digital cameras.

Beyond the days and nights spent on the lakebed documenting the trackway, I think the real opportunity to 'observe the enemy' came afterward, in the woods surrounding the Cottage Grove Reservoir. In the subsequent days and weeks, teams of eager researchers led by Todd and Toby fanned out in search of other indications of sasquatch presence. The more I think about it, the more I think that the tracks were just the bait and the trips that were made through the nocturnal woods by the local research teams and their children were the real plan, the real incentive behind the London tracks. If that was the hidden sasquatch agenda, then the local researchers cooperated perfectly.

Pulling the last of twenty-two casts from the mud of the lakebed at Cottage Grove Reservoir

Paranormal Sunday

They took the rest of Saturday to recover, and then Toby and Beth gathered their team and headed for the woods. If there was ever any doubt about the authenticity of the tracks that had been collected over the past few days, all doubt would be eliminated by the end of 'Paranormal Sunday'.

It was a sunny Sunday and Toby's nine-year-old son Jude wanted to go on a hike with his dad. Beth was still in town and the buzz surrounding the

London tracks was in the air. It was the perfect opportunity to head into the woods for a daytime hike under the auspices of 'bigfoot research.' Toby's idea was to hike through an area where four sasquatches had once been sighted. On a weekend afternoon and in the company of two very competent outdoors people, it didn't seem like it was dangerous to take his son along on a hike into the place where a sighting had once occurred.

They were enjoying every moment of their Sunday hike. The group split into two teams. Toby led his son to a wetland location that he knew very well. He had even gone to the trouble of hiding a park bench at this favorite resting spot of his. The pair enjoyed their break, basking in the sunshine as they sat next to a big stump on the edge of a wetland. Being a devout Christian, Toby felt compelled to carve a cross with his little pocket knife into a large toadstool. Pleased with his handiwork, Toby decided to leave his carved symbol of Christianity on the stump as a token, or even a gift. Toby placed his gift on the big stump and took a picture of it. If it did disappear, a photo would help document the place where Toby's 'gift to the sasquatch' was last seen.

It was a joyous moment in a very uplifting day in the woods. His son watched as Toby took a photo of his carving in the toadstool. In a most uncharacteristic fashion, Toby's son began to whoop and yell, stomping his feet into the dirt. Toby laughed, and felt feelings of inner pride at the sight of his son's vivid expression of joyfulness in nature.

Shortly thereafter, Toby became suddenly aware of the fact that he and Jude had not seen Todd and Beth in quite a while. Together, they walked back toward the car. As they neared the car, Toby caught sight of Todd and Beth heading purposefully in their direction. As soon as they were reunited, Todd did something that was completely out of character: he walked right up to Toby and gave him a huge hug. Not only did the man-hug take Toby completely by surprise, but it seemed to also be an awkwardly long hug, especially coming from such a salt-of-the-earth country fellow as Todd. All at once, Todd was face-down on the ground; lying flat on his stomach with his arms and hands outstretched. Toby gave Beth a look of both question and concern, being that she had just spent the last hour or so in Todd's company. Toby couldn't help but wonder what the heck had happened back there in the woods when Todd and Beth were alone. Beth gave Toby a wink and whispered, "We'll talk later." Toby's son was watching all this, looking a bit mystified. Not wanting to give his son any cause for concern, Toby shrugged

117

off the whole matter, deciding that it was getting late anyway and probably time to get his son home.

After taking Jude home, Toby met up with two friends who lived up the McKenzie River valley east of Springfield, who had also heard about the newly discovered London tracks. They, too, were eager to go for a night hike in the name of 'bigfoot research.' Toby, having a passion for night-hiking, was only too willing to oblige them. In typical Toby fashion, he explained to Dave and Dylan that they should be cautious though, and even guard their minds with the power of Christ. The two new arrivals, while not being devout Christians like Toby, had spent ten years as firefighters and emergency medical technicians (EMTs). They may not have been ready to share a prayer with Toby, but they could relate to the idea of being cautious and strong, both physically and mentally. As first responders to accidents and emergencies, Dave and Dylan had seen their share of unspeakable horror.

The team headed for a tavern in the town of Cottage Grove to have some dinner and plan their evening outing. They were joined by veteran local researcher John Bull. At one point, Toby asked the other five researchers if they could go outside and pray. The prayer, led by Toby, asked for God to "keep them safe and to keep their discernment strong." Toby also asked that, "all six of us may see His handiwork, and that those who have not seen the supernatural in action may see its reality tonight."

One must be careful what one asks for. You just might get it.

It was well after dark when the group loaded up three cars and headed to an area where a large rock had been tossed at John Bull once, and a twenty-two inch footprint track was also found. As they got out of the cars, Toby felt suddenly compelled to leave the pack and run up the old skid road alone in the dark. Once away from the group, Toby called his girlfriend to say hello and tell her about the events of the day.

After waiting a bit in a clearing, Toby heard Beth coming up the hill toward him. Although she did not have a flashlight on, Toby seemed to instantly know, even in total darkness, that it was Beth who approached. As Toby and Beth talked, they saw flashlights and headlamps coming up the road. Toby and Beth called to them to turn off their lights, using words to the effect that, "You can see better long term without lights. Your eyes will adjust for walking...until ya fall! Murphy's law!!"

Walking up, now with no lights, was the rest of the team: Todd, Dylan, and David. John and his dog were missing, which was not a matter of huge concern. Of all the night walkers, John was the most familiar with the area. He had seen a sasquatch once before in the very same area, and was totally gung-ho to see one again, hopefully soon.

They waited and waited. Thirty minutes had elapsed and John was still a no-show. Toby called him on his phone to see what was holding him up. John answered the call and told Toby, "When you told the others to turn off their lights Toby… I did not even have one on….I felt as though I had to leave then…Something urged me to get in my car and just go. It was not my time to go hiking that night….I am pissed right now and have no idea why I'm home….I should be back with you guys…I sat in my truck for a while and could do nothing but leave the mountain….this is not how I do things…!"

This left Toby thoroughly confused. At first he explained it away as though John was feeling moody around the unfamiliar faces, or perhaps Toby was a bit too gruff in the way he asked them to turn off the lights. As the rest of the group gathered together, they talked about John's weird exit. Then, they decided to break off into two groups. Toby and fire chief David were in one group. Beth, Todd, and Dylan were in the other.

As they walked along, talking and sharing in the cold rainy night, Toby and David came upon some power lines in a clearing that crossed overhead. Then, journeying past the power lines, they entered a mature stand of fir trees that looked like good cover to block the rain that was now falling steadily. Toby was a bit underdressed for this cold wet weather but David was not. He was extremely well dressed, not only for the weather, but for pretty much every other eventuality right up to a hostage crisis. David was basically wearing brand new, all black, SWAT gear. Each team had a radio and as they ducked into the trees, Toby radioed the other team to notify them that he and David were hunkered down in the trees. Please keep radios quiet and listen for a while.

The other team agreed.

At that point, Toby looked over at David who had gone from standing up to lying face down, on the wet forest floor. Meanwhile, he was still talking to Toby about the same casual stuff as before, all the while lying flat in the mud in his expensive tactical gear. At that moment, Toby flashed back to the fact that had seen Todd do the exact same odd behavior

Having attended a number of sasquatch conferences, and even organized a few of them himself, Toby knew a thing or two about the sasquatch's powers of intimidation. He knew well that the sasquatch are reported to employ smells, sounds, and even a palpable sense of fear to repel intruders. Toby told David that he thinks the sasquatch may be making him feel ill and that *they* may want them to back off a little. David then goes on hands and knees, grabbing his stomach. He tells Toby he's about to vomit. Not really knowing what else to say or do, Toby suggests that Dave try to walk a few more steps, just to see what happens. Meanwhile, Toby was unaffected. He felt no particular sickness or fear, just a bit of confusion over what to make of this sudden turn of events. David tried to take another step, then immediately turns to Toby and said, "I'm frozen! I can't move. *They* want me to leave! I have to go home! I gotta go, *NOW!*"

With that, Dave turned and headed back down the hill. Toby followed along, trying to reassure his stricken comrade. He told Dave that everything will be alright. He should feel normal once he gets out of *their* area. As they walk downhill, past the clearing and the power lines, Toby sees David lift both his shoulders, and especially his right shoulder, as if to guard his vision. Meanwhile, David kept saying over and over, "I am gonna cry! Oh my Lord, why am I gonna cry? I have to leave...."

Toby tried again to reassure him, saying to David that they are protected; they are covered by Christ, and they'll get him home OK. They proceeded to carefully but steadily make their way down the darkened forest road until they were reunited with Beth, Todd, and Dylan. David immediately moved toward his friend and firefighting partner Dylan, who is 6' 5" tall, grabbed him by the collar and emphatically told him, "We're going home!" And with that, Dylan and David silently strode off into the darkness, toward their truck about a mile down the hill.

The remaining three, Beth, Todd, and Toby, stood there in the dark and drizzle, staring at Toby and waiting for an explanation. They listened intently as Toby explained what just happened a short distance up the hill. Beth, like Toby, had been around the sasquatch game for a while, and had a pretty good idea what was giving David his sudden health problems. Then Todd suddenly felt compelled to tell Toby the reason why he gave him a big, long, man-hug earlier in the day. It was because *they* wanted to see Toby at a certain spot, maybe even this spot, on a particular night, maybe this one.

This was all news to Toby. The fact that a serious-minded, no-nonsense guy like Todd was sharing something that a sasquatch telepathically told him earlier in the day was so far out of character that Toby just didn't know what to say. But what Todd said to him next left Toby even more speechless. "*They* like your son. *They* heard him in the woods earlier in the day and they were curious about him. *They* appreciated his voice in the woods."

At this point, Toby didn't know whether to be angry, or just thoroughly confused. He was suddenly not sure what part of this evening was reality and what was part of some crazy fantasy. While listening to all this, a wave of relief overtook Toby as he reminded himself that his son was safe at home. Toby questioned Todd a bit more on his and David's strange behavior. That's when it dawned on him that perhaps it was also related to the strange behavior and sudden change of plans by John Bull. As the single explanation for all these strange events dawned on Toby, he suddenly had yet another realization: All three of them may have been somehow led up there to that particular spot, at that very moment, by an extended series of events that began with the discovery of the London tracks last Wednesday afternoon!

The conclusion suddenly seemed so obvious, now: It was *Sasquatch Calling* and this was The Clash. Toby suggests that they should once again pray, which they did, and following that, all three of the self-anointed sasquatch researchers commenced walking UP the hill, back toward the clearing, the power lines, and the dense timber stand where David had just been so thoroughly undone. Strangely, they felt no fear. Toby describes his feeling at that point as one of great awe and curiosity. The sense of normalcy he felt was almost bizarre, even as they headed toward the scene of such ominous recent events. Toby felt strangely protected by something; maybe his faith. Despite his sense of invincibility, Toby was also really tired of being cold, wet, and not well-dressed for the weather. In any case, the hapless trio wasn't quite 'out of the woods,' yet. The biggest clash of all was just ahead.

As they walked up the hill, past the power lines, and ultimately back into the same area where David had been repelled, Toby was hit with the feeling that they had just walked right into something invisible but tangible. As the trio advanced side by side; Todd on the right, Beth on the left, and Toby in the middle, Toby felt like they had walked into an invisible wall of quicksand. Their motions were slowed by a palpable thickness. It became difficult to move. Toby likened it to being on the moon, in a very heavy and restrictive pressure suit, with no ability to make quick gestures. Toby felt reduced from about 90% mobility to 30% mobility, in a single step. Toby insists he still was not scared, just stricken by a sense of awe. He suddenly realized that numerous stories he had heard of being immobilized by the presence of a sasquatch were completely true!

As he walked further into the invisible force field, Toby recalls smiling and saying, "I am just barely allowed to function. I'm not scared, Beth, but you're gonna have to be the one to help me. They're gonna let me come in!"

And, by all appearances, that's just what she did because they advanced, together. And as quickly as Toby felt he had entered that wall of quicksand that slowed his movement, he popped right out of it!

Toby looked over at Todd and noticed he was shaking his hands, as though to get the 'pins and needles' out of them. At that same moment, as they entered the broad clearing by the power lines, Toby found himself doing the exact same thing. It's a feeling I have experienced, myself. Beth, Todd, and Toby were 'getting zapped.'

Courageously, they forged ahead. Within a few minutes of entering the clearing, Beth was drawn to the darker part of the forest, wandering off alone and talking to the night. Beth was then heard singing Bible songs and giggling. Meanwhile, Toby looked over at Todd, who was holding his arms out with palms up and turning in circles. Todd turned and said to Toby, "They're mad because I brought my gun. They don't want me to have a gun in here."

Toby stepped a bit further from Todd and decided to try talking to the woods, himself. Toby recalls asking them to leave his son out of this, in the same way they would be bothered if he were there looking for their kids. Toby went on to explain to whomever was listening, that *we* are God's children and that we have dominion over *them* (the sasquatch). Toby felt no particular response. Meanwhile, Todd was still saying that they were angry about his gun. Todd moved much closer to Toby, closer than Toby had ever seen this fearless man ever move before. As they moved in unison through the forest clearing, they thought they could hear, and even sense, the presence of at least one sasquatch.

Impulsively, Toby stated out loud that he was sick of being rained on. Then, they move into the woods toward Beth. Toby asked Beth, whose nick name is Sasquatch Whisperer, to tell *them* that they are coming into their area and, by the way, they are sick of the cold and rain.

Beth responded with words to the effect that, "Well, OK, just know that they are really close." The trio moved together, side by side, into a very dark pocket in the forest, beneath a tree. Beth then said, "Oh, brother, they want us to sit down in the mud and rain. I am not sitting in rain fellas. No way!"

Toby wasn't feeling quite so intransigent. He turned to Beth and said, "Well, *I'm* sitting down."

In an instant, all three are sitting cross-legged (Indian-style) on the wet ground. The next thing Toby recalled was feeling a great sense of relaxation, as though he was, "inside a French press coffee maker filled with Novocain and morphine." In Toby's words, "It felt like the afterglow that follows some really great sex. It was a state of deep and utter relaxation, and I commented on it out loud. I heard Todd say, 'Me, too, I am totally gonna fall asleep right here in the mud and snooze...but they still want me to take my gun off.'"

To this, Toby said to Todd, "Just take it off and throw it in the field."

Beth chimed in, "No, we're going to set some boundaries here. That's his gun and you have no right to dictate this. Todd, keep your pistol on."

Todd and Toby were feeling their knees gradually weaken and their facial muscles relaxing, as they felt overcome by intense relaxation. Their muscles felt like Jell-O. Sleep tugged at their consciousness from within. It was so dark that Todd cannot be sure he saw it outright or in his 'mind's eye' but he was now aware of the sasquatch that was standing over them.

Todd's words were, "I felt I had been turned to Jell-O by its presence. Then it took one big step and it disappeared from view."

The struggle to stay awake was finally over. Todd said, "I'm getting sick. I gotta go. They want me to go. I gotta leave."

The team got up slowly and began heading down the hill, feeling targeted by the same uneasy feelings on and off as they descended the hill.

As the cold, wet trio stumbled down the hill, the ring of a cell phone emanated from Toby's pocket. They were still high enough on the hill to get pretty good cell coverage. It was me calling Toby.

"How did your outing go?"

"Oh, man, we're still out here. We're just heading down the hill now. We're almost back to the car. To be perfectly honest, we're wet, cold, and actually pretty traumatized." Toby did his best to summarize the events of the evening.

"Yikes! Sounds like you guys just got zapped," I observed, with my usual knack for stating the obvious.

"No doubt about it. We just need some time to recover."

I hung up. I felt a bit sorry for their predicament but I still couldn't help but smile. It may not have been a daylight sighting, but I knew full well what it all meant. They had encountered a powerful adult or maybe a group of adult sasquatches. The eager-beaver researchers had gotten too close and they got a taste of the power that these beings can bring to bear. It sounded like they got a taste of the sasquatch intimidation trifecta: Todd got the physical illness,

Toby felt the invisible wall, and they all got zapped with 'the tinglies' and the sleepiness. It's the sasquatch's way of immobilizing intruders and sending the unmistakable message, "That's far enough. You will not come any closer."

The next day, Joe Beelart and I returned to the scene of the London track find to take more photos and have another look around. We also met up with Beth, Toby, and John Bull. Toby, Beth and I headed up the road to the scene of the 'zapping.' We walked the long logging road up Straight Creek as they recounted all the experiences of the night before.

Beth, John Bull, and Joe Beelart at the Straight Creek gate.

Somewhere in last night's adventure, Beth had lost a glove. I strongly suspected we would not only find the glove, but we would find it under slightly mysterious circumstances. We did. It was lying in the middle of the road, right in the clearing where they had been zapped. A foot-long stick had been neatly placed atop the glove, as if to keep the glove from blowing away. We found a curious configuration of sticks in the woods twenty feet away from the glove. Other than that, it looked and felt like a very ordinary patch of woods. Toby and Beth showed me the clearing, the power lines, and the deep dark patch of woods where the excitement happened the night before and they recollected the whole story. We left some gifts of food and trinkets and headed back down the hill to the Cottage Grove Reservoir where we had parked our vehicles.

Cherry Tomatoes

An experience like the one Toby's crew experienced will affect a person in one of two ways: either they never go 'squatchin' again, or they pursue the subject with more enthusiasm than ever before. At first, Todd had no interest in following up on his experience, but he *was* a lifelong hunter, tracker, and outdoorsman. It was really just a question of how long it would be before he returned to the woods. By Todd's own assessment, it took him a few weeks to recover from the ordeal, but eventually he was again camping with Toby and back on the trail of the sasquatch.

Todd, Toby, and Beth have accumulated quite a catalog of interesting locations throughout the McKenzie River drainage where sasquatch activity and/or UFO activity have occurred. So, when TV crews come to town to do a show on the paranormal side of the wilderness, Toby is a valuable resource. That summer, the crew from TV's *Finding Bigfoot* announced that they were coming to Cottage Grove to film an episode on the London track find. The emphasis was going to be placed upon Cliff Barackman's role in collecting the casts. No mention was going to be made of the nighttime adventures of Toby's 'paranormal Sunday' experiences up Straight Creek.

There was, however, interest in filming a 'night investigation' with Bobo (James Fay) and his dog 'Monkey.' One of the production crew, a Northwest field man named Tyler Bounds, explored the upper McKenzie valley for locations. Using BFRO reports to guide him, he found a nice camp spot with a very wild character off the Boulder Creek Road in the Willamette National Forest. It was an area that was well-known to local bigfoot enthusiasts for past sightings and encounters. Meanwhile, Bobo's dog was flown from his home in northern California and reunited with his master in Eugene.

Tyler, Bobo, Monkey, and a cameraman from Animal Planet headed up Boulder Creek to film their night investigation. To no one's surprise, it didn't include any of the drama of Paranormal Sunday. There were no eyeball cryptid sightings for the benefit of the Animal Planet crew, but they did hear mysterious noises and disturbances in the woods all night long. Monkey behaved oddly, becoming agitated and barking at stirrings and noises in the surrounding forest, leading the crew to suspect that they had some mysterious forest visitors checking them out from a distance.

James (Bobo) Fay, Monkey, and Craig Flippe.   Monkey

Beyond the forest noises, something interesting was found at the edge of camp the next morning. It was Bobo's custom to leave his favorite piece of jewelry, a necklace, draped across his boots outside his tent. The necklace consisted of a flat piece of agate carved into the shape of a sasquatch profile in mid-stride. It was, of course, Bobo's hope that the necklace would be accepted as a gift by any hirsute forest visitor that might be keeping an eye on their camp. Tyler decided to leave his boots outside the tent, right next to Bobo's. When they went for their boots in the morning, Bobo and Tyler were surprised to find that, rather than Bobo's necklace being taken, another necklace, some beads strung on a leather thong, had been left on Tyler's boots.

I'm not sure whether this event was deemed worthy of inclusion in the episode that was filmed, but upon completion of the camp out, Bobo offered his candid assessment of Tyler's campsite on Boulder Creek: very 'squatchy.'

Todd was ready to try a new camp spot, so he decided to spend a night with his son up at Tyler's camp on Boulder Creek. It was September of 2012, one week before the beginning of school when Todd and his high-school-aged son, Jake, headed up the McKenzie River. Soon after they left home, Jake happened to mention that he wanted to try out for the basketball team that year, so he would need a new pair of basketball shoes. Todd swallowed hard at this news, knowing that basketball shoes were a lot more expensive than the Converse sneakers that he would have worn a generation ago. No matter, it was a worthy pursuit and Todd agreed that they would chase down some proper basketball shoes when they got back to town.

Less than an hour later, they arrived at Bobo's camp and began unloading their camp gear. They had brought the usual fishing and camping gear, as well

126

as some 'gifts' for the local sasquatches. In this instance, they had a big bag of cherry tomatoes that they had acquired unexpectedly.

Todd and his son found a lost dog a few days prior to their camping trip. They were able to track down the owner by paying attention to publicly posted bulletins in their neighborhood. As an expression of his gratitude, the dog owner gave Todd and Jake the only thing he had in abundant supply: cherry tomatoes that he had grown in his garden. They weren't quite sure what to do with their bonanza of cherry tomatoes until the idea of their camping trip materialized. Todd knew enough about sasquatch field research techniques to know that home grown garden produce is much more attractive to the local sasquatches than store-bought stuff. They would leave cherry tomatoes somewhere near their camp as 'gifts' to the local wildmen.

When they got their camp set up, Todd and Jake then loaded up a plastic grocery sack full of tomatoes and headed into the woods. Just outside their camp were some springs with lots of soft, boggy, saturated earth around them. If tracks were hoped for, it was the perfect spot to leave their gifts. They hung the sack of tomatoes from the stub of a branch on one of the trees by the spring. Then they headed back to camp to build the evening campfire and relax. That's when the strange things began to occur.

Todd was taking photos of the campsite and the surrounding forest. Suddenly, his camera battery went completely dead. He had fully charged the battery just before he left home. It should have been good for a few days of photography. They decided to take a walk along the creek bed after dark. Both of their flashlights stopped working within minutes of each other. The bright full moon illuminated the forest so they continued walking along the creek bed. That is when they heard a large rock land nearby then shatter into fragments.

They continued their loop back toward camp, now with a very much more heightened level of alert. They could hear something moving in the shadows to their right. Then there was something else shadowing them in the darkened forest off to their left. They arrived back in camp. They could hear faint movement in the woods all around them, now. It was not heavy footfalls or crashing around, but rather soft snapping of twigs, almost as though small, light critters like chipmunks were stirring in the forest. Suddenly, Jake began to feel nauseous.

One moment Jake was contentedly sitting by the fire, then he was doubled over and feeling very ill. Then, a moment later, Jake's head was up, and he was peering intently into the forest. Todd was somewhat alarmed by the fact that Jake was sitting silently, not moving, with his eyes transfixed on some random point in the woods. Todd looked into the darkness of the moonlit forest, trying to see what was holding his son so spellbound. All at once, it came into focus. Todd discerned the distinct outline of a large upright creature standing in the shadows right on the edge of their camp! As Jake continued to stare at the immense form in stunned silence, Todd decided to turn on his flashlight and illuminate the intruder. The instant that Todd made the decision to turn on his flashlight, the creature stepped silently and quickly into the forest and disappeared from view. What baffles Todd, even to this day, was the immediacy with which the creature was able to perceive Todd's intent. As Todd tells it, it was as though the creature read Todd's mind. It *knew* that Todd was about to hit it with a beam of light and it wasn't going to let that happen.

Now the pair was thoroughly spooked. Their senses were on full alert and their hearts were pounding. They struggled to suppress the fear that built in their minds. Sticks were heard to snap overhead as something else came flying through the forest and right into camp. A rock hurtled into camp and landed with a heavy thud. Another rock landed in camp. At that point, the two men were out of their chairs and on their feet, with their backs to the fire.

In a moment of courage born of fear, Jake picked up a rock and threw it *back* into the forest. That was enough! Todd couldn't take any more. The decision had been made and they were outta there! They both grabbed only what they could carry and jumped into their car. The tent, sleeping bags, and all their fishing gear remained in camp as the terrified campers abandoned the scene and took off for town. At first they drove in stunned silence, hands trembling as adrenaline coursed through their veins.

Perhaps some tobacco might calm their rattled nerves, Todd thought. He produced a pair of cigarellos (small cigars with plastic tips) and they lit up. After a few drags, Jake turned to his dad and said, "Why do I taste tomatoes while I'm smoking a cigar?"

Todd shrugged, but at that moment, his mind flashed on the sack of cherry tomatoes that they left on the tree branch by the spring. After a few more minutes of awkward silence, Jake turns to his father and said, "Dad, I've always believed your stories about sasquatch, but now I KNOW…" His voice trailed off.

If Todd hadn't been driving the car, he would have given his son a hug. In those few, well-chosen words, Todd's son was able to reward his father with both pride and a sense of vindication. Up until a few moments ago, his son wasn't completely sure what to think about his father's interest in the whole sasquatch business. But now, in the mind of his son Jake, Todd was anything but crazy. Their father-son campout did not end well, but it did have an unexpected outcome: In the mind of his son, it validated Todd's interest in the sasquatch phenomenon. The sasquatch was now a fact of nature that Jake had seen with his own eyes.

As they headed down the McKenzie highway toward Springfield, Todd pulled over at the truck weigh station in Walterville. He called Toby and told him that they just got scared out of the woods by the sasquatches. Toby was sympathetic but also of the feeling that they needed to get back up there right now in the name of bigfoot research.

"That's not gonna happen," Todd said flatly. "But I did leave all my fishing gear and most of my camp gear up there, so I guess we have to go back up there tomorrow and get my stuff."

The most interesting thing Todd said to me in the process of describing this terrifying experience was that, after that night, "My wanting to know finally passed my fear." Todd went on to say that, "The hostility I felt, changed to probing and curiosity."

Todd wasn't ready to head right back up there with Toby that night, but still, a transformation did occur in Todd Bailey's thinking. His need to know, that is, to understand the sasquatch phenomenon finally surpassed his fear of what the sasquatch could do to him. His fear changed to curiosity and a desire to understand the confusing situation he had experienced.

Perhaps, without knowing it, Todd was also speaking from the perspective of the sasquatch. Whatever trepidation that the sasquatch may feel when first encountering specific people may eventually change. Distrust is replaced by curiosity and a even a desire to continue the relationship, especially after the intentions of the individual are assessed. In a sense, Todd, his son, and the sasquatch, had managed to exchange introductions. Both sides had lost a little of their distrust of each other's intentions. If they were going to build the relationship, they just had to go back. They didn't *have* to go back, but if they did, it would be a big step. They did go back, and Todd was about to find out that he and his son may have indeed bonded with a sasquatch.

At 10 a.m. the next morning, Todd, Jake, and Toby rolled into the hastily abandoned camp at Boulder Creek. By light of day, all of the intimidating feelings of the previous evening were gone. None of the camp gear had been touched in their absence. Everything was exactly as Todd and Jake left it.

The tomatoes! The team went off to check the tomatoes by the springs. On the trail to the spring, they happened across two nine inch barefoot tracks! When they arrived at the spring, they could see that most of the cherry tomatoes were gone. The plastic grocery sack had tears in it but it was still hanging in the tree exactly where they left it, about five feet off the ground. A few tomatoes remained in the corners of the sack. It's a pattern that has been observed by others for decades. It seems that when a sasquatch takes the food, the gift, the bait, or whatever you want to call it, they never take it all. They may take most of it, but they always leave some. It was a pattern that was reminiscent of the Skookum expedition.

The track found by the cherry tomatoes

The team carefully searched the whole area around the springs for more tracks, tomatoes, or any other possible indication of sasquatch presence. Then, they took the bag down from the tree and headed back to the car for a closer look. There was hope that the bag might contain finger prints, a hair, or something else by way of physical evidence. Back at the car, they examined the bag more carefully and dug out their casting material.

Toby and Todd mixed and poured their first footprint cast since the London track find. Owing to the enormous experience they gained at the

Cottage Grove Reservoir, they proceeded with much more confidence and skill. As they waited for the plaster to cure, Todd suggested to his son that they try to keep the good feelings going by leaving something else for the sasquatch by way of gifts. The only edible material that remained was dog food. It wasn't gourmet, but it would have to do. They put dog food in a large trash sack and dispatched Jake to hang it on the tree by the spring while they checked on the track casts.

A moment later, Jake returned from the springs carrying a pair of Converse low-top sneakers.

"Where did you get those?" Jake's dad asked.

"You're not going to believe this, but they were on the ground, right where we hung the tomatoes."

Toby and Todd looked at each with the same incredulous look.

"That's impossible. We just searched the whole area for evidence fifteen minutes ago. There weren't any sneakers there a few minutes ago."

Jake with the 'gifted' shoes moments after they were found.

The trio abandoned the tracks and hastily returned to the spring. Jake showed them where he found the sneakers. They were in plain sight, Jake insisted, neatly placed side by side, just as though they were sitting on a shelf at the shoe store. Both laces were tied into neat bows. Tiny threads of moss were lodged in the corners of the trademark Converse insignia on the sides of the shoes. They were well worn shoes, but they were dry and still functional. The three men stood in a circle, dumbfounded, struggling to understand how a pair of sneakers could materialize at a place that they had thoroughly searched a few minutes ago.

A new chill travelled up Todd's spine. "Jake, remember the conversation we had in the car on the way up here yesterday. You told me you needed a pair of basketball shoes..." his voice trailed off.

If this was a coincidence, it was one of the strangest coincidences of all time. Yet, it was just too remarkable to dismiss as mere coincidence. It was supernatural. It was paranormal. It was also very funny.

Try to imagine a sasquatch having an affinity, a fondness, for a certain father-son team that had been observed several times lately, coming and going from the local woods. Now, imagine that the same sasquatch were able to remotely eavesdrop on a conversation between the same father and son about the athletic apparel needs for the upcoming school year. Imagine also that a sasquatch was sympathetic to the fact that the son had needs that the father was hard-pressed to provide. What if, by some chance, that the sympathetic sasquatch happened to know where there was a pair of sneakers that were just about the right size? Perhaps the sasquatch had to rummage around a bit in the back of his or her cave for that pair of sneakers that was left behind by campers a few months or years ago. Could a sasquatch actually take such an opportunity to bestow a pair of saved sneakers upon some worthy humans? Could this be yet another indication that the sasquatch understand English, can eavesdrop on conversations, can exhibit compassion, empathy, and maybe even a sense of humor?

The most curious, even ironic twist of all was that the team searched the area for simple evidence that sasquatches exist. Instead, they found evidence that the sasquatch are excellent practical jokers. What's funny is how lame the sneakers are, by today's standards.

Imagine a kid showing up for basketball try outs at a modern American high school wearing twenty year old, low top tennis shoes with moss growing on the Converse logo. He would get laughed off the court, *until* he told the story of how he got them. Only a few short years ago, that story would also get him laughed off the court, but not any more. A large percentage of the kids in every American high school have seen *Finding Bigfoot* on cable TV, and quite a few of those kids love not only the show but the whole concept of 'Bigfoot.' Imagine the team mates hearing that the new kid got his shoes delivered by

Bigfoot, and all it cost him was a sack of cherry tomatoes. Who could ever top that story? That kid *has* to be on the team. The whole narrative, no matter how you want to fill in the missing details, is just unbelievably funny. The fact that the shoes essentially fit Jake's feet, though, is a bit chilling.

Is it even possible that a sasquatch could somehow *know* enough, and then also *do* enough to put those slightly inadequate but still serviceable sneakers in front of the intended person? It certainly challenges even the most unconventional-minded sasquatch researcher to understand just what a sasquatch is capable of, in light of these events. To me, it also may be a clue as to how strongly and affectionately the sasquatch regard certain people, especially kids. Indeed, after all the laughter has died down, this is an episode with some of the most profound implications ever to be considered in the dubious science of bigfoot research. Not only is it paranormal with a capital "P," but there is actually a bit of a pattern here, as well.

The old Converse logo complete with strands of moss.

Recall that, after the London tracks were cast, Todd and Toby went off to explore the wood and Toby's son Jude was along. In a move that Todd didn't fully understand even as he did it, he informed Toby that *they* (the sasquatch) were charmed by the presence of Toby's son. Some see this as a very threatening, even menacing thing to reveal, but I do not, especially in light of the fact that nothing bad happened to any of the kids or grownups in this story. Six months later, it is Todd's son who first has a sighting in camp. Once the trauma of the initial introductions subsides, the same lad is bestowed with

133

tennis shoes that, by all appearances, came from the local bigfoots. Recall too, that as they fled the camp the night before the sneakers were found, Todd's son Jake has the mysterious experience of tasting tomatoes in his mouth, right about the time that the sasquatch may have been helping themselves to the tomatoes that were left for them back at the springs.

Not long ago, I was introduced to a 'sasquatch whisperer' by my friend Guy Edwards. Her name is Tish Paquette and she would describe herself as a sasquatch communicator. Tish was kind enough to come out to my place and walk the trails of my favorite areas with me and provide her take on what may be going on. One of the most fascinating observations that she offered without any prompting from me was that the local wildmen liked to observe *my son* as he walked the trails.

When I was invited to study the goings on at the Hoyt household in 1998-2001, it was clear that Nina, the teen-aged daughter was the member of the household with the strongest connection to the sasquatch. She had the most encounters and the sasquatch activity seemed to gravitate toward her more than the other members of the family. To a lesser degree, her mother April and Allen's grandmother (who lived on the property) also had a stronger connection to the sasquatch activity. Women enjoy a greater degree of trust than men, but kids seem to experience the highest degree of trust and acceptance of all.

A minor pattern begins to emerge that the sasquatch are more interested in young people than grown-ups. This idea has been around for a long time. Campers or rural residents with sasquatch encounters often report that the mysterious beings seemed particularly interested in the kids. In my own mind, the question is not *whether* the sasquatch are interested in kids, but *why*.

Perhaps it is simply because the sasquatch, while equally interested in all humans, recognize that kids are inherently less threatening and more trustworthy than adults. Another possibility is that the sasquatch are looking toward the eventual maturation of the human race to the point when humans no longer shoot at, or even fear the sasquatch. And, while the sasquatch may even be working behind the scenes toward that eventual moment, they understand that it is still a long way off. The current generation of adults is already too far gone, but the next generation is not. Also, the sasquatch are consummately patient. They may be working the next generation since they are a more promising prospect for eventually achieving a spirit of mutual acceptance between sasquatch and humanity.

If I was Todd's son, I would wear those sneakers with pride. Maybe not on the basketball court, but certainly whenever I was in the woods. Imagine the pride and sense of camaraderie that the sasquatch might feel if they ever saw him wearing the sneakers he was given.

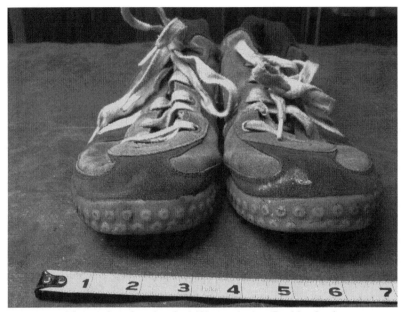

The sneakers found at the 'gifting station' on Boulder Creek

The Outcrop

Four weeks after Paranormal Sunday, Todd Bailey was again ready to head into the wilds. He loved exercising his tracking skills, and what could be more challenging to track than a sasquatch? Todd headed up Whites Creek, one of the most active areas in the past, and sure enough, he came upon some very large barefoot tracks.

As Todd followed the tracks, he could see that the creature that left them was traveling parallel to an open ridge, but while the tracks followed along the ridge, they also avoided the open ground of the ridge top, which would have been an easier travel route. Elsewhere, the tracks paralleled the established trails, but avoided the actual trail. Interestingly, these are exactly the kinds of things that the 'special ops' commandos are taught to do when moving through hostile territory.

At other times, when Todd felt that *he* was being stalked, and indications were that it may have been a sasquatch, the noises that followed him were surprising soft. Todd's only conclusion was that the sasquatch can sound like a bulldozer moving through the woods when they want to, but the same massive creatures can travel so softly that they sound like chipmunks.

I can relate. When Paul Graves and I were sitting beside the Moclips River behind Jim Henry's house, we could hear the very faint popping of brush that emanated from the other side of the river. It was so soft and faint that there was absolutely no cause for concern on our part, or even the suspicion that it was a sasquatch on the move. Only later did we learn that two young neighbors were very alarmed by noises coming from essentially the same woods just before our arrival on the scene. At that point, the softer noises we heard became much more suspicious. Maybe Paul and I were hearing a sasquatch after all.

In 2000, as I was staking out the woods around the Hoyt homestead, it was pretty much the same story. Allen Hoyt and I would sometimes sit in a clearing that we called the 'dance hall,' owing to the numerous tracks he had seen there over the years. As we staked out this area in hopes of catching a glimpse of a sasquatch, we both heard very light brush-popping coming from the thickets all around our position. Allen confidently stated, "That's them. That's how they move."

At the time, although I didn't say it to Allen, I just could not believe that he was correct. My view was that if it sounded like chipmunks, it *was* chipmunks. Now, fifteen years later and fifteen years wiser, I am much more inclined to agree with what Allen was saying back then. To anyone who is ever in the position of being circled by a sasquatch or even a group of them, I would submit that, when they want to, the creatures do indeed move with incredible softness, considering their massive proportions. I am much more convinced of this now than I was previously, especially in light of the fact that an experienced tracker like Todd Bailey has the exact same take on the situation.

There is another observation that Todd Bailey passed along that I had encountered myself, but just could not bring myself to accept. To use the words of Todd Bailey, "One minute, you know you're looking at a sasquatch track, and then there are no more tracks."

Sasquatch tracks in mud, dirt, and snow have all been observed to abruptly end. There is no simple explanation for how this is done, but there is a definite pattern to this observation, made over many years by many field researchers:

track ways do mysteriously and abruptly end, as if the creature that made them disappeared into thin air.

It is also a bit of a relief to know that serious and sober individuals such as Todd are willing to corroborate this mysterious observation that has been kicking around the bigfoot research community for years. Many people who observe this have been afraid to mention it, even to other researchers, for fear of ridicule.

And when it comes to fear of ridicule, many sasquatch researchers seem to have a few other experiences that they are extremely reluctant to share. Everyone who delves into paranormal research of any kind will eventually have some such experience that will leave them scratching their head. Whether one is investigating sasquatch, ghosts, extraterrestrials, crop circles, or something else, sooner or later something really strange and unexplainable will happen to you. Some people just plain do not notice. Others fail to grasp the mystery as it happens or dismiss it as illusory. It really becomes a test of one's ability to notice these subtle events as they occur, usually at the most unexpected of moments. Personally, I have had so many bizarre experiences that I felt it was time to put them into a book. As I set about trying to chronicle my own unexplainable experiences, I have encountered still more from the other field researchers in my circle of acquaintance.

On a warm summer night in 2013, Todd, Toby, and Dave headed up to a camp spot they found up in the hills outside of the town of Vida. They set up camp by a very scenic outcrop that provided a great view up the McKenzie drainage in the direction of the Three Sisters Wilderness. The trio set up their camp chairs and enjoyed one of life's greatest pleasures: a warm summer evening, a cold beer, friends, a campfire, and just a few yards away, a rock outcrop with a great view of the wilderness to their east. Unfortunately for Toby, he had to work the next day, so around 11 p.m. he bid Todd and Dave adieu and headed back to town. By now the fire had died down and Dave set to work building it back up to a big, roaring 'white man fire.' At that point, Todd began drumming rhythmically on the lid of the ice chest and chanting in a manner that was decidedly Native American. This was not a typical behavior for a regular guy like Todd, but Dave did not object. If anything, it seemed somehow to be appropriate atmospherics, given their remote location in a place that was once the heart of Indian country. They left the fire and went out to the outcrop, where they sat on the ground, looking out over the landscape for what seemed like the next hour.

Suddenly, both men sat up at the same time and noticed a great deal of light in the eastern sky. Todd noticed that he was not sitting next to Dave anymore. He was in a slightly different spot. Meanwhile there was a glow on the horizon that resembled an imminent sunrise, which was impossible since Toby had left only an hour ago and that was 11 p.m. They both stared at the glow on the horizon and struggled to understand what they were looking at. Dave turned around and looked at the fire. The big bonfire he had built only an hour ago was a weakly glowing pile of embers. Todd pulled out his cell phone to check the time and was stunned to see that it was just after 5 a.m.

Todd and Dave slowly came to the realization that they were the recipients, the experiencers, or the victims (however one wants to look at it) of the 'missing time' phenomenon. They two men shared at least four, and perhaps as much as five hours of missing time. One moment it was midnight, and the next moment it was sunrise. Their exact positions at that moment, with respect to each other, were slightly different than where they remembered sitting. They had not consumed more than a single beer each.

They were both upset, even angry. They both felt exhausted. They made coffee and then took a nap. The experience bothered them for days. In fact, it still bothers them. I spoke with Dave a few months later. I asked him if he was aware of the thought that is widely held in paranormal research that missing time is indicative of some sort of alien abduction. He was. Did he think he and Todd may have been abducted, and of course, put back in approximately the same location? That thought had, indeed occurred to both of them, but they seemed to be looking for a more ordinary explanation, even when there wasn't one.

"Did either of you notice any marks on your body that you had never seen before?" I asked. I don't claim to know anything about alien abductions, but I did happen to pick that item up from a book on the subject that I once read.

"Yes," was the surprise answer Dave gave me. "We both did," he continued. "Todd had a dot behind his ear that he had never noticed before. I had a wart-like bump on the back of my hand. There was a hard object inside the wart and I dug it out with the tip of a pocket knife. It was a tiny piece of some kind of metal. I still have it."

I didn't want to make a bigger deal out of it than it needed to be. All's well that ends well, and Dave and Todd were still enjoying life on planet Earth, but it did seem that their mutual experience had all the hallmarks of a fairly standard alien abduction. I had the opportunity to speak with them both, separately, about the event. Their stories were perfectly consistent. Neither person ever embraced the idea of UFOs, or ETs, nor were they really aware of the view that such abductions do happen and they are probably much more common than most people realize. Dave is a career firefighter, and emergency medical technician (EMT), and even a teacher/trainer of firefighters at the local community college. Certainly, it is not in Dave's career interest to be thought of as a guy who was abducted by aliens, sasquatches, or anything else. Dave would just like to know what did happen on that fateful summer night after Toby cleared out. I didn't want to say too much to poor old Dave, especially since I wasn't there. I can never be sure. But Toby put Dave in touch with me because he knew of my interest in paranormal phenomena. It is my view as a career teacher of science and the scientific method that, when one wants answers and cannot find them, one needs to branch out, cast a broader net, and generally widening the search to related topics, until some clues emerge that shed additional light upon the unresolved mystery.

By broadening my base of information into related paranormal, I think I have happened upon clues as to what happened to Todd and Dave on 'the outcrop.' I didn't really go looking for the clues. The clues found me, but that's the way it often happens when one probes the realm of the paranormal. Serendipities and synchronicities seem to abound. In any case, the best possible answer to the mystery of what happened to Todd and Dave on the outcrop that night found me at the Robert Gray Middle School science fair.

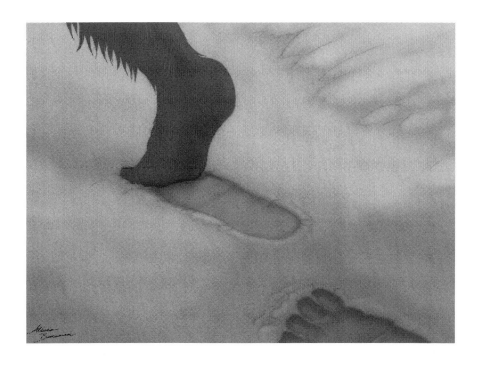

Chapter Five: The Science Fair

You always learn something new at a science fair. I learned that there really are alien abductees. In fact, I actually met one at the school science fair.

Those two words, "science fair" strike fear in the hearts of parents throughout the school community. Gearing up for a science fair inflicts enormous stress and turmoil on every household in the neighborhood with school-aged children. The decisions, the expense, the poster board, and especially the time required; it's enough to send shudders up the parental spine.

It began like every other science fair. You start with a school gymnasium. You fill it with a maze of folding tables then fill the tables with a forest of display boards. Finish with an array of hardware: gerbil cages, jars, electrical components, steam engines, Lego robots, and of course, the proverbial paiper-mâché volcano. My personal favorite is the tornado machine. There's something awesome about the conglomeration of hundreds of tri-fold project boards jammed into a school gymnasium. It's a diverse presentation of scientific ideas, from the petty to the profound.

The preparations are stressful but once the projects are finally assembled, all that ends. Then, the gym fills with proud parents and hyperactive kids. At that point, my job as a science teacher becomes relatively easy. I just stand there being cordial to parents and praising the efforts of their children: "Yes, little Ryan's bread mold experiment is very scientific. You must be very proud." The most common line I hear from parents on science fair night, is, "You have no idea how stressful it was to get that simple project done."

Out of the sea of faces on science fair night emerged one that was as pretty as it was familiar. She smiled as she strode over. This was one parent that I knew from experience was not the least bit stressed by the science fair.

"Hi, Janet. Nice to see you, again."

Janet and Jim Cornell were well-known around the school. The Cornells were model parents of remarkably perfect children. Janet was a fixture around the middle school. She helped out in the attendance office and tutored ELL (English Language Learning) students. She was often seen in the halls of the school. The Cornells were there at every open house. They came to every parent conference. Jim was a doctor at the big hospital in the neighborhood. Janet was a member of that endangered species known as 'the stay-at-home mom.'

This was the third year that I had one of Janet Cornell's kids in my eighth grade science class. Typically, a family with multiple children has an under-achiever and an over-achiever. Not so with the Cornells. Their kids were all brilliant. The joke among the teachers was that, even though Janet came to every parent conference, there was nothing to talk about. Her kids were perfect.

Our little public middle school in southwest Portland is uniquely blessed with a plethora of similarly committed and involved parents. They tend to be a bunch of left-leaning liberal Democrats who can afford private schools, but who send their kids to the neighborhood public school anyway, because they believe in public education. But, even in a neighborhood full of dedicated parents, Janet Cornell still stood out. She was one of the nicest, most involved, most supportive parents in a community that is chockablock with involved, supportive parents. Her kids were uniformly polite, quiet, studious, athletic, and happy kids.

I remember one parent conference with Bill and Janet Cornell. At the time, their third child was a student in my science class. This kid was every bit as perfect as her siblings, so there was nothing much to discuss at the parent-teacher conference. But there they were, both Cornell parents, dutifully attending the conference anyway.

After about fifty or sixty of these ten minute sessions, the monotony sets in. In an attempt to preserve what remained of my sanity, I decided to take the conversations in a different direction. Just to be a wise guy, I asked the Cornell's how they manage to produce a steady stream of such perfect children.

They both turned and looked at each other and shrugged. "We just try to be there for them," Janet replied after a bit of a pause. "We try to keep a calm household. We try to be consistent about what we expect. We keep the kids busy with sports. We eat dinner together every night. The kids are expected to sit down with their books every night, and I always help them if they need it."

"Would you mind writing a book, or at least a brochure, on how to raise children, so I can circulate it around the neighborhood? You've obviously got it down," I kidded.

Janet blushed, and we all laughed.

That was the fall of 2002. Now it was February of 2003, and I was again standing in the Robert Gray Middle School gymnasium chatting it up with Janet Cornell at the science fair.

It wasn't more than a few seconds into the conversation that Janet surprised me with this question: "My kids tell me you do a science lesson on UFOs."

"Um, well, yeah, I actually do. It's all in good fun. I bring it out every year on the day before Christmas vacation. You know, half the class is already gone to Maui and the ones who are there are wired on sugar. It's hard to keep them in their seats on a day like that. Since we're finishing an astronomy unit at that point in the year, I pull out an old film strip about UFOs. I make a bunch of jokes. It holds their attention pretty well on the day before a vacation."

"They also tell me that you talked about abductees," Janet fired back.

Yikes! It began to seem like this lady was about to nail me to the wall. She was nice and everything, but she also was serious about education, and it suddenly seemed like she was about to take me to task for squandering instructional time on matters that were not even close to being a part of the school district's approved science curriculum. A little damage control seemed like it might be a good move, maybe even an apology for contaminating her children's mind with some decidedly unscientific stuff.

"Uh…yeah…I guess I did bring that up. The filmstrip mentions the case of Betty and Barney Hill. They're the first people to ever go public with claims of being alien abductees. I also show the kids a video that mentions the Hills. I kept things light, though. Like I said, it was the last day before vacation. I'm really sorry if I caused any kind of problem…"

I was on the ropes and I knew it. I expected that my teaching methods were about to be questioned in a big way. I was expecting to be scolded for contaminating young minds with pseudoscience. This conversation was about to go in a most unexpected direction, and I was about to get one of the biggest shocks of my life.

"Oh, don't worry," Janet reassured me. "There's no problem. I rather appreciate what you did. You see, I learned I may actually be an abductee."

I was stunned. Absolutely speechless. These were words I never expected to hear from any person, much less the one parent I respect most out of the entire school community. It's not often that I am caught speechless. I did my best to act like I was unfazed, but I don't think I did a very good job.

All that came out was a single word. "Really?"

"Well, that's what I've come to understand, anyway. Frankly, I didn't originally have any recollections of the experience at all, but apparently it did happen. I *think* I was abducted. Can you imagine?"

"No, I can't imagine." I was still stammering and trying to recover from the surprise direction in which Janet just took this conversation. "I don't get it. You're *told* that you're an abductee? How does that go?"

"I know this all sounds pretty strange. The only reason I'm bringing it up is because my kids told me you brought it up in class as an example of a scientific mystery. I never took the subject seriously. Then one day, out of the blue, I got a phone call from this researcher whose name was Walter Webb. He was the assistant director of the Hayden Planetarium in Boston. He told me he was investigating an unusual case and he needed my help."

For the next hour, I completely lost track of the fact that I was standing in a hot, stuffy school gymnasium crammed with hundreds of science projects and almost as many bodies. I was spellbound as Janet Cornell unfurled a story that was more fascinating than all 500 of the science projects in that room put together. I was transfixed by the words coming out of her mouth. It was as if she and I were the only ones in the room.

Janet explained that Walter Webb, senior presenter at the Hayden Planetarium and part-time UFO researcher, was sought out by a person who felt he was a UFO abductee. This guy, Michael Lapp, was working as a counselor and waterfront assistant at a summer camp when the abduction happened. According to this man's story, he and another counselor were abducted off a dock at this particular summer camp on Lake Champlain in western Vermont in August of 1968. In 1977, when he sought out Walter Webb, Michael still vividly remembered the details of this alleged abduction and he detailed the entire traumatic event for the benefit of Walter Webb. In an attempt to verify the details of this incredible story, Webb needed to contact the other person who supposedly shared in the abduction. That person was Janet Cornell. Janet related that Walter Webb was on the phone, asking if she was Janet Cornell, and if she had once worked with Michael Lapp at a summer camp in Vermont called Buff Ledge. Yes, she had, indeed. She and Michael were fellow waterfront instructors.

"What's this all about?" Janet wanted to know.

Walter Webb confessed that this was a strange thing to say, but Michael Lapp was claiming that the two of them, he and Janet, were involved in some kind of odd incident on the camp dock one night. Did she have any recollection of that evening, Webb wanted to know.

Janet recalled that Webb was very mysterious in his initial questions. "He was very guarded in his questioning. He never let on that he was investigating UFOs, or abductions, or anything like that."

As we stood in a corner of the science fair, Janet explained to me that Walter Webb was polite and seemed very serious so she took his most peculiar question seriously, even though her first suspicion was that she was being pranked.

Webb asked about any unusual objects or light that she may have seen that night. After thinking about it, Janet told him, "I do remember watching odd lights in the sky. One of the lights came right at us and I thought it was going to hit us. We ducked. That's all I remember."

"Would you be willing to tell me what you do remember about that night?" asked Walter.

Janet explained that that she and Michael were left to watch the camp while the rest of the counselors and campers either went off to a swim meet or an overnight campout on Mt. Mansfield. She restated that they were sitting on the dock just after sunset, talking and looking at the lights on the far side of the lake. They noticed several lights in the sky that moved silently, changing direction frequently. One of the lights became very bright and accelerated, moving directly toward their position on the dock. It looked like it would collide with them. Janet hit the deck. That was all she could remember.

Webb confided that there were more details that Michael was claiming but he was reluctant to share. He didn't want to implant any false memories. What Walter Webb really wanted to know was whether Janet might be willing to be hypnotized. He sensed her reluctance and did his best to assure her that it was a serious scientific effort. It would all be done very professionally and seriously.

As we stood at the science fair, Janet explained that she wanted to be helpful to this guy on the phone who was claiming to be conducting a serious, scientific investigation. After all, her husband was a scientist too. This guy seemed so sincere that Janet felt he merited at least a little cooperation.

The irony of standing in a school science fair talking seriously to a person about their alien abduction scenario was not lost on me. I felt like I was talking to a human science project. The fact that this person was such a competent parent gave me pause, so I decided not to make a joke out of the slightly awkward circumstances. Instead, I just kept my mouth shut and listened.

Walter Webb explained to Janet the convoluted means by which he managed to find her. He was a veteran UFO researcher. Indeed, he was one of the original team of researchers to personally investigate the Betty and Barney Hill case when it was first reported. He had been approached by Michael Lapp who was troubled by recurring nightmares and the memory of an alleged abduction that occurred while he worked as a counselor at Camp Buff Ledge. Walter Webb explained to Janet that the camp was no longer in business so the employment records were unavailable. But, using Michael's scant information, Webb eventually located another counselor who worked at the camp. That former counselor had received Christmas cards from Janet, so she was able to provide Webb with Janet's married name and her current address in Atlanta.

Gradually, Janet began to feel more comfortable with the sincerity of Walter Webb. His position at the planetarium provided her with some reassurance that this was a serious effort that justified her involvement. She finally confided that she planned to return to Boston soon on business. Rather than have him fly out to meet with her, why didn't he just stay put and she would meet him at the airport when she made it to Boston. Webb was thrilled with this suggestion. She took his contact information.

It should be emphasized at this point in the story that psychologists do not place nearly as much confidence in recovering repressed memories through hypnosis as they used to. There is also experimental evidence that suggests that memories can be planted or 'installed' in a person's brain during hypnosis, simply by discussing artificial events with a hypnotized subject. Twenty years ago, when Walter Webb was investigating this case, there was much less recognition of how hypnotism can backfire in this way, so there may have been more validity given to experiences described under hypnotism back then.

On the other hand, I happen to know a professional hypnotist named Doug Meecham. I met him through my friend and fellow paranormal researcher Guy Edwards. From Doug, I've learned, first of all, that hypnotists actually call themselves NLPs, which stands for neuro-linguistic programmers. Most of Doug's NLP work is with people who want to control pain, quit smoking, lose weight, or break some other unhealthy habit like gambling. Doug also happens to be a teacher of NLP (hypnotism). It was Guy Edwards' idea to have Doug hypnotize sasquatch eye-witnesses in order to take them back to the moment of their slightly traumatic encounter. This might afford the opportunity to learn more about the encounter or even verify its authenticity. I attended a presentation by Doug Meecham and learned that, while it is possible to implant false memories in a hypnotized subject, there is a definite protocol that is now used by NLPs to avoid implanting false memories. When it is properly done by an experienced practitioner, NLP is very effective at getting to the truth behind repressed memories.

It is indeed rather chilling to watch an NLP practitioner work, and it is most fascinating to see the involuntary transformation in the witness at the moment when hypnosis takes effect. The subject, who is being guided back to the past experience by the hypnotist, suddenly shifts from using the *past* tense to refer to what once happened, to using the present tense, as if it were all happening at that very moment. It is such a distinct and involuntary transition that it is very unnerving to observe. Guy has watched Doug work on multiple occasions with witnesses and he says it gives him goose bumps every time he sees the hypnotism process take effect.

The point here, is that while there will always be eminent psychologists who dispute the authenticity of hypnotism, I think it is a very authentic, very credible practice when properly done by experienced practitioners like Doug Meecham.

In any case, Walter Webb was able to reassure Janet Cornell that his efforts were appropriately scientific. After some initial hesitation, Janet decided she would cooperate with his efforts to explore her potentially repressed memories. When she arrived in Boston a few months later in February of 1980, they arranged a meeting at hypnotist Claire Hayward's office and Janet Cornell was indeed 'put under.'

We're still standing in the science fair as Janet is explaining to me that, when you are hypnotized, you are not unconscious. You are in a trance but you can hear everything that you are saying. When she began to discuss, under hypnosis, the events of that August night in 1968, she couldn't believe

The dock at Buff Ledge Camp, circa 1968. Lake Champlain sunset from the camp. Note date stamp on side of the old Kodachrome photo. (both photos courtesy of Janet Cornell)

the things that were coming out of her mouth. She described first the lights in the sky, then an intensely bright beam, and then being aboard a strange craft. She and Michael were together at this point and they were (need I say it) petrified with fear. There were strange, presumably alien beings that reassured them that they would be returned to their world as soon as some tests were completed. They were then separated and subject to the kind of tests that are now described on cable TV shows. Such TV shows did not exist when Janet was being hypnotized, so it is much less clear where her descriptions would have originated from if they were not based on experiences that she actually had.

Janet described a guide that stayed with her and watched out for her. She communicated telepathically with this guide, and he reassured her that she would not be mistreated. She would be returned to the camp shortly.

Janet consented to be hypnotized a second time, after which she was so creeped out by the details she was describing that she decided she had enough. She didn't want to do any more hypnosis.

"No problem," Walter Webb reassured her. They wouldn't bother her any more, and he thanked her profusely for her generous cooperation. "There was something interesting, though…" Webb offered.

Every single thing that Janet Cornell recounted under hypnosis perfectly matched the descriptions that Michael Lapp provided under hypnosis!

Janet told me that this statement surprised her greatly. It seemed to validate the whole idea that Janet really had been abducted. It also served to convince her that she would remain available to this man in the future if there was some other help she could be to his investigation.

Even though I had done a presentation on UFOs for the benefit of the kids in my science classes, I would not describe myself as a believer in the phenomenon, at least not at that point in my life. What I did not tell Janet Cornell was that, when I did present the story of Betty and Barney Hill, I actually ridiculed any investigation of the whole event as pseudo-science. For the sake of entertainment, I made every joke I could think of. I certainly did not encourage the students to take abduction claims (CE-4 cases) seriously.

The irony of it all was the fact that, by raising the issue in a light-hearted, even skeptical way, this information now came my way, causing me to seriously re-evaluate my whole skeptical take on the subject. And despite the fact that this person who was relating her CE-4 account had absolutely impeccable credentials, I still found myself wondering whether I should take her anecdotal account at face value. Then came the real 'clincher.'

"He ended up writing a book about the whole investigation," Janet announced. "In fact," she added proudly, "There are reviews of the book that say it was the best and most thorough investigation of a CE-4 case ever done."

"Really," I remarked. Inwardly, I was thinking something else, like, "This is so amazing. And this is the last person I would have ever expected to hear this from. I've known this person for years. She was always very sober, serious, but most of all, an impeccably credentialed parent and respected member of a fairly affluent community. I thought alien abductees were supposed to be attention-hungry kooks. This lady was anything but that."

I decided right then I needed to see this book.

"What's the title of the book?" I inquired.

"Encounter at Buff Ledge," she replied.

"And do you, by any chance, have a copy?"

"I do, indeed," she assured me. "Signed by the author, of course."

"This whole thing sounds so fascinating. I wonder if I might read this book. I promise I will take good care of it and return it promptly."

"That would be fine. Tell you what, I'll send it to school with my kid tomorrow." Janet paused then added, "Now, please understand two things. First, my kids don't know anything about any of this and I don't want them to. Maybe someday I'll tell them the story or just show them the book, but not right now. So please don't mention anything about our conversation or this book. I'll send it with Emma (her daughter) but the envelope will be sealed. The second thing is that I do not want to be known as the UFO lady of southwest Portland, so please don't say anything about this around the neighborhood or the school."

"Isn't your name in the book?"

"No. When Walter told me he was writing a book, he asked me if it was OK to use my name. I said absolutely not. He completely understood, in fact, he agreed it was better that he did not. So my name in the book is Janet Cornell."

"OK, 'Janet,' your secret is safe with me," I said with a wink.

The next day, right on schedule, a tall, good-looking kid walked up to me handed me a manila envelope. "My mom said to give you this," she said blankly.

"Thank you, Emma." I did my best to act casual and indifferent, even though I couldn't wait to open the envelope. It was a hectic day of disassembling the science fair. I didn't get a chance to open the envelope until I was home that evening. I read late into the night. I finished with the book in forty eight hours.

It's not a thick book. It is very factual in tone, almost clinical, but it was fascinating especially in light of the fact that I knew the central character, and all of her perfect children.

The description of the abduction was chilling. Michael said it began with a bright white beam of light and in an instant they were aboard a vessel. They were together at first and they were told that they would be returned to Earth soon. They were then separated and subjected to a battery of tests and medical procedures. Michael saw Janet on an examining table. Janet also described being put on a table and feeling cold. Egg cells (ova) were presumably extracted.

At one point, one of the ETs expressed surprise that Michael was still asking so many questions. This meant that he would remember the entire episode afterward and this would only increase his mental turmoil. The same ET was quite confident that Janet, on the other hand, would remember nothing.

Then, as promised, they were returned to the same dock where their ordeal began. According to Michael, Janet was in a daze at that point and needed help finding her way back to her cabin. So, Michael escorted her back to the women's cabin area. Later, he was still concerned about her condition but being that she resided in the women's cabin area, he was not allowed to see her. The next day was the end of the session for Michael. The session as not over, but Michael had to begin football practice. Janet felt a strong need to talk to Michael but she had no idea why. Due to the hubbub of events, she was never able to talk to him before he left the camp for the summer. Later, Michael confessed that he was very concerned for Janet's well-being, and wanted to know what she remembered. Michael remembered the entire episode but, by all appearances, Janet apparently had no recollection of the bizarre events whatsoever, so he decided it would be best if he just left her alone.

One of the most interesting parts of the book for me was the fact that the researcher, Walter Webb, expressed to Janet his frustration that stemmed from his inability to locate other counselors who were at a camp when the alleged abduction took place. To his amazement, Janet volunteered that she could help him with that problem. She was a dedicated sender of Christmas cards. She had the current address of nearly every counselor she had worked with at Buff Ledge Camp in her address book.

The contact information provided by Janet Cornell's address book was mentioned in the book as being immensely helpful to the author in reconstructing the events of that unique evening. Through interviews with the other counselors, Webb was able to determine that there were two separate sightings of the same UFO that night, some two hours apart. Janet and Michael saw it the first time just before they were abducted. The second sighting was witnessed by some of the counselors in their rooms above the dining hall, and by some of the campers as they returned from the swim meet. In fact, there was so much commotion over the second UFO sighting that Michael was able to take Janet all the way back to her cabin in an area of the camp where males were not supposed to be. Webb surmised that the second sighting was consistent with Michael's claim that the aliens returned Janet and him to camp just as the campers were returning in the camp bus. The addresses Janet provided were *the* key to verifying the details of Michael's previously unverified claims. Sure enough, using the accounts of former camp counselors, all the elements of Michael's description were corroborated by multiple witnesses! After exhaustive investigation, and through the use of Janet Cornell's address book, Walter Webb was able to confirm many of the details of Michael Lapp previously unverified descriptions. The CE-4 event really happened!

The other fascinating aspect of the book was the fact that Walter Webb was so effusive in his praise of Janet Cornell. The fact that she did not have any interest in aliens and no conscious memory of the entire ordeal was actually a point of considerable reassurance for him. She did not want any recognition and she was not even sure she believed the descriptions that came out of her own mouth under hypnosis. She had never communicated with Michael in the eleven years following their CE-4 encounter. And of course, Webb found Janet Cornell to be the very same articulate, clear-headed, intelligent, and personable individual that I knew her to be. In all, she was what might be called the perfect witness. Walter Webb found her credentials to be, in a word, impeccable.

From everything I knew of Janet Cornell, I could not agree more. In fact, by knowing all of her kids over three successive academic years, I am able to say I know Janet Cornell and her family, better than Walter Webb did. Everything I know of the whole family, and Janet in particular, is in complete agreement with the very positive impression that Janet Cornell made upon Walter Webb. At the end of his book, he observed that Janet's involvement was critical. Without her help, he could not have done the research as thoroughly as he did. By his own assessment, she was the best witness he could have ever hoped to find. On the title page, Webb wrote an inscription to Janet thanking her effusively and acknowledging that he could not have completed the research effort without her.

Upon finishing the book, I was on the phone to her asking how I could return her book. I offered to send it back the way it arrived, in a sealed manila envelope delivered by her reliable eighth grade daughter. Janet declined my offer and offered to stop in and pick it up the next time she was in Robert Gray Middle School.

The next morning she walked into my vacant classroom fifteen minutes before the daily stampede of students began. I handed her the book and thanked her for loaning it to me. She reminded me not to divulge her identity, and especially to not broach the subject with her child. I wholeheartedly agreed.

I did have a few questions I wanted to ask her. The time was short and she offered that she really did not want to dwell on the entire episode. She just wanted to live her life and raise her kids. In fact, she confided in me, she wished the whole thing had never happened and she was trying her best to forget about it.

"Thank you for sharing it all with me," I said. Then I added, "I don't know much about the whole subject, but there is one thing I think I've heard about the CE-4 scenarios, and that is, I think, they come back."

She didn't even have to ask what I meant. She was moving toward the door and she stopped abruptly, wheeled around and said, "Oh, I know!"

I didn't say anything. I just stood there experiencing the same feeling of amazement that I felt in the science fair when she dropped her first bombshell on me.

"Every once in a great while," she continued, "I wake up in the morning feeling like I didn't sleep a wink; I mean not at all. On other mornings, I wake up feeling like I slept for a solid month. And on these mornings, I always find two small parallel marks, about an inch apart, on some part of my body. Once they were on my leg. Usually they're on my arm. Once they were on my forehead."

"What do you make of it?" I asked.

"I have absolutely no idea," she replied. "And I don't really want to know. As I said, I just want to forget about it. I try to put the whole thing out of my mind."

The bell was about to ring and my morning was about to begin in earnest. She continued moving toward the door and I escorted her in that direction. She paused and looked a little bewildered. I could see that there was something on her mind.

"There's just one thing I want to know," she finally said as we got to the classroom door.

I somehow knew just what she was going to say next.

"Why me?"

"I'm not sure. I think you have to look at what you do best, and that thing you do better than anybody else I've ever met, is raising perfect children *perfectly*. Your kids are absolute works of art. All of them. And I'm not just saying that to be nice. I've been aware of it for a while now. Remember when

I asked you and your husband to write a brochure about how to raise kids. You really are the best there is in that area. So, if you want my opinion about why they are interested in you, I'd guess it has something to do with your way of raising children, or your DNA, or both."

She thanked me for the kind words and left. I haven't had much contact with Janet Cornell since then. I do run into her coming out of the dry cleaner or the grocery store in Hillsdale. When I pass her on my way to the school, we wave to each other.

Since she was in the neighborhood, I asked Janet to read a draft of this chapter. On a rainy winter afternoon I met her at the local Starbucks. She gave me a photograph, which also she asked me not to print. The photograph was taken in 1979 by Walter Webb in Logan International Airport on the occasion of Janet and Michael Lapps first and only reunion eleven years after the encounter at Buff Ledge took place. I must say I was struck by how sharp looking both of these twenty-something folks looked in that picture. I'm not really sure what the ETs may be after in the human DNA that they are apparently harvesting, but if physical attractiveness is one of their priorities, they certainly got their alien money's worth.

Janet e-mailed me the following message after reading the chapter:

Hi Thom

Wow! You did a great job of getting the details right. Science Fair Part II was even more interesting; so many specifics. Quite the chapter!

One tiny thing: it is Buff Ledge Camp, not Camp Buff Ledge.

By the way, my youngest son graduates from medical school this May, and it was most definitely in your class that he first became interested in science. You made science cool. You got him psyched for science in high school. Many thanks for your years of great teaching.

My best to you,

Janet

Alien Hill

Once I was coming out of the same neighborhood Starbucks and a trio of former students were sitting at one of the sidewalk tables outside the store. They remembered the discussion we had had in class about UFOs and abductees, and wanted me to know that they had actually seen something in the sky that they could not identify. After giving them a chance to admit that they were 'jerking my chain', they insisted that they were dead serious. They were out in the neighborhood one evening around dusk when they saw three small, dark objects arranged in a triangular formation and hovering in the sky over a neighborhood hill.

"Really," I intoned, still waiting for them to bust up laughing. But their faces showed no sign of squelched amusement, and I did reflect on the fact that these particular kids were pretty solid, cooperative, and hardworking souls back when they were in my science class. So I obliged them with a serious question. "Where did you see these object hovering? Which hill?"

"That one over there," said one, and they all three pointed in unison in precisely the same direction, toward the hill which held, among many others, the house of the Cornells.

"Yeah," added another of the trio. "Ever since we saw them, we call that 'Alien Hill.'"

"You don't know the half of it," I thought to myself. I wondered whether Janet Cornell woke up that morning with two small parallel marks on her arm. I should have called her up and asked her, but I also remembered that she didn't really want to dwell on it, so I thought better of it. The boys couldn't remember the exact date, anyway. I didn't have time to explain but I thanked the boys for the neighborhood update. I encouraged them to keep their eyes open.

"Alien Hill," I thought to myself as I drove home. "I like that."

It has a real name. It's called Healey Heights. It's visible, indeed conspicuous from just about everywhere in greater Portland because, perched atop it, is the city's largest radio antenna. It's an immense red and white structure that accommodates the most powerful radio transmitters in town.

I should also add that Healy Heights had me wondering even before I became aware of its connection to the *Encounter at Buff Ledge* story. In the thirty years I have been teaching in that neighborhood, I have observed a bit of a pattern when it comes to the kids who come to my classroom from Healy

Heights. They're all smart. Real smart. The Cornell kids were shining stars but they were also not surprising based on what I've come to expect from that part of the school's feeder neighborhood. To be fair, there is an absolute abundance of nice, bright, well-reared kids in southwest Portland, but it seems like some of brightest, most compliant kids in every class, year after year, walk down off Healy Heights to get to school each morning.

In December of 2014, I again broached the topic of UFOs on the day before Christmas vacation. This time, six different girls became wide-eyed and eager to share their story. Apparently, one of the girls lives on Fairmount Street, which sits at the very summit of Council Crest, the highest point of land in the Portland metropolitan area. On June 20th, 2014, the girl was having an end-of-the-year sleep-over. She and five of her girlfriends were in a tent in the yard. It was 3 a.m., they were still awake, and of course, telling ghost stories. A loud buzzing noise was heard and they all stuck their heads out of the tent and witnessed the same multi-colored orb directly over their heads.

When science fair time came around a month later, I encouraged the girl who lived on the property to do a comparison of the written descriptions offered by all six girls. We found an on-line UFO reporting form on the MUFON website and she collected written statements from everyone involved. Interestingly, there was very little agreement on the exact details of shape color, distance to the object, and duration of the sighting. The project was a very interesting study of difference in human perception. On this point all the girls wholeheartedly agree: a fast moving object came to a complete stand still directly over their tent on that summer night. It then left as quickly as it came.

By way of context I will offer that this particular household produced three students in my science class over a ten year period. The girl who reported this incident is the youngest of the three. All three kids were excellent students. They were all very intelligent, hard-working, had very pleasant personalities, and are very good-looking, just like the Cornell family. The oldest sibling came back to my classroom for a visit recently. She is studying engineering at an eastern college.

Council Crest and Healy Heights are neighboring high points on the same ridge of the Tualatin Mountains. The two topographic high points are about a mile apart.

I have been teaching the offspring of Healey Heights and Council Crest households for thirty years. The uncanny consistency of the children who live there continues to amaze me, not that I think extraterrestrials have anything to do with it, but it seems they may *know* about it.

A cosmic explanation isn't necessary to explain what's going on here. It's just good, old-fashioned proper parenting. Mind you, proper parenting is not something that is completely understood, even in this world full of psychological and behavioral research. Yet, the demographics of Healy Heights, I think, tell the whole story.

Any local realtor can tell you that, as a neighborhood, Healy Heights has the lowest crime rate of any neighborhood in the greater Portland area. It also has one of the highest average incomes and one of the highest average property values on the whole west coast north of San Francisco. Healy Heights is a neighborhood of steep, San Francisco-style streets leading to houses with small, steeply terraced yards and homes with impressive views of either Mt. Hood to the east or the Tualatin Valley to the west. On the opposite side of the hill from the middle school where I work is the largest complex of hospitals in the state of Oregon. This means that the greatest percentage of bread-winners in Healy Heights work at OHSU, the Veterans Hospital, or Doernbecker Children's Hospital, all of which are crammed into a steep ravine on the back side of Healey Heights. So what you have on Healey Heights is a very highly educated, very affluent, very liberal, and very dedicated collection of households, and a whole lot of them. So, it follows that the kids from that neighborhood are a reflection of the affluence, education, and dedication that embodies nearly every household in that exceptional neighborhood.

And, even though most do not put much stock in any alien intervention in the neighborhood, I would submit that if someone from this planet, or any other planet, wanted to study the accumulation of factors that lead to the proper rearing of high-achieving human children, Healey Heights is the perfect fishbowl to peer into. It's also an easy place to find. Just zero in on the big red and white radio tower. You can't miss it.

It does seem there is some kind of alien thing going on here. Those who speculate in books on CE-4 cases say the same things over and over again. They feel that reproductive material is being harvested: human egg cells (ova) and sperm. I just hope the extraterrestrials understand that there is more to it than just obtaining good genetic material and the stem cells needed to make the tissue grow. Human reproductive tissue should have assembly instructions to go with it. That these unwritten assembly instructions are so well understood by so many people in one place is the magic of Healey Heights.

Having taught in this particular neighborhood for so long, I feel qualified to point out the very clear connection between good child-rearing practices and high-performing students. That, I think, is the real lesson for everyone, terrestrial and extraterrestrial alike: good parenting is as important as good genetics, maybe more so, when trying to cultivate superior human offspring. Janet and Jim Cornell are good examples of both, so I guess I'm not surprised that extraterrestrials know their whereabouts. Nice to see that the ETs have done their homework.

The Science Fair, Part 2

You need a really good lesson to hold the attention of a classroom full of eighth graders on the day before the Christmas break. For me, the story of Betty and Barney Hill works every time.

Year after year, the eighth graders say they loved learning astronomy. There aren't a lot of hands-on activities, and the terminology is a bit rigorous, but the kids seem to enjoy the intellectual leap. Unfortunately, most schools teach very little astronomy, or astrophysics, as it is properly known today. When they do teach it, most schools limit their study of astrophysics to our solar system.

They seldom venture into 'deep space.' Grade school astrophysics stops at Pluto.

Knowing how students are fascinated by deep space astrophysics, I always cover it anyway. I prepare the students to write a big paper explaining the evidence that supports the Big Bang Theory. Once the students finish this writing assignment, they can articulate the red-shift of distant galaxies, the percent of hydrogen and helium in interstellar space, and the role of background radiation in supporting the Big Bang Theory. After that paper, their brains are also slightly fried.

By then, we are on the verge of Christmas vacation. That's when I pull out the UFO lesson that caught the attention of Janet Cornell. And I can't resist showing the students an article and a film strip on the strange case of Betty and Barney Hill, the first two people ever to stand up and declare that they were abducted by aliens.

On one such day, I happened to have another teacher present in my classroom. She was a 'para-educator,' that is, a person who is there to assist a 'special needs' child with learning disabilities. She was actually a substitute para-educator. The regular person was absent that day. As the kids were filtering in, she introduced herself as Miri and reminded me that four of her kids had once been students in my science class.

"They still talk about you," Miri said with a smile.

The student that she was there to assist that day sat near my own desk, so I suggested to Miri that she might just sit at my desk until her efforts were needed. I also mentioned that my lesson was 'bomb-proof,' so she might not be needed at all.

"You might just sit back in my desk chair and enjoy the lesson. It'll be something a little different, but on a day like this… "

"You don't have to tell me twice," Miri replied, and plopped down in the soft chair.

Inwardly, I was also hoping that this new face in my classroom didn't have any strong opinions about what constituted an appropriate science lesson for middle-schoolers. If she did, she might even be slightly outraged when I squandered an hour of educational time on aliens and abductees. I thought about switching to a different lesson for that period but I didn't really have anything else ready to go. Also, I knew the material would hold the class' attention, including the special needs child. I was betting that Miri the para-educator would not much care what I taught as long as I kept a lid on the situation. So I launched into the lesson, reading stories of UFO sightings by astronomers and astronauts, and then showing a film strip about UFOs and the strange case of Betty and Barney Hill.

Meanwhile, the teacher aide was sitting at my desk, taking copious notes. This had me a little concerned. Might these notes be shown to a principal or supervisor as evidence of my irresponsible approach to public education? I decided it was too late to do anything about it. I reminded myself that this person was looking comfortable and taking it easy while I did all the work. I tried my best to ignore her note taking, instead focusing on the twenty-eight kids that needed to be kept busy.

To my surprise, despite the big class and the unsettled day, I buzzed right through the material in record time. I was finished with my planned material and the period was still a few minutes from over, so I finished with a brief description of the abductee that I had met a few years ago at the school science fair, and the book about her famous case. The kids loved the idea that somebody in the neighborhood might be an abductee. More jokes and laughter ensued. Meanwhile, I couldn't help but notice out of the corner of my eye that the para-educator at my desk was taking notes more furiously than ever. I was getting very concerned. Maybe I should have switched to a different lesson, I thought. Maybe I shouldn't have offered the local tie-in to the abductee thing. I was now feeling very insecure. I was pretty sure I would be hearing about my science lesson on abductees in the future and it would not be good.

The bell rang. The kids sprang to their feet. They were one period closer to vacation and one period away from their lunch break. The stampede for the door was underway and out of the corner of my eye, I watched the para-educator gather her notes and follow the students to the door. Then she took a sudden detour in my direction. She stopped in front of me and locked eyes, saying nothing. I felt a little uncomfortable. I tried to break the awkward silence.

"I hope you don't mind the presentation on abductees. We just finished a long and demanding astronomy unit. Today was sort of a reward," I stammered. "You know a 'throw away' lesson on the day before vacation."

"I'm an abductee," she replied flatly, still looking me squarely in the eye.

"Excuse me?"

"I'm an abductee. I had heard about Betty and Barney Hill before, but I had not seen that interview with Betty Hill. It was fascinating. I loved every minute of it. I wanted to remember every detail so I did my best to write it all down."

It took me a moment to register what she was saying. I was hugely relieved. I smiled a weak smile. "I have another class coming in but it sounds like we need to talk. Can you come back here at lunch?"

"See you then," she replied. Miri turned and headed for the door, hurrying to catch up with the student that she was supposed to be keeping a close eye upon.

Before the next period was even over, Miri was back at my desk, quietly focusing on the final moments of the same lesson I taught the period before.

The period ending bell rang, the usual stampede ensued, and I was now alone in the room with Miri. It was easily the most unique lunch conversation I've had in thirty years of teaching.

Unlike Janet Cornell, who remembered *nothing* of her abductee experience, Miri claimed to remember quite a bit. She was claiming multiple encounters with multiple beings. They had been inside her house, which was about a mile from the schoolroom in which we were sitting.

"I was able to ask them questions," Miri explained.

"In English?"

"Well, I spoke to them in English. When they answered, their lips didn't move. I heard their answers, loud and clear, in my head. They use perfect English, though. They even used slang."

"How many were there?"

"There were at least three different kinds of beings. One was big and blonde and very human looking kind of Swedish. The others were much more alien. One was a small bodied, big-headed guy with dark, almond-shaped eyes and two holes for nostrils. The other one was almost lobster-like in appearance, like a large, upright-standing praying mantis. The small one with the almond eyes did most of the talking. He was my guide. Apparently, everyone that they abduct is assigned a guide who stays with them throughout the process. I asked my guide where they were from. 'The closest star,' was his answer."

Miri told me she knew enough astronomy that she was able to respond, "Oh, Alpha Centauri! That's the closest star to our Sun, right?"

"Well, that's not what we call it," said the big-headed one.

(At least five years after Miri first related her abduction experiences, planets were indeed discovered orbiting Alpha Centauri. Using data obtained from the

Hubble Space Telescope, it was announced in March of 2015 that the existence of two planets, Alpha Centauri Bb and Alpha Centauri Bc, had been verified. While these two planets are thought to be orbiting too close to their parent star to be habitable, it is strong evidence that Alpha Centauri does indeed host a system of at least two planets, just as Miri claims she was told by her guide!)

As I listened to Miri's unfolding story at the time, I didn't really know how much faith to put into this account, but two thoughts reassured me. First, I didn't go looking for this account. It found me. Strangely, I'd now met two abductees without leaving my classroom.

Also, Miri wasn't ballyhooing her experience. She told me that I was only the second person to whom she had ever told her story. She had also told her mother. She fully understood that her story was just too incredible to discuss with anyone else. It would only make her appear crazy. She was relieved that she was finally able to talk openly about it to someone, and the only reason she brought it up for my benefit was because she had just learned so much background information from my lesson.

I tried to appear nonchalant, but inwardly I was stunned by the amazing synchronicity, that she of all people happened to be in the classroom on this particular day. The spooky coincidence of her presence, as a substitute, filling in for an absent person, on the day I happened to present the most daring and unconventional lesson of the entire year, seemed bizarre. I still wasn't sure she was on the level, but any way I sliced it, this was the most interesting lunchtime conversation ever. Knowing that the lunch period was only thirty minutes long, I tried my best just to keep her talking.

Miri recollected that, as the ETs stood in her darkened living room in the wee hours of the morning, they seemed to be very uneasy around all the children's toys that littered the floor. They seemed to be afraid of falling. Her guide, the one with the big head and almond eyes, seemed especially concerned about his safety around all the toys.

They took her away for a period of time that she estimated to be between two and four hours. They hoisted her aboard with a light beam that seemed to grab hold of her bones. It was very painful. Once aboard, her guide stayed with her the entire time. She was told by her guide not to touch anything. It was her impression that the ETs viewed humans as generally 'unclean' beings. When Miri saw what she thought was a window, she went over and touched it. Her guide explained that it wasn't a window, and then impatiently reminded her not to touch anything.

It seemed to Miri that the craft they were on was behind the moon. She said that at one point she could see the Earth. Aboard the craft, she observed at least four kinds of ETs. Her guide was one of the small, grey-skinned humanoid figures with big eyes. What struck Miri the most was that his eyes never blinked and the lips never moved. Miri began to suspect that she was looking at a being that was actually wearing some sort of suit that covered the entire body. The grey ones had long, curved fingers that were all nearly the same length.

Another group of beings were small, shiny, and blue-black in color. They were very giggly and very rude. There were two taller groups, one set of beings that were essentially human in appearance and very blonde. Another group of individuals had very distorted facial features on otherwise human bodies. They had a very menacing demeanor and an unusual smell that reminded Miri of the scaly place on the inside of a horse's leg. Miri was very suspicious of them and very careful when talking to them. Her guide also seemed nervous about talking to them.

One of the Swedish-looking ones, who was also female, proudly explained to Miri that it was *her* job to make the abducted Earthlings feel comfortable. Toward that end, she directed Miri's attention toward a corner of the vessel that she had personally decorated in an Earth-like manner. Miri could not believe how tacky and decrepit the furniture was that this being described so proudly. It looked like worn out motel furniture. Miri thought it best to keep her decorating opinions to herself. She did not comment on the furniture to this somewhat arrogant being.

One particularly frightening being she encountered was a cat-like female who seemed to be some sort of scientist. This being was interested in Miri's appearance and she was offended that Miri didn't want to be touched by her.

As she was led about the vessel by her guide, Miri saw other humans in sleep wear being led around by their guides. Clearly, multiple humans were being processed at a given time. Most of these people appeared to be in a trance-like state. One poor fellow was wearing a night shirt and was otherwise naked from the waist down. Miri's guide was somewhat apologetic about this sight and suggested she avert her gaze.

"How do you choose who you take?" Miri asked.

"You are mentally reachable. That is why you were chosen." The lines between statement and thought are blurry when telepathic communication is happening. Miri said she had the thought that, "We can mentally control some of you, but there are limits. Not everyone can be controlled. We cannot control people when they are in large groups."

Despite their obvious sophistication, they also seemed to be naïve in other ways. They were very impressed with her intelligence, so much so that they thought she must be some kind of leader. Miri assured them that she was not. She explained that she was simply a housewife with five kids. Unconvinced, they pressed her for any details she could offer about humanity's weapon systems. This surprised Miri. She insisted that she knew absolutely nothing about weapons, and that they should be asking military leaders these questions.

"I asked them how they manage to come and go from Earth without being detected," Miri told me.

"It's easy," her almond-eyed guide declared. "We operate at night. Our crafts can't be detected. We come and go anywhere we want. Walls, doors, and roofs mean nothing. Oh, and that big red and white antenna is a great landmark," the almond-eyed guide said without moving his lips.

"I asked him how long it takes to get here.

"Two weeks."

"Wow," I thought. "I wonder what kind of short cut they have worked out. I knew that Alpha Centauri is five light-years away, and Einstein said it's not even possible to travel at light speed."

"So, I asked him 'What is your means of travel? Is it gravity wells?' He answered, 'No, but it is something your people are just beginning to consider.'"

Toward the end of her time on the vessel, her guide asked Miri what she would like to see.

"The Earth," she replied.

"Of course," the guide replied. "That's what everyone else wants to see."

"I was shown a view of the Earth," Miri explained. "From our location, it was about the size of a softball. I tried to look at, and remember as much as I could. Then I was asked if there was anything else. I asked my guide what his planet looked like. On a screen, I was shown a scene of grassland dotted with trees that looked much like baobab trees of Africa. There was also a standing, sloth-like creature in the view. My guide explained that it was an ancestor of theirs that still lived. I was told that I was seeing a real-time view of their planet. I could not understand how that was possible."

"Wouldn't the view be at least two weeks old if that's how long it takes to get here?" she asked.

"No," he replied flatly. "That's right now."

Miri tried to word her next request so it did not sound so cliché. "May I meet your leader?" Her guide obliged her request and took her to the captain of the vessel who, oddly enough, was actually wearing a cap. She described him as looking like a mix between a Japanese person and an alien.

He was pleasant enough so I asked him, "Why do you come here?"

Miri confided to me that she already knew full well that they were here for genetic material. She just wanted to see if he would give an honest answer.

"We need the reproductive material. We don't reproduce well," was the frank reply.

She decided to press the situation. "But what you do is so invasive," she objected. You take such liberties with people. Why do you do this to people?"

"It's my job."

The captain did not like her argumentative tone. He responded by stabbing her with a needle-like instrument. At that point she was returned to her home in southwest Portland. After that night in the mid-1990s, she never saw the ETs again.

Many of these incredible specifics were related to me as Miri and I sat in the Hillsdale Starbucks. She had written copious notes on the backs of the printed pages I had given her. She elaborated and explained her notes as I frantically wrote. We never did get around to ordering any coffee.

If Miri were manufacturing her entire story for my benefit, as some readers no doubt expect, she had to be a very creative yarn spinner. I never would have expected answers that, in many cases, contradict principles of interstellar travel that we are given to understand by either science or science fiction. Often, the improbable answers offered by Miri also make perfect sense. Of course extraterrestrials have jobs, just like we do. Some of those jobs suck just as much as some of our jobs do. But we do our jobs because we have to. We have to pay bills and keep the family fed, and so must they.

The more I thought about it, the more illuminating that particular statement seemed to be. Not only did it suggest an oh-so-human detachment from his day to day grind of harvesting genetic material from unsuspecting earthlings, but, if it was true, it also implied something rather profound. If they all had jobs, then their presumptive extraterrestrial civilization, where ever it was, must have a market economy. Competition, the need to make money, and the struggle to survive necessitates working a job, even on a planet that is presumably much more advanced than our own. And on this planet, somebody has the job of driving the intergalactic bus from Alpha Centauri to

Earth whenever they need more human DNA. They probably sell it to Alpha Centauri couples who are plagued with alien infertility.

"You say they've visited you more than once?" I queried.

Miri confided that she had been visited many times before, but not recently. At one point, one of the extraterrestrial beings asked about her pre-school aged child. She suddenly became very concerned for her children's safety and well-being. Miri then told them that her children were off-limits. She wanted the kids to be left alone. After one of these late-night encounters, Miri said she found the courage to tell them that she didn't want them to come back any more. Her family was too important and these unannounced visits were very intrusive. Miri told me that was the last time she ever saw the ETs.

One might wonder why Miri was able to describe such vivid recollections of her multiple encounters, yet Janet Cornell had absolutely no recollection of her encounters. I think one possible answer lies in the fact that the other person involved in the *Encounter at Buff Ledge* story, Michael Lapp, also claimed to recollect all the details of his harrowing experience, even as Janet remembered nothing. Again, assuming that all parties are being truthful, (and if I wasn't assuming that, then I wouldn't have gone to the trouble of writing all this down), then it begins to look like it's just a matter of personal constitution. Some people seem to remember their extraterrestrial encounters, much to the detriment of their long-term emotional well-being. Others, like Janet Cornell, are mercifully unable to recollect the terrifying details of their abduction experience. According to Michael Lapps own recollections, his guide on the vessel was surprised that he remained so lucid and full of questions throughout his ordeal. It meant he would also remember the experience after it was over, and that would cause him lasting turmoil. Indeed, in her later contact with Michael, Janet told me that he did carry much turmoil, especially about the fact that he could not share his experience with anyone else.

"He was definitely suffering from post-traumatic stress syndrome," Janet observed for my benefit.

I have observed a similar situation with some of the sasquatch witnesses that I interviewed. In the case of campers whose tent is approached by some ominous nocturnal form, quite often one person in the tent, typically the female, is paralyzed with fear but utterly aware of every moment of the whole terrifying situation. Meanwhile, the other occupant of the tent, the boyfriend or husband, remains blissfully asleep throughout the episode. As often as not, the boyfriend is so soundly asleep that their terrified tent-mate is unable to awaken them. It begins to appear that there may be certain human dispositions that are easy to nullify by some manner of external control, while others are more autonomous and difficult to externally manipulate. As the ET ostensibly explained to Miri, "We can mentally control some of you, but there are limits."

There is one final point of interest that Miri shared with me before our memorable half-hour conversation came to an end. On one of the nocturnal invasions of her home, she observed playful interactions between the dramatically different-looking extraterrestrial beings. The lobster-like one, whom she described as resembling a huge praying mantis, also seemed to be the most mentally elevated, and the most sensitive. Indeed, he was very sensitive to remarks from the others about his Crustacean-like countenance. When the other ones teased him about his appearance, he would draw himself into layers of exoskeleton that would close around his head. What a curious observation that seemed. I would not expect a person who is observing extraterrestrials to report immature behaviors like ridicule about matters of appearance. Nor would I have expected a person to report that the lobster/praying mantis ET became embarrassed and self-conscious when teased. Could bullying be a common practice throughout the galaxy?

As usual, it is difficult to know how seriously to take such an account. Any skeptically-minded person would reject the whole story as delusional. As always, I find myself just looking for patterns. Miri described the same extraterrestrial entities that are prevalent in UFO literature. Of course, it will be assumed that she gleaned her descriptions from existing media treatments. Indeed, much of what I presented to the class was so new to her that she felt the need to take notes.

I'm a little bewildered by the fact that two very sincere individuals, with very different alien abduction claims, who live just a couple miles apart, shared their abduction tales with me just because I seemed supportive. The first one, Janet Cornell, seemed to have decided that she would share her story with me. My encounter with Miri, on the other hand, was so accidental as to be an extraordinary synchronicity. If these accounts are valid, then abductions must happen a lot more frequently than anyone realizes. It also leaves me to wonder whether that particular neighborhood, Healy Heights, really is on someone's list of shopping stops for great human DNA.

I am also inclined to wonder whether it is really random chance that these two abductee tales found me at my workplace. I didn't even have to cross the street. My keen-eyed copy-editor, Molly Hart Lebherz, after proof reading all these chapters, tells me I must be some kind of a 'weird magnet.' She's using a more polite term than the one I'm more used to hearing: a 'shit magnet.' Molly supposes that paranormal experiences are being steered my way because *they* know I'm a writer and *they* want to see it all written down. Whoever *they* are, they may want to enlighten humanity about what occurs in the unseen world that surrounds the human experience. Do they want to facilitate the awakening of humanity? I do not know, but it's beginning to look that way.

Whenever I write down a person's description of paranormal events, I always send them a copy of the chapter for review. Both of the abductees interviewed for this chapter live in the Hillsdale neighborhood where I teach. They both graciously offered to meet with me and go over the corrections that would make my descriptions more accurate. In both cases, we agreed to meet at the local Starbucks. I could not help but be struck by the coincidence that, when I met Miri, she was sitting and waiting at the very same table where Janet Cornell chose to sit when I met her a couple weeks earlier. I try not to put too much emphasis on such peculiar coincidences, but the more I delve into paranormal matters, the more I seem to notice such coincidences.

I offer these descriptions to the reader, but not as unassailable facts. I invite the reader to accept or reject the accounts as they see fit. I am totally convinced that Janet Cornell is the real deal. Her case may be the most rigorously investigated case in the history of the abductee phenomenon. I feel very privileged to have personal contact with such a prominent figure in the world of paranormal phenomena. The fact that a second alleged abductee then surfaced in my classroom (on UFO day, no less) is probably too much for the skeptically minded readers to accept. To me, it's downright spooky.

In 2004, I was invited to speak at a paranormal conference in Denver, Colorado. I met very many devotees of the extraterrestrial phenomenon. One interesting point that I was given to understand at this conference, was that there is more than one kind of extraterrestrial that seems to have an interest in planet Earth. Based on her alleged personal experience, Miri would most certainly agree. John Keel, author of *The Mothman Prophecies* and one of the most prominent paranormal researchers ever, also makes the point there may be competing extraterrestrial entities that meddle in terrestrial affairs while keeping mostly to the shadows. A fascinating thought. Not just one, but several different groups of entities have an awareness, maybe an interest, in happenings on our planet.

I find that idea to be plausible, although I have no way of verifying it. I favor it because it suggests that Healy Heights isn't the only place where strange things happen that may have extraterrestrial connections. If we could just identify other such places and debrief enough abductees, we should get a lot closer to understanding our exact role in the galactic community.

As a science teacher who has hosted thirty science fairs at the little middle school in the shadow of Alien Hill, the most interesting thought is this: if there's more than one kind of extraterrestrial, and if more than one of these alien cultures meddle in and experiment with human lives on planet Earth, then our little planet is, in a manner of speaking, a big science fair.

It may be a bit alarming to suppose that we humans are being toyed with, abducted and maybe manipulated by unseen entities. It's also funny, since there's not much we can really do about it. I'm grateful that, at least most of the time, they put us back where we belong when they're done. We would prefer to deny that this is happening and most people do exactly that.

Are there multiple, even competing and conflicting alien agendas? Perhaps. If there are, this really isn't a new idea, either. Indeed, it's as old as The Bible. Satan and the demonic forces from below oppose and obstruct the almighty Triad from above: the Father, Son, and Holy Ghost.

Maybe, all I am doing in my pursuit of paranormal truth is verifying the authenticity of Scriptural themes. So be it. I didn't set out to verify Scripture but, let the chips fall however they may. My twenty years of paranormal research is summarized in this volume and hopefully will produce accurate insights as to what is really going on behind the veil that conceals entities that come and go from planet Earth.

Could the Earth be a zoo, with the humans acting as the exhibits? In a zoo, visitors are asked not to interact with the creatures on display, out of concern for the well-being of the animals on exhibit. At a science fair, on the other hand, one is invited to interact with the exhibits, as long as you don't mistreat them. Be gentle. Do no harm.

Welcome to the science fair.

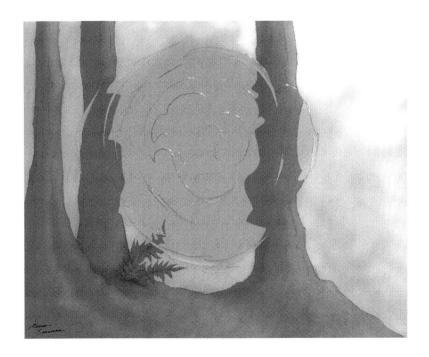

Chapter Six: The Quicksilver Curtain

A torrent of rain blasted the skylight above my head. I sat at the desk, with a cup of tea beside me, contentedly typing on the computer keyboard. The clicking of keys momentarily stopped as I marveled at the intensity of the deluge that washed the pane of glass over my head, as though it was being sprayed by a direct blast from a garden hose.

"I wouldn't want to be in the out-of-doors hiking today," I thought. The clicking on the keyboard resumed.

Lots of other people *were* in the mountains on that September weekend in 2013. Four separate missing-person cases resulted from that one day of surprisingly strong weather. All four missing souls had been hiking the Washington Cascades between Mt. St. Helens and Mount Rainier. Two of the missing people were Pacific Crest Trail hikers who were nearing the end of their arduous journey that began at the Mexican border. As the storms raged, travel on the PCT became temporarily impossible. Two separate backpackers missed their scheduled rendezvous to resupply. As heavy snow blanketed the high country, they hunkered down and rode out the intense weather. At lower elevations, torrents of rain tested the foul weather gear of hikers throughout the region. One day hiker was missing from a trail near Stevens' Pass, Washington. A spelunker (cave explorer) was missing in the Big Lava Bed south of Mt. St. Helens. Search and rescue teams were stretched to the limit.

On Monday morning, I plopped down at my desk chair in a cluttered classroom like I have done literally a thousand times before. I set my coffee on the desk, and opened the e-mail program. A message from the principal was highlighted as urgent. "Please be aware that, over the weekend, our beloved French teacher's boyfriend went missing in the Gifford Pinchot National Forest."

I was not prepared for the local connection of this unfortunate wild weather. And I mean local. I jumped up and dashed through the open door of the classroom directly across the hallway. Shawna was sitting in a chair at the front of the classroom, looking distraught and bewildered.

"I'm so sorry," I offered feebly. "Is there anything I can do? Why are you even here?"

"I don't know. Beth [our wonderful principal] encouraged me to stay home. I guess I just needed to get my mind off of it, so I came in to work. Besides, there's nothing I can do. Kris' family is up there at the command center. I'm just the girl friend. I wouldn't be any help."

"The weather's still horrible up there right now," I added. "Without the right gear, you'd be in a survival situation, yourself."

Shawna somberly agreed. She kindly explained the circumstances as she understood them. He boyfriend, Kris Zitzewitz, and his friend Caleb had been searching for a cave to explore in the Big Lava Beds, a rugged jumble of black lava rock from a historically recent lava eruption in the volcanic wonderland just south of Mt. St. Helens.

Shawna had been in touch with Caleb by phone from the Goose Lake campground on the edge of Big Lava Beds. The search for Kris was being hampered by the persistently wretched weather and the shortage of manpower. As Shawna understood it, Kris and Caleb had been looking for a specific cave they had read about that was situated somewhere within the four-by-six mile expanse of jagged rock and scrubby pine trees that is the Big Lava Beds. No trails or roads traverse this extremely rugged piece of real estate, although forest roads do completely encircle the rugged jumble of eight-thousand-year old cooled lava

On that ill-fated Saturday, Between 1:30 and 2 p.m., the pair of spelunkers split up and travelled on opposite sides of a long pressure ridge, looking for the opening to the cave they sought. At that moment, the duo was inundated by one of the torrential downpours that had been hammering the region all day.

When the downpour abated, Caleb called for Kris. No answer. He backtracked and searched the other side of the lava feature where they split up. Caleb made his way back to their car, just as they agreed to do if they became separated. He was sure Kris would be waiting there. No Kris. Caleb left notes and up and down the FS-60 road that flanked the lava bed. Still no Kris. By this time Caleb must have been fighting back panic. At 5:30 p.m. he felt he had no choice but to make the phone call we all hope we never have to make. He dialed the Skamania County Sheriff and reported Kris Zitzewitz missing.

As Shawna related these details, I got a very bad feeling. As much as anything, it was the intense rainstorm that had me wondering. I knew the area was very rugged but it was also very contained. Between the jumble of lava rock, steep-sided chasms, and the blanket of ten to twenty-foot high trees, travel in the lava beds was confusing and treacherous. It is said that compasses and GPS units are unreliable amidst the iron-rich lava landscape. The pair of adventurers were, however, experienced outdoorsmen. Kris was suitably dressed with rain gear. He had a helmet and a daypack that contained some emergency supplies.

The searchers supposed that Kris had fallen into one of the myriad deep cracks or caves in the lava rock, was injured, and unresponsive. By late Tuesday, all of the other missing hikers had been located. Search crews could now focus their efforts on the last of the missing hikers.

The weather on Wednesday was still nasty. It was wet and cold at 4000 feet where the search was being conducted. The winds blew and snow fell from time to time, preventing the helicopter that was expected to aid the search effort from getting airborne. The weather finally abated somewhat by week's end, and one hundred searchers combed the area on Saturday. By then, so much time had passed with absolutely no sign of Kris that the effort was more focused on recovery than rescue. At one point, some footprints were found but it was unclear whether they belonged to Kris or another one of the searchers. One empty energy drink can was found, but it may have been a piece of random litter. After finding no trace of Kris on Saturday, the search was suspended.

The Big Lava Beds. The white patches are snow. The cinder cone where the lava originated is seen in the distance (top-center).

My heart went out to my neighbor-teacher across the hall. She was trying to cope but was hurting badly. I wanted to help but had no idea how. Then it occurred to me. I'm a paranormal investigator! In my quiet investigation of paranormal matters, I felt I had stumbled upon this almost magical phenomenon I called the 'coconut telegraph.' What would be the harm in trying to use it to get some answers? Why didn't I think of this sooner?

During the previous year, I had been working with an indie movie producer and friend named Christopher Munch. We had been taping interviews on recent advances in the understanding of the sasquatch phenomenon. I met another contributor named Kathleen Odom, an experienced psychic and animal communicator. Like Steve Frederick, Kathleen seemed to possess an ability to send and receive messages from 'the sasquatch people.' Over the years, I had encountered two or three such folks, so Kathleen was not the complete oddity that some might suppose. She didn't advertise her capabilities, but I certainly knew about Kathleen's alleged ability to communicate with cryptids.

I e-mailed Kathleen and asked if it were possible to use the coconut telegraph to get some idea what happened to Kris. Kathleen said she would need some details about the person and the exact location where he disappeared. A photo of the person would be really helpful. I said I would ask, but before I got back to Kathleen, she e-mailed me to say that her husband had gone on-line and found news reports about the incident. They found all the specifics of time, date, and place that they needed. They even found a picture of Kris Zitzewitz.

I received an e-mail from Dave Paulides, a friend and author of a series of books on unsolved missing person cases world-wide entitled *Missing 411*. Dave had seen the news reports about Kris Zitzewitz.

I asked Dave, who may be the nation's foremost expert on this grim subject, what he could tell me about any patterns that surface in these missing person cases.

Dave replied that he and his research partners have currently identified fifty-two clusters of missing person reports throughout North America. One such place is the Cascades of Oregon and Washington. He further explained that there are also certain factors, that he called 'profile points,' that recur in the police reports on these cases. One such profile point was very rocky terrain. That fit the Big Lava Beds to a tee. Another profile point that is common to many disappearance cases was sudden bouts of extreme weather.

Chillingly, according to Dave's compiled records, two women hikers disappeared from the Craters of the Moon National Monument in Idaho only a week earlier. Both bodies were eventually found, the second one showing up twenty-eight days after the disappearance.

Craters of the Moon is quite similar to the Big Lava Beds. Big Lava Beds is more forested. 'Craters' is much larger (over 1000 square miles), more stark, and less vegetated.

Dave Paulides describes another bizarre case in which an elderly mushroom hunter, Hildegard Hendrickson, disappeared in the forests around

Wenatchee, Washington on June 8th of 2013. Dave observed in his book that the Summer of 2013 had an alarming cluster of missing persons around the Pacific Northwest. The Zitzewitz case added to that cluster.

Eventually a pair of sneakers was found that was thought to belong to Hildegard Hendrickson. My good friend and fellow sasquatch researcher Paul Graves (see Bigfoot Magnets, Chapter 3) is a trained Search and Rescue volunteer. Paul assisted in the coordinated grid searches for Ms. Hendrickson. Paul told me that the searchers on that case reported a strange whistling that seemed to follow them at times.

During the search, Paul went into the woods and set up a camp in the middle of the search area. He returned to the same spot a few weeks later and discovered that the site of his camp had been marked with an elaborate structures made of bent and twisted sticks.

I asked Dave what or who he thought was behind all these disappearances. "We've never speculate about what may be going on. It just gets too weird. We try stay with facts and leave the speculation to others," Dave explained. "The facts do show that the Cascades Mountains have a high rate of disappearances in which the missing people are never found. There's definitely a cluster there."

I pressed Dave to speculate, anyway. He reluctantly replied that there is a short list of possibilities that do come up when others speculate about the cause of these missing person cases. That list included sasquatch, aliens, and mass-murderers, but Dave just wasn't going to go there. As a former cop, Dave prefers to stick with the facts and leave the speculation to someone else. (After reading a draft of this chapter, Dave did offer that I might want to add to the list one particular kind of presumed ET. 'Reptilians' are specifically mentioned by responding readers as culprits in missing person cases.)

A day later I heard back from Kathleen. She was much more willing to speculate as to Kris' fate, although 'speculate' may not be the best word for what she does. Kathleen *reports* on what she got from what I like to call the coconut telegraph. On October 12th, about two weeks after the initial disappearance, Kathleen had this to report:

> Thom,
>
> I wanted to update you on the missing hiker. I checked in with the Sasquatch at 3 AM Friday regarding this situation. When I first heard about it, my immediate take was that he was abducted.....but I just kept shaking my head trying to "turn it off" until I could get into true sacred space with Spirit and Sasquatch. Well, when I did

that, what I 'got' from the Sasquatch was alarming. They told me that Kris (the hiker) had been very quickly abducted by the 'green ones' and that the Sasquatch had tried unsuccessfully to prevent this from happening; that this is not uncommon especially in this particular area between Mount St. Helens, Mt. Rainier, and Mt. Adams. They commented that these 'green ones' are not good ones, that the Sasquatch can ward them off, but that the hairless humans have no defense. They went on to say that they (the Sasquatch) always try to warn and protect the hairless humans who usually think they are in a relatively 'clean' place. It was really clear to me that the Sasquatch are totally on our side. Apparently, this abduction scenario happens in the blink of an eye. As an intuitive/trance medium/clairvoyant, I have rarely (if ever?) been unable to get a channel on a deceased (or living, for that matter) human. Some connections are clearer, stronger than others, but I always get a connection...however, in this case, I absolutely could not get anything on this Kris (and I even had a photo which can help)...it was like his spirit was completely GONE!

-Kathleen

If her sources are correct, and of course we have no way of verifying the authenticity of Kathleen's sources, things did not look good for the missing hiker. I immediately went to the internet and asked Google for the color most commonly associate with 'Reptilians,' the species of ETs that are said to originate from some star in the constellation Draco. Several colors are possible, but the most common one is (you guessed it) green!

Meanwhile, in the Gifford Pinchot national Forest, the search for Kris continued, off and on, until a late fall snowstorm blanketed the area and roads became impassable. A couple months later, I made a trip to the Skamania County Sheriff Office and requested a copy of the police report on the Zitzewitz case. In voluminous detail, it presented the initial 'missing person' report, the grid search details, the log of all participants in the search, and even the interviews with roommates about the mental state of the missing person.

Perhaps the most interesting and unusual item in the entire police report was the statement by several of the searchers that, while they were actively searching the Big Lava Beds and calling the victims' name, they kept hearing some unusual whistling. Recall that the searchers looking for Hildegard Hendrickson reported the same thing. On the Yakama Indian Reservation,

177

which is near the Big Lava Beds, the elders say the Stick Indians (sasquatch) communicate by whistling.

As far-fetched as the information from Kathleen Odom may seem to some, to me it was hauntingly accurate. If so, then the sasquatch may, by and large, be protectors and custodians of humanity, although they also may be powerless to intervene in some situations.

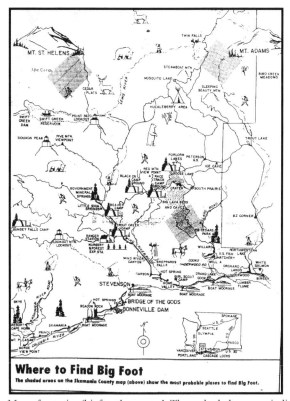

Where to Find Big Foot

The shaded areas on the Skamania County map (above) show the most probable places to find Big Foot.

Map of putative 'bigfoot hotspots.' Three shaded squares indicate 'best locations', one being adjacent to the Big Lava Beds. (One wonders what kind of sightings, and how many, led to the creation of this map.) Graphic courtesy of *The Skamania County Pioneer.*

Could it be that, as the searchers were conducting their grid search, their motions and actions were being monitored by the sasquatch? It is Paul Graves' view, and mine, that as they were searching, they were being shadowed by the sasquatch. If that were so, then it seems to add more credibility to Kathleen's report from the sasquatch.

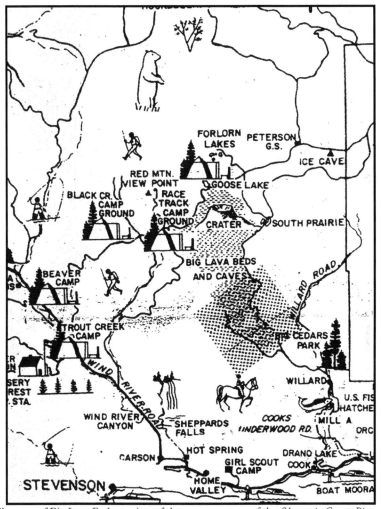

Close up of Big Lava Beds portion of the map, courtesy of the *Skamania County Pioneer*.

Not everyone is inclined to assign paranormal explanations to these missing person cases. In researching this chapter, I was in touch with a retired editor Joannna Grammon of the Skamania County Pioneer. She shared:

> "My personal theory on some of these disappearances is falling into a lava tube (down the rabbit hole, so to speak.). About 1986-1987, two young guys were hiking near Ape Cave and one leaned over to pick up something he'd dropped and fell into a greenery-camouflaged tube. His buddy went for help. As it got dark, he was lying in some water with a broken leg and crawled further into the

tube. He was finally pulled to safety through a 'chimney' in the middle of the night. Datus Perry said that the bigfeet sometimes live in lava tubes. In any case, there are certainly holes around big enough to swallow a person. Old mines in northwest Skamania County would work."

It's impossible to be absolutely certain of anything in paranormal research. As previously stated, the best you can do is look for patterns. One pattern that I have seen emerge is that some people who go to the woods looking for evidence of the sasquatch come back with very strange experiences of an entirely different type. Are these strange and unexpected experiences related to the sasquatch in any way? Might sasquatch researchers just bump into entirely different paranormal phenomenon from time to time?

The idea that bigfoot is somehow connected to other paranormal phenomena is hardly new. John Keel, author of The *Mothman Prophecies*, was emphatic in his view that the sasquatch was just one star in the paranormal constellation. Keel saw a definite connection between hairy, two-legged beings with glowing red eyes, the mothman (a demonic, winged human form), and the aerial lights which most people call UFOs. One of Keel's most important points resonated with my own experience: as one studies one paranormal entity or another, the paranormal entity will begin studying you.

In studying the sasquatch at the Hoyt's place near Mt. Rainier, it became increasing clear that the sasquatch were studying me. It even seemed that they knew where I lived. I read *The Mothman Prophecies* only after I had ended my project at the Hoyt's place, but that book opened my eyes to the fact that early paranormal researchers like Keel had many of the same experiences and had arrived at many of the same conclusions I had. That realization prompted me to take a harder look at other key ideas raised in Keel's book. Here are three important ones:

1. Don't operate in a vacuum. Communicate and cooperate with other people's investigative efforts.
2. The past is the key to the future. Familiarize yourself with historical efforts and previously written books.
3. Clues, and even answers, can come from anywhere. Study and be familiar with other paranormal phenomena.

After reading Keel's book, I was less afraid to wear the 'paranormal researcher' hat. Keel was adamant in the view that the sasquatch was just one tile in a much bigger paranormal mosaic.

Not long after reading Keel's book, I was invited to speak at the World UFO & Paranormal Expo in Denver. The conference, in November of 2004, featured speakers on the subjects of crop circles, Loch Ness Monsters, UFOs, and the 'portal' phenomena. There were other sasquatch research presentations but to my surprise, the sasquatch presentations, mine included, were not nearly as interesting as the other topics.

Freddy Silva, for example, a serious crop circle researcher, made a very persuasive case that crop circles were not uniformly attributable to the two infamous British hoaxers, Doug and Dave. This took me by complete surprise. I assumed all crop circles were hoaxed. Silva agreed that some crop circles were indeed hoaxed, but most are not. Genuine crop circles do indeed bear hallmarks of extraterrestrial intelligence.

I was also humbled by my own ignorance when it came to the Loch Ness Monster. I was pretty sure that *that* one was all a fake. But, when I shared a meal with a devotee of the Loch Ness Monster, he thoroughly dismantled my provincial views. This researcher hailed from Inverness, a North Sea port eight miles from Loch Ness. He assured me that sightings of Nessie are much more common than outsiders realize. There are even credible sightings of Nessie crossing a highway before disappearing into the lake. This polite fellow, whose name I did not record, made the comparison that sasquatch sightings are as common in the Northwest as Nessie sightings are around Loch Ness, yet people who do not live near the nexus of either of these paranormal phenomena tend to be completely unaware of just how frequent the local sightings really are.

Every region of the world seems to have its own particular paranormal concern. Scotland has Loch Ness and its so-called monster, the English own the crop circle phenomenon, the Pacific Northwest used to lay claim to bigfoot (they don't anymore), and the southwestern U.S. is a hot bed of UFOs and portal activity.

The UFO crowd was well represented at the Denver conference. I attended a few very interesting UFO presentations, and I shared a meal with a few very serious UFO researchers from New Mexico and Colorado. Sure enough, their central point was the same as the Loch Ness guy: "You have no idea how much stuff goes on in the southwest if you don't live there."

Two things surprised me about the UFO researchers I met at the Denver conference. They were, as often as not, very well dressed, and they were very scholarly. The uniform of the bigfoot researchers seemed to be jeans and a flannel shirt. They dress like outdoorsmen. The UFO people were more sharply dressed. They wore ties or turtleneck sweaters and blazers. Another fascinating realization I made about UFO researchers: a lot of them are also Bible scholars. A big reason why UFO buffs are bible scholars, I learned, is that the original Bible, written in Hebrew, contains a great deal of putative reference to UFOs. Not being a Bible scholar myself, this idea surprised me, though it was not news to any of the Bible scholars/UFO buffs at that dinner table.

"I grew up reading The Bible in Catholic school. How did I manage to miss all that?" I asked.

"Because you haven't ever read the Hebrew Bible," they explained. "If you haven't read The Bible *in Hebrew*, you haven't really read The Bible. You've just read a loose, simplified translation with a lot of omissions and a lot of missing specifics."

"So, all you UFO guys can read Hebrew?" I asked.

"Not everybody, but the real serious ones can."

"Wow, what else do you guys have in the Southwest that I'm missing?"

"Well, portals, I guess. Do you know about portals?"

"Not a bit. What's it about?" I inquired.

"It seems that there are certain places where a window or doorway to another realm opens up and things come into our world, at least temporarily, from someplace else. For a while, sightings of various kinds occur, including bigfoot, pterodactyls, chupacabras, you name it. Then, they all seem to leave as quickly as they came, the portal closes, and life returns to normal, at least for a while."

"Wow, where does this happen?"

"Sedona, Arizona is the most famous place. There are several portal areas around Sedona, but there are lots of places where portals seem to appear only occasionally. Freddy Silva seems to be on the right track with his crop circle research. He says that the planet is crisscrossed with magnetic 'ley lines.' In places where they intersect, portals sometimes open up. All the sacred sites and ancient cathedrals in Europe are located where these magnetic ley lines intersect. Mysterious things occur on a semi-regular basis. Cathedrals were not randomly located. They were built on sacred sites."

The Denver conference opened my eyes to a lot of ideas, the main one being just the reminder to keep an open mind. So when local sasquatch researchers in the Pacific Northwest started sharing stories of a very different kind, I had already been humbled by enough examples of my own ignorance that I didn't just laugh and walk away.

The portal business really intrigued me. Were portals really connected in some way to the sasquatch phenomenon, like John Keel emphatically maintained? I didn't go looking for any connection, but one day, it found me. Author and researcher Kirk Sigurdson was the first person to bring a personal experience with the portal phenomenon to my attention. Kirk described an encounter with a shimmering region in the atmosphere right in front of his position. It rippled and distorted the light, like a fluttering curtain made of quicksilver (liquid mercury).

Kirk's experience began when he and his girlfriend were camping at Cayuse Meadows, near Mount St. Helens. Here are Kirk's own words:

> At a time in my life when I was experimenting with remote viewing and telepathy, I drove up into the Lone Butte area of Washington State with my girlfriend, Meg, who happens to be a veterinarian with a genius IQ. We set up camp in a favorite spot for mushroom picking that was located next to a rather large swamp.
>
> Meg and I set up our tent and decided to take a nap around four o'clock in the afternoon. As she drifted off to sleep, I dabbled with a bit of "sending," a new technique of mine which involved "asking" for a response from the bigfoot community by sending out a mental picture of what I thought one of their faces might look like.
>
> I sent the mental face out over the forest—a kind of invitation that begged a response. As I hovered between wakefulness and sleep, I found my attention being pulled in a specific direction, almost like a psychological planchette on a OuiJa board. I was surprised to see how clearly and vividly the topography looked from on high. It really did seem as though I was getting an aerial view from remote viewing—a kind of soul-loosening ritual that used to be termed "astral flight."

In my near-dream state, I noticed a clearing that I recognized right away as Cayuse Meadow. I soared up the cliffs overlooking the meadow until I came upon a group of trees on both sides of a gravel road. The trees were noticeably broken, as if one or more sasquatches had snapped off the tops.

When the remote viewing session came naturally to a close, I arose, ate a little snack, and hopped onto my new KLR-250 Kawasaki motorcycle. The lure of what I had seen beckoned me. I tucked a topographic map into the back pocket of my jeans and rode off excitedly.

In about an hour, I knew that I was fairly close to the area with snapped trees that I had "viewed". I began exploring side roads in an attempt to find the right road. After a few false starts, I was fairly surprised when I found myself right back in the exact same place I had been before. There were the same snapped trees on both sides of me; and so many of them. I could see the sap still leaking out of a few of the breaks. They had definitely not been caused by winter winds or snow load.

Without warning, my motorcycle died. The engine didn't sputter out. Rather, the bike simply turned itself off. Could the electrical system of my new bike be faulty? I tried to restart it, but no luck. I worried that my battery was defective.

I dismounted from my bike and removed my helmet. I could sense right away that a kind of heavy energy was in the air. It felt as if anything could happen. I stopped worrying about my bike and took a deep breath. All of my senses were operating at a heightened level.

As I pushed my way into the forest, a "woo woo woo" sound came from behind a tree to my right. It almost sounded like a person trying to imitate an animal. I turned and began walking toward the vocalization. Then another "woo woo" came from behind me. I wheeled around, and once I had turned, a third "woo woo woo" came from a third direction.

I began charging the vocalizations more boldly than I ever had done before. The calls seemed to speed up a bit. Were they toying with me, or just agitated? I picked up a big stick and hit a tree with it, not so much like a sasquatch knock, but just an attempt to sound strong and confident. The "woo-woos" stopped as soon as I struck the tree.

A silence fell over the forest. I remembered that in my pocket, I had two magnets that I'd brought camping. They were toy magnets that sizzled and crackled loudly when one threw them into the air. I threw the magnets very high into the air, and they sizzled loudly like a zap of electricity.

The area had obviously been clear-cut maybe twenty or thirty years or so earlier. All of the firs were second-growth 'reprod' about 20-25' tall. They looked like overgrown Christmas trees.

Suddenly, a loud crashing noise demanded my attention. A tree was pushed to one side, and then another and another. Underbrush was also crashing out of the way. Something was charging toward me, but what? I was able to discern a huge body approaching through the woods—not by virtue of seeing the thing itself—but by the steadily approaching sound of trees and brush that were being trampled. Judging by all the racket of breaking limbs, the creature sounded even bigger than a sasquatch.

My conscious mind resorted to the most logical assumption: a bear was charging me, and I needed to get the hell out of there! I jumped back on my bike, kicked the engine over, and much to my relief, it started right up. I was afraid to turn back. The crashing brush had been in the same relative direction as the road upon which I had come, so I rode as fast as I could in the opposite direction.

After riding for about a quarter mile, I let up on the accelerator and listened. The forest was strangely quiet, aside from the idling of my motorcycle engine. Over the hum of the bike engine, I heard a distant crash up on the hill.

"Holy shit!" I thought. I took off down the fire road, jumping my bike over some fallen alders. Thankfully, the diameters of the logs weren't big enough to stop my front tire. After about another quarter mile of travel down a very steep hill, the gravel road became little more than a trail through rough grass.

The whole situation had a surreal quality about it. Something that could not logically exist was still loudly smashing its way toward me. Yet, I managed to put some distance between it and me, and I began to relax. I finally reached the end of the steadily dwindling trail. The trail ended at a steep drop-off. From my vantage point, I gazed down upon Cayuse Meadow. I could see elk grazing far below me in a swampy clearing. I dismounted my motorcycle, and took off my helmet.

The forest was very quiet now. No bird, squirrel or insect noises could be heard. I walked over towards a little stream that meandered through a grove of scraggly fir trees. It was then that I caught a whiff of a really terrible odor. It reminded me of the smell of certain places in the New York Subway system: an eye-stinging stench resulting from accumulated decades of homeless men and women peeing and defecating in hidden corners. My eyes began to water. I felt a shortness of breath, almost as if I were inhaling concentrated ammonia. I'd smelled 'sasquatch reek' before but never like this! This stench was overpowering!

I walked cautiously back toward my motorcycle. As I did, a shimmering vortex caught my attention. It seemed to be hovering in mid-air, about ten feet beyond the edge of the cliff. The whole shimmering blob before me emanated rainbows of light, like sunlight striking a layer of oil floating on a mud puddle. I noticed that the land and sky behind it looked altered, duller and darker, almost as if I were looking through a giant suspended sunglass lens.

As I studied this "portal" or whatever it was, a skulking presence seemed to be very close at hand and it seemed intent on herding me right off the cliff in the direction of this shimmering curtain of light. Something was very close to me and very huge, though I could not see it.

I felt an urge to leap off the cliff as a gesture of surrender, but I resisted. I prayed. Suddenly I found the strength to resist, and I turned, leapt onto my bike, and kicked the starting lever. Thankfully, it started right up. My helmet felt much heavier than usual. I wanted to cast it off, but I didn't dare. I began praying a fragment of the Scientific Statement of Being that I'd learned in Christian Science Sunday School: "All is Infinite Mind, and its infinite manifestation, for God is All-in-All." The motorcycle seemed to drive itself. I found myself riding at incredible speed.

My heart was pumping very fast, and I was worried that I might crash, but I pressed on borne of fear, over deadfall logs, over rotten, punky fragments of logs, through brush and grass, onto loose gravel and then up a steep incline with deep ruts eroded by once-flowing water. It took all my concentration to keep the bike's wheels out of the cavernous gullies in the road. One miscalculation and I would have been wrecked.

Once I reached the top of a hill, I felt safer. The heavy, stifling feelings let up and I could breathe normally again. My heart was still racing. I wanted to see if anything was still following me, but I was too afraid to let up on the throttle. In a way, I felt the instinctual need to NOT LISTEN, as if the act of listening might allow that huge invisible force to locate me once again.

About an hour later, I pulled up in camp. Meg was puttering around the picnic table, getting ready to make dinner. She smiled when I dismounted. When I removed my motorcycle helmet, Meg studied my face and instantly knew something was very wrong. I stumbled over to the water cooler and drank as much water as my stomach would hold. Meg put an arm around me, asking what had happened. It was a while before I could even speak to answer her questions. Bigfooting was never the same after that experience. Hearing crashing sounds in the trees always stirred memories of those terrifying moments.

It wasn't until several summers later that I once again heard that same terrifying sound. I was camped at a quarry on Devil's Ridge in the Mt. Hood National Forest with my good friend, Joe Beelart. Joe had warned me not to bang my djembe drum too loud. We were sitting around the fire, waiting to see if anything rattled the tins of little fruit pies that we had placed strategically around the quarry. After an hour of being hushed, I'd had enough. I banged my drum loudly and shouted into the darkness. Deep tones echoed out over the valley below, along with my howls. Suddenly, a huge tree was pushed over very near our camp, in the outer darkness, its thick roots yanked from the earth. The crashing sound instantly took me back to the terrifying afternoon at Cayuse Meadow. Joe, on the other hand, was elated. The crashing tree was a kind of confirmation: Yes, I had definitely pissed off something big, most likely a sasquatch. I regretted banging the drum so disrespectfully, but now Joe wanted me to do it again. No way, Jose.

In all, it was a magical night, but I was very glad that the crashing sound stopped when it did. In the morning, Joe and I searched but could find no sign of any freshly downed tree. Months later, at a barbecue, some hunter friends of mine explained that bears sometimes push trees over. They told me bears could also make "woo woo" sounds. I didn't have the heart to tell them about the other events that most certainly were not the work of bears. They wouldn't have believed me, anyhow.

In the years that passed since that experience on the cliff above Cayuse Meadow, I've heard other people speak about invisible things walking through the woods, or even crashing through the woods. Torrie Randles, Derek's wife, spoke of a similar situation that happened to her while she had been hunting in the Olympic Peninsula. Torrie never stated that loudly crashing creature, presumably a sasquatch, was "invisible." Rather, she marveled at how well it remained hidden and out of sight, even as it came loudly crashing toward the position where she held her ground, wide-eyed and tightly gripping her deer rifle.

It's very hard, I think, to really grasp the ability that these creatures have to effectively cloak such an imposing presence. I certainly understand Torrie's unwillingness to accept the fact that the trees were not big enough and the woods was not thick enough to fully conceal the approaching sasquatch, yet nothing of the approaching creature could be seen.

If I had it all to do over again, I would not have followed the urge to penetrate that logging road above Cayuse Meadow on that one summer afternoon. It was a traumatic experience to have been in the presence of a huge, invisible creature, and to have faced a portal that this creature seemed intent on herding me toward.

The whole traumatic experience did help me to understand why early pioneers named certain forbidding forest places after devils or spirits. I also understand why Native Americans traditionally avoided these menacing places. Whatever it was that approached me, it certainly did not seem benevolent, although it did allow me to escape in the end. I do not carry any physical scars from the experience, but my mind bears a wound that has not fully healed. I carry a post-traumatic stress that leaves me feeling uneasy, sometimes nauseated, when I enter forested places that hearken of bigfoot activity.

The cover of Henry Franzoni's book, In the Spirit of Seatco, bears a map detailing locations place names like 'devil' and 'spirit' that are now associated with bigfoot activity. Cayuse Meadow is located next to Skookum Meadow and near Spirit Lake, Devil's Backbone, Devil's Peak, and Devil's Creek. Something devilish was certainly afoot that day in late summer. One need not be a Christian to keep one's distance from devils and their accursed "magick." In my view, Cayuse Meadow, Skookum Meadow, Squaw Butte, and Tillicum Swamp are all haunted by devils, spirits, ghosts, aliens, monsters, giants, bigfoots, demons--whatever one chooses to call them. Native Americans and even early white settlers were correct about the evil nature of many sasquatch hot spots.

At least two other sasquatch researchers I know have also had encounters with some sort of quicksilver curtain. Dedicated outdoorsman Todd Bailey, of the London trackway fame, has seen the quicksilver curtain on three occasions. Todd describes it as a very limited circular area where the air has a rippling, shimmering look about it, very much like the surface of a pond or lake in a light breeze.

When faced with this mirage-like shimmering, Todd rubbed his eyes and tried to check his vision. The air was distorted in front of him, but the image, or illusion, or whatever it was, hung in the air in a specific place just a few feet off the ground. I asked Todd if he ever approached the quicksilver curtain that rippled in an unseen breeze. Todd confessed that, not only did he *not* approach the mysterious phenomenon in front of him, but his instincts told him to run the other way.

In January of 2014, fellow field researcher Cliff Barackman was giving a talk at the Columbia Gorge Discovery Center in The Dalles, Oregon. Also on the bill were a couple of First Nation bigfoot researchers, Mel Skahan and Oliver Kirk. I've had occasional contact with both of these gentlemen over the years. Not only are they very experienced, but they're both very well known in their respective tribal communities. Oliver is a career law enforcement officer in the Natural Resources Department of the Warm Springs Reservation in north-central Oregon. Mel Skahan has pursued paranormal phenomena, principally the sasquatch, on the vast Yakama Reservation in south central Washington state. Both of these researchers spoke to the audience of sightings and encounters that occurred on their respective reservations. Theirs was some of the most interesting and useful information of all, because it is ordinarily not accessible to Caucasian researchers like me. Like the slogan used to promote Las Vegas, things that happen on the reservation tend to stay on the reservation. These two experienced researchers shared sasquatch encounters on 'The Rez' that we white folks seldom get to hear about.

After their presentations, I had the chance to chat it up with both fellows. They agreed that, although they were there to talk to the audience about the sasquatch, they each had multiple encounters with aerial lights and other phenomena that fall loosely into the category of UFOs. Both men were aware of places on their reservation where fast moving orbs of various colors are seen to be moving about, where intensely bright lights emanate from the trees, or other unexplainable phenomena.

I asked both gentlemen if they'd ever seen "the shimmer."

"I haven't, but my research partner has seen it multiple times," Mel immediately replied. He gave me the number of his research partner, Jon Sampson.

Mel Skahan (left) and Oliver Kirk

Jon drives loads of timber out of the center of the Yakama Reservation in connection with tribal logging operations. He travels remote roads day and night. He and the other drivers have quite a list of orbs, lights, and other strange phenomena that they've seen over the years. Usually, they're too busy driving loads to stop and investigate, but Jon does like to spend his free time investigating sasquatch sightings and other paranormal phenomena around the reservation.

I asked Jon about the shimmer. He had seen it a few times. He described it as an area that shimmers like the surface of a pond, but it hangs vertically in the air, just above the ground. In one case, Jon saw spheres of light circulating around this shimmering curtain. In another instance, the shimmering area had an arrowhead shape. Did he try to get closer to it and probe it, I asked? Definitely not. Discretion is the better part of valor, and Jon got the heck out of there. Like Todd, Jon wasn't about to probe anything that strange and ominous.

Could the 'quicksilver curtain' be just a weird local atmospheric phenomenon? Do we have any reason to think it is really a portal to someplace else? Has anyone ever tried to enter the shimmering zone?

Larry Kelm does not consider himself to be a bigfoot researcher nor a paranormal researcher, either. Larry is a pretty regular guy, but he did have a surprise encounter with the 'quicksilver curtain,' and he states in no uncertain terms that it nearly cost him his life. Larry Kelm is a high school shop teacher in southern Oregon. Here are Larry's words:

> I'm a 54-year-old college educated professional person. In the fall of 1980, I ran a small business as a construction contractor in Eugene, Oregon. During the slow times between jobs, I would don my backpack and hiking boots and disappear into the mountains for weeks at a time, enjoying the peaceful solitude of long hikes. At that time I was single and didn't answer to anyone so I was free to do what I wanted when I wanted. I decided to hike the old Molalla Indian Trail that followed the ridge tops from Saddle Blanket Mountain to Oakridge, one of the Native American's favorite summer camps and trading centers. It was a beautiful August day. Two days into the hike (I expected to be gone about two weeks), literally out of the blue, the most terrifying event of my entire life occurred. It would change the way I perceive reality forever.

> I was walking along the trail, enjoying the strong breeze and bright sunshine when, in the middle of a step, everything around me started to turn gray and blurry. The only way I can describe it is that I was suddenly looking through someone else's prescription sunglasses and everything was out of focus. I finished the step and started another. Every inch I moved forward the darkness increased and the gray blurring turned into a jumble of shapes that made no sense. I then seemed to pass a barrier and everything started to return back into focus by the time my foot reached the ground on the second step. Now, everything around me had changed. Day had turned into night and there was no wind. All the Douglas fir and pine trees had been replaced with thick, jungle-like growth. The cool thin mountain air was replaced with thick, humid air. There

191

were no stars in the sky, but there was a diffused light that let me see everything clearly. I could see, but I couldn't tell what the light source was.

As often happens when the human body receives a massive dose of adrenaline, the entire incident appeared to be in slow motion, so even though I was only there for a second or two I had plenty of time to observe my surroundings. The silence was broken by a continuous high-pitched keening sound. I was nearly overwhelmed with a sense of fear and danger. My forward momentum carried me for one more step before I stopped dead in my tracks. I was so terrified I actually felt my heart stop for a moment. I opened my mouth and gasped in a huge gush of the thick, humid air. I recoiled backward.

This is what I feel saved my life. I recoiled backwards in the same footsteps that I had travelled when I entered wherever it was I was in. Just as I reversed my direction, I heard the statement, "Gotcha!" and a very hairy, very massive arm brushed across the front of my neck. Had I not reversed direction just when I did, the massive arm would have grabbed me around the neck. I avoided being grabbed by the slimmest of margins. I quickly took two more steps backwards and everything reversed itself from what had just happened. The world around me became lighter, the fir and pines gradually came back into view and by the third step I was back on Saddle Blanket Mountain.

I continued to walk backwards in terror, and as I did, I observed that where I had just come from was a shimmering oval patch of air about the size of a large door. The woods behind it looked like it was under water. By the fifth backward step the shimmering area seemed to just evaporate and everything was back to normal. By then my lungs had nearly burst from the volume of air I had inhaled during the huge gasp I had just taken. My body felt like it was on fire from the adrenaline surge. I spun around and ran back down the trail as fast as my legs could carry me, and didn't stop until I reached my truck. I was nearly two days getting to that place and about three hours getting back.

On my way home I was absolutely horrified at the thought of what would happen if I were to drive my truck into something like that. I had terrible nightmares for years, and still haven't come to grips with what happened. My fingers are trembling and the hair is standing up on the nape of my neck as I write this.

Since then I've read everything I could get my hands on about people who have mysteriously disappeared throughout history, and discovered several instances where people have vanished in plain sight of others. The quantum physics people have a theory about parallel universes. They just might be right.

I had been in touch with Larry Kelm by e-mail but we had never met until I attended a Ray Crowe-sponsored gathering of bigfoot enthusiasts in Sweet Home, Oregon. Larry thought it would be the perfect opportunity to meet midway between our respective homes so he could explain a bit more about his experience. On a rainy summer weekend, Larry Kelm and I finally met at Longbow Campground. A rather interesting situation transpired around that meeting.

Larry showed up with his wife and we decided to look for a place where we could talk in private. After reading his written account, I knew his story was a paranormal doozy. Meanwhile, Ray Crowe's conference was well attended by serious minded 'flesh and blood' researchers like Tom Steenburg and Chris Murphy. I didn't want to embarrass Larry by having some 'flesh and blood' bigfoot researchers happen along and hear about his very paranormal experience, which may or may not even be bigfoot-related.

The rain finally stopped, so the three of us drifted off to the fire pit. We pulled three lawn chairs close to the smoldering coals and I tried to rekindle the fire. In the presence of his wife, Larry recounted his entire story. His wife had obviously heard it before but she listened intently. I watched her reaction from time to time. She seemed familiar with, and supportive of, all that he described. As Larry neared the end of his account, a few of the other participants in the bigfoot conference drifted over to see what we were talking about. Here came Chris Murphy and Tom Steenburg, the two visiting Canadian authors of a couple of very 'flesh and blood' bigfoot books. To my chagrin, they both pulled up lawn chairs and plopped down in our midst. Then, they wanted to know what we were talking about.

Larry stopped talking in mid-sentence and looked at me. I shrugged. Larry was hesitant to continue. It dawned on me that this might be an opportunity to test the sincerity of Larry's story and to get some very skeptical feedback from two stalwart 'flesh and blood' bigfoot researchers.

"What the heck, Larry. Tell 'em what we're talking about."

Larry Kelm paused, took a deep breath, and patiently retold his entire account from the beginning. It occurred to me that my reputation as an investigator of the bigfoot phenomenon might now be in serious jeopardy, especially if Chris and Tom spread the word that I was giving serious consideration to this most outlandish of paranormal accounts. I completely expected the two distinguished Canadians to roll their eyes, stand up, and walk away shaking their heads.

To my amazement, they did not. Not only did Chris and Tom *not* walk away, but they listened very attentively. And when Larry finished the second go-around of being drawn through the quicksilver curtain, or whatever it was, Chris immediately responded by saying, "That reminds me of something really strange that once happened to me."

Then Chris launched into an account of his own. Once, he was driving down a two-lane highway with two cars in front of him. Suddenly, the front car veered into the roadside ditch and crashed. The car immediately in front of him slammed on the brakes, stopped and the driver of that car began to get out of the car to render assistance. Chris slowly pulled around the site of the wreck by driving in the oncoming lane. As he pulled slowly by, he could see the driver of the wrecked car was motionless and slumped over the steering wheel. He appeared to be either seriously injured or dead. The motorist ahead of Chris was already out of his car and heading for the wreck. For that reason, Chris decided against stopping. A few moments later, Chris had second thoughts. Chris changed his mind and used the first available opportunity to turn around and return to the scene of the wreck. This is where things got strange. Chris was out of sight of the wreck for only seconds, a minute at the most, but when he returned to the scene, there was absolutely nothing there! No wreck, no assisting motorist, no nothing; just an empty stretch of highway.

All of us sitting around the smoldering fire sat silently for a second. Tom Steenburg broke the silence. "Let me tell you about the haunted house I once investigated…"

"Wait a minute!" I interrupted. "Before we change the subject, let me ask you a question, Chris. What the heck happened? How do you explain the total disappearance of the wreck you witnessed?"

"Well. I don't quite know, but I *think* that what happened is that I witnessed a wreck that *once* happened there. It's like a piece of cosmic video tape replayed itself. That wreck happened in the past and I saw a replay of it."

"It's like the events that witnesses describe who live in northern Italy," Chris continued. "The stone highway built by the Romans, called the Appian Way, lay buried and undiscovered in many places. It was discovered after people living along its route in modern times reported seeing columns of Roman soldiers, marching along in battle dress, moving along a definite route but waist-deep in the earth. Roman soldiers were marching on some sort of a path or road that was three feet below the present surface of the earth. As a consequence of these odd sightings, some of these areas were excavated and, to everyone's amazement the Appian Way, the three foot thick stone roadway, was uncovered. The soldiers that were seen were marching on a road that was buried beneath the earth. So how is any of this possible? It isn't. It's impossible. But it happened. And other events like this have happened elsewhere."

I once took a class called 'Haunted Mt. Hood.' We toured old homesteads along the former Oregon Trail that was used by so many thousands of emigrants in the 1800's to relocate to the Oregon Territory. Cascade Geographic Society curator Michael P. Jones has made an occupation out of collecting historical and even paranormal anecdotes from historic sites around the greater Portland area, and then conducting tours like this.

One pattern that Michael Jones has discovered, is that people who live along the Oregon Trail today do sometimes look out their window and see human forms wearing pioneer-period clothing and doing things that pioneer homesteaders might have done: surveying their homestead, or standing solemnly with heads bowed before the grave of a dead child. The apparitions aren't doing different things each time the modern residents see them. It's the same thing every time. As with the witnesses who saw soldiers marching on the buried Appian Way, the Mt. Hood witnesses report seeing essentially the same event replaying multiple times.

I think Chris Murphy described it best. It's as though a piece of videotape is being periodically replayed against a backdrop of modern surroundings. Ancient events are replaying themselves in front of modern witnesses. Are the witnesses seeing tormented souls whose ghostly form is doomed to relive a period of earthly suffering? It doesn't seem that way to the modern witnesses. One witness who periodically sees the ghost of a pioneer homesteader did enough background research to find out that the deceased homesteader was actually very content with his station in life. In his day, he was known for sometimes performing heroic rescues of other stranded immigrant families on the harrowing 'Barlow Road' section of the Oregon Trail. Nor do the ghostly forms in period clothing *seem* particularly tormented when they are witnessed by modern residents. To the contrary, the one apparition seemed content, even happy as he patrolled the perimeter of what was then his modest homestead.

On the other hand, the pioneer family that is sometimes seen standing with heads bowed before a grave does not seem so happy. Still, the gravesite that the ghost family are seen to haunt endures in the vicinity of Summit Meadows on Mount Hood. The grave is that of a child that died *en route* and was buried beside the Oregon Trail, as were so many others.

People who live near battlefields also report similar observations. Residents living near Civil War battlefields such as Gettysburg occasionally witness the replay of tiny portions of the historic and horrific battles that once took place at these locations.

It may be too much of a stretch to try and identify a common thread in all these events, but here goes. Perhaps time itself does not always proceed in a linear fashion. Perhaps bits of time replay themselves. Perhaps significant events get burned into the fabric of time. Non-scientists often describe these puzzling manifestations as "coming from other dimensions." A physicist who is versed in quantum mechanics might call these parallel universes "brane worlds." Brane is short for 'membrane' and branes are places with either more or less than the three physical dimensions that we earthlings inhabit.

String Theory is the outgrowth of quantum physics that validates the idea that there are more dimensions than we are directly experiencing. Physicists are more accepting than ever of the suggestion that there are worlds with more dimensions or fewer dimensions than the three physical dimensions and one temporal (time) dimension that we routinely experience. It is possible that these dimensions are all around us although we cannot experience them directly. Mediums that make contact with the dead may be accessing these additional dimensions. Dead people may reside in another universe, or another realm within our universe. Windows or "portals" to these universes, dimensions, or realms may open up from time to time, allowing beings to access our world in the form of an apparition that temporarily manifests itself in our three-dimensional world.

Don't laugh. There are tiny particles that could be used to probe these hypothetical multidimensional universes. Neutrinos are sub-atomic particles like electrons, but with no electrical charge. Since they are electrically neutral, they are not affected by electromagnetism and they are barely affected by gravity. Therefore, these particles can travel great distances and they can be spotted by detection systems that identify their perfectly straight paths that stand out against all the particles in our universe which travel in curved paths.

Could the quicksilver curtain be the manifestation of temporary portals; that is, openings into other 'brane worlds' that, once entered, may not be so easy to get out of? I wish I knew. It seems that it's not as far-fetched of an explanation as it might first seem. There is indeed some theoretical physics that describes it. Whatever it is, it will probably not be well understood for a long time, but it certainly seems to be a very real frontier of paranormal research. Based on the experience of Larry Kelm, it may be a situation that is much too dangerous to even explore. Fortunately, encounters with the quicksilver curtain are beyond rare, although it seems that there are individuals like Todd Bailey and Jon Sampson who have seen it more than once. What I do know, is that if I ever see even a hint of a quicksilver curtain, I'm getting the hell out of there as fast as I can.

One statement made by Larry Kelm does keep coming to mind. Since Larry is the only person I know who may have actually entered this realm defined by the quicksilver curtain, I will allow him to speculate that it is indeed some sort of very menacing portal. As Larry said, such portals may be an explanation for at least some of the 'missing person' cases that are never solved.

One of the earlier cases that Paulides reports in *Missing 411* (Createspace, 2014) is nine-year-old Murray Walkup Miller who disappeared in Montana while helping his father cut firewood on October 24, 1936. On his second trip to the creek to fetch water, he vanished. He was found days later, alive, and said that on his way back from his second trip he found himself in a place he did not recognize. This sounds a little familiar in light of Larry Kelm's story. If Murray *did* end up in a portal that placed him somewhere else, it is some extraordinarily good fortune that he managed to find his way out, especially after languishing in some nether-world for days.

I still find myself wondering if Kris Zitzewitz's disappearance, and many others, began with some sort of accidental interaction with a portal. Sadly, I do not think we will ever know, since so few of these victims are ever seen again. Murray Miller and Larry Kelm are the only cases I could find where the person returned to tell the tale.

I find myself wondering why Larry Kelm managed to escape a tragic fate. By Larry's own description, he entered the portal-like region and was very nearly grabbed by something that looked to him like a big, hairy arm. It seems that it (or they) had Larry trapped, yet he managed his escape by the narrowest of margins.

I shared Larry's account with a couple of paranormal researchers who feel they know a thing or two about the whole portal thing. Interestingly, Beth Heikkenen and Tish Paquette both offered the same thought as to why Larry escaped. Although they do not know each other, both women insisted that, when the portals manifest themselves on the Earth's surface, they are guarded, perhaps by the sasquatch, so that hapless people like Larry do not go stumbling into them. Both women whom I consulted felt that one of the jobs, or roles, that the sasquatch serve is to guard the portals. Consequently, they both felt that Larry was essentially repelled by the being that was guarding the portal. Larry felt he escaped, but Tish and Beth agree: "Nah, he didn't 'escape.' He was just chased out of someplace where he didn't belong." Essentially, the being that was guarding the portal, probably a sasquatch, did his job by scaring Larry out of the portal with a deliberately feeble act of aggression.

Why then, was Kris Zitzewitz was not afforded the same consideration? Perhaps, Kris did fall prey to a much more dangerous group of entities; the ones Kathleen Odom's contact referred to as 'the green ones.' It seems reasonable to speculate that in some of the unsolved missing persons cases, the victims are falling into the hands of some very ruthless entities, quite possibly the Reptilians or 'green ones' mentioned by both Dave and Kathleen.

Speaking of Dave Paulides, he also related to me one incident he heard of in which a hiker happened across the quicksilver curtain phenomenon someplace in northern Colorado. The hiker approached the shimmering curtain with extreme caution. He carefully inserted his hand and, to his utter amazement, he watched as it disappeared up to his wrist. He yanked his hand back, spun on his heel and didn't stop running until he was back to his car. Dave could not give me specifics on this case, but if it is factual, then not all encounters with the quicksilver curtain end in tragedy.

The reason it is so difficult to speculate on what is going on in these missing person cases is that it appears that there is more than one thing going on. Obviously, not all missing people cases have the same root cause. Sometimes people do get lost and then perish before they are found. Sometimes the remains are found. Other times, they are not.

Sometimes, it appears that the sasquatch are in some way involved. These are usually missing children situations that eventually turn up alive and unharmed (see: 'The Guardians' chapter in *The Locals*). In other cases, a person randomly ventures into or is perhaps even lured into some kind of portal or wormhole, or whatever it is. Sometimes they escape or are returned. Other times, they are not so lucky. In some cases, it seems that some sort of abduction by extraterrestrial entities is at work. As often as not, it appears that these entities emanate from subterranean enclaves. I suspect that the process of being abducted may sometimes begin with a forced entry into a subterranean base or enclave and from there, who knows where the poor soul ends up?

Perhaps Kris Zitzewitz found a cave in the midst of that torrential downpour, but it was an opening to a place that was occupied by menacing beings. In traditional Christian theology, it could then be said that he entered the realm of the devil. I don't think the sasquatch are the devils in these cases, but they may well know of these entities and know from where they originate. It is as sad as it is mysterious, since most of these unfortunate souls are never seen again.

Interestingly, some New Agers make a definite distinction between portals, vortexes, and wormholes but there does not seem to be any agreement on the use of these terms. Heck, most people see all of them as fictional concepts. If someone did stumble upon the entrance to one, it will probably look like a shimmering curtain of quicksilver. I will confidently state that venturing into it would be a very bad idea.

The biggest benefit in writing about such speculative matters is that, no matter how rare or uncertain it all is, it may help somebody a great deal to know what *not* to do if they do happen across one. Do not enter it. I think the only consolation is that such phenomena are extremely rare.

The bad side of writing about this stuff is that it might motivate some to stay out of the forest or the wilderness altogether. That would be most unfortunate. Avoiding strong downpours may be prudent. Paying attention to one's surroundings is always a good idea. Paulides says don't hike alone, especially in the vicinity of Wenatchee Lake, Washington.

Personally, I rather enjoy hiking alone. I do not plan to completely avoid it simply because certain people, in extremely rare cases, meet with some unknown fate.

Soldiers who survived horrible battles often wonder why they were spared, when so many all around them died. Their only way of explaining it is that, if your number is up, then you are almost powerless to avoid it, but if it is not your time to die, then you just will not die that day, no matter how many others do. Those who survive against all odds tend to shrug it off, knowing that there is not much they can do about it, either way. If you thought about it too much, they say, you wouldn't be able to even cope.

That's why I don't worry about disappearing as I travel the wilderness. I pay attention, I'm careful, and I stay out of intense weather as much as possible. That's all I can do. I'm not going to stop living my life just because something bad *could* happen. If I did that, I'm not really living anymore, so I'm already dead. Based on the vast numbers who do travel in the mountains without incident, and the miniscule few who tragically disappear, I think the odds are still heavily in my favor.

Chapter Seven: The Goblin Universe

The Goblin Universe, as described in a profound book by Ted Holiday and Colin Wilson, refers to the 'phantom menagerie' of other-worldly creatures that seem to reside in the shadows of our physical world. Various mysterious beings sometimes manifest themselves for our inspection, only to dissolve away, especially when we make a serious effort to document their existence. Holiday was mainly concerned with the Loch Ness monster and similar beings that appear to inhabit lakes of the British Isles and beyond, but he recognized the existence of still other creatures including big cats, hairy hominids, and ETs. In the 1982 book, published by Llewellyn's psi-Tech series, Holiday described his serious but unsuccessful efforts to photograph the Loch Ness monster in the 1930s. He was frustrated by unexplainable camera malfunctions that always occurred exactly when the elusive being made its long-awaited appearance. Anyone who has ever tried in earnest to photo-document the sasquatch should be able to relate to this pattern.

As previously stated, each region throughout the world seems to have at least one element of 'paranormality' that regularly manifests itself. Some regions have multiple phenomena.

For students of the paranormal in the Pacific Northwest, obviously the sasquatch is the most accessible manifestation of the goblin universe. Clearly, the sasquatch do not confine their activities to the Pacific Northwest as the early researchers believed. The sasquatch phenomenon muscled its way into the public consciousness as a consequence of sightings and track finds in the PNW.

More and more, the view that the sasquatch are wild apes is being replaced by the view that they are essentially people, perhaps Indians, that were not evicted when the huge nineteenth century migration of Europeans evicted most Native American tribes.

The idea that the sasquatch are just a tribe of Native Americans has problems as well. There are sasquatch sightings by credible individuals that also include aerial lights. There are sightings that end with the sasquatch disappearing from view at point blank range in broad daylight. More people than ever seem willing to attribute essentially mystical powers to the sasquatch. Toby Johnson and his crew of researchers (Chapter 4) are not the only ones who would insist that the sasquatch can stop us in our tracks, that they can command us to leave an area, and that they can confuse our perception of time.

"If bigfoots exist, why don't we ever find their bones?" the skeptics often ask. A possible answer to this familiar question is offered by the experience of Ron Lewis of Maple Heights, Ohio. Ron and a friend were combing the forests of Ashtabula County, Ohio for indications of the sasquatch that they believed to reside there. In the midst of one thick and very remote patch of forest with a view of a distant lake, they found an unusual, rectangular rock formation that measured five feet wide by ten feet long. The rocks that formed this massive cairn were all about the size of bowling balls and their jagged edges interlocked very tightly. It looked for all the world like they discovered a grave, and a very large one at that. After examining the site and weighing the other possibilities for quite some time, the two men became increasingly suspicious of the possibility that they had stumbled upon the proverbial sasquatch grave. Of only one thing were they certain: in order to find out, they would have to dig it up.

From there, I will turn the narrative over to Ron Lewis, himself:

> Those involved: My brother Nick Lewis (our look out), my partner "Dave," and me.
>
> (I'm Ron Lewis from Mayfield Heights, Ohio.)
>
> It was a beautiful, July day when we arrived at the site of the mysterious cairn in the middle of that Ashtabula County woods. Our plan was to exhume what we were certain was a bigfoot grave. We began in the middle of the rock pile, believing that the best way to uncover anything was to start from the top-center of the stack. The rocks were not like any kind of demolished building or any other randomly arranged pile of rubble. Rather, the rocks were carefully and intelligently arranged. They were tightly interlocked to form one solid structure. When I say structure I use the term loosely. There was no trace of mortar or any other form of bonding agent.
>
> We had bug spray on that day, but it didn't stop the mosquitoes. Being surrounded by swampland, the mosquitoes there are always rather ravenous. If you forget one area of your body, they will relentlessly swarm and bite that area. They were going after our eyeballs; the only place on which we couldn't put any repellent. This was the first and only time that we ever encountered such an aggressive and directed mosquito attack.
>
> We had been exploring this area for a year or so before we discovered this particular structure. During that time, we had many interactions with the bigfoots in this area. We had seen them, been followed by them, been charged by one, and missed several golden opportunities to get really good pictures. We had even heard them speak. They can imitate just about any animal, and even some not local to our area. They are excellent imitators. I even heard them

mimic my own voice and, I have to say, it is very bizarre to hear something you said get restated by some unseen being in the woods.

The "Dig"

The structure of interest was approximately 5 feet wide by 10 or 11 feet long. We started our expedition early in the day knowing full well it would take the better part of a long summer's day to get to what we hoped would be some great physical evidence. My partner and I were going to remove the rocks. My brother was there to keep watch in case we had some of our friends (the bigfoots) come in for a visit.

We spent the better part of the day separating and unstacking the rocks. This was a hot, humid, beautiful summer day, and separating and lifting out each rock was sweaty, demanding work. For every stone that would get out, we would have to loosen several surrounding stones. The rocks were interlocked with a surprising amount of care that did not at all resemble any other feature in the surrounding area. Most everything else was covered with some plant life, yet this particular structure was comprised entirely of bare, moss-free stones. In fact, this is why the structure gained our interest in the first place.

There were almost no other rocks of the same size around the area, and definitely no other rock structures that even remotely resembled this structure that we had decided to excavate. The surrounding area was very swampy, and it was close to a big lake. By the time we excavated to a depth of about three feet, it was becoming a bigger and bigger problem to proceed. We had to pretty much remove every stone in a layer before we could begin excavating the next layer. We finally gave up around 5 p.m. or so, due to exhaustion and lack of meaningful progress over that final hour or so. We decided *not* to put the rocks back. This turned out to be a bigger mistake than messing with the rock stack in the first place.

The Ghost

For a few weeks after our excavation, strange things began happening at our homes. It would take a while to explain how or why they knew where we lived, but I think Thom covers that idea elsewhere in his book. Suffice to say we had been in contact with the local bigfoots for a long time and we knew them to be very,

very, smart. They have quite a sense of humor, too, and they love pranks. For example, my partner would wake up to find his firewood pile thrown all over his yard. On one occasion he heard laughter coming from the wooded area by his backyard. Several times, he restacked the firewood into a neat pile, only to find it thrown all over the yard again.

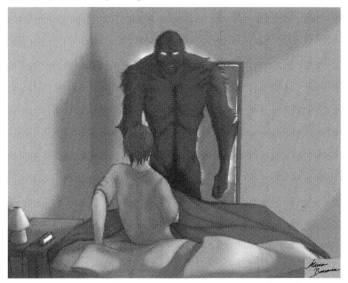

In retrospect, I realize now that we were ignoring subtle hints that we needed to replace the stones we had removed. The clues gradually became more difficult to ignore. On countless nights, I would hear loud, forceful smacks on my exterior garage door that would shake the whole house. Even this did not fully convey the message. Finally, things became impossible to ignore.

I will remember the final event until the day I die. On the night of The Great Northeast Blackout (August 14, 2003), a chain reaction of power outages plunged the entire region into darkness. Among other things, the blackout stripped away my safe haven of light.

Bigfoots will exploit *any* advantage they can get, and they definitely had an advantage now. It wasn't yet late, but without electronic entertainment or even electric lights, most people around me had already gone to bed. That's when I saw two huge red eyes on my front porch, looking right into my house.

Next thing I knew, there were more loud smacks on my garage door. There was no mystery. By then, I knew who was doing it and I'd had enough. I went out and told them to go away. I sternly stated to whoever might have been listening that I was not coming out to entertain them.

I was a little on edge. Between the noises, the red eyes on the porch, and the whole power outage, I was a little on edge. It felt like I was living a scene from a horror movie. I reminded myself that if they wanted to hurt me they had already had plenty of chances.

Then, I went to bed. In the middle of the night, I awoke to the horrifying sight of a bigfoot in my bedroom! It was glowing. I could see right through it. As I sat up in stunned disbelief, it sternly spoke to me in two short sentences.

"Fix my resting place! You are now responsible for anything that happens to it!"

Then it turned. It faded away as it walked through the closed door.

I didn't sleep any more that night. Early the next morning I called my partner and said "We *have* to go...."

He finished my sentence, "...Fix the grave. *I know*."

When I began describing the hairy apparition, Dave completed the description for me. He informed me that the same ghost I described had visited him last night.

I must point out that Dave and I are well educated. We did not believe in ghosts before this incident, but we certainly wasted no time going back and fixing that grave to the best of our ability.

After we put back every single stone, we prayed. We asked for forgiveness. For good measure, we left an offering of peace. At that moment, **I swore I would never mess with this or any other bigfoot grave, ever again!**

I would advise everyone else to make the same vow. Even if someone has the opportunity to obtain some groundbreaking physical evidence of the existence of these "people," I would strongly emphasize that it should be done with the utmost respect for their living and their dead.

Of all the various paranormal elements of this story, the most interesting aspect of this whole experience is the claim that the deceased creature, presumably a sasquatch though we cannot be certain, communicated with Ron in his bedroom. Ron was not trying to, or expecting communication from, the apparition. Yet, it not only came and found him, but also his research partner Dave, on the same night. If this were the only account of its kind, it would be easier to dismiss as random chance or the stuff of an overly vivid imagination, but there is enough of a pattern to these kinds of experiences that I feel it justifies a little more evaluation. It seems that Ron is not the only one who is reporting an unsolicited communication with a putative sasquatch, although I know of no other report that suggests that the communication also came from a *dead* sasquatch.

It's one thing if a person sets out to communicate with a sasquatch then claims to have succeeded. Naturally, sober-minded individuals will attribute the whole affair to the powers of suggestion: the person wanted the communication so badly that their mind made it happen by virtue of their own hyper-active imagination. I find it a bit more compelling to receive such reports from persons who not only did not consciously attempt to communicate, but who did not even consider such things to be possible. Ron's concept of the sasquatch got a paradigm shift.

Paranormal investigation is all about assembling patterns. It is the only way of identifying elements of 'paranormal reality' from a data set consisting of unverifiable observations and anecdotal data. In searching for such a pattern in the anecdotal stories of sasquatch communication, consider one particularly vivid account. The following experience speaks to the suggestion that communication with the sasquatch is not only possible, but that the sasquatch can even initiate this communication with *unwilling persons* if the situation is sufficiently dire. This account was kindly provided by a veteran sasquatch researcher Kent Ballard, of Brazil, Indiana. Kent writes:

> "Well, they say a confession is good for the soul. I used to be one of those folks who snickered and laughed at people who thought bigfoot was telepathic. I kept this opinion right up to the moment several of them telepathed me all at once.

I had a contact who claimed to have several bigfoot on his property. They were apparently hanging around an old dump in those woods. No one knew what they were up to but periodically we could hear them banging on metal and moving things around while we were some distance away. The contact wanted very much to get rid of these creatures. I wanted to learn what they were up to in the dump. We armed ourselves to the teeth and began the short hike to the dump.

We were stopped dead in our tracks, surrounded, and ordered to leave. It's that simple. At one point we were back-to-back, me holding a specialized police/military Benelli shotgun with magnum deer slugs in it up and at my shoulder, ready to fire, safety off. My contact was armed with a WW II M-1 Garrand rifle, .30-06, semiautomatic. His weapon was at *his* shoulder, safety off. We were both carrying extra ammo and each wearing the largest side arms we owned.

It was made clear to us, after they surrounded us at very close range, that if we so much as pulled a trigger neither one of us would ever see home again. They were that blunt about it. By the way, that was their phrase, not mine: we would "never see home again."

The shift into telepathy--this all took place in broad daylight-- was ridiculously easy. For a few fleeting seconds I thought my friend was talking, then I realized I was not *hearing* words. They were inside my head. The English language is not constructed to properly discuss telepathy, as I have found out over the years since. This encounter was in 2003.

For a few very tense moments it was a Mexican standoff--I believe to this day we would have taken at least two, possibly more with us. But there were a minimum of eight bigfoot around us and we heard more coming, very noisily. I should point out to those not familiar with the Midwestern woods in deep summer that it is heavy jungle. You cannot see more than four or five feet--if that--in some areas. I saw one move and stop behind some pond willows. He was the nearest to me so I trained my weapon on him. I heard kind of a choked gurgle behind me--it was my contact--and he hissed that he had seen a bigfoot "the size of a house" zip from one tree to another forty feet ahead on the path we had been following. I heard the crashing sounds myself but did not turn around.

Grunts, huffs, snarls, and the sounds of undergrowth being crushed around us let us know they were not the only two in the area. We heard what sounded like one or two of them beating something hard--not wood--and later assumed they were beating their chests. We heard popping-clacking sounds which we later assumed to be them popping their teeth.

I'll admit it. We were both frightened and thunderstruck. This kind of thing was not supposed to happen in central Indiana in broad daylight. We were outside any frame of reference. It was totally unreal and completely unexpected. We had no idea what to do.

Finally, telepathically, it became clear they had a "leader" of some kind. We could hear/sense/understand that some of them wanted to kill us on the spot. Others were arguing with them. The whole affair was like listening to an old telephone party-line or a room full of people all talking at once. We were terrified and could easily sense they were terrified too, but they were not going to allow us near that old dump in the woods regardless of any casualties-- or killing--they had to accept.

The end was, thankfully, anticlimactic. The 'leader' seemed to come in clearer than any of the others and told us very clearly to lower our weapons. I thought back, "ARE YOU NUTS?"

Again, we were told to lower our weapons, click the safeties back on (he actually used the term "safeties", possibly picked from our minds), and if we did that, we would be allowed to leave. There was a whirlwind of thoughts and emotions going through my head. We were in genuine and immediate danger of being torn apart by what I then considered gigantic animals, and yet these "animals" were willing to let us walk back out the way we came, provided we did them no harm and lowered our weapons. In essence, they were telling us to surrender.

We had no choice. In a dreamlike state, I lowered my weapon. I had control over myself. It was my choice. I just could not believe I was surrendering to an animal.

When I lowered my shotgun and clicked on the safety, I could feel wave after wave of sheer relief. That broke much of the pressure. They were delighted I had done that and thought maybe we would all part that day without any disaster taking place. And I felt relieved too. I wasn't going to be torn apart after killing at least one or more of them. There were simply too many to fight.

My contact kind of lost it down there. I had to walk around to his side, take my left hand, and gently press down on his rifle barrel. His aim was still locked in on the area where he had seen his giant bigfoot take cover on the other side of the trail. And he was in shock. I told him to click his safety on. His answer was to glance at me with eyes as wide as saucers. He was in shock. I was mighty close to it myself, but could function. "We're going home now. Put your safety on and take your finger off the trigger. We're going home. They'll let us out if we just go. We're going home." He later told me he had 'heard' everything that I picked up in my mind, too. He said he even heard me arguing with them. And he knew I wasn't speaking out loud. He just simply could not believe he was taking part in a telepathic process.

It wasn't long after that we were both sitting in his kitchen. His family and my associates said we looked like ghosts walking in the door. We could do little more than babble for several minutes despite the questions they were all hurling at us. We just sat and stared at each other. It would be another full half hour or more before we could begin to tell the story in any kind of coherent manner. And even then it didn't make any sense. And I will be the first to admit that it still doesn't make any sense, at least not in any manner that I can understand.

Several permanent changes in my thinking came about after this:

I walked into those woods willing to kill any bigfoot that challenged me. I walked out strictly a no-kill person, which I remain to this day.

I now know we are not dealing with any kind of mere 'tall ape.' They are more than that. Much more.

I stopped laughing at any or all of the "Twilight Zone" stories that I have heard associated with the presence of bigfoot. Sometimes, I may still have doubts about them, but I damned sure do not dismiss them out of hand.

I remember making two radio calls while we were surrounded to the rest of my team. They all swear I made four. I have no memory of making that many calls. I was telling them to get out of the woods and head for the contact's house and stay there. They said I sounded like a robot, no emotion in my voice. I thought I was almost crying when I made the two calls I remember. They say differently. This remains a mystery.

The bigfoot were very obviously defending that dump. There was some kind of strong reason they did not want us there; a reason they were willing to kill for. I don't know what it was. It could have been females giving birth (the month was July), it could have been something else entirely. I will never know.

Did the bigfoot allow us to leave peacefully--if somewhat addled--because of mercy? Or was it simply because they thought two missing men would only bring more men with more guns? Did they show us a kindness, or did they handle the situation in the manner that gave them the least amount of trouble? Either one? Both? Or did they do it for another reason?

We were never "skunked" with any intensely bad smell. I have no idea why. I have a lot of speculation about that, but no real answers. It's now assumed their 'skunking scent' includes a heavy proportion of hydrogen sulfide (H_2S), which has been proven to knock animals--including human beings--unconscious, seriously warp their sense of time, and even cause serious and permanent lung damage. Why then did they not use this tactic? Could there have been too many together in close proximity? Would they have "skunked" each other? Would this have had a bad effect on the mothers or children being born, if that was the case? And if not, what were they protecting from that scent and the powerful gases within it? Were we all too close to something to make this defensive/offensive weapon of theirs too powerful to use in that area? Again, I don't know, but I'd sure like to.

I've relived and thought about this encounter for four years. I still have many more questions than answers, and the few answers I do have only lead to more speculation and questions. I am certain that the bigfoot have a professional military sense of how to set up ambushes. They picked the ground where they stopped us; we didn't. And it was to their advantage. They could see us clearly. We only got glimpses of them. One of my team members, armed with a telephoto lens on a very good 35mm film camera, took a shot of us coming out of the woods. There is a 'blobsquatch' in the background behind us. It could easily be the play of light and shadow through the trees and brush. If it is not, that bigfoot was much larger than me and my contact combined. We realized that we were being escorted out of the woods. They made no effort to cover the sounds of their movements and I think they were hurrying us along, making sure we didn't change our minds.

I ask you all to consider the powers that a true telepath would have over a human being. They could simply send a message to your mind saying, "You don't see me" and perhaps gain 'invisibility' in that manner. Conversely, they could tell you that something is moving and visible to your right when nothing is actually there, while all the real mischief was going on to your left. Taking this to the extreme, they could force you to walk around one of them in the woods while you would swear by all that's holy it was just a tree, not a living animal standing there watching you. What limits does this power have? What ranges does it work at? Another extreme thought is this--could they simply tell you that it would be a wonderful thing, the best thing in the world, if you put your gun barrel in your mouth and pulled the trigger? This is all sheer speculation. Until such a time comes when we understand this phenomenon more, all we can do is speculate.

But the skunking scent is different. That apparently follows the laws of known physics and science. We need to get a fresh and strong sample of this someday, and someday somebody will. I do not know if a standard military gas mask--the kind sold in Army surplus stores--would protect a researcher with a vacuum bottle attempting to obtain a sample of the skunking gas. But I imagine it will be tried sooner or later.

I wish them luck. It'd take a brave person to try this, but there are many courageous people in this hobby. And happily, there's another generation coming up behind us. I talk to many young people with a deep interest in bigfoot. Possibly some of them will become researchers. And as our technology advances, while it will not make any of us telepaths or invincible to poison gas, it will give them an edge we do not yet possess.

People have been actively searching for bigfoot for over a century now. All we have so far are mere scraps of information. But I believe that will change, that the great days of this research lie in the future, perhaps the near future."

Sometimes people find reason to doubt the authenticity of a person's account only because it is too good, or too vivid; as though the person who submitted the story is some kind of talented novelist or screenwriter. Certainly, Kent Ballard tells his story in a very engaging manner. But knowing Kent for as long as I have, I am very satisfied that Kent is sincere and his account is authentic. Obviously, it is the implications of the account that are so troubling: there are more of these creatures than we realized and they have capabilities that we are a long way from fully understanding. Perhaps these suggestions are much easier to embrace in light of the information gathered and presented in this book from other sources like Allen and April Hoyt, Jim Henry, Kathleen Odom and Toby Johnson that will make Kent's account and his conclusions more believable.

I have been aware of Ron Lewis' and Kent Ballard's accounts for seven years now. Even though it is consistent with the extraordinary claims of others, it is always reassuring if one can test these claims by trying to use some form of telepathic contact, oneself. This is perhaps the ideal, but telepathy seems to be something that some people have more than others. That said, I have heard from a few gifted telepaths who insist that everyone has the skill; one just has to develop it. I am not sure how much of this skill I have been able to develop. In any event, science does not allow the experimenter to participate in the experiment, even though I sometimes do. I still prefer to test these ideas as empirically as possible, by employing a third party who has developed this particular skill set to a considerable degree.

Once, my friend Guy Edwards and I escorted a mutual friend, Dr. Robert Faust, to one of our favorite spots in the Mt. Hood National Forest in the vicinity of the Roaring River Wilderness. It's a place with a pretty good history of sasquatch activity. Once we were comfortably ensconced in the woods, sitting around the campfire, Bob Faust went to work trying to open a channel with the mystical beings that were strongly suspected to inhabit these woods. In no time at all, Bob is in a trance and, by all appearances, dialoging with one of these creatures. It was a fascinating session.

"What is your name?" Bob asked.

"Pulina," was the answer.

"How many of you are there?"

"Two of us...me and my son."

"Where is your mate," Bob inquired.

"The star people took him," was the immediate reply.

(Could this mean he is dead?)

"Will he be back?" Bob continued.

"Yes, I think so, but I don't know when."

Then came the clincher. "Can we see you?" Bob asked, boldly.

Long pause, then, "No."

"Why not?"

"There is one among you who cannot be trusted."

"Yikes!" I thought. I knew who *that* was. I felt like a wanted felon in a donut shop full of policemen. I just wanted to blend into the scenery in the worst way. I had spent years as a BFRO operative, setting cameras in every known bigfoot hotspot. The results were always the same. The suspected sasquatch activity would suddenly shift to another nearby location. The cameras never got the results we were hoping for, but one day April heard a telepathic comment that she never asked for or expected: "Quit trying to trick us!"

Bob adroitly offered the perfect response. "We don't have any cameras. We just want to see you."

"Among our people, it is considered a blunder to be seen by your people. I have never been seen by one of your people. I'm not going to let that happen. Now, I have to go."

"We would love to see you but we respect your wishes. Peace."

Guy and I looked at each other and were probably sharing the identical thought: "That was entertaining. Who needs a television when you have Bob Faust?"

If this putative conversation were the only one of its kind, I guess that I, too, would be inclined to discount it. But it isn't. In presenting this account to other self-proclaimed telepaths, I have received a very consistent reply, "That's exactly what you always get."

The sasquatch are very committed to staying in the shadows. It is essentially their role here on earth. At least one other person who has dabbled in telepathy, Kirk Sigurdson, articulates it this way: among the sasquatch, there are different stations, or roles, that are being lived out. The sasquatch that are fully cooperative with the ETs have access to the subterranean redoubts and perform sometimes arduous tasks on behalf of their agenda. They often raise their young here, in the relative comfort and security of this idyllic planet. As parents, the sasquatch sometimes need to leave their young and take care of other matters. Habituation sites where they can trust the human residents to leave their young ones alone are very valuable to the parents.

When the young become mature and have developed their advanced mental and physical skills, they sometimes leave and venture out 'elsewhere.' Other sasquatch individuals remain here. Sometimes, especially among older sasquatch, they grow to resent the degree of control that must be endured in deference to the ET agenda, whatever that is. These individuals 'go rogue' and live their life on Earth's surface, making a living independent of the comings and goings of the other entities.

Is any of this fact? I cannot prove anything. I can only put the reports I have gathered from seemingly reliable field researchers out there for future researchers or telepaths to consider, to try and verify, or conversely, to refute. Paranormal investigations do not really fall into the category of 'science.' Nothing in this realm is truly testable or verifiable, but that fact does not necessarily render all of these observations or ideas to be false or fake. It is quite possible that events or ideas can be both factual and at the same time unverifiable. This is often, maybe always, the case with the spurious bits of information that are acquired by international spies in the name of 'intelligence gathering.' Paranormal research is more like intelligence gathering than strictly scientific inquiry.

What the 'intel' seems to be saying on the question of communication with the sasquatch, is that it *is* indeed possible. The communication can even be involuntary, especially if you happen to have done something to piss them off, as Ron seems to have done, or even frighten them, as Kent Ballard may have done. The communication does indeed take on the appearance of telepathy. For certain, there seems to be *no* language barrier when this form of communication is used.

The Muse Effect

Although I have certainly tried, I cannot really claim any definite successes with my own attempts to communicate directly with the 'forest people,' also known as the sasquatch. About the only thing I can report from my own personal experience is there may be another, more *one-way* type of communication *from* the sasquatch. Essentially, it takes the form of inspiration. When I am working on a problem, whether it is a literary problem or another kind of problem altogether, it seems that a walk in the woods always generates some very useful ideas. Sometimes the ideas will suddenly and intensely descend upon me, like a collapsing wave at the beach. I have learned to pull out a pad and scribble some notes as the ideas flow, for they are easily lost amid the torrent of other ideas that cascade into my mind from some unknown source. While this whole concept may sound pretty imaginary, it is actually a concept with a very well-established history.

In ancient Greek and Roman cultures, the muses were entities that provided worthy individuals with artistic inspiration. Indeed, the Greeks and Romans both instructed those who searched for the inspiration of the muse to walk to a wild place. For them, the muse was not a force or entity that resided within a person. Rather, they were spirit beings who resided in a specific place in the physical landscape. It was there that one must go to access the phenomenon. In Greek mythology, as described by Pausanias (110-180 A.D.) there were two generations of muses. The first generation of muses were the daughters of Uranus, god of the sky and heavens, and his wife Gaia, the Earth mother. The other generation of muses consisted of the nine daughters of Zeus and Mnemosyne.

In Roman mythology, the muse were synonymous with the 'nymphs of the springs,' which one accessed by going to a specific place, namely a spring. For the Romans, then, flowing fresh water was the realm of the muses. Indeed, I have had the most success with accessing my muses when I venture into my local landscape, especially after dark. Interestingly, I walk along the river for miles. When I do, the muses do indeed provide flashes of inspiration, as long as I know what ideas or questions I want answers to. The Romans may have been on to something. Walking along the river at night definitely works for me every time.

I would encourage anyone who is wrestling with creative challenges to take a walk with their ideas and focus on the questions that they are trying to explore. Naturally, the psychologist would tell us that the muse is just a capability within our brain that is stimulated by the increased blood flow, and maybe the fresh air, that combine to stimulate creative thought. It does seem, however, that the muse effect happens best for me in a very specific patch of woods. That, too, may be nothing more than the powers of suggestion. Whether the muse effect exists internally in our brains or externally as a result of some unseen physical entity, I guess I don't really care.

I tend to side with the Greeks. The muse feels like an external force that one can access if you just give it a chance. Whether it is a spirit being, an ET, or just a mental process that we activate by walking in the woods is not nearly as important as just making the effort to access it. The pursuit of inspiration has never been a purely scientific matter. Artists just do what works for them.

For me, the creative spark is most accessible when I walk in the woods, at night, without a flashlight. That may not be the best move in a more urban environment, but it works for me in the very rural setting in which I reside. Others report that daylight walks can offer as much inspiration as nocturnal strolls. As with most paranormal matters, different things work differently for different people. Like a lot of other paranormal matters, it can be right there in your immediate surroundings, but you won't find it until you go looking for it.

The 'Muse' phenomenon may or may not have anything to do with the sasquatch. It may be a completely separate entity or set of entities within the phantom menagerie that occupies the Goblin Universe. Another entity from Greek mythology that is an excellent candidate for the being we now know as the sasquatch is Pan, the Greek god of fields, groves, and wooded glens. Son of Zeus, Pan was not worshiped in temples, but rather caves, grottoes, and sylvan settings. The analogous figure in Roman mythology was Faunus, but in Greek mythology, Pan was also the god of fertility, spring, and theatrical criticism! Go figure.

Author Jim Brandon suggests in his 1983 book, *The Rebirth of Pan*, that Pan, the god of Nature, is real. Various paranormal phenomena suggest that the Earth itself is alive, and the sasquatch is a creation of this "American earth spirit" that is meant to teach us something. Getting one's hands on a copy of this book is very difficult. 'Jim Brandon' is a pseudonym for the real author, William Grimstad, and the book has long been out of print. The least expensive copy currently sells on Amazon.com for $200.

Regardless of which mythological being is synonymous with the sasquatch of today, I am quite certain that this same set of entities did manifest itself in ancient Europe and elsewhere, thereby earning itself a place in the mythology and theology the Ancients. I have learned to regard the sasquatch as a potential manifestation of the same Muse phenomenon that existed in ancient mythology. This thought has also altered my approach to the investigation of the sasquatch phenomenon, which does manifest itself occasionally in my rural surroundings. On many of the outings I conducted in the name of 'sasquatch research,' I did not take home any tangible evidence much less direct sightings, but I did get some very useful inspiration.

In October of 2002, for example, I was walking in the woods and pondering possible titles for my first book on the sasquatch subject. The very clear thought popped into my head that, "We are *the locals*," and I knew at that moment that I had the title I was looking for.

I will add that it does not seem utterly necessary to *walk* in the woods to access this inspiration. I have a fairly long drive from my rural home to the urban neighborhood where I work, and I have noticed that useful inspiration happens with a certain consistency at two places in my long commute. Both of these places are large tracts of intact forest that envelop the highway. I also found that turning off the car stereo as I approach these two patches of forest improves the chances of extracting useful ideas and inspiration. Essentially, this entire book was written from notes and ideas that were collected on countless walks, and drives, then hastily scribbled, often in the dark, onto a handy notepad.

People who want to tease me about my long-standing interest in the sasquatch will often say to me, "Hey Thom, have you found Bigfoot yet?"

To this I cheerfully reply, "I don't go looking for Bigfoot. I know where Bigfoot lives *and* Bigfoot knows where I live. I leave Bigfoot alone because I know that's what *he* wants, but if Bigfoot wants to find me, he knows where I am."

Notice, I play along with the widely held misconception that the sasquatch phenomenon consists of a single entity whose name is 'Bigfoot.' This is not the fact of the matter, but I have no interest in correcting the misconception. I just baffle the person with a seemingly insane statement that actually contains several grains of truth that are lost on those 'unwashed masses' who are disdainful of the whole bigfoot idea in the first place.

Brian Smith of Walla Walla, Washington was once explaining the Native American 'take' on the sasquatch, as it was explained to him by an elderly member of the Yakama Nation. "They're not starving," he intoned, "but they will accept food 'offerings' if they are appropriately presented. They won't take apples, but they will take an apple pie. They won't take a raw chicken, but they will take one that is baked and sprinkled with a little paprika. They won't accept food that is left on the ground, but they will take it if you leave it on a stump or fallen log."

I carried this thought around for a long time before I finally decided to try it out. It was late summer and there was an abundance of ripening apples in my orchard. I made two pies, one for the family and one for the 'wood nymphs' or whatever they are. That evening, Kirk Sigurdson and I took a drive up to Fish Creek, a tributary of the Clackamas River some thirty miles distant from my house. We parked near the mouth of the creek and headed upstream just as darkness descended. In the absence of a moon, that tract of forest was particularly dark and forbidding. We both carried flashlights but tried not to use them. We walked at least a couple miles before we came to a meadow in the forest, and there we stopped, sat, listened, and thought. I went to the edge of the meadow and hung a grocery sack, containing the freshly baked pie, on the stub of a tree branch. We walked and listened some more, before gingerly making our way back downstream along Fish Creek to Kirk's car.

It was 2 a.m. by the time Kirk dropped me off, and headed home. I took in the cool night air as Kirk drove off, headlights stabbing the dark and tires crackling down the long gravel driveway. I impulsively decided to take a midnight stroll around the property before turning in. Being on a level and very familiar trail, I didn't carry a flashlight. At one point, the trail traverses the base of a very steep hillside that is blanketed with a mature stand of moss-draped maple and cedar trees that typify the mid-latitude rain forests of the Pacific Northwest.

Suddenly, I heard a loud crashing noise emanate from the hillside high above me. I stopped and strained to hear. Having seen deer wandering the property earlier in the day, I assumed that the same deer were just making their nocturnal circuit, as I was. The noise of a creature crashing through the underbrush grew steadily louder, as it descended the steep hillside toward my position. I suddenly felt somewhat vulnerable, standing in the open on that trail. I was still thinking it was probably a deer or even a small herd. What did not make perfect sense was the fact that the hillside that the sounds emanated from was too steep to safely climb or descend, even in daylight. Still, I've seen deer ascend slopes that were too steep for me, so I just accepted the idea that there were deer coming down the hillside toward me, unaware that they were approaching a person standing on the trail in the middle of the night. At that moment I recollected that one of the deer I had seen earlier in the day was a buck with a fully developed set of antlers. If that deer were feeling threatened, it could do some real damage to a guy like me. I decided it would be prudent to get off the trail and find a more defensible location next to a tree.

The leaves crackled beneath my feet as I stepped through the undergrowth, sending the tell-tale sounds of movement through the forest. The forest fell silent. The crashing of feet or hooves came to an immediate halt. I, too, stood motionless and strained to hear. Nothing moved. I waited. Still nothing moved. I waited so long I began to doubt there were still other creatures in the forest near me. At least ten, maybe fifteen minutes elapsed. Still no sounds of movement. At this point, I finally decided I could not stand there all night, waiting for indications of presence. I slowly stepped back down the slope to the trail and made my way along it, feeling for the path with my feet in the absence of any light at all. Just ahead of me and to my left was a bench I had built for sitting and communing with nature. As I approached the bench, which rested at the base of a particularly large cedar tree, I again heard the footfalls and motion descending the slope. Now the sound of crashing through brush had descended the steep hillside to the level of the trail. When the footfalls met trail, the sounds took a new direction, now travelling along the trail right toward me. I quickened my pace, trying to make it to the safety of the trail-side bench before the deer caught up to me. When I felt the bench against my knees, I turned and listened again. Sure enough, the sound of footfalls was still coming down the trail right toward me.

At this point, I was still thinking "deer," in fact I was thinking, "deer with dangerous antlers," so I jumped up on the bench and embraced the tree behind it with both arms, doing my best to put the tree between me and the approaching sounds. I peered out from behind the tree, trying to distinguish the outline of any moving shape or form. I peered into the inky, moonless night, unable to see anything at all. Still, the sound of feet or hooves drew

220

steadily nearer until it felt like it was less than ten feet distant from where I stood on the bench, hugging the cedar tree. Then, all noise and motion stopped. The woods fell completely silent, again. I peered out from behind the tree. What puzzled me most at that point was the extreme darkness of the forest. A few minutes ago, I could make out the vague outline of trees and tall bushes, but now I was essentially blind. Yet, as blind as I felt, I was certain that something was standing right there, motionless, ten feet from me. I had no flashlight but I needed to figure out what the hell was going on, and more to the point, what exactly was confronting me in this nocturnal stand-off. That's when it dawned on me that I actually did have a source of illumination with me: my twelve-dollar Casio digital wristwatch. (These days one would use their phone to illuminate the surroundings. I did not have that option in 2004.) I raised my right wrist and faced the crystal face of the watch in the direction of the trail and pushed the tiny button which caused the number display to illuminate. The tiny, feeble glow of the dial did absolutely nothing to resolve the mystery of exactly what was silently confronting me. Again, I was puzzled by the complete blackness into which I peered. I could not resolve the outline of a single object in my surroundings.

All my attention was now focused in the direction of the apparition confronting me. I held the glowing face of my watch out in a desperate attempt to illuminate whatever it was. Things were about to take a turn for the worse. At that precise moment, from *behind* me came another noise that resembled the sound of someone clearing their throat. At precisely the same moment, I felt something touch the back of my right ear. Had my bladder been full, I'm sure that at that point I would have wet myself. I was simultaneously stunned and terrified. I spun on my heels to face the new threat, still holding the tiny button that illuminated the dial of my wristwatch. Instinctively, I held my watch out, as though it were some sort of *Star Trek* weapon capable of defending me from the unseen forces of evil that surrounded me. I suddenly felt both incredibly vulnerable and incredibly ridiculous.

What I did next, I still do not fully understand. I had often tried to mentally rehearse that which I would do if I were ever confronted with a sasquatch. I resolved to stand my ground, make no threatening gestures, and just try to take it all in. Yet, as Scottish poet Robert Burns wrote, "The best laid plans of mice and men always go asunder." They certainly did in my case. I jumped off that bench and sprinted for the house. How I managed to stay on the narrow bridge that crossed a small creek, I'll never know. I broke out of the woods, and crossed the open pasture, still at a sprint. I arrived at the back deck of my house and caught my breath, then sat down on a lawn chair to unlace my boots.

As I did so, a loud cackle erupted from the impenetrable thickness of an overgrown tree farm on the next-door neighbor's property. It was so loud it positively echoed off of the surrounding hills. I feared it would awaken the neighbors. I turned and looked up at my bedroom window just in time to see the light snap on. I finished removing my shoes and went inside.

"Why are you up?" I asked.

Her only reply was, "What the heck is that noise?"

My wife has always been more skeptical of the 'sasquatch hypothesis,' even as we sometimes heard odd creature calls in the night that didn't quite seem like ordinary coyote howls. So, it was with a certain relish that I answered her question with another question: "So do you agree that *that* is *not* coyotes?"

"In the fifteen years I've lived here, I have *never* heard that sound before."

"You'll be fine. Go back to bed."

I went back outside. I sat down on the back deck and listened some more. Nothing. The overgrown tree farm where the cackling noises originated was only fifty yards and one low fence away from my position. After what I had already been through that night, I wasn't about to go there. Once again, all of one's planned courage melts away like a snowman on a warm spring afternoon. I went back inside and retired for the evening.

It wasn't until the next day, under the comforting light of the midday August sun that I reflected upon the events of the previous night. All at once, I recollected the fact that I had left a fresh pie in the Mt. Hood National Forest earlier in that same evening. It all clicked. After the excitement in the wee hours, I had all but forgotten about leaving the pie up Fish Creek. For the first time, the possibility of a connection between these two events seemed inescapable, even though they happened almost thirty miles apart.

A year or two later, I picked up an essay written by a friend fellow sasquatch researcher, Henry Franzoni. His paper summarized the legends of hairy men that he had gleaned from a host of Native American sources. One particular legend jumped off the page: "Amidst the Clackamas Tribe of the Chinook Nation exists a legend that, among the hairy people who inhabit the upper reaches of the Clackamas River a juvenile sasquatch demonstrate their eligibility for 'manhood' by successfully touching one of the 'hairless people' (us) without being seen."

If there is any truth to that legend, I'd like to think that my clueless behavior of that summer night helped a juvenile sasquatch along his path to manhood. That general thought helps explain the cackle that emanated from the tree farm immediately after the embarrassing encounter at the bench. Somewhere in that grove of overgrown Christmas trees, a few sasquatch were 'high-fiving' each other, and celebrating at least one creature's achievement. If that were so, then the cackling I heard may have been laughter, in which case they may have been having their fun at my expense. I take no offense. I am even honored, for the whole episode also benefitted me greatly in my journey as a student of the paranormal in general, and student of the sasquatch mystery in particular. My paradigm got shifted. I learned that I probably don't need to go 'looking for bigfoot' anymore. The experiences of that August night served as a pretty good indication that they do indeed know where I live, and that they know how to find me.

When I tell people, "I don't look for bigfoot anymore. I let bigfoot find me," it sounds like the most arrogant thought imaginable. I don't have the time or energy to convey the whole story of Fish Creek and the apple pie. It probably wouldn't change their thinking, anyway. Henry Franzoni knows this. He would say, "I cannot tell you what the sasquatch is. If I tried to tell you, you wouldn't believe me. You just have to figure it out for yourself."

True that, Henry. To these wise words I would add only that real understanding of paranormal matters seems to begin with a paradigm shift that pushes the observer right up to the edges of science.

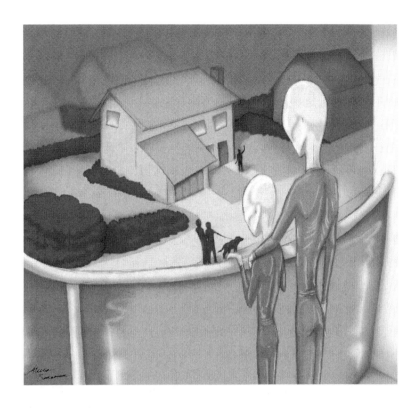

Chapter Eight: The Zoo Hypothesis

When Enrico Fermi estimated, people listened.

Among prominent physicists Fermi had a reputation for making very accurate estimates and projections based on very limited data. So, while working on the hydrogen bomb, three other prominent physicists listened to and remembered Enrico Fermi's off-the-cuff assessment of the possibility that extraterrestrials may be visiting Earth.

Fermi, Edward Teller, Emil Konopinski, and Herbert York were working together at the Los Alamos National Laboratory in 1950 to develop the hydrogen bomb. As the foursome of physicists went out for lunch one day, conversation turned to the recent, well-publicized UFO sighting by pilot Kenneth Arnold. It was Kenneth Arnold who first used to phrase 'flying saucer' to describe the fast-moving crafts he saw while piloting his light plane near Mt. Rainier, Washington.

As they walked to the restaurant, the physicists discussed the sighting and the probability that it was indicative of life existing elsewhere in the cosmos. Fermi did what he was famous for: making quick calculations with impressive accuracy. It was Fermi's view that there *should be* advanced civilizations elsewhere in the galaxy. He went on to speculate that not only should extraterrestrials have visited Earth by now, but they probably would have first visited Earth a long time ago. The conversation again shifted, this time to a discussion of the chances of achieving faster-than-light travel. At the lunch table, the conversation ranged to other topics but then, out of the blue, Fermi blurted out, "Where are they?"

Despite the lack of any clear conversational connection, the other physicists immediately and uniformly understood what Fermi was referencing. His fertile mind was still puzzling over why there were no conspicuous extraterrestrial visitors here on Earth. He couldn't let go of the idea that they should exist and they should have made their presence known by now. This contradiction, the lack of evidence of extraterrestrial visitors, despite the fact that they *ought* to be here by now, has become known as the 'Fermi Paradox.'

Fermi couldn't let it go. They must be here. Maybe they *are* here. What if they're here and we just can't see them? To Fermi, it seemed like a logical possibility, maybe even a probability. In that case, we would be just like animals in the zoo, blissfully ignorant of the fact that we are being observed by unseen entities. Are we captive? Are we simply entertainment? Are we being managed for some utilitarian purpose?

People want to see the animals that their tax dollars pay for, but the animals in the zoo are much better off when they cannot see the zoo patrons. More and more, modern zoo keepers understand that if the animals cannot see the public and the zoo keepers, they behave much more naturally. They get less stressed. They interact more normally with each other. Previously unattainable goals like reproduction begin to happen. More and more, in order to facilitate these objectives, zoo keepers employ two-way mirrors that let zoo patrons see in while staying out of sight of the animals on exhibit.

When all is said and done, then, *we* could be the animals in the zoo, Fermi concluded, and that thought has become known as the 'zoo hypothesis.' It's a scientific guess; a hypothesis, but it suitably addresses the nagging question of why we never see the ETs, even as logic dictates that they must be here.

In a way, this is a very comforting thought. It means we will never have to defend ourselves from alien invasion, any more than the animals in your local zoo have to worry about a human invasion. After all, why would we invade a zoo that we already own and control?

On the other hand, if we accept the zoo hypothesis, one of Hollywood's favorite movie themes, alien invasion, becomes absolutely irrelevant. No worries. There are just as many new movie themes that come to mind if we accept the zoo hypothesis. In fact, that theme has already been exploited by screenwriters. The 'prime directive,' as articulated in a few episodes of *Star Trek*, dictates that more advanced space-faring cultures must not interfere with the affairs of the unsuspecting beings that inhabit the planets they visit. If ETs made their presence known to the local population, it would upset the delicate balance on any planet, including ours. It would destabilize the natural function and evolution of the resident species. Just like the sign at the zoo: "Please don't feed the animals."

I guess a few more philosophical questions arise if we are to take the zoo hypothesis seriously. *Why* would extraterrestrials be so interested in planet Earth? They don't appear to be plundering our most precious natural resources like petroleum or gold. We're doing that pretty well without any help.

What else could we possibly have that they would travel so far to get? It may be wrong to assume they want anything at all. We go to the zoo to satisfy our curiosity about the other members of the animal kingdom and that's about it. We don't hunt the zoo animals or take their resources. In fact, we go out of our way to make their lives stable and happy. If the analogy is correct, then we are a similar scientific curiosity. Let's hope so. That means we enjoy a measure of protection from our unseen captors.

The very first modern author to think and write extensively on this whole question was not Enrico Fermi; it was American writer Charles Fort (1874-1932). His writings were very popular in his lifetime and are still widely read. Fortean phenomena, as they came to be known, were the mysterious events of his time that Fort assiduously collected. He attributed some of the mysterious events that occur on Earth to extraterrestrial visitation of planet Earth. Fort was also convinced that alien abduction of humans was occurring, and he was the first modern thinker to publish this radical perspective. Charles Fort used to say that, "The Earth is a farm." In light of a previous chapter of this book, I would have to add, that if Earth is a farm, we may be the crop. The most likely reason for extraterrestrial visitation of Earth is for purposes of harvesting human genetic material. It may not be limited to human genetic material, but human genetic material would certainly be a very valuable, maybe *the* most valuable terrestrial commodity.

Increasingly, electronic and print media have taken on the question of ancient aliens. Logically, it implies that extraterrestrial interest in the affairs on planet Earth may be so longstanding that indeed there exists an alternative to evolution and natural selection when pondering the origins of humanity. The idea that our God or gods would fit the modern definition of extraterrestrials is an idea that has been circulated so thoroughly and persistently that no one, I think, can be shocked by this suggestion.

Let's take another look at the zoo hypothesis in light of what Charles Fort, and others, have written. Fermi was suspicious of the possibility that extraterrestrials come and go from planet Earth, but he could not really devise an answer to his one famous question: "Where are they?" Fermi was an exceedingly bright guy but he may have missed the answer to his famous question. We may not be as bright as Fermi, but we do have access to new sources of information that Fermi did not have. Certain modern scientific discoveries in seemingly unrelated fields may point us toward an answer to Fermi's famously unanswered question, "Where are they?"

Could they be hiding in other dimensions or moving too fast for us to see? If Occam's razor is correct, then the simplest answer is the preferred answer. In that case, a one word answer might merit the greatest consideration. Here is a one word answer: They're *underground*. The extraterrestrial phenomenon may originate from elsewhere in the galaxy, but, once it intersects with our planet, it may emanate from underground redoubts (hiding places). It may not be possible to *prove* this, but there exists some totally overlooked *evidence*.

Mima Mounds

My first awareness of the Mima Mounds came while I was actively investigating bigfoot sightings for the BFRO. I saw one report come in that no one else wanted to touch. If it wasn't baloney, it was decidedly paranormal; probably the most unusual sighting report I have ever encountered. The woman who submitted the report, thirty-one year old Angela Cawthon, claimed that she and her mother saw a sasquatch-like being in the parking lot of the Mima Mounds Natural Area and it was dressed in an awkward combination of men's and women's clothing.

Angela offered a pretty good description on the on-line form. She also offered her phone number and promised to elaborate further if she were called. I obliged her request. Angela and her mother were travelling I-5 on their way home from Seattle. They were looking for a break from the monotonous freeway driving and they saw the Mima Mounds, only a couple miles off the Littlerock exit, just south of Olympia, Washington. They decided to check them out.

As they pulled into the parking lot, they observed another couple walking toward the woods that surrounded the parking area. As they drew nearer to the pedestrian couple, Angela's eye was caught by one person's unusual physical proportions as well as their very strange choice of outfits.

Here are Angela's words that described what she and her mother saw as they pulled into the parking lot for the Mima Mounds Natural Area:

"It had on a brand new red sweatshirt with a hood. The hood was pulled up on the head, but not tightened around the face. It was wearing sunglasses. They were medium sized but did not sit close to the eyes. I could see behind them from the side as it passed. Over the sweatshirt, it had on a new red knit sweater that buttoned up the front. It was pulling up the top corner of it to try to cover its face. It was carrying a bundle up under the sweatshirt and sweater with the other arm. It had on a brand new pair of bright yellow men's work gloves like the leather ones with the big stiff cuffs that you would buy at Home Depot. Amazingly, it was also wearing a red skirt that hung down just below the knee. It looked to be a finer knit. It had on shear black pantyhose and through them I clearly saw matted thick dark fur, in lumps, with no skin showing through. It also wore tennis shoes which were brand new and white, as if they just came out of the box.

When it passed our car, it was no more than twenty feet away; the distance of the parking space we would have turned into. It was loping quickly along the sidewalk at the front of the parking spaces. It was larger than most large men. It hunched slightly forward as if it were being pelted by heavy rain. When it turned to look at us, it twisted its upper body from the waist up.

I could not see fine details of the face, just a darkness where the eyes would be, and the rest of the face was thick fur. I did not see the nose. The gloved fist holding the sweater up was covering it. When my mother and I went over what we saw, I asked her if she thought the face was wrapped in some kind of scarf. We both agree that there was no scarf.

I am 31 years old. I have seen many strange things in my life, but never before have I been stricken with fear through my soul, even before I had a chance to see the object that would make me so afraid. It was as if this thing was emanating fear itself and wanted us to be very afraid and go away immediately, no questions asked, which we did.

I would like to think that that thing was a bigfoot. What is most prominent in my memory, even now, is the powerful fear that I felt and that it was instantaneous and extremely strong and deep and hit me the instant we drove around the trees into the view of the creature. The fear struck, as I said, before we even really knew someone/something was there. This indicates to me that it was not

230

a bigfoot, but something more frightening; something not of this world.

I am shy to admit or talk of the possibility of this, but I have felt desperate fear before. I know what I experienced in those cases were nothing like this creature, and the fear was from within myself, from fearing what I did not know or understand. The fear that came from the thing at the mounds was pressed into me from the outside. Like an electric shock, it was pounded right through me, intensely and deliberately. This experience was different because of where the fear came from. It was not mine."

This sighting report, submitted in 2002, was my introduction to the Mima Mounds. Since this report was so unique, even among sasquatch reports, I can't blame anyone for dismissing it as fiction. After seeing this report, I decided I needed to know more about this Mima Mounds place, which I had never heard of before. I also gave the witness a call.

Indeed, Angela thanked me for giving her a serious listen, for she confided that she expected to be dismissed, even though she insisted she was on the level. One of the things that impressed me about this report was that it carried a ring of truth, especially in the manner in which the witness described her peculiar sense of projected fear. In my experience, sasquatch eyewitnesses sometimes describe a very similar sensation, especially when they find themselves in very close proximity to one of these mysterious beings. It seems like the sense of fear and foreboding was being projected at Angela and her mother from the moment they pulled into the parking area. I suspect that the two women stumbled upon a situation of which they were not welcome to be a part. Clearly, they were being repelled just like Toby, Todd and Beth experienced (Chapter 4, London Calling). I mentioned this to Angela on the phone. She wholeheartedly agreed. She and her mother felt utterly unwelcome and they never even got out of the car. They just got the heck out of there. It's hard to say what was going on that day at the Mima Mounds, but Angela and her mother, for whatever reason, were probably showing up at the wrong place at the wrong time, and they were effectively made to feel that way.

Angela's report also bears a certain similarity to other reports that surface in the world of UFO research. There are other reports of a sasquatch wearing clothing but it is generally a single item of clothing: a torn white t-shirt, an Oakland Raiders jacket, and other single items of sartorial adornment. I have never investigated another reported sighting of a sasquatch wearing a combination of Home Depot work wear and full-on drag. There are, however, numerous reports of apparent extraterrestrials that were doing a bad job of blending in by virtue of their clumsy, if not ridiculous attire. We are told by UFO researchers that there are multiple categories of extraterrestrials: the grays, the reptilians, Swedish-looking humanoids, and the 'wookies,' that is, sasquatch-like extraterrestrials. With all this in mind, I am inclined to think that the sartorially-challenged tourist that Angela Cawthon observed in the Mima Mounds parking lot was perhaps an extraterrestrial. Of course, there are those who feel that all sasquatch are ultimately extraterrestrial in origin, and that possibility cannot be categorically ruled out.

One must also wonder what this extraterrestrial, or sasquatch, or both, was doing in the parking lot of the Mima Mounds Natural Area. I have only one guess: sightseeing. I discovered that the Mima Mounds were at the center of a long-standing scientific debate. There was absolutely no agreement as to how they were formed.

The next time I travelled the I-5 interstate south of Olympia, Washington, I took the Littlerock exit for a look at the Mima Mounds. Nothing of interest took place when I pulled into the empty parking lot, but I certainly took an extra long look around before I got out of the car. I took a few photos of the mounds, read all the interpretive placards, and walked around. I recall that there was also a lot of distant gunfire. There was a nearby shooting range and apparently it was so well-established that one of the interpretive signs mentioned that gunfire could be coming from a nearby gun range. It was not, according to the sign, a threat to visitor safety. As I walked around the Mima Mounds, I could find no reason why the place would be of any particular interest to the terrifying apparition that Angela and her mother encountered. I did learn, from studying the interpretive signs, that there were several competing theories to explain the formation of these mysterious geologic features.

The Mima Mounds as seen from the air.

I kept reading about the continent-wide mound phenomenon and the fact that Mima-style mounds occur worldwide. They are still called Mima mounds, even when they occur in far-flung places. The mounds near Mima, Washington were among the first to be scientifically studied. That makes the Mima Mounds in Washington the 'type-locality' for these geologic structures world-wide. Mima doesn't even exist anymore, but the village of Mima did exist when the mounds were first studied by prominent University of Washington geologist, J Harlan Bretz. It was Bretz (whose first name really was the single letter "J"), who first named the curious configurations in the 1930s. Since then, other mound fields have been found at various locations all around the North American continent.

A ground-level photo of Mima Mounds Natural Area, Littlerock, Washington

The more I read about the place, the more I could see that it really is a scientific enigma, and that none of the various theories as to the origin of the mounds stand up to serious scrutiny. When I then learned that these mound fields are found all over the place, the mystery widened even more. Still later, I learned that Mima-like mound fields are found in some of the same places where lots of sasquatch reports originate, including northern California, southeast Oklahoma, and southern Ohio. That's when I first began to wonder whether the mound phenomenon had some sort of connection to other paranormal phenomena, such as the sasquatch, extraterrestrials, or both.

Mima-style mounds typically consist of a well mixed combination soil and rock. The mounds typically range from six to eight feet high and about twice that width at the base. Mima mounds appear to consist of about one very big dump truck load of rearranged or moved earth. They also contain much more organic matter than the surrounding soil. There is no clear layering as one finds in all undisturbed soils that form in place. Often, the crushed rock fragments in Mima mounds do not match the local rock. There is no one characteristic that all Mima mound fields have in common. Some Mima mounds consist of local material, but other mound fields are made from material that has been moved from somewhere else. Certain mounds, such as ones in Louisiana and California, contain rock that seems to have come from great depth.

Shading indicates larger mound field localities in the U.S.(Reprinted from *The Rebirth of Pan*, by Jim Brandon, 1983)

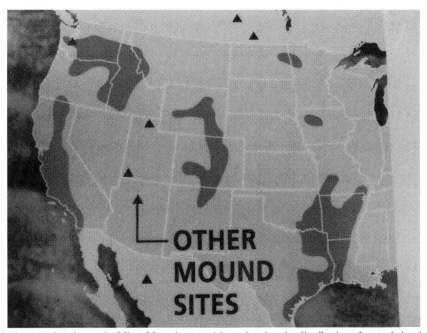

An interpretive sign at the Mima Mounds natural Area showing the distribution of mound sites in the western U.S. Note it generally agrees with Jim Brandon's map from *The Rebirth of Pan* (previous page).

Mima mounds have many other locally used names. In the far western U.S. they are called hogwallow mounds, biscuit mounds, or Mima mounds. In the Gulf coast, they are called pimple mounds. In the upper Midwest, they are variously known as natural prairie mounds, pimpled prairies, freckled lands, and prairie blisters. Geologists generally use the term Bretz coined: Mima mounds.

Mound fields are not limited to North America. They also occur in South America and Africa, and Europe. Mysterious mounds also occur on the moon, where circular mounds of unknown origin occur on the floor of King Crater, on the backside of the moon.

King Crater on the Moon. Mysterious mound formations are pimple-like formations seen in the top third of the crater. (NASA photo taken on Apollo 16 mission.)

There is absolutely no consensus as to how Mima mounds occur, but there certainly are theories. One early researcher, E.W. Schmidt, considered them to be anthropic, meaning they were built by humans. Indeed, there are elaborate and artistically formed mounds in Ohio that are widely attributed to early

Native American tribes. The Serpent Mounds of Ohio, and other extensive mounds, are attributed to the Edena and Hopewell cultures, two prehistoric Indian tribes with mysterious origins. There are paranormally-inclined researchers who insist that the presence of rare elements like iridium suggest that these mounds have an extraterrestrial origin. In any case, the presumed anthropic origin of the mound fields in Ohio has opened up a debate as to which mound fields around the continent are natural phenomena and which ones are anthropic (man-made).

Other suggestions for the origin of Mima mounds fall into five general categories:

1. Erosional (water or wind)
2. Depositional (glacial outwash debris or river deposits)
3. Shrink/swell (some kind of uneven soil heaving, presumably due to freezing and thawing)
4. Seismic (earthen piles formed by violent earthquakes)
5. Biotic (formed by the action of fossorial (burrowing) animals.

Mounds are found in so many places with such varied landscapes that one thing seems to be agreed upon by all researchers: All mounds do not have the same origin. Indeed, one researcher even observed that no two mound fields are exactly the same. That said, the favored scientific theory at present, for the origin of most mound fields throughout the continent can be summarized in two multisyllabic scientific words:

Polygenetic Bioturbation

Polygenetic: multiple sources of origin (*poly*: many; *genesis*: origins)
Bioturbation: disturbed or moved by living things (*bio*: living; *turbation*: disturbances)

OK, they're basically saying mounds throughout the continent are being formed by a variety of living things that are moving the soil around in their search for food or to create domiciles. The principal suspect is gophers, specifically pocket gophers (*Geomyidae thomomys*), but other fossorial suspects include ground squirrels, prairie dogs, ants (specifically Towne ants), and badgers. Particularly in the mound field near Mima, Washington, pocket gophers are very definitely the favored explanation. All other possible explanations (earthquakes, glacial melting, erosion, and deposition) have been thoroughly discredited by careful scientific scrutiny.

While pocket gophers may be the principal suspects, there are some very definite problems with this theory. First of all, no population of pocket gophers, or any other fossorial (burrowing) animal *currently* lives in the Mima Mound complex! That means pocket gophers built the mounds over thousands of years and hundreds of generations, then completely and utterly moved out, for no apparent reason. Further, pocket gopher populations live in many locations, including my own yard, yet they build no mounds. Indeed, moles make bigger hills in my yard than the pocket gophers. The thinking goes that pocket gophers build the mounds as domiciles for their colony when the water table is near the surface or where solid bedrock is very near the surface. They build the mounds when the soils are not thick. It is thought that the critters are making domiciles by piling up the earth so that the lodges don't flood when the water table rises during the rainy season. Since pocket gophers do not currently inhabit most Mima mounds, it begs the question of why they would go to so much effort to create these homes, then leave.

Still other problems exist with the pocket gopher theory. No one has ever seen pocket gophers build huge mounds. Kangaroo rats have been observed to build mounds in parts of New Mexico. Two adult kangaroo rats can build a three foot high mound in just twenty-three months. Kangaroo rat mounds are smaller and much more irregular than the massive and densely spaced mounds that characterize the Mima-style mounds. Badgers, with their muscular bodies and impressive claws, are very efficient at moving the earth. Unlike pocket gophers, they also currently occupy mound fields throughout the western U.S. Still, they favor arid regions and so there are absolutely no badgers in the rainy climate of the Mima Mounds in western Washington. In other places around the western U.S. where badgers do build mounds, they are low, messy affairs with very large cavities throughout, owing to the size of the hefty bodies that must travel through the tunnels that they construct. Badgers did not build the Mima Mounds proper, and badgers are not likely candidates for most Mima-style mounds found in other regions.

The mound phenomenon, on a continent-wide basis, does coincide with a whole suite of other burrowing animals, but several scientists dispute the view that these critters even made the mounds that they currently occupy. A.L. Washburn (1988) contends that gophers and other burrowing animals opportunistically move into the pre-existing mounds that are formed by some other mysterious process. He further asserts that gopher activity actually accelerates the *destruction* of the mounds, not their formation. Mounds atop the Laguna geologic formation near Merced, California are aligned in straight rows (Reed and Amundsen, 2012). No one has any idea what kind of burrowing rodent is capable of creating mounds in straight rows.

In the Midwest, especially Ohio and Wisconsin, the general term 'anthropic' is used because not all human-built mounds are burial mounds. Some mounds are thought to be earthen lodges. Burial mounds contain artifacts and even bones. Some burial mounds in the Midwest have rodent tunnels in them, suggesting that rodents do indeed move into mounds that were originally anthropic in origin.

Sometimes, natural mounds are also used for burial, especially in localities where digging is difficult due to a high water table or thin, rocky soils. The dome-shaped Mima mounds, and the conical shaped mounds found in other parts of North America absolutely lack any kind of artifacts. Anthropologists are so confident that most mounds are *not* anthropic in origin that they raise no objection when the mounds are obliterated for farming. In Iowa, 80% of the mounds that once existed have been plowed under. A similar percentage of the mounds in California's Central Valley have been obliterated for farming.

This fact may actually be a bit of a clue. Mounds are made from very fertile soil. They contain lots of organic matter and thoroughly mixed soil with no natural layering (horizons). When rocks are present in mounds, they are small. Often but not always, the rocks are broken up rock fragments. Mounds generally occur on ground that has a high water table, or on very thin soils that lie atop solid bedrock. Mounds are only rarely found atop well drained, fertile soils. They are so often found on poorly drained landscapes that one early geologist suggested that mounds were *put there* by someone or something to "create *terra firma* from the water world." Farmers throughout the west found that plowing the mounds under made excellent farmland. This is a big reason why so many mounds no longer exist to study. Interestingly, in Mima, the whole south end of the historic mound field *was* flattened for farming. It is now occupied by Weyerhaeuser's Mima Tree Farm.

One of the most fascinating bits of Mima Mound research was an attempt to put a date to the formation of Mima mounds. Concentrating his efforts on four mound fields around the Columbia River basin, a mound researcher named Fryxell found that mounds in two locations were constructed over a period of 14,000 years, and at the other two locations, the mounds were built over a period of 3,000 years. Of greatest interest, Fryxell found that mound formation at all four locations stopped at the same time, 7,500 years ago. Since then, there has been no mound formation at any of the four sites he studied.

One unprovable statement kept coming back to me: the suggestion that the mounds were put there by someone or something to "create terra firma from the water world." As I pondered the question of mounds one day, that thought seemed to resonate with the words of Charles Fort: "The earth is a farm." This set me to thinking about conversations I have had with devotees of other paranormal phenomena. Many a UFO researcher will insist that mysterious crafts may sometimes come from space, but as often as not, they emanate from underground. Indeed, there also exists Unidentified Submerged Objects (USOs) that seem to emanate from underwater hideouts.

From a host of such observations, UFO researchers theorize that there are underground and underwater redoubts that are safe havens for extraterrestrials that visit planet Earth. Indeed, the 'hollow Earth' idea has been around for decades, but modern ET researchers hasten to point out that this suggestion is misleading. Certainly, the interior of the Earth is molten hot as we get to the lower parts of the crust and into the mantle. For this reason, the possibility that there are habitable cavities deep in the Earth's crust seems highly unlikely. Does that mean there cannot be large subterranean bases? Not even close. There are many, many mountain peaks, especially in volcanic and limestone terrain that could contain very large natural cavities. Large cavities in mountains and hills would be every bit as removed from the searing heat of the Earth's interior as is the Earth's surface upon which we live.

Recently, I was having a conversation with Oregon's most distinguished and insightful sasquatch researcher, Henry Franzoni. It is Henry's considered opinion that the sasquatch very definitely emanate from underground. Henry insists that not only do the sasquatch have subterranean hideouts, but they are very large. When I pressed him for how he happens to be so certain of this, all he would say is that it is widely held by informed Native American sources. Further, Henry observes that sasquatch activity seems to emanate from known cave country. Beyond that, Henry asserts, it just makes good logical sense. The only question becomes how these subterranean redoubts are accessed yet so well hidden from prying human eyes. The most obvious answer to this question is that entrances to subterranean cavities are made through bodies of water.

New Agers have long insisted that aliens, sasquatch, and still other entities emanate from a large redoubt within the enormous composite volcano known as Mt. Shasta in northern California. I have heard the same thing from Native American sources in reference to other locations. Mt. Adams in western Washington is a location that gets a lot of mention. Like Shasta, Adams is a dormant composite volcano that has erupted in historical times. There are most certainly large cavities that have been vacated by molten rock as a consequence of these historical eruptions. Volcanic landscapes are typically riddled with long hollow lava tubes. Many of them, like Ape Cave near Mt. St. Helens, are well known. Many more probably are not.

Mt. Adams sits astride the border of the Yakama Indian Reservation, rendering half the mountain 'off limits' to non-Indians. Local Indian lore supports the view that Mt. Adams is also a place of sacred mystery. But the snow-capped peak is also a dormant volcano that periodically erupts. It seems too active to allow for a long-term subterranean base of some sort that is hidden from humanity.

In trying to reconcile the history of volcanic activity with the Yakama Indian view that the mountain is a haven for mysterious beings, one must study the eruptive history of Mt. Adams. There have indeed been numerous eruptions of Mt. Adams in the not so distant past, but, just east of Mt. Adams is Goat Butte; a shield volcano that has not erupted in 200,000 years! If one were looking for a stable formation beneath which one might find a huge natural cavity, Goat Butte is an excellent candidate. Or, a large cavity could be constructed beneath the huge, thick, cooled lava disc of the shield volcano that is Goat Butte. The fact that Goat Butte is also on the Yakama Reservation is a bonus from the point of view of anyone that may wish to be left alone.

If a huge cavern were created beneath Goat Butte or another such feature, then large amounts of tailings (mine waste) will be generated. Hundreds of tons of crushed rock is going to have to be disposed of somewhere. Depending on the size of these underground caverns, a potentially enormous amount of debris is going to have to be stashed somewhere on the Earth's surface. That brings us right back to the Mima Mound phenomenon. Dollops of rock and soil appear to have been deposited around the continent in such a manner that it actually benefits humanity. By leveling the piles of earth, excellent farm land is generated out of land that was not suitable for agriculture in its original form.

In the process of investigating the Mima Mounds, I tried to take on some of the paranormal possibilities as well as the ones that are acceptable to conventionally minded scientists. One website that focused primarily on extraterrestrial matters even suggested that Mima Mounds continent-wide are put there just to confuse scientists.

This idea was thought-provoking but somehow incomplete. It makes a bit more logical sense to suppose that the mounds exist for a more utilitarian purpose, namely to get rid of unwanted material, but perhaps the mounds are still configured with an eye toward confusing scientists who seek to understand their origin. An ET presence on planet Earth would be presumably astute in all ways. Not only would staying out of sight be a priority, but so would there be an expectation that all changes to the planet, like changes to a zoo, must be beneficial, not detrimental to life on the planet. Concealing tunneling waste would be a priority, but reconditioning it into useful, arable soil would accomplish multiple objectives. Sophisticated ETs would place a high priority upon multiple agendas. Doing things to the Earth, and on the Earth, that accomplish only a single purpose would not be the hallmark of an advanced culture.

One morning I was standing in my yard, drinking a cup of coffee and patrolling my garden for slugs. I was also thinking about how the mysterious mound phenomenon might somehow relate to my suspicion that ETs and sasquatches are operating out of underground hideouts. I stared blankly at the compost pile in one corner of the garden. All of a sudden, the compost pile came into sharp focus and at that moment, a light bulb came on in my brain and the answer to my question appeared like a lightning bolt. The mounds are compost!

Composting is one of two miraculous processes that occur naturally on planet Earth. The other one is photosynthesis. Both processes are essential to maintain terrestrial life on Earth. The thing that makes these processes miraculous is that, even with all our modern technology, humanity has not learned how to artificially duplicate these remarkable processes, nor do we really need to. The planet seems to be almost hard-wired to encourage these processes to happen without any help. Photosynthesis and composting happen all by themselves, and thank heavens that they do. Without composting we would have very little soil, and without photosynthesis, we would have very little oxygen and way too much carbon dioxide in our atmosphere.

As a gardener, all this knowledge was stored away in my brain, thanks to detailed articles I had read in numerous issues of *Organic Gardening*. It all became suddenly relevant as I pondered Charles Fort's, and Enrico Fermi's view that extraterrestrials must be operating in the shadows right here on planet Earth. As Henry Franzoni, and countless others have said over the years, they must be staying out of sight by working out of large subterranean hideouts. That's when it occurred to me that, if potentially sizeable populations of beings are comfortably ensconced right here on Earth and right under our noses, they must be very good at concealing their presence. Being extremely advanced, they must also be very efficient at recycling the inevitable waste products of their existence. They're not going to produce glass, plastics, and other non-recyclables. They would have to get rid of all that somehow, and that would complicate their existence in ways that any advanced culture would have learned to avoid.

No matter how efficient and advanced the ETs are, their underground bases are going to unavoidably generate two types of waste. One would be tailings from ongoing excavations. The other would be biological waste. The biological waste from an underground series of bases might be huge, depending on the number of beings that occupy these citadels. The biological wastes and the tunneling debris, in their raw form, would be too recognizable, providing too much of a clue as to what is really going on underground. The prying eyes of intelligent humans must be distracted.

To accomplish this, a certain reconditioning of the waste would be necessary. The easiest way to accomplish this is to mix the biological waste with the crushed rock and soil. Then allow biotic action to heat it up and compost it. Composting is a natural means of cooking down the biological material into an unrecognizable, untraceable, but highly valuable soil amendment. Then, it would be necessary to move the stuff a certain distance away from the places where it is generated in order to avoid providing too much of a clue as to its point of origin. The Mima Mounds are eighty miles distant, as the extraterrestrial crow flies, from Mt. Adams. Mt. Rainer is fifty miles from the Mima Mounds. Mound fields in the central valley of California are very similar distances from Mt. Shasta, a proverbial ET redoubt in that state. These would by no means represent the only possible locations of subterranean extraterrestrial bases. Indeed, if there is anything to this whole line of thinking, the mound phenomenon on a global scale may suggest the scope of the subterranean activity. If that were true, then the scope of the subterranean activity is absolutely staggering, given the sheer volume of material that is represented by the mound phenomenon world-wide.

Some mound fields probably *are* created by some natural process such as burrowing rodents. It then becomes possible that highly intelligent beings understand this very well and are actively trying to obfuscate, that is, confuse the situation, by leaving the tailings of their excavations in configurations that look like natural or anthropic features. That would render some mounds we find to be the result of natural earth processes. Other mounds may indeed be 'anthropic.' Other mounds are probably the work of extraterrestrials; although 'extraterrestrial' might not be the best term for beings that live here, at least temporarily.

In any case, the scientifically acceptable phrase, 'polygenic bioturbation' actually fits all these scenarios, including the paranormal one, to a tee. Polygenic means multiple sources of origin, but it does not confine those sources to rodents or even terrestrial beings in general. Bioturbation means that material is disturbed and even transported from elsewhere. Again, this is completely consistent with some very paranormal possibilities such as subterranean excavations by very intelligent biological beings. Any way you slice it, polygenic bioturbation is the correct phrase, even if one embraces the admittedly far-out possibility that at least some mounds, on a world-wide level, are tell-tale indications of large-scale excavations that have occurred or are still occurring somewhere beneath the surface of the Earth.

Perhaps two or more separate paranormal phenomena intersect underground. It's an idea that has been around for a long time: the sasquatch and the extraterrestrials are somehow in cahoots. It's a pretty simple concept, really. When it comes to managing the farm (Earth), you need a combination of brains and brawn. The ETs are the brains, and the sasquatch are the brawn. And the farm house (or 'the office' if you will), is actually a *series* of offices. If ETs *must* be here as Enrico Fermi postulated, then they must have offices or bases somewhere and these redoubts, as Henry Franzoni and others speculate, *must* be underground.

Personally, the idea of living underground sounds dismally cold, dark, damp, and decidedly unappealing. If there are subterranean bases, they must have a way of modifying the surroundings to provide some much needed bright light and fresh air.

What defies understanding, though, is how a very large amount of subterranean material is moved tens or miles from its point of origin. It implies the existence of technologically advanced, presumably aerial earth-movers. Do the ETs drive aerial dump trucks? Yes. One interesting detail of the Mima

Mounds and some other mound fields is that the bases of the mounds are concave. They penetrate into the ground they rest upon more deeply at the center of the mound than they do at the edges.

If fifteen cubic yards of earth were dropped upon the ground from a height of ten feet or more above the ground, then the material would impact the ground with such force that it would compress the soil it landed upon. That compression would be deeper at the center of the mass than at the edges of the pile. This is exactly what one sees in the rare instances when a mound is excavated so it can be viewed in cross section. When we view a mound in cross section, we also see that the earth that comprises the mound consists of a different, darker solid than the soil horizon upon which they rest.

The concave base of mounds has been noted by researchers of other mound fields around the continent. It begins to appear that many of North America's mounds were formed from material that was dumped onto the earth, all at once, from a certain height above the ground. If the material was placed gently on the ground by ancient Indians or just pushed into piles by the action of fossorial rodents, the mounds would not show these convex bases.

What cannot be provided in this discussion is definitive proof that extraterrestrials and/or sasquatches are operating out of subterranean bases. It is an undeniable fact that the most secure places on Earth, where the military and key government officials plan to go in the event of nuclear attack, are large underground installations. The most famous of these citadels sits beneath the Greenbrier Hotel in rural West Virginia. This shelter was built during the Cold War, it was a big secret at the time, but it is no longer used as a potential shelter for Congressmen. During its construction it was code named Project Greek Island, and the on-site supervisor was Fritz Bugas. Raven Rock Military Complex in Adams County, Pennsylvania, is another extensive underground military bunker that is in active use today.

Anyone who asserts that large underground installations are impractical or technically impossible is quite naïve. Many such enclaves have been built by mere humans, and some of them, like Project Greek Island were quite opulent in their day.

The real question is not whether subterranean establishments exist, but whom, exactly, is using them. Specifically, do extraterrestrials currently reside on planet Earth in 'Greek Island' citadels at various subterranean locations around the planet? Enrico Fermi, one of the planets most gifted technical thinkers ever, thought they must be here, but he could never quite come up with the specifics of their whereabouts. Indirectly then, the Mima Mound phenomenon, as it manifests itself continent-wide, seems to suggest a solution to Fermi's unanswered question, "Where are they?"

This mound in the Mima Mound complex has been excavated to provide a cross-section view. Notice that the mound extends deeper into the surrounding soil at the thickest point in the mound. All excavated mounds show this same structural feature. The surrounding soil is also a paler shade than the mound material.

As far-fetched as it may seem to some, it is not nearly as far-fetched as the suggestion that is made by ostensibly serious scientists that fossorial rodents are the force responsible for moving enormous amounts of earth into piles of uniform size, uniform shape, and uniform spacing. No example of such industrious and ingenious rodent behavior can be found among currently-existing rodent populations anywhere on Earth. Perhaps the most telling detail is the fact that the mounds are indented upon the ground upon which they rest. The implication that the material was dumped upon the Earth all at once is the only explanation I can devise. The linear arrangement of certain mound fields, and the fact that mounds contain rock fragments that match formations found at great depth, is impossible to explain within the dominant scientific paradigm of fossorial rodents.

The Hum

As a science teacher, I often get asked by the students how they might earn "extra credit" to improve their grade. First I give the standard teacher reply: "How about just turning in all in your assignments?"

Then, I make an open-ended invitation to research and report on a science-related topic of their choosing. I keep it deliberately vague, and when they ask for specifics, I usually offer that, personally, I would much rather read an extra-credit report on a scientific mystery than some familiar science topic like whales, Saturn, or Isaac Newton. A couple days after making these flippant remarks, a particularly delightful 8th grader named Gabriella handed me a report on the Taos Hum.

This was a new one by me, and I read with interest. I learned that there are many places around the globe where people report a persistent hum that begins one day, right out of the blue. There are localities where these reports are clustered, like Taos, New Mexico, and Bristol, England. In such cases, the hum that is being reported takes on the name of that location.

Not everyone in a particular locality claims to hear it. Older people hear it more than younger ones, but those who do claim to hear it say that it sounds like a diesel engine idling somewhere underground. The interesting thing about the Taos Hum is that a panel of scientists was commissioned to study the phenomenon and try to come up with a plausible source for the persistent hum. They were able to rule out nearby machinery, tinnitus, other hearing disorders, and other sources of ambient energy like cell-phone towers and radio transmitters. In the end, no plausible source of the Taos Hum was identified. As with all paranormal matters, there is a great deal of conjecture that can be read on the Internet, and even some fairly rigorous discussion of the possibilities by engineers.

Having been to a few too many performances by The Who, my hearing is not as good as it once was. I cannot make any claims to ever having heard faint machinery sounds emanating from the Earth, but I do know others who have. In one case, my old buddy from the world of bigfoot research, Rick Noll, was camped out with his brother in the wilderness near Mt. St. Helens, Washington. On this particular night, Rick's brother was awakened by a hum that seemed to emanate from below. He tried to awaken Rick and alert him of this unusual event but, no matter how hard he tried, his brother could not awaken Rick. The following night they both listened intently for the hum, but there was no such sound.

After reading as much as I could on the Internet about "The Hum," I tend to side with the researchers who assert that it is attributable to Very Low Frequency (VLF) naval communication systems that create resonant frequencies. It is observed that certain frequencies of sound and energy may be detectable at great distances from the powerful transmitters than emit them. Two very powerful VLF transmitters, one near Cutler, Maine and another at Jim Creek, Washington are mentioned as likely sources of the frequencies that may be resonating and becoming audible, even as far away from the transmitters as the opposite side of the Earth.

Going into the study, the scientific panel that investigated the Taos Hum strongly suspected that US Navy ELF (Extremely Low Frequency) transmitters were the source of the Taos Hum. Upon concluding their study, this was their published finding:

> "Since the US Navy ELF stations in the Michigan peninsula and in Wisconsin were widely suspected to be the source of the hum, we looked carefully at the 65 to 75 Hz region of the electromagnetic spectrum, the frequency range where ELF signals would be prominent. We could find nothing above [background level] noise. Considering the spread spectrum of this broadcast, its limited antenna length and the distance from the transmitting site, it is unlikely that the signal would be above the [background] noise level in northern New Mexico.
>
> As a result, we are left with a mystery. There are no acoustic signals that might account for the hum nor are there any seismic events that might explain it. There are no unusual lines at suspect frequencies in the electromagnetic spectrum recorded near Taos. In fact, other than the signals generated by the power grid or in the case of the golf course, a power generator located at the course headquarters, we found no clear lines at all in this spectrum."

By now, the reader must know that my personal *modus operandi* is to roll the unsolved mysteries together, to employ Occam's razor whenever possible by favoring the simplest explanation, and to suspect a certain extraterrestrial presence that is operating here on Earth, but from 'behind the veil.'

When pondering the possible sources of the mysterious and widespread hum, I think it is most important, then, to listen carefully to what the witnesses themselves are saying. If they say it sounds like a diesel generator that is idling, and that is without a doubt the most common description of the perceived noise, then why not consider the possibility that they actually are hearing some sort of mechanical generator?

Quite simply, the suspected subterranean inhabitants may also need a subterranean source of electricity for their power grid. Or, perhaps mechanical tunneling equipment is being used. Perhaps both kids of machinery are in use.

"The Hum" phenomenon is very widespread. As with the mound phenomenon, it may have multiple origins. Some of it may be attributable to Naval ELF or VLF communication. It *does* seem like that possibility has been thoroughly investigated, and those who have done so conclude that, in some cases, naval communication can be ruled out.

All I am doing in this essay is exploring a possible connection between various paranormal phenomena. It makes good logical sense to combine mysteries wherever possible, but admittedly, this may not always be appropriate. I try to keep an open mind and I welcome any and all new sources of information, even ones that serve to refute my ideas. I will say that I have never before seen a suggestion that these various mysteries (extraterrestrials, sasquatches, mounds, The Hum) are in any way connected.

Is this theorizing based in reality? Only time will tell. In any case, fourteen elements of this theory are summarized below.

The Extraterrestrial Bioturbation Theory:

1.   The presence of thousands of mound fields around the Earth, containing millions of mounds, suggests that there are extensive underground excavations planet-wide.

2.   Rock and soil is piled in densely concentrated configurations, of completely uniform size that imply intelligent placement, not the random work of burrowing rodents.

3.   Lens-shaped bases to the mounds that curve downward beneath the center of mass can be explained only by dropping that material from height, allowing it to impact the Earth with considerable force.

4.   Mechanized transport by aerial crafts with uniform earthmoving capacity is being employed to form many of the mounds found worldwide.

5.   Some mounds are formed by natural or man-made process but most are not. The intelligent forces behind the mound formation do try to confuse the situation.

6.   Rodents occupy the mounds opportunistically after their creation. The mounds are usually tailings from excavations and composted materials that have been deposited on the landscape, *then* inhabited opportunistically by fossorial rodents.

7.   The creation of earthen mounds may have shifted or ceased around 7,500 years ago. Either the excavations ceased around that time or the disposal of debris shifted to water bodies where the dumped earth cannot be detected so readily.

8.   The debris is relocated a good distance away from its point of origin, presumably to conceal the location of the underground redoubts that have been constructed.

9.   Pulverized rock and biological waste from subterranean bases is comingled and composted to produce good soil which is moved to the surface and deposited in concentrated mound fields.

10.   The mounds are placed in locations that render marginal lands suitable for agriculture or just to encourage terrestrial flora and fauna. The soil layer on the surface of planet Earth is or was *definitely* being enhanced over time.

11.   ETs and sasquatch comingle in subterranean redoubts worldwide.

12.   The Hum, as heard in various locations such as Bristol and Taos suggests the use of subterranean mechanical equipment; probably for the purpose of excavation, electricity generation, or both.

13.   ETs don't do anything for a single purpose. All overt action by super-intelligent beings serves carefully considered multiple agendas.

14.   The multiple purposes behind ET actions reflect definite ecological awareness and commitment, as well as concealment of their subterranean presence.

General Conclusion:

1. ETs are heavily invested in planet Earth.
2. The speculations of Enrico Fermi, Charles Fort, and Henry Franzoni are correct.
3. The Earth is a farm.
4. We are a crop.

Chapter Nine: Down the Rabbit Hole

One of the most enduring enigmas in the field of anthropology or archeology is the cluster of mysteries surrounding the origin and demise of the Anasazi culture. The Anasazi Indians of the American southwest developed a high culture that was rich in astronomical traditions, sophisticated agriculture, and advanced construction technologies. That much we know. What else they knew we are not sure, but they left behind clues that suggest they possessed skills in weather control and inter-dimensional travel that still cannot be duplicated by modern science.

No one knows what the Anasazi called themselves. *Ancient Puebloan* or *Ancestral Puebloan* are currently more acceptable titles. Anasazi is seen as a bit of a put-down since it is a Navajo term that translates into 'ancient enemies' or more precisely, 'ancestors of our enemies.' Another translation that has been offered is 'ancient ones not like us.' This translation comes closer to raising the implication that Anasazi were completely different, and possibly from *someplace else* entirely. Obviously, the Navajo language did not have a term for extraterrestrial, nor did they have a concept in their mind for 'beings from earth-like planets found elsewhere in the galaxy' but this possibility has been raised again and again, especially in light of their apparent grasp of some pretty sophisticated science.

The Navajo were nomadic hunters for the most part, like the Utes, Paiutes and Mojave Indians that eventually acquired Anasazi territories. The Ancient Puebloans (Anasazi), on the other hand, were much more settled. They established large, permanent, apartment-like dwellings, called pueblos. Their culture was more agriculturally-based than almost any other North American tribe or Indian nation.

The Anasazi, by all appearances, appear to have been the bearers of a global culture. Their circular ceremonial structures, called 'kivas,' contain striking similarities to the Stonehenge edifice in southern England. Not only was their knowledge of astronomy extremely advanced, but the glyphs that we find chiseled into sandstone rock faces throughout their former range suggests that they understood the mechanics of the solar system. Anasazi *pictographs* (rock paintings) appear to document an astronomical event of the century, the Crab Nebula supernova explosion of 1054 A.D. Researcher Gary David has discovered that the geographical configuration of numerous pueblos in northern Arizona perfectly matches the configuration of stars in the constellation Orion.

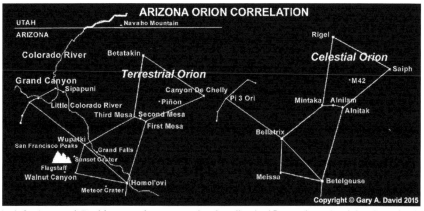

At left: Ancestral Puebloan settlements and culturally significant sites. At right: Stars in the constellation Orion (Courtesy of Gary A. David, Kivas of Heaven 2010)

Based on archeological evidence, it appears that the Anasazi emerged as a culture on the American landscape around 500 to 700 A.D. Their appearance was very recent and very sudden but it is relatively easy to document with tree-ring data derived from logs they built with. Where they came from is just one of the mysteries of this enigmatic culture. Most archeologists say they split or evolved from earlier tribes, specifically the Basket Makers, which appeared on the landscape around 1200 A.D.

Oral histories from more modern tribes offer interesting insight. Zuni and Hopi peoples, members of the Pueblo people, are thought to be modern descendants of the Ancient Puebloan/Anasazi. Hopi oral history contends that their ancestors emerged from The Sipapuni, a hole in the Earth that is located near the mouth of the Little Colorado River in the Grand Canyon. Hopi legend connects the Sipapuni to the Third World, a subterranean realm that was destroyed by flood. The Ancestral Puebloans were rescued from this flood and kept alive by the Ant People, who fulfilled their commitment to guide them from the subterranean Third World. (Gary David, a scholar of Ancestral Puebloan culture, corrects me on this point. His understanding is that the Ant People helped the Hopi survive the destruction of the First World and the Second World, but not the Third World. In any case, recall that the image of the Ant People invokes a very strong similarity to the 'praying mantis-like' appearance of one of the ETs encountered by Miri in Chapter 8, *The Science Fair*.)

The Anasazi were very advanced with respect to the other indigenous people that inhabited the northern half of the New World. Mummified parrots have been found in Anasazi burial sites, as well as sea shells from the Pacific Ocean. These imply that the Ancestral Puebloan has some interaction and trade with the Aztec and Inca nations of Central and South America. If there were trade, there was certainly exchange of ideas as well. The Aztec, Inca, and Mayan cultures bear many indications that they too were aware of and even interacting with extraterrestrial influences. The Mayan people may be the most credited astronomers of all. Anasazi knowledge of astrophysics bears many similarities to the astrophysical awareness of these cultures to the south.

Hidden Cities

In the remote and inaccessible canyon country of southwestern Colorado, an extensive complex of six hundred cliff dwellings at Mesa Verde lay concealed and completely undisturbed for six hundred years. One of these pueblos, the 'Cliff Palace', is the largest cliff dwelling anywhere on Earth. Richard Wetherill and Charlie Mason were two cowboys looking for stray cattle in a snowstorm in 1888 when they ventured up a steep canyon that rose from the Mancos River in southern Colorado. To their amazement, the two cowboys stumbled upon the Cliff Palace at Mesa Verde, a 'magnificent city' as they later described it, and spent several hours exploring it. So numerous were the tools and utensils seen throughout the rooms of the cliff dwelling that, by all appearances, the pueblo complex had been utterly untouched by anyone since the final day of its occupation six hundred years earlier! If the Anasazi had migrated or been forced to evacuate, the useful and valuable tools *could* have been transported and put to good use at some future location. But instead, they were left behind in plain sight at the abandoned pueblos. There was no sign of struggle or violence. Either the pueblo occupants were expecting to return or they knew from the start that they were going somewhere else where all that stuff would not be needed.

When the Ancestral Puebloan culture was thriving, large-scale agriculture was being employed to feed a burgeoning population. By all appearances, their agriculture had been elevated to an art form that has not been improved upon to this day. For example, the Ancestral Puebloan people used their agricultural lands on mesa tops and valley floors to maximum efficiency, growing three complementary crops, the 'three sisters' in perfect association.

Corn, the basis of the Ancestral Puebloan diet, is a heavy feeder that depletes soil nutrients in just a few years. Beans, on the other hand, are nitrogen-fixing *legumes* that replace the same soil nitrogen that corn depletes. The tall corn stalks also support the climbing bean vines. Meanwhile, the spreading, broadleaf habit of squash plants receives shade from the corn and beans, serving as 'living mulch' that shades the soil. This naturally suppresses the germination of pesky, sun-loving weeds. It is a brilliant association of plants that maximizes crop space, soil nutrients, and available water. This perfect agricultural symbiosis has not been improved upon by today's agricultural scientists and it may never be improved upon. In agriculture, it is the best that one can do.

The gravity-fed irrigation system developed by the Ancestral Puebloan also remains a standard-bearer of non-mechanized irrigation systems, even by modern standards. The sophistication of their agricultural science, compared to their contemporaries everywhere else on Earth at the time, raises justifiable suspicions as to exactly how such primitive-living people developed this impressive level of technological and agricultural sophistication. And it does not end there. Not only were they capable farmers, but the Ancestral Puebloan were also excellent engineers.

The Anasazi built some impossibly elaborate pueblos in some incredibly inaccessible and forbidding locations. Their level of engineering and materials management achievement alone rivals anything that can be done by modern construction engineers. How the Anasazi managed to acquire and transport heavy building materials so far, without the use of wheels or horses, is but one of the mysteries surrounding the Anasazi. Heavy logs were transported long distance, yet bear absolutely no scar from rope or other sign of being dragged. How a population of about two thousand people could have transported and assembled thousands of cubic yards of raw construction materials into domiciles at such impossibly steep locations still boggles the mind. Stone masonry is so perfect that a knife blade cannot be inserted between massive interlocking blocks. The time frame of this massive construction is impossibly narrow. Huge domiciles were being built in multiple locations at the same time. It is a series of ancient construction feats that rival the equally inexplicable building of the Great Pyramids of Egypt, Stonehenge, or Machu Pichu.

At the same time that the Anasazi were building these enormous pueblos, the rest of the human inhabitants of the North American continent were living in a virtual stone age. Even stranger is the fact that, only a couple generations after they built these enormous complexes of domiciles, the Ancestral Puebloan just up and left them, never to return. They walked away from the largest and most durable structures on the continent, in some cases only a few short years after they were completed. Then, these same durable villages remained utterly untouched for the next five-hundred-fifty years.

The enormity of these pueblos, and the suddenness with which they were abandoned, makes the departure of the Anasazi even more puzzling. Twelve great pueblos were built at what is thought to have been the capital of the Anasazi culture, the Chaco Canyon site in northern New Mexico, between the tenth and twelfth century (900-1100 A.D.). Each pueblo contained hundreds of rooms, the largest ones being five stories tall. The roofs were supported by large timbers that could not have been acquired locally in the desert of northern New Mexico.

Up until very recently, the origin of the estimated 200,000 timbers that were used, each weighing hundreds of pounds, was a mystery. Then Nathan English, a geochemist at the University of Arizona, used strontium isotopes analysis to determine that the beams were harvested in the Chuska and San Mateo Mountains some sixty miles distant from the Chaco Canyon site. Each log was fifteen feet long and they averaged nine inches in diameter. The fact that the Anasazi population at Chaco Canyon, which is thought to have numbered in the thousands, managed to transport hundreds of thousands of three-hundred pound logs a distance of sixty miles, through mountainous terrain, absolutely boggles the mind. The condition of the logs is impeccable. No scratches, drag marks, or signs of rope friction provide clues as to how the Ancestral Puebloan managed to move these building materials so far. Every aspect of the pueblos' construction, the largest human-built structures in North America prior to the mid-1800s, defies easy explanation. Tightly interlocking stones and adobe walls of enormous size were built in locations that, in some cases, could only be accessed by ladders or by rock-climbing.

Three of the largest installations, Chaco, Aztec National Monument, and Gila cliff dwellings were somehow positioned perfectly on the exact same meridian (108 degrees E. longitude). This is not seen as accidental. Without the invention of a compass, which supposedly did not exist in pre-Columbian America, it becomes extremely difficult to explain how this could have been accomplished. More importantly, it begs the question of why such an alignment of distant dwelling sites was a priority. Thirty-foot-wide roadways radiate outward from New Mexico's Chaco pueblo complex. The only pre-Columbian public works project of similar scope is the Appian Way road complex that was built to project the Roman Army into outlying areas of their empire. It is not believed that the Ancient Puebloan culture kept a standing army, so what exactly was the purpose of these roads that have runway-like widths? The 'Northern Road' that radiates from the Chaco site is explained by Puebloan belief systems as leading to their place of origin. It is said that along this route, the spirits of the dead travelled, which manifested themselves as monstrous beings with glowing eyes. Forgive my preoccupation with other paranormal matters but this description bears a striking similarity to the description of the sasquatch that is rendered from modern sighting reports.

That brings us to the central location of religious and spiritual significance in the pueblo complexes: the *kiva*. What exactly was their purpose in Anasazi society? The conventional thinkers and Park Service tour guides call the kivas 'Anasazi churches' or religious gathering places. They were cylindrical structures dug into the ground. Some were small and some were so enormous that they were sometimes mistaken by early archeologists for water reservoirs.

It is said that only men and boys were allowed in the kivas, which had no doors or windows, but were entered by ladder through a smoke hole in the roof.

There was one kiva for every eight rooms in the earlier pueblos. There were also 'great kivas' that included enormous roofs made from hundreds of the aforementioned stout timbers that were transported very long distances from their point of origin. Some great kivas had roofs that weighed hundreds of tons, supported by huge timbers, which in turn rested on large limestone cylinders that were also transported mind-boggling distances. The strontium analysis performed by Nathan English also indicates that timbers from different great houses at Chaco Canyon were harvested in the same year.

Clearly, the scope of the construction was immense, it was performed in a short period of time, and it was just as quickly abandoned. In at least one case, construction of a pueblo happened less than ten years before it was abandoned. Meanwhile, the building materials were hauled forty miles distant and the labor pool that somehow accomplished this is thought to be much smaller than what the Egyptians or the Maya had available to them.

Whether they were small or huge, the kiva was a cylindrical room with a central fire pit, a ventilation system to feed the fire, and a small hole in the floor, called the sipapu, which was in line with, but opposite, the fire pit. The sipapu is said to be the 'place of emergence.' Essentially, the sipapu was seen by the Anasazi as a portal, which led either to the underworld, or another dimension, depending upon how you look at it. The implications of the sipapu in the kiva are nothing short of enormous. Either the Ancestral Puebloans were able to venture across dimensions, or realms, or they were just taking very potent drugs like peyote or, more likely, datura that made them feel like that is what they were doing. Naturally, a science-minded person who does not wish to embrace the idea that the Ancestral Puebloans could physically leave our plane of existence would favor the view that all these spiritual beliefs were chemically induced.

Another possibility is that the kivas served as sweat lodges where hot rocks were doused with water to create a steam filled room. Some researchers suggest that the kivas were not all ceremonial, but actually served as dwellings, though this seems to defy the extra effort and the specific design details that went into the kivas' construction. It is often suggested that the kivas were symbolic representation of human emergence, as in birth. It is even argued, with a straight face, mind you, that the sipapu represents the birth canal from which we all emerged to begin our time on Earth.

One clue to the real purpose of the kiva is suggested from their locations within the pueblo complexes. Kivas often occur in clusters, rather than being dispersed evenly throughout the larger pueblos. If they were just churches, temples, or gathering places they ought to be more dispersed for easy access. Clustering of the kiva probably relates to magnetic ley lines or some other external factor that dictated their location. Enough beating around the bush. The kivas were not round living areas, men's clubs, or Anasazi churches. And they certainly weren't just symbolic representation of the female reproductive system. To assign any of those explanations is to trivialize the real and profound purpose of these enigmatic structures.

Based on their sophisticated and precise design, as well as their juxtaposition in the pueblo complex, the kivas probably defined the Anasazi culture, from its origin to its ultimate fate. As told by modern Puebloan sources who do not want to be named, kivas were indeed portals, either to other dimensions, or to an underworld, the Third World, from which the Ancestral Puebloan originated and to which they ultimately returned. Either way, they enabled the Anasazi to cross realms, to come and go from this existence as we know it. They also enabled other entities, both living and dead, to enter our three-dimensional, physical realm. The Anasazi are not the only culture to have developed this capability. Other cultures, both past and present, such as the Nez Perce of modern Idaho, possess similar capabilities that are a closely held tribal secret.

The Departure

Why did the Anasazi leave so suddenly and so utterly? Were they the victims of severe drought? That *was* the favored explanation for a long time, but climate data has been used to challenge this view more recently. And if it was a planned relocation as a consequence of drought, why didn't they take any of their useful and valuable tools with them? Perhaps it wasn't climate change at all. It is also suggested that they were attacked by hostile neighboring tribes. That too was a favored explanation. It may even be the current favorite among anthropologists and archeologists who study this question. But there is no evidence of any kind of struggle or battle in the abandoned pueblos, and archeologists know what the aftermath of violent overthrow should look like. In fact, the careful and undisturbed placement of artifacts, as seen by the two cowboys and other early explorers of the abandoned pueblos, suggest that it was as peaceful a departure as it was sudden. Further, if they were chased out by hostile tribes or marauding bands of nomadic Indians, why didn't the victors of this battle stay and enjoy the spoils of war? After all, these were the largest and most durable structures on the continent.

Not only did no invaders take up residence in the vacant pueblos, but neighboring tribes, such as the Utes, scrupulously avoided the Anasazi's former residences, even when they knew they were vacant. They considered the abandoned pueblos to be sacred places. Apparently the Anasazi, far from being some vanquished foe, were so feared and revered that other tribes didn't even mess with the places where the Anasazi *used* to live. Clearly, they were the most powerful and well-organized culture in that whole region of the continent. Toward the end, the Anasazi were surrounded by nomadic tribes. These nomadic bands are thought to have originated in the Athabascan culture of Canada. None of these late-arriving tribes were in any position to challenge the pre-eminence of the Anasazi culture.

Were the Ancient Puebloan (Anasazi) then the victims of internecine squabble and social decay? It is sometimes suggested that the Anasazi culture was marginalized by the effect of competing cultural influences that trickled up from the south. Some combination of these factors is usually endorsed by the academically-inclined, university-oriented anthropologists and ethnologists of today. Again, this is not consistent with sudden and total departure. Social decay and dissolution of such a well-established culture would be a much more gradual process and be evidenced by a steady dismantling of the pueblos. All valuables would ultimately be consumed or disappear. In truth, even food supplies were abandoned at some of the pueblos. This defies the logic of gradual departure in the wake of the cultural decline.

For a long time, the demise of the Anasazi culture was unquestioningly blamed on the Great Drought. Between 1150 and 1350 A.D. there was a planet-wide climatic shift that we now call the Great Drought. Oddly, this is also the time of what was known in other parts of the planet as the Little Ice Age. Some regions were beset with crippling drought, while places closer to the poles were beset with persistent and unseasonably cold temperatures.

In the American southwest, drought was the name of the game. It was assumed to be an unprecedented disaster for an agrarian culture like the Anasazi. Not only would they have experience relentless crop failures for decades upon end, but they would also be subject to much greater pressures from aggressive and better armed nomadic tribes that surrounded them, like the Navajo, Utes, Paiutes, and more.

In response to the droughts and subsequent raids by neighboring tribes, it is said that the Anasazi/Puebloan abandoned their large complexes of domiciles in the center of exposed valleys and retreated to well-hidden and well-fortified cliff swellings like the spectacular Cliff Palace at Mesa Verde. Eventually, these remarkable fortifications also had to be abandoned for the same reasons, and at that point the Anasazi are said to have undertaken a long and arduous migration to the more favorable Zuni lands of western New Mexico and the Rio Grande watershed of Texas and Mexico. At that point, the Anasazi culture was kaput, or at least, it was assimilated into other Native American cultures to the point where it essentially disappeared. This is the official version for why the Anasazi did a disappearing act, according to eminent historians like Frank Cushing and Alfred Kidder.

More recently, some upstarts have upset this apple cart, beginning with a certain heretic from Washington State University by the name of Carla Van West. In 1990, Dr. Van West spoke at a well-attended anthropological conference in Crow Canyon, New Mexico to share her closer look at The Great Drought. She calculated the rainfall rates (based on tree growth-ring data), the soil type, and the estimated crop yields that the Anasazi would have been able to achieve. She concluded that the Great Drought would not have been nearly as ruinous as was originally supposed. It should not have completely displaced such a well-established culture as that which the Anasazi had achieved.

Bone analysis at Anasazi burial sites does suggest that there were periods of malnutrition and increased infant-mortality during the Great Drought, but it should not have, according to Dr. Van West, completely ended such an established culture. Perhaps a certain 'balkanization' (fragmentation) of the cultural landscape did occur, but not enough to evict the occupants of the most magnificent structures ever built by any Native American tribe.

After that conference in which Dr. Van West challenged the conventional thinking that the Great Drought was the main reason for the demise of the Anasazi culture, the mystery of what brought an end to this great culture was again a wide open question. Since that conference, the search for a root cause for the demise of the Anasazi culture shifted to social dimensions. Some researchers have concluded that a new, flashier religion to the south, the 'Kachinas' of the Zuni and Hopi lands, supplanted the existing religion and culture, kind of like the way The Beatles and their new brand of rock and roll supplanted the 'big band' sound and the Sinatra-style crooners of the fifties. Again, such cultural shifts just don't seem to justify the abandonment of an entire existence and way of life that was more comfortable, and more technologically advanced, than anything else on the continent at that time.

So, what did happen to the Anasazi? A big clue may lie in the shift in the architecture of pueblos that took place after the Anasazi packed up and left the planet in the 1300's. It seems likely that some of the Ancestral Puebloan/Anasazi did indeed relocate. The Zuni, one group that is thought to descend from the Ancestral Puebloans, are now found in in western New Mexico. Another people, the Hopi, are centered in northern Arizona.

When the newer pueblos are analyzed for differences in architectural styles, a marked de-emphasis in the kivas is distinctly evident. Modern pueblos feature fewer or no kivas compared with earlier Anasazi pueblos that featured whole clusters of kivas, great and small. Dr. Ware concludes that this implies a spiritual crisis within the Anasazi culture. Gary David observes that the Hopi still use kivas that are rectangular rather than cylindrical.

The departure from their time-honored homeland, and its elaborate and durable architecture, is known to anthropologists as the 'Process of Abandonment.' Dr. David Wilcox cites a certain social dimension to this process of abandonment that anthropology is just beginning to grapple with. He concedes that the Great Drought may not have been bad enough to evict the Anasazi, but it may have been more of a 'last straw', especially when heaped upon other factors that created profound instability within the Anasazi culture.

The Ancestral Puebloan/Anasazi society did indeed disappear in the late thirteenth or early fourteenth century, leaving behind the largest pre-Industrial Revolution structures on the continent. The extensive pueblos, some containing hundreds of rooms, remained abandoned and untouched for the next six hundred years. It is speculated by academics that this was part of a purge directed at the dark arts that certain members of the Anasazi nation had become so proficient at manipulating. Owing to the fact that almost all kiva roofs were burned, I suspect that the fires were deliberately set on the heels of the departing Anasazi, as a way of sealing the portals to prevent future use.

Either way, the kivas found at many of the Anasazi pueblos appear to have been deliberately burned during a narrow time frame that is consistent with the general abandonment of the great Anasazi pueblos. Did the Anasazi become a little too big for their metaphysical britches? According to this thinking, their metaphysical efforts, centered on the kivas, may have brought about a certain cultural and even environmental ruin.

Whatever it was, it had to have been profound, because in locations like Hovenweep in southeastern Utah where the Anasazi were very well established, they suddenly wiped the slate of their existence totally clean. One of the most compelling ideas that has ever been suggested is one offered by the Hopi of today. These Hopi are members of the Puebloan Nation who are the presumptive descendants of at least some of the disaffected Anasazi.

In answer to the question of what ultimately happened to the Ancestral Puebloans, Hopi legend states that these Ancestral Puebloans used the power of the mystical 'kiva' structures to return to the subterranean 'Third World' from which they originated. Perhaps this Third World is just a jumping-off point on a journey to another planet. This would render the Anasazi essentially a space-faring race of extraterrestrials. If so, then they resided here on Earth for a millennium, building their population as an agrarian-based culture, then returning to their mysterious place of origin. The remarkable sophistication that is evident in everything they left behind is one big reason why so many suspect that the Anasazis were indeed a terrestrial culture with another-worldly origin.

In essence, the Anasazi, through the use of these dimensional doorways, became extremely powerful, both spiritually and metaphysically. It is held in Hopi lore that the Anasazi originally came here, the Fourth World, from the subterranean Third World. This suggests that the Anasazi were either arrivals from another dimension, or another planet, or both. They maintained a connection to the Third Realm through the sipapu hole in the floor of the kiva. This provided them with considerable power, which they exercised to great effect, even to the point of manipulating the weather.

Yet, according to Hopi legend, in their sometimes successful attempts to manipulate the *weather*, they also unintentionally changed the *climate* (average weather) of their region in ways that were absolutely unforeseen. According to Puebloan teachings, the Anasazi may have even brought the Great Drought upon themselves. It became obvious that one element of Anasazi culture, the sacred rituals practiced in the kivas, were having a deleterious effect on the Anasazi culture as a whole. If social conflict led to the balkanization of the once powerful Anasazi civilization, then it may have resulted from the shamans becoming too powerful through these rituals. The reason for supposing this is that researchers have observed that later pueblos had few or no kivas, although this is also a matter of some dispute. Researcher and author Gary David maintains that Hopi and Zuni villages of today have many kivas.

Climate Control

If this all sounds a bit far-fetched, that is certainly understandable, for this suggestion is not supported by much physical evidence, only legend and oral history. Still, there is an interesting allegory that does exist in modern science and history.

Cloud seeding had been experimented with since the 1950's. Cloud seeding involves the burning of silver iodide in furnaces aboard aircraft. Silver iodide smoke, when released in sufficient quantities, provides a potent artificial source of condensation nuclei. The trillions of tiny smoke particles from the burned silver iodide provide the catalyst that triggers this "three-phase process" of raindrop formation. It is this process that forms the basis of rainfall formation at high altitudes. The release of dry ice (frozen carbon dioxide) is yet another way to artificially accelerate the three-phase process. Cloud seeding, in essence, brings about a big artificial acceleration in the process of rainfall formation. Along with this rainfall formation is a huge, concomitant release in 'latent heat.' This means the atmosphere in the vicinity of the cloud seeding becomes suddenly much warmer.

In and around hurricanes, this process was used by the American military and civilian weather scientists to try to create a new eye wall outside the existing eye wall of hurricanes. It was theorized that this procedure could theoretically fragment or reorganize a hurricane.

In 1947, the Army Signal Corps launched Project Cirrus with the intention of trying to steer hurricanes. A hurricane that was headed safely out to sea was seeded with silver iodide. The hurricane subsequently changed direction and made landfall near Savannah, Georgia. Threats of lawsuits over the damage caused were deflected only after it was shown that another hurricane had taken a similar path on its own. In any case that was the end of Project Cirrus, but it was not the end of the attempts to artificially control extreme weather.

For twenty-one years from 1962 to 1983, Project Storm Fury also made several attempts to steer hurricanes. After some promising initial results, it was finally shown that there was no way to be sure that the behavior of hurricanes under natural conditions was any different than the hurricanes that were supposedly steered with silver iodide or dry ice.

In 1984, only a year after the official end of Storm Fury, Hurricane Diana followed the most unusual path ever observed. It circled and crossed its own path twice before making landfall at Southport, N.C. on September 11th, then heading *back* out to sea and eventual extinction in the north Atlantic. The Army denies all involvement in this curious hurricane behavior. During this same time, Fidel Castro was going public with statements that the American military was trying to militarize hurricanes. The statements were labeled "outlandish" by the American media but in retrospect, his claims do not seem as outlandish as they were made to seem.

Regardless of Hurricane Diana in 1984, did all attempts to artificially influence weather end with Project Storm Fury in 1983? Definitely not. Modern attempts to change the weather have culminated with the work that has been accomplished by scientists working for a Swiss company under the direction of Sheikh Khalifa bin Zayed Al Nahyan, the president of United Arab Emirates. Scientists and engineers working for Metro Systems International built huge fields of ionizers in the desert of the U.A.E. to generate waves of negative ions. The ions rise into the upper atmosphere where they attract dust particles. As previously stated, the dust particles serve as condensation nuclei that trigger raindrop formation. When the drops become too heavy for the updrafts in the cloud to support, it rains. Weather control is technologically possible, to be sure.

How the Anasazi, and even some modern tribes, are supposed to be able to perform similar tricks through some metaphysical means is officially unknown, but there are indeed other tribes today such as the Hopi and Utes that are said to be capable 'rain-makers' in the literal sense. Hopi legend further holds that the Anasazi were given a device by Maasaw, the caretaker of the land, called a water jar. It could be used to cause a spring to issue forth from the hillside where ever the Anasazi decided to establish a pueblo complex. Plans were even included with the water jar to construct a new one if the original one was broken. How this mysterious water jar worked is not at all clear, but it was this ability to supposedly generate water anywhere they went that enabled the Anasazi to construct pueblos in some very arid and very out-of-the-way places.

If there is any truth to the idea of these water jars, then this begins to support the view that either the Anasazi were extraterrestrials or they were being assisted by them, for their technology was out of this world. Even if the reader doesn't buy into the idea of magical water jars, it is an undeniable fact that the Ancestral Puebloans established relative large settlements in places where the lack of natural resources, specifically water, should have prevented them from doing so.

Not only does it seem that the Ancestral Puebloans had some pretty impressive tricks up their sleeve, but some of these abilities may still exist in the skill set of modern tribal shamans. Specifically, the ability to manipulate inter-dimensional portals, or something like that, may still exist among some modern tribes. Members of the Nez Perce Nation privately acknowledge that within sweat lodges, tribal elders are indeed able to conduct two-way communication with deceased relatives. Similar ceremonies occur or did occur around the geographic location on the Grand Round Reservation known as Spirit Mountain.

Metaphysical travel, through kiva-centered ceremonies in the case of the Anasazi, or other tribes in more recent times, may not be just the stuff of myth. It is not totally explainable by modern science but it may still occur through sacred and secret rituals conducted by these modern tribes. It is just one of many remarkable feats that Native Americans could share with the rest of humanity if we just embraced their wisdom and power.

Crossing Realms

What about this "Third World" from which the Ancestral Puebloans are said to originate? Is it a place in some other set of cosmic dimensions? Is it perhaps another planet located elsewhere in our galaxy? Is it just a subterranean world here on Earth?

The Ancestral Puebloans seem to have disappeared very suddenly, but perhaps they never actually left the planet when they returned to the Third World from which they originated. Perhaps the Hopi creation myth can be taken literally, rendering the Third World to be same underground redoubt, presumably constructed by extraterrestrials, that was referenced in Chapter Eight. Perhaps the Anasazi were even complicit in the construction of certain underground redoubts within their region. This would explain the Anasazi's impossibly gifted skill at constructing their own dwellings on the Earth's surface, which they did in their spare time, while commuting to the subterranean world. I humorously envision the Anasazi gathering at the kiva every morning, lunch boxes in hand, to catch their morning bus through the sipapu hole in the kiva, (down the rabbit hole) to the subterranean construction site. If there is any truth to such fanciful speculation, there should be Mima mound fields found in the southwest. It turns out, there are. Then there is also the persistent Taos hum that emanated from the Earth right in the center of the Anasazi's ancestral homeland. Hmmm.

Hopi legend says their ancestors emerged from this subterranean Third Realm that was destroyed by flood, just as the Second Realm was frozen in ice. If the Third Realm is a subterranean world, could groups of Anasazi descendants still live there? In that case, the sipapu in the floor of the kiva just delivers a person to this subterranean world right here on Earth, as opposed to some other mystic set of dimensions, or another three-dimensional world on another planet. But the idea that the kiva provided a portal to another realm altogether, another 'dimension' if you will, is an idea that has gained strength as theoretical physicists began exploring the concept of wormholes for the first time only in the past century.

Worm Holes

A portal, as described by New Agers and paranormalists, would probably qualify as a wormhole to theoretical physicists, and a wormhole is essentially synonymous with what an astrophysicist would call a black hole: a singularity of infinitely dense matter created by the collapse of a star fifteen times greater than our Sun. Black holes were theoretical constructs first described by English geologist John Mitchell in 1784. Cygnus X-1, an intense X-ray source in the constellation of Cygnus, was the first black hole to be identified in the heavens over a hundred years later. We now understand that black holes reside at the center of most, perhaps all, larger galaxies.

It was Albert Einstein and colleague Nathan Rosen who first published a paper that mathematically proved that such objects, that we can never see, actually exist. Einstein and Rosen showed that not only do solutions to the general relativity equation allow for the existence of black holes, (or as they called them back then, 'dark stars') but they represent wormholes than may lead to somewhere else in space-time. Hence, they became known as 'Einstein-Rosen bridges.' Much like the wormholes in an apple that enables a worm to cross the mass of an apple without having to travel all the way around the apple's surface, Einstein-Rosen bridges are short cuts across space-time.

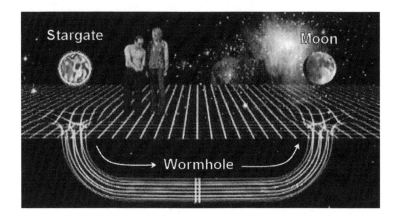

While black holes, Einstein-Rosen bridges, or 'wormholes' have been recognized features of outer space for a long time, it is now being suggested that such wormholes could exist right here on Earth. If they did exist on Earth, they would be a means of instantly crossing huge amounts of space, and probably time as well.

The problem with using this wormhole as a shortcut across space, as Einstein showed, is that they are inherently unstable. They don't stay open long enough to allow an object travelling at the speed of light (or slower) to get spit out the 'white hole' on the other side. Also, the intense gravitational tides would rip an object apart as it passed through the 'event horizon' and into the infinitely dense singularity at the center of the black hole. In 1963, a mathematician named Kerr suggested a rotating black hole that would allow one to pass through a black hole and miss the singularity that would rip you apart. Still, Kerr's black hole concept had the same instability problem that Einstein suggested. Then, in 1988, Cal Tech physicist Kip Thorne and his student Mike Morris suggested that a strong source of negative mass/energy could be used to hold the portal or wormhole open. Finally, someone had come up with the mathematics that validates the possibility of a *traversable* black hole.

All black holes observed by astrophysicists in the universe are Schwartzchild wormholes (a.k.a. Einstein-Rosen bridges) that would collapse before a traveler had time to traverse them. Thanks to Thorne and Morris, now there was a possible kind of black hole that *was* traversable, and it is called, of course, a 'Morris-Thorne wormhole.' It had to be held open by a sphere of 'exotic matter,' which is some sort of mysterious, negatively charged mass. Dark matter is one such substance that is presently undetectable but thought to pervade the universe in great quantities. It may be one source of the intense negative mass/energy that could be used to keep a traversable black hole or wormhole open long enough to navigate it. Notice, too, that modern physicists are suggesting that we essentially 'seed' the vortex of the wormhole with *negative* mass-energy to keep it open, just as the atmospheric physicist would seed a hurricane's vortex in order to redefine its structure.

Recall, also, that the most modern method of rain-making, as employed by engineers hired by the U.A.E., involves seeding clouds with *negative* ionic energy. There seems to be an uncanny similarity in the language used to describe two very different phenomena, cloud seeding to produce rain, and wormhole seeding to keep traversable wormholes open. Interestingly, both phenomena are alleged to have been under Anasazi control. Could we be looking at two sides of the same coin, or at least two applications of the same principle of vortex manipulation through seeding with negative energy?

Another paper by Matt Visser in 1989 came up with a path through a wormhole that enabled one to miss the region of exotic matter. By embracing 'String Theory,' the mathematics of general relativity are modified and extra dimensions or *branes* are added to our three dimensional universe. String Theory makes it theoretically possible, not only to have a wormhole that is held open without exotic matter, but also to have other dimensions that can be accessed to travel to beyond our familiar three-dimensional universe.

This is pretty much where we stand with string theory today. The universe consists of at least seven dimensions, and it is possible that there are 'parallel universes,' or that our universe is but a tiny point within a much larger universe. Consequently, the term 'multiverse' has found favor with string theorists.

We're not yet to the point of being able to open up a worm hole and dive in, but the mathematics of string theory does allow that such traversable wormholes might even have been naturally created in the early universe. It has also been shown by Thorne and others that to travel across space using wormholes, one not only can, but must also travel across time!

The theoretical idea of wormholes is even being applied to certain technological problems. One of the pioneers in this field is Dr. David Greenleaf (and some co-authors) who are working on applying the 'wormhole technology.' As of right now, it is possible to make objects invisible to microwave radiation. Microwaves are but one small part of the electromagnetic (EM) spectrum that includes light and all other types of wave energy. Solutions to the general relativity equation allow for the same invisibility in other forms of EM radiation. Greenleaf suggests a tube that is coated with some sort of still-undiscovered meta-material. You would pass an object into the tube and watch it disappear, then re-emerge out the other end. This idea has an obvious use in medicine, where MRI machines use magnetic waves to see inside the body without using dangerous x-rays. MRI's cannot be used to guide surgeons' tools at present because the intense magnetic fields of the MRI imager will rip the metal tools right out of the surgeon's hands. Surgical tools could theoretically be made invisible to magnetism by inserting them into this tube, and only the tips would be visible to the MRI imager. This basically makes the wormhole technology into a cloaking device. While creation of the technology for this device is still a long way off, the mathematics say it is certainly possible. What may be of greatest interest in this discussion is the fact that the shape of the objects Greenleaf envisions is always *cylindrical*. Recall that this is the shape always used in the construction of kivas by the Anasazi, as well as the shape of the sipapu (hole) in the floor of the kiva that was the conduit to the Third World. I doubt this is a coincidence.

Such cloaking has other interesting applications that are theoretical but probably won't stay that way for long. If clusters of wires could be made invisible over short distances, then they could be used to deliver light energy to pixilated displays that would appear to be floating in space. This would enable the creation of truly three dimensional television displays. The TV images would float in the center of the room yet be as vivid and well illuminated as the brightest high-definition flat screen TV of today.

What *has* to be the most interesting attempt to apply wormholes to a technological problem was Carl Sagan's attempt to apply the idea of time-space travel to his 1995 novel, *Contact*. In his fictional story of extraterrestrial contact, Sagan sought to portray an engineered wormhole that could be used for time-space travel right here on Earth, instead of traveling all the way to some far off black hole like Cygnus X-1. Further, Sagan wanted a structure for this space-time machine that did not violate the general relativity equation, so he actually turned to Kip Thorne at Cal Tech and asked him to work out the math for such a construct. Dr. Thorne has acknowledged that Sagan's request was the impetus behind his initial involvement in wormhole theory, which then led to Thorne's groundbreaking work in this area.

Specifically, Thorne, like Einstein, understood that any object, like a spaceship, would create gravitational waves ahead of it that would cause the unstable wormhole to turn into a singularity and slam shut, destroying the spaceship and its occupants. But perhaps a source of negative energy could be used to create opposing gravitational waves, or *negative feedback* as it is known. That would cancel out the waves created by the offending object that was attempting to traverse the wormhole. It is analogous to the idea of noise-cancelling headphones that create a sound wave that negates the offending sound waves, thereby generating silence inside the headphones. Or, think of a negative-energy substance that, when pushed into a balloon, caused the balloon to *deflate* rather than inflate. Is there such a substance? If there is, it would fall into the category of *exotic materials*.

'Dark matter' is one such candidate for such an exotic material. Astrophysicists are fairly certain that dark matter exists, but it is a theoretical construct that is currently impossible to detect. The work being done with super-colliders becomes instrumental in trying to quantify and capture these exotic materials. At present we are far too technologically primitive to move such vast amounts of matter and energy around. Kip Thorne's mathematical work for Sagan suggested that, if there were a super-advanced civilization that could keep a traversable wormhole open, it would have to be kept open permanently, and 'forever' is a mighty long time. Still, the math says that it is indeed possible.

Could the Anasazi have had a deep understanding of the same string theory that we are just barely beginning to understand today? If portals, as they are described by metaphysical and spiritual devotees, are the same as the wormholes of theoretical physics, how is it possible that they already exist, and that they open and close at certain locations on Earth? Naturally, the physicist would say it *isn't* possible and that the whole suggestion that the Anasazi had access to such a phenomenon is a myth.

Perhaps the Anasazi and others have or had access to some scaled back version of this phenomenon, and the negative energy that drives it is found where the magnetic 'ley lines' of the planet intersect. There are indeed such locations on Earth where magnetic fields intersect in intense ways, and they have long been known to correspond with the location of European cathedrals and other 'sacred sites' around the planet. It also seems that the Anasazi, the

Maya, and many other cultures had identified these 'sacred sites.' Like the early Europeans, the ancient Americans located their sacred structures at these sites. Whether the sacred kivas and the rituals that took place within them were able to conjure open worm holes is highly speculative indeed, but in light of the new knowledge of traversable wormholes that we have acquired just in the past century, we are definitely getting closer to an eventual intersection of science and mysticism.

It is too much of a stretch to accept that the Anasazi were the terrestrial manifestation of a space-faring culture? At the very least, it again appears that they were getting substantial help from a space-time faring culture. To me, the most plausible explanation for the advanced capabilities of the Anasazi lies in the possibility that Maasaw was the physical manifestation of the extraterrestrial intervention of which the Anasazi were the recipients. And as beneficiaries of the extraterrestrial assistance, one wonders what *quid pro quo* arrangement the Anasazi had with the ETs. The world-wide mound phenomenon suggests that, at one point in the past, a big construction project was taking place on Earth to build large subterranean bases. Perhaps the Anasazi had a role in this project. Based on their obvious competence in constructing the elaborate pueblos for which they are famous, their skill at constructing large structures from native materials would have been extremely handy.

Perhaps Maasaw has manifested herself at other times and in other places, and has been given other names in these other situations. The clear implication is that the three letter word 'God' which we use to explain everything about this world that we do not yet understand may be the same entity the Anasazi called Maasaw. It may indeed be an unseen but ever-present being, just as most modern theologies suggest. Science and religion may yet prove to be strange bedfellows.

Mainstream archeology sees nothing mysterious about the disappearance of the Anasazi. They were totally assimilated into contemporary tribes such as the Hopi and Zuni of the Rio Grande River basin. When the bulk of the Anasazi abandoned their terrestrial realm, some of the Anasazi *did* remain and establish or comingle with these contemporary tribes, but certainly not all. Can we verify any of the suspicions as to where the rest of the Anasazi went? One point on which all archeologists seem to agree is that there should be many more graves associated with the Anasazi Puebloans complexes than have been found so far. It is estimated that the total number of identified graves found surrounding the large Anasazi villages is less than five percent of what there should be. This is particularly true at Chaco Canyon. Indeed, a great deal of time and effort has been spent looking for these missing graves, since they contain a wealth of artifacts that give us a window on their artistic and cultural achievement. For example, some of the turquoise jewelry pieces found in Anasazi interment sites are equal to or even superior to anything that can be constructed by modern jewelers. The missing bodies are a very real problem for archeologists with purely academic orientation. The opportunities for paranormal speculation are wide open:

-They left the planet to die.

-The bodies were sent somewhere else through the kivas.

-The bodies were transported to the Third World (the underworld) where they are interred and will never be disturbed by the prying eyes of archeologists.

We can ask these tribes who claim to have Anasazi ancestry but they are tight-lipped about specifics, even as they claim to hold written record (in addition to the oral histories) that describe what actually happened to the Ancestral Puebloans. We can also study the only written record that the Anasazi left behind for us to examine: the petroglyphs that decorate rock walls through the Anasazi's former domain. The code of the petroglyphs is not universally agreed upon but the images found on rock faces around the southwest U.S. do indeed point in some very intriguing directions.

The Petroglyphs

The Anasazi are considered to be the antecedents of the Hopi Indians of today. Like virtually all early Native American cultures, they did not really have a written language, but they did create images and figures on rock walls and outcrops throughout their sphere of influence. A bright red paint, called ochre, was used to create pictographs which, in a much faded state, can still be found, particularly in the Four Corners area where the borders of Arizona, New Mexico, Utah, and Colorado intersect. This was the land of the Anasazi. Also found in this same area are thousands of *petroglyphs*: shapes and figures that were chiseled into the dark stain of 'desert varnish' that coats many surfaces of the native sandstone bedrock. A harder rock, like agate, might have been used as a chisel, and using some sort of hammer, petroglyph 'rock art' was created that was more enduring than ochre pictographs. This art form was practiced throughout the domain of the Anasazi. Through the petroglyphs, the Ancestral Puebloans are speaking to us across the millennia about their ideas and objects of deep spiritual significance.

Although I was already familiar with the idea that the Anasazi were allegedly the terrestrial manifestations of a space-faring culture (thanks to my friend Joe Beelart), I did not venture to the southwestern U.S. with the purpose of investigating this possibility. I went to the Southwest, specifically Las Vegas, to watch my son's high school baseball tournament. In the free time between games, on my wife's encouragement, we ventured into the Nevada desert and right into a stunning synchronicity. In pursuit of scenic natural attractions, we ended up at Valley of Fire State Park.

Valley of Fire State Park, Nevada

To my amazement, even as I was probing the Anasazi enigma back home, I found myself face to face with dozens of well-preserved petroglyphs that have been attributed to the Anasazi and even the Basket Maker culture that is said to precede them. Based on what I had already learned about the Anasazi, not to mention other potentially paranormal enigmas, I was stunned to find that, at least in some cases, the message that the petroglyphs conveyed to me over the millennia was immediately obvious. I got chills when I found myself inspecting petroglyph images that appear to reference astronomical concepts, portals, interactions with the cosmos and even space-faring beings. Most remarkably, I even stumbled upon multiple petroglyphs that suggested an Anasazi familiarity with, and even a partnership, with the sasquatch!

Initially, all I had to go by was my personal impressions of the rock art I was witnessing. I had to find out whether there were generally-accepted interpretations of the petroglyphs; maybe even interpretations based on an enduring knowledge of Anasazi lore. I found this particular interpretive sign (below) that offered translations of petroglyphs images, yet it did not speak to some of the most intriguing images that I was seeing. I then beat a path to the interpretive center at Valley of Fire State Park and found the only person who was dressed in an official green uniform. He was sitting at a computer terminal in an office and he was kind enough to allow me to interrupt his work for the purpose of answering a few pointed questions. He was also honest enough to acknowledge that which he really did not know. In brief, this helpful park employee told me that virtually all petroglyphs are thought to be of a certain spiritual or mystical significance. Whoever made these ancient petroglyphs, which are estimated to be up to 4000 years old, did not put them there for trivial reasons. They weren't just tagging the landscape with ancient graffiti.

The Anasazi, or the Basket Makers, created these petroglyphs to depict their most profound and sacred concepts. It was the Anasazi's only known form of written language. In fact, the Anasazi petroglyphs are probably the most extensive example of ancient communication found anywhere on the North American continent. They are clearly a window into Anasazi culture; maybe the only window we will ever get.

"So what are they telling us?" I asked the park employee.

"No one really knows," was his candid answer. "But when you've been doing this job a while and talking with people who may or may not know what they are talking about, you get some pretty strange ideas."

"Great," I replied, "Because I have some potentially strange ideas myself. Do you mind if I ask you what you think of them?"

"Shoot."

"Well, (full disclosure) I'm a serious devotee of the sasquatch phenomenon, but I swear I saw a petroglyph which clearly depicts two scrawny humans holding hands with two much more massive beings, that look suspiciously similar to sasquatch people. Are you familiar with that particular petroglyph?"

"Yes, indeed," the park ranger replied. "That is a famous one and it is called 'The Family.' That's how it's generally interpreted: A family. Two grown-ups, and two kids."

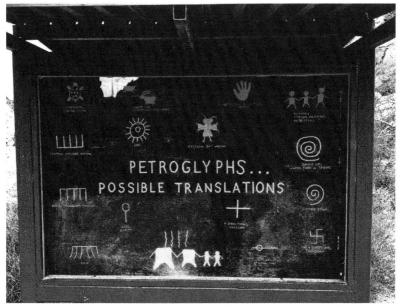

Interpretive sign at Petroglyph Canyon, Valley of Fire State Park

"But you said petroglyphs always had always spiritual significance," I insisted. "That sounds more like a family portrait, not an expression of Anasazi spirituality. What about the wiggle-lines coming off of the bigger creatures? When I saw those I immediately thought of the strong smell that is so often described by sasquatch eye-witnesses."

"Those are said to be snakes."

"Why do they only emanate from the big creatures?"

The park employee shifted his weight from one foot to the other. I was putting him on the spot and he clearly did not want to debate the significance of petroglyphs with some random park visitor.

"Look," he replied. "Like I said, no one really knows. If you want to write a book saying the Anasazi were extraterrestrials, *and* that certain petroglyphs indicate that, then there is no one, repeat *no one*, who is truly qualified to challenge that view. In fact, I've heard as much said many times. There just isn't any way to dispute it, or to verify it. No one, not even in the tribal communities, really knows what those petroglyphs are saying. So, if you think they show a connection between the Anasazi and the sasquatch or aliens, you're probably OK."

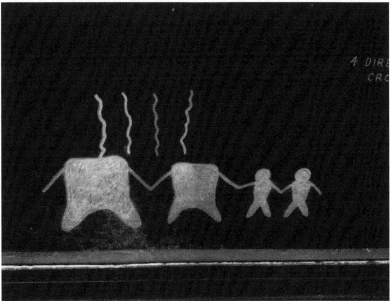

A close-up of the Snake Dance (also called (The Family) on an interpretive sign at Valley of Fire State Park. This glyph appears at several Anasazi petroglyph sites.

"Funny you should mention that," I thought to myself. "That's exactly what I had in mind." I thanked him for his time and information. He added one more suggestion.

"You really ought to go to the Lost City Museum down the road in Overton. It's a restored Anasazi village with artifacts that were removed from a pueblo complex before Hoover Dam and Lake Meade submerged the site. You might find some great information there."

Unfortunately, it was too late in the evening to add another stop to our impromptu exploration of the Anasazi heartland. It was getting dark and we had to get back to Las Vegas. Maybe the information I missed at the Lost City museum would have corroborated my suspicions about the Anasazi and the sasquatch, maybe not. I may never know. At least I have my own interpretations of the petroglyphs, and as the park employee told me, nobody really knows for sure what the Anasazi were trying to tell us in those petroglyphs. We'll never know for certain whether the Anasazi were ETs or just knew them well. It seems scientifically impossible that a supposedly primitive culture could be able to manipulate string theory in ways we still do not understand in this technological era. Yet, the Anasazi were almost impossibly advanced, in their architecture, in their agriculture, their astronomical knowledge, and their apparent grasp of metaphysics, with respect to all other contemporaneous Native American and European cultures. For the foreseeable future, it will remain an enormous enigma, but it is such an interesting one to ponder, that I, for one, might even be happier by *not* knowing for sure.

The spiral is a familiar theme in petroglyphs. It is also said to represent the point of origin of the Anasazi: the sipapu. Interestingly, the object next to the vortex (wormhole) appears to be a flying object, half bird, half plane. and it faces downward toward the underworld from which the Anasazi emerged by way of the sipapu.

Post script:

By embracing the paranormal, some interesting possibilities for further information open up. Almost by definition, 'paranormal' implies 'unverifiable' but it is often interesting enough to report anyway.

In April of 2014, I was invited to an informal symposium in the Portland area that was organized by Jeff Roane and hosted by Rich Fiala. The symposium was entitled 'Footstock' and its focus was a recognition of the paranormal events that sometimes surround otherwise ordinary encounters with the sasquatch phenomenon. Each of the twenty or so attendees was invited to share experiences of that general sort as well as their impressions of what might be behind such enigmatic events. Having just returned from Nevada, I shared the photos of Anasazi petroglyphs and asked the attendees to speculate as to their potential significance.

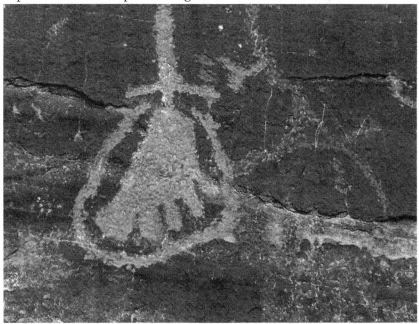

Of particular interest was the glyph that portrayed the broad, sasquatch-style foot with the circle around it. People offered some immediate impressions that were generally humorous in nature and we all had a few laughs. The general consensus was that no one had any real idea what the petroglyph meant but they agreed that it was certainly a reference to the sasquatch. The trademark 'big foot' seems to have been a cultural icon for a lot longer than we ever realized.

A few days later I got a call from Tish Paquette, one of the attendees of the conference who has a great deal of experience with harnessing and channeling psychic energy. Tish informed me that she didn't have any real impression of the glyph to share at the conference, but later on that week, an image of that petroglyph came into her mind while meditating. It seemed as though an answer was being offered as to what the petroglyph portrayed. Tish told me that the interpretation of the glyph I projected at the conference was indeed meant to represent the foot of a sasquatch, and the band that encircled the foot represented the Anasazi artist's awareness of the power, or perhaps barrier that the sasquatch possess, enabling them to repel unwanted contact, and to protect themselves from potential sources of danger or harm. Fascinating, indeed, that such an idea came to Tish while meditating. Her interpretation seemed utterly valid in light of what we think we understand about the capabilities of the sasquatch. They definitely possess considerable power, and the power to repel unwanted intruders is among them.

Another pattern that has been discussed in hushed tones for years within the community of sasquatch researchers is the view that the sasquatch have the ability to come and go from our plane of existence; that the sasquatch are indeed inter-dimensional travelers. If there is any merit to this venturesome thought, and if there is also any merit to the suggestion that the Anasazi, too, had within their culture the ability to travel between realms, dimensions, or whatever else one wishes to call them, then, from a strictly logical point of view, these similarly powerful beings ought to know each other. Indeed, they ought to be encountering each other on a semi-regular basis as they travel the same metaphysical highways.

For me this renders the famous petroglyph, 'The Family' to be a petroglyph of enormous spiritual, cultural, and even scientific significance. In my view, it is a virtual certainty that this glyph is meant to portray a partnership and camaraderie between the Anasazi and the sasquatch people.

Later, I learned while reading on petroglyphs that certain sacred beings were drawn without heads because the Anasazi understood that those beings wanted to keep their identity concealed. Such entities essentially carried their head with them and attached them only when they were present. In deference to these powerful beings, their heads were not portrayed on petroglyphs. I also read that the squiggly lines are interpreted by others as being signs of strong power. How curious that so many modern researchers of sasquatch lore have now come to the realization that the sasquatch are indeed completely averse to being photographed. Those who claim to have a dialogue with the sasquatch maintain that the sasquatch tell them it is a serious misstep in sasquatch society to be photographed by us 'hairless humans.' Petroglyphs suggest the Ancestral Puebloan understood this idea over five hundred years ago.

The Mayan culture centered in present-day Guatemala had the largest collection of written documents in all of Mesoamerica until the Spanish invasions of the 15th and 16th centuries. One of the only pieces of writing to survive the tragic destruction of virtually all Mayan written documents at the hands of the marauding Spaniards was the *Popul Vuy*. It is not seen as a historically factual document owing to the fact that it largely a narrative that reads like a series of parables. Like many collections of cultural myths and legends, it is seen as containing some factual underpinnings although it is by no means easy to distinguish fact from fiction. Nonetheless, the Popul Vuy is seen to say that the Mayans had an awareness of their powerful Anasazi neighbors to the north. Further, the Popul Vuy suggests that the Mayans had more than a passing awareness of the powerful, hair-covered beings that we have only recently come to understand in the context of our more modern, but not always so enlightened Western culture. The Mayans, through the Popul Vuy, also embrace the existence of a vast underworld.

Indeed, many tribes in North America embrace creation myths that bear remarkable similarities. To name only the three I am specifically aware of in the Northwest, the Nez Perce, the Umatilla, and the Chinook nations all have creation myths that describe a single ancestor, or small group of ancestors that emerged from the underworld, naked and freezing. Over and over again, in the Native American lore, references are made to an underworld inhabited by powerful beings. We might do well to take these so-called 'myths' literally, but it is an admittedly difficult matter to scientifically investigate. Truly, we may also be tampering with beings and forces that we are not meant to interact with, at least for the time being. Again and again, the message in historical and present-day tribal lore is that these beings are quite powerful and certainly not to be messed with.

It might just help the general human condition, though, to promote a wider understanding of this idea, for it might go a long way toward improving our understanding of our exact place in the physical and metaphysical universe, and even help us grasp what exactly is meant by our own three letter word that we use to explain almost everything we do not understand: God.

By trying to understand the Ancestral Puebloan concept of supernatural beings, we uncover big clues to the concept of Deity as it (or they) exists across time. It is clear to me that the Anasazi concept of supernatural beings overlaps with and therefore pertains to our own. And achieving a better understanding of the nature of supernatural beings, and the role they play in our world, is perhaps the best reason to have ventured down the 'rabbit hole' in the first place.

Chapter Ten: First Contact

No terrestrial enigma is more difficult to resolve than crop circles. They are either the work of hoaxers *or* they are attempts to communicate directly with humanity by extraterrestrials that do not trust the news media to do the job. There really aren't too many other possibilities. Beyond the question of who is making these creative yet ephemeral patterns is the deeper question of what exactly they mean.

One big question that is often asked is why most crop circles are found in southern England. After all, what's so special about the English countryside? There are huge fields of cereal crops all over the place that are just waiting for messages from space. Are English crops, or English people, special?   More than likely, we are told, southern England happens to be the stomping ground of two wise-guy tavern chums named Doug and Dave, who have made a hobby of smashing cereal crops with boards and ropes just to make people who study the crop circle phenomenon look stupid. That is precisely what the unquestioning news media has told us all along.

So, it may come as a surprise to hear that not all crop circles are found in Hampshire, the home county of Doug and Dave and the pub where they plan their nocturnal capers. Ninety percent of crop circles are indeed found in southern England, but not in Hampshire County alone. Crop circles are also found in other English counties, and even other *countries*. Dave Chorley is now dead, and Doug Bower is 90 (as of 2014). Not only do crop circles continue to appear, but, in some cases, they are more elaborate than ever. Doug and Dave acknowledged in 1991 that, although they were taking credit for the entire crop circle phenomenon in the mid-eighties, they were not responsible for crop circles outside of Hampshire County. Years later, after Dave's death, Doug Bower also stated that they were indeed being encouraged to put themselves before the media by a shadow entity or organization that they themselves could not identify.

Veteran crop circle researcher Freddy Silva has been able to connect Doug and Dave's motivation to British military intelligence, also known as the Ministry of Defence (M.o.D.) In Silva's landmark book, *Secrets in the Field* (Hampton Roads, 2010), he does a better job of explaining the connection between Doug and Dave and the British military than I ever could. It all seemed pretty far-fetched at first, but I confess that I, too, was a crop circle skeptic until I had the chance to hear Freddy Silva speak in 2004 at a paranormal conference in Denver.

Among other things, I learned that there are a lot of dedicated and serious researchers, most of whom are indeed English. This discriminating bunch of field researchers are quite capable of distinguishing the fraudulent work of hoaxers from the genuine crop circles that do indeed seem to have extraterrestrial origin. According to Silva, Richard Hoagland, Peter Sorenson, Colin Andrews, Lucy Pringle, and others, the American, British, and German intelligence agencies simply do not want the general public to take the crop circle phenomenon seriously.

Instead, intelligence agencies in these three countries have exercised their considerable influence over the mainstream media to obfuscate and trivialize the truth. Crop circles, or 'crop formations,' as they are more properly known, represent the most profoundly important phenomenon of our time. Stalwart and courageous English researchers have tenaciously articulated this remarkable thought despite a well-organized and very well financed opposition. This suggests one possible reason why 90% of crop formations are indeed found in England: the English really *are* smarter than the rest of us, or at least more open-minded. Apparently, they are also more difficult to mislead with concocted media treatments that deliberately avoid a balanced presentation of the real and abundant evidence showing that many, even most crop formations do indeed have extraterrestrial origins.

When strange patterns are found in crop fields, they are properly known as 'crop glyphs' or 'crop formations.' (For purposes of brevity, permit me to abbreviate as CFs.) Mysterious circular impressions have been found since at least the 1890s, and probably much earlier still. That pretty much rules out Doug and Dave right there, but don't expect the media to point that out. Nor could Doug and Dave show us the frequent flier miles that they must have earned if they were indeed the force behind CFs as they occur worldwide. According to experts like Freddy Silva, there have been over 10,000 reported crop circles found to date and a hundred more appear every year. Despite the demise of Doug and Dave, crop circles continue to re-occur every summer as the vast fields of ripening cereal crops again become inviting palettes for profound artistic expression.

Just as most, but not all, CFs occur in southern England, most, but not all, CFs are found in crops. More than once, 'crop circles' have been found to be etched into forbidding desert landscapes. One notable example is an elaborate and beautiful pattern that was discovered in the hard-pan surface of a dried up, desert lake bed in Oregon. This 'geo-formation' or 'geo-glyph,' found in August of 1990, is certainly beyond the range of Hampshire County's Doug and Dave. If the public is to be persuaded that all CFs are the work of hoaxers, another set of hoaxers would have to be found for this one.

It all started when Lt. Col. Bill Miller guided his fighter plane along an aerial training route high above the eastern Oregon desert in the summer of 1990. Lieutenant Miller was returning to his base, Gowen Field near Boise, Idaho, when the immense geo-glyph, etched into the surface of Mickey Basin, caught his eye.

Mickey Basin is part of Oregon's vast Steens Mountain Wilderness. At 170,000 acres, the Steens Mountain Wilderness is a stark, desert landscape that straddles the transition zone from the high altitude desert of central Oregon to the even-drier basin-and-range landscape of the intermountain west. Nearly treeless mountain ranges alternate with flat-iron sage brush valley floors. Spring snow melt from Steens Mountain collects in parched valleys that surround the range. As summer heats up, the water evaporates, leaving an accumulating crust of dissolved minerals. Miniature versions of the Utah's vast Bonneville Salt Flats are formed. Mickey Basin is one such land-locked salt flat, or playa.

In 1990, the Steens Mountain desert landscape was not yet the federally protected Wilderness Area that it is today. Rather, it was a still a Wilderness Study Area, enjoying temporary protection while it was being considered for eventual inclusion in the National Wilderness Preservation System (NWPS).

As Lt. Bill Miller flew his training route over this arid landscape, an unusual geometric pattern caught his eye. Miller's Vietnam-era RF-4C Phantom II jet fighter carried no weapons, but, as fate would have it, his plane was fitted with high-resolution reconnaissance cameras. The landscape below Lt. Miller was all very familiar to him, making the huge and elaborate pattern in the desert lake bed all the more curious. From 9,000 feet, Miller snapped a picture of the geo-glyph, and then continued the final seventy miles to Gowen Field, where he dutifully reported his unusual observation. With his on-board camera, Miller documented the first-ever geo-glyph to appear in the United States on August 10th, 1990. Miller's discovery was not reported to any news outlets right away.

Artistic recreation of the Oregon Sri Yantra by Guy Edwards. To view photos of the original Google: Oregon Sri Yantra (The rights are held by Bill Witherspoon)

Lt. Miller was attached to the 124th Tactical Reconnaissance Group, which is part of the larger 190th Tactical Reconnaissance Squadron based at Gowen Field. The photo analysts there studied his photograph but had absolutely no explanation for the elaborate, quarter-mile wide, geometrically precise pattern of triangles, circles, and squares that had been perfectly inscribed into the rock-hard lake bed of Mickey Basin. One of the baffled photo interpreters even took the photo home and showed his wife, Alicia Gloeckle, who was able to match the photo with a picture in one of her Time-Life series of books on the occult. Ms. Gloeckle became the first to correctly identify the design on the desert floor as a mandala.

Most people are familiar with verbal mantras, like the word "ohm," that are used to focus the mind in meditation. Similarly, a mandala is a pictorial mantra that focuses the mind during meditation. The pattern that was so precisely etched in the Oregon desert wasn't just any old mandala; it was the most powerful and beautiful of all mandalas: the centuries-old Sri Yantra.

In her website, scholar and author Kathy Doore explains that the Sri Yantra, the holiest and most significant of all yantras, is composed of nine interlocking triangles that surround a center point, or 'bindu.' The inner pattern of interlocking triangles are surrounded by a series of petal-like curves, all that being enclosed within a series of closely-spaced squares, each side of each square containing a t-shape tab at its respective midpoint. The precise geometry of the Sri Yantra is very difficult to draw without errors, even on a piece of paper.

The Sri Yantra

293

Back at Gowen Field, the photo analysts were still scratching their heads. At one-quarter mile in width, this ancient Hindu mandala in the Oregon desert was profound not only for its size but its utterly perfect presentation. In all, it consisted of 13.3 miles of closely spaced, perfectly-placed lines. Other pilots from Gowen regularly travelled the same training route used by Bill Miller, but no one had seen the curious geo-glyph before Lt. Miller, either in its finished form or while it was still being created. Architects consulted by the Idaho Air National Guard estimated that the surveying alone of such an immense glyph would cost at least $75,000. How it so suddenly appeared, and why it was there in the first place, baffled the photo interpreters at the 190th Squadron.

Being part of a Wilderness Study Area, the remote location was off limits to the motor vehicles and mechanical devices that would be needed to complete such a huge project in such an inhospitable place. Not only was the location of the breath-taking glyph impossibly remote, but the surface of the lake bed it was etched upon was impenetrably hard.

News of Bill Miller's discovery was finally released to the media on September 12th, 1990. During this same period, crop formations were regularly appearing in England and their authenticity and origin was a matter of much debate. Such formations were, however, virtually unknown outside southern England. But a Boise TV station changed all that when they reported Bill Miller's fascinating discovery. Two days later, the story was first reported by Rick Attig of the *Bend Bulletin*, picked up by the Associated Press, then reported a day later in Portland's *Oregonian* newspaper. In Rick Attig's *Bend Bulletin* story, the public was reassured that, in late July, Charles "Sambo" Smith, a local ranch hand, saw two men pulling a garden plow across 'the desert' as he observed a third man walking along behind.

According to the story, 'Sambo' Smith did not bother to stop his pick-up truck and find out what the hell these men were doing. Nor did reporter Rick Attig bother to explain exactly how he managed to find 'Sambo' Smith amidst the plethora of ranch hands that must circulate throughout Harney County, Oregon. Indeed, 'Sambo' Smith never specified that he witnessed this unusual activity *in Mickey Basin proper*. The article said only that 'Sambo' Smith saw three men and a plow 'in the desert.' Interestingly, no road comes within view of the Mickey Basin salt flat where the geo-glyph appeared. The closest road is three quarters of a mile away. The disinformation begins.

Local UFO investigators Don Newman and Alan Decker saw the September 14th story in *The Bend Bulletin* and hustled out to Mickey Basin the very next day. One of the pair, Don Newman, was a military man himself, having flown B-17 Flying Fortresses during World War II. Newman had also served as a flight instructor in those historic and durable aircraft. He and his associate, Alan Decker, drove their own vehicle out onto the lake bed and observed that their vehicle left only slight, but still definite impressions in the lakebed. Yet, they found no other footprints or tire tracks of any kind in the vicinity of the glyph, which was situated in an otherwise pristine alkali flat.

This surprised Newman and Decker, since the *Bend Bulletin* story quoted Sgt. Charlie Swindell, head of photo quality with the 190th Tactical Reconnaissance Unit, as saying he personally visited the site and found surveyor's stakes at the corners of the design, as well as nails and strips of surveyors' flagging. Swindell also told the reporter that it was he who consulted local architects and obtained the estimate that the survey work required to achieve this enormous and elaborate design would cost between $75,000 and $100,000. Swindell further observed that the precision of the 1,563 sq. ft. design was "pretty doggone good." Rick Attig further reported that the Bureau of Land Management, who administered those particular federal lands, was investigating the incident, since, as agency spokesman Mark Armstrong noted, creation of the geo-glyph represented a blatant violation of land use rules for an official Wilderness Study Area.

Forty-four days after the geo-glyph was first discovered, an Iowa artist surfaced in the media. He took responsibility for the symbol that he claimed to have created in the name of 'outdoor art.' Bill Witherspoon claimed that he created the pattern in Mickey Basin using a non-mechanical garden plow that was alternatively pulled by his son Miles, James Ansley, Robert Hoerlin, and Anthony Lawler.

This is where the whole story gets really interesting. Witherspoon produced a video that purported to demonstrate how he and his companions managed to perfectly execute the creation of this enormous and elaborate pattern.

This video was viewed by the Bend-area UFO investigators Newman and Decker as they looked into the origin of the Mickey Basin glyph. They described Witherspoon explaining that his team carried their plow and related items two miles from their camp every day. Using a simple blueprint, they first staked out the shape with aluminum wires, then they followed the wire courses with a crude garden plow pulled by various members of his team. Witherspoon purports to demonstrate in the video the process of pulling the plow across the dry lake bed. Newman and Decker dispute the authenticity of this video tape. It was their observation that, on the video, Witherspoon and company generally followed the course of an already-made line of the geo-glyph.

I never saw this video although I looked for it. The UFO investigators who did view the video observed that the furrows created for the sake of the video were not as deep or as wide as the perfectly laid trenches in the original glyph. They further observed that the video clearly showed parallel hills of dirt unevenly falling on either side of the furrow as the soil-cutting action of the plow was being demonstrated. Unlike the furrows created for the video, they said, the lines of the Sri Yantra geo-glyph were incised *into* the ground with no such hills of raised earth to be seen anywhere.

Bill Witherspoon held a news conference, attended by Newman and Decker, at which he stated that it took ten days to create his outdoor art, and that he began his work on September 10th. (The glyph was discovered on August 10th.) No mechanized equipment was used. Witherspoon had no photos of the work in progress. On the question of how he hauled all the necessary construction and survival gear, Witherspoon now claimed that he and his compatriots travelled only three-quarters of a mile each day on foot, from their camp to the Mickey Basin site.

The central question was how this well-dressed, middle-aged artist and his team managed to endure ten days of arduous work in ninety-plus degree heat, with absolutely no natural shade, all equipment being hauled around on foot. According to Newman and Decker, after his interview with the assembled media, neither they, nor any of the other UFO or crop circle people, were buying Witherspoon's story.

Yet, the news media accepted Witherspoon's story at face value. TV and print media attributed the Mickey basin glyph to Bill Witherspoon. Meanwhile, Newman and Decker turned their field report over to their associate, retired Oregon State professor of atmospheric science James Deardorff. Dr. Deardorff publicly disputed Witherspoon's claim to being the originator of the lake bed geo-glyph. Deardorff calculated that something like fifty-three dump trucks of earth would have had to have been removed in order to achieve the tidiness of the final geo-glyph. Witherspoon, on the other hand, was not claiming the use of any dump trucks. Nor did Witherspoon convincingly recreate even a fraction of the glyph on the video Deardorff had seen. Dr. Deardorff went public with his considered opinion that Witherspoon's video was a ruse. In a story published in the *Spokane Spokesman-Review* on November 19th, 1990, Deardorff noted that Witherspoon's attempts to recreate even one line of the glyph were unpersuasive. Exerting great effort, Witherspoon was able to carve only a half-inch furrow; nowhere near the eight inch wide, three-inch-deep lines that comprised the Mickey Basin geo-glyph, as carefully measured by Newman and Decker.

Deardorff went on to insist that the thirty-three days that transpired between discovery of the glyph and the first official announcement of its discovery was extremely suspicious. This was more than enough time for some government entity to concoct the improbable story that an Iowa artist and a few friends used a plow, a blueprint, and a lot of wire to perfectly etch thirteen miles of complex geometric symbols in Mickey Basin in the name of 'outdoor art.' His human-pulled plow did not seem like the right implement, and humans were not the right power source, for carving such an extensive array of lines in such a forbidding location.

A year later, Deardorff learned from another UFO investigator, Jennifer Brown-Jacobs, that a UFO sighting had occurred around the same time and in the same area as the appearance of the Mickey Basin glyph. Two men camped with a sail plane group on the edge of the Alvord Desert eight miles from Mickey Basin observed three very bright lights hovering in the sky over a ten minute period, after which they observed the formation of a strange stationary cloud. Jennifer Brown-Jacobs was able to narrow down the date of this sighting to July 5th or 6th and to determine that, based on the direction and distance away, the UFO activity was directly over Mickey Basin. Yet, Capt. Michael Gollaher, of the 124th Tactical Recon Group told *The Bulletin* it was unlikely the glyph was made before mid-July, because other pilots who flew the same training route would have seen it sooner.

Faced with this unresolved conflict, I decided I needed to hear from Bill Witherspoon. I found that he still lived in Fairfield, Iowa and, ironically, he founded a company in 2002 that *manufactures illusions!* The Sky Factory makes and sells artificial skylights that display projected images of blue sky and moving clouds. The skylights are popular in dentist offices and medical facilities where patients must lie in one place for long periods during medical screening or dental procedures.

I asked him for rights to use the aerial photo he owned of the Mickey Basin glyph. He explained that would not grant rights to use the photograph until he saw the essay I was writing. He said he wanted to be sure I was not "adding to the misinformation" that was already out there. I sent him a draft of this chapter and after he read the draft, he not only refused to give me permission to use the photograph, but he got a little nasty about it:

Dear Thom,

I have read your version of the events surrounding the Sri Yantra project and unfortunately, your story does not contribute clarity but rather adds yet another layer of misinformation. This, and previous stories, reminds me of the children's game in which one child begins with a sentence whispered to the child sitting to the right, who continues the process by whispering what was heard to the next child in the circle. By the time it returns to the originator, it has become unrecognizable.

Your version is filled with incorrect (but easily verifiable) information; dates, people's names, sequences, events that never occurred, even distortion of the simplest traditional knowledge. It is hard to imagine how, starting with this poor research and scholarship about something that is completely transparent and known, you can develop sufficient credibility to meaningfully unravel what may well be a genuine mystery.

In any event, I had hoped you might bring a bit of clarity, but since that is not the case, you do not have permission to use my copyrighted images.

Sorry it didn't work out!

Best regards,

Bill Witherspoon

Ouch! I expected a negative reaction but not such a personal rebuke. Yet, it was also a reaction I had seen many times before. When a teacher catches a middle school student in a lie, a common reaction is an exaggerated degree of indignance, even outrage. Such a reaction, I have learned from in thirty years in a classroom, is an attempt to mask a degree of guilt. Another typical reaction is the tendency to resort to *ad hominem* (personal) attacks, rather than just sticking to the issues. I couldn't prove Mr. Witherspoon was lying, but his reaction did not help reassure me that the glyph was his creation. Rather, it aroused further suspicion. It began to appear that, "Something is rotten in the state of Denmark," as Marcellus observed in Shakespeare's *Hamlet*.

I tried to respond to Mr. Witherspoon's with politeness and even a *mea culpa* for my misuse of the word 'mandala.' I stated my desire to get the story right and my willingness to change anything that was not true. I requested he correct me. He replied that he didn't have time to go through my story chapter and verse. I understood. He was a busy man. He toned things down a bit:

> Dear Thom,
>
> Sorry the game analogy seemed impolite. Try this. In all information transmission the signal to noise ratio declines with every new iteration or copy. When humans are communicating, because, among other things, of their own agenda, the distortion is greatly accelerated.
>
> "Complete, accurate information about every aspect of the Sri Yantra construction was freely given out verbally and in writing shortly after its discovery. Since then, the "internet story" has changed due to those who, for personal reasons, have a need to believe that it is not a product of human effort.
>
> Without exception, these modifications, when viewed with even modest critical thinking, completely fall apart. For example, something new to me is the 13.5 mile long ball of twine…What we did use, as was disclosed, were various lengths of aluminum electric fence wire -the longest being about an eighth of a mile in length. There was no demo or after-the-fact video. There was video footage of the actual construction made by a professional videographer who was part of the crew.
>
> Those who were not happy with the humble human origin "proved" the video to be fraudulent in the following way. They correctly observed a slight disturbance of the playa surface ahead of the plow. This they asserted was because we had filled in an existing line and then plowed. (BTW, these were the same folks who labeled us as paid CIA cover-ups).
>
> An artist, or anyone who has ever made a large complex drawing would realize that to maintain accuracy, the plow must follow a predetermined path. A line-drawing of this sort can't be done free hand. The path for the plow was a line scratched into the playa surface. The layout of these lines took about 7 days, the plowing only 3.
>
> Bill Witherspoon"

As far as specifics, Mr. Witherspoon was giving me very little to support his story. Note that he said he used "various lengths of aluminum electric-fence wire" in the construction of the glyph. I'm not sure what folks were using in 1990, but today's electric fence tape is largely woven polypropylene (plastic) with strands of aluminum inlaid in the weave. Aluminum wire alone would be heavy and much more expensive. That wasn't important. What was important was seeing some sort of evidence to support Witherspoon's claim, video or otherwise.

I asked if I might rent, borrow, or buy a copy of the video he mentioned in the above letter. I also asked if there are any other creations of his that resemble the complexity of the Mickey Basin glyph. He replied:

> I just got off the phone and found that Jim Ansley, the videographer on our crew died several years ago. I never knew. He had all the video masters and I'm sure they are long gone. I do not believe I have any copy of the full plowing footage. However a short segment is included in the PBS/Iowa Public Television program that was done on the Sri Yantra and subsequent work. I believe that is posted online.

http://www.skyfactory.com/about/billvid.html
http://www.skyfactory.com/about/billvid2.html

I was a little surprised to read that Bill did not keep even one copy of the video that purports to display the creation of his artistic *magnum opus*. Surely the accomplishment of such a Herculean task would be a matter of enduring pride. Also, with all that 'misinformation' out there on the internet, one has to wonder why Bill Witherspoon has not done a better job of documenting his claim to authorship of the Mickey Basin glyph. All he had to do is post a copy of his video on YouTube for all to see. The case would have been closed.

But all copies, and the master, were destroyed when Jim Ansley died? Having nothing else to inspect, I eagerly studied the video segments attached to the links Bill provided. What I viewed was a TV segment produced by PBS affiliate IPTV, in Iowa. I was again surprised.

I encourage the curious reader to study the video and formulate one's own opinion. What I saw on the video was certainly not a probing expose of this enigma. Instead, it is a decidedly 'soft ball' treatment that aggrandizes Bill

Witherspoon as an outdoor artist, accepting every claim as fact and questioning nothing. The producers seemed completely unaware of the fact that there is controversy as to whether Bill Witherspoon is the legitimate creator of the Mickey Basin glyph.

In 1991, Witherspoon 'returned' to the Oregon desert. This time he got permission ahead of time from rancher Ed Davis to use a dried up lake bed on the Davis Ranch. This time everything was videotaped by Walden Kirsch, a reporter for KGW-TV, Portland. The 1991 glyph was constructed by mechanically spreading volcanic cinders on another playa using a very large, tractor-mounted fertilizer spreader. Everything was done mechanically, using tractors and quad cycles as power sources. The hand drawn plow was completely irrelevant, yet they made a point of including a brief four-second demonstration of its use.

I studied the video clips very carefully. All of the video seemed to show the construction of the Davis Ranch effort. The construction of the Mickey basin glyph was not shown, but it *was* shown in a completed state. Mechanized equipment was essential to the construction of the Davis Ranch glyph, but the story on the 1990 Mickey Basin glyph remained that the whole glyph, all 13.3 miles, was done by human power, alone. This discrepancy was never addressed in the IPTV video, nor was it mentioned in any part of the KGW video that was included. Most tellingly, aerial photos of the *finished* Mickey Basin glyph are spliced between shots that depict the creation of the *Davis Ranch glyph*.

The IPTV video raises more questions than it answers. It in no way lays the Mickey Basin matter to rest. It becomes obvious that there is some video sleight-of-hand going on in the way the IPTV segment was edited. After studying the video, I felt even more certain that 'something is rotten in the state of Denmark.'

I e-mailed Mr. Witherspoon and asked him where he camped while creating the Mickey basin glyph. He did not answer that question. I asked him whether he encountered any legal consequences for making the Mickey Basin Sri Yantra. He told me the Bureau of Land Management fined him $100 for defacing.

That seemed like a remarkably small penalty. Why didn't the BLM prosecute Bill Witherspoon to the fullest extent of the law? He publicly admitted to essentially defacing federal property. People who get caught chopping down a saguaro cactus or tagging a cliff face with graffiti on federal land are ordinarily fined $10-15,000 dollars and convicted of a felony. I would have expected much more severe consequences to befall Mr. Witherspoon if the government truly believed he carved thirteen miles of lines in a lake bed that was, at the time, a Wilderness Study Area. Convicting him would have been simple. He publicly admitted that he committed this crime and produced a video that would have been *prima facia* evidence of felonious behavior.

The key question, especially to the skeptic, is *why* Bill Witherspoon feels compelled to claim he created the glyph if he really did not. Dr. James Deardorff provided an answer to that question and Bill Witherspoon seems to be well aware of this. It was the view of Deardorff and others that Witherspoon's involvement was intended to dismantle the allegations that ETs, not Iowans, created the Mickey Basin Sri Yantra. In the 1980s and 1990s, at least one government on the other side of the Atlantic Ocean was actively obscuring the true origin of crop formations, presumably because the public was not ready for the truth. Crop circle researchers also speculate that the military or government people thought the whole phenomenon would go away in a few years.

There is definitely a grain of truth to this view. The cover story that Doug Bower and Dave Chorley were the perpetrators of all crop formations in southern England has been thoroughly discredited, and after the demise of Doug and Dave, crop formations continue to appear.

But, what possible incentive could be provided to a guy like Bill Witherspoon to maintain a phony cover story even twenty-five years after the fact? Wouldn't it be perfect if Bill Witherspoon were compensated for his cover story with some kind alien technology that the government acquired by way of a UFO crash? Conspiracy theorists would have a field day.

It turns out that Bill Witherspoon founded a company in 2002 that makes extremely impressive displays of artificial sky. They are essentially huge digitized video displays that look like giant picture windows that are built into ceilings or walls.

I found myself wondering how an 'outdoor artist' who used to drive a converted school bus around the Oregon desert scratching patterns into playas, managed to come up with a such spectacularly useful piece of advanced technology. The IPTV video mentions that Bill has a background in business. So I asked him who came up with that nifty invention he sells. I also asked him, once again, for the best evidence he could provide that he created the Mickey basin glyph. He replied:

Thom,

I believe that I am one of the people shown in the Mickey basin plowing video. If a person wanted to go to the trouble, they could be assured that it was in fact shot on the site by a careful matching of the background which is the north eastern side of Mickey Basin. But that's a lot of trouble and one would have to go on site. None of us took photographs of the process - just Jim's video. I had a 35 mm SLR which is what I used when I was flown over the site by the rancher at the Mann Lake Ranch. That was a few days after the completion and I shot about 2 rolls of slides from the air and maybe less than a roll from the ground. I'm sure that Hoyt Wilson (Mann Lake Ranch) would vouch for the fact that it was done by me and my crew. He is someone I knew before 1990 and he was fully aware of what was happening at the time. (He did send the BLM on a goose chase when they tried to probe him for my identity before I sent the public letter). I also believe that if the slides were properly enlarged, some would show the school bus parked at the edge of the playa.

The Sky Factory was founded by me in 2002. The technology, which is not rocket science, was developed to create *illusions* of sky that would be so convincing they would trigger the same relaxation response that is brought about by real sky. I was the artist and engineer behind the first products. Now we have electrical and mechanical engineers who are building the Digital Cinema products and new iterations of our SkyCeilings using LED and micro-control technology.

Bill Witherspoon

If and when a manned mission to Mars actually happens, big artificial windows like the ones Bill Witherspoon sells *will* be installed on the spacecraft. Psychologically, the astronauts would benefit greatly from a view outside the spacecraft. Real windows, especially big ones, would be vulnerable to damage from fast-moving particles in space. Instead of windows, digitized projections supplied by external cameras make much more sense. Gene Roddenberry knew this when he created his fictional starship *Enterprise*.

Like touch-screen computers and other recent technological innovations, Bill Witherspoon's sky view technology *will* be used on the spacecraft to Mars. It would be foolish *not* to use it. According to Miri (Chapter 8), the ETs she met are already using this technology.

To say the very least, Bill Witherspoon's involvement in the Mickey Basin geo-glyph is still a very open question. After all the communicating I did with Mr. Witherspoon, and after viewing the scant video evidence he provided, I am *not* convinced that he created the Mickey Basin glyph. Dr. James Deardorff's opinion that Bill Witherspoon did *not* create the Sri Yantra in Mickey Basin still has validity.

On a personal level, I got to know Bill Witherspoon a bit through his correspondences. He was condescending, but also a very articulate guy. As far as his role in creating the Mickey Basin glyph, as James Deardorf said, I'll believe him when he does it again, the exact same way. That has not happened, nor is it likely to. He made a glyph the year after the Mickey Basin glyph appeared, but his method of creating the Davis Ranch glyph bore no similarity whatsoever to the Mickey Basin glyph. Indeed, the Davis Ranch glyph looks a bit like a 'red-herring' meant to distract public scrutiny.

While Bill Witherspoon's role in the Mickey basin glyph remains an open question, what is certainly not an open question is that he had nothing at all to do with the hundreds of crop glyphs that appear in the English countryside over the past four decades. In the 1980s those glyphs were being officially attributed to Doug Bower and Dave Chorley. The pair were never prosecuted either, despite the fact that they publicly admitted to vandalizing numerous farmers' crops. When Doug and Dave went on television to demonstrate their crop-smashing equipment and technique, the absurdity of their claim also became readily apparent. Since then, 'Circlemakers' and other groups now claim to be creating the crop formations, yet their attempts to take credit for the whole crop circle phenomenon worldwide are equally unpersuasive.

Certainly, some CFs are the work of hoaxers. Just as certainly, most CFs are well beyond the capability of those who stand up and try to take credit for them. To name a single example, the breathtakingly beautiful Milk Hill crop glyph is so remarkable in its geometric precision and complexity that no one can replicate it persuasively.

Here is a crop circle constructed by Doug Bower and Dave Chorley to demonstrate their skill (or lack of). On the basis of this pathetic effort, the media failed to see any reason to doubt that they were the perpetrators of all crop circles.

Sheer, profound artistic perfection. Did Doug and Dave do this? Perhaps the Circle (fakers)? Not likely.

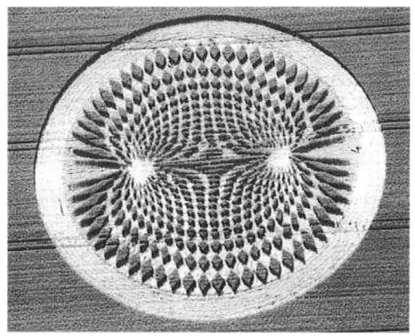

Genuine CFs are often pictorial displays of complex mathematical theorems or other scientific principles. 'Magnetic Fields' is clearly the theme of this highly detailed CF.

Freddy Silva offers a list of specifics that enable CF investigators to identify the genuine CFs.

1. Fake crop circles smash the stems of the wheat or other cereal crops, and separate many of the fragile heads from the stems of the plants. Genuine crop glyphs manifest stems that have been stretched unevenly at their base without any damage to the plants. Remarkably, the plant structure in a genuine CF is intact and the plants are still growing! Stems are perfectly bent at ninety degree angles just above the ground but they are not smashed, broken or pulverized in any way. Fake CFs are a mess of smashed and ruined plants.

2. The delicate seed heads of the wheat, rye, or canola (rapeseed) in a fake CF are often completely separated from the plants. The seed heads in real CFs are carefully and delicately 'laid' side by side, usually in interlocking or interwoven configurations that are up to five layers deep. Seed heads are completely intact in real CFs.

The largest crop circle ever: the remarkable Milk Hill glyph appeared on August 12, 2002, is 878 feet across, and consists of 409 separate circles. (Definitely not the work of Doug and Dave.)

3. Stems of altered crops in genuine CFs occasionally show signs of surface burning, even as the stems are otherwise undamaged. Sometimes the stems are hugely elongated. Often the nodes (where branching occurs along the stems) are blown open. It appears as though the plants are subjected to rapid bursts of intense heating that causes the stem to droop but not crease or break. It has been shown that this effect can be accomplished by exposing plants to intense bursts of infrasound (sounds below 12hz. that are inaudible to humans). Ultrasonic vibration may also be capable of producing this same effect on plants.

4. The soft, chalky English soils are particularly good at preserving the impression of footprints. Footprints abound in fake CFs, and are absent in genuine CFs.

5. CFs typically appear between 2 and 4 a.m. in late summer, during the shortest darkness period of the year which, in southern England, is only four hours of total darkness.

6. Crystalline structure of plants and soil are dramatically altered in real CFs. The soil in real CFs is dramatically drier than the surrounding

307

soil. Many tons of water are mysteriously absent from the soil in genuine CFs.

7. Seeds that are collected and germinated from mature seed heads in genuine crop circles grow five times more vigorously than ordinary seeds of the same plant species.

8. Electromagnetic irregularities are easily detected in real CFs. Batteries in digital cameras and camcorders often go dead. Digital watches go dead. Cell phones malfunction. In one instance, car batteries of an entire nearby villages failed. In another instance, a whole nearby town lost power. Aircraft flying low over new CFs often experience instrument malfunction. People with pacemakers and other electronic medical devices are strongly advised not to enter genuine CFs since the ambient electromagnetic disturbances associated with genuine CFs will cause those devices to fail. Human-built (fake) CFs bear no such electromagnetic irregularities.

9. Edges of genuine CFs are crisp, clean, and essentially perfect. Complexity of the patterns and imagery is not only stunning, but it has been gradually increasing in complexity over the decades during which the phenomenon manifested itself for closer scrutiny. Fake CFs are simple, even crude patterns that rely heavily on string-guided, circular patterns. Even the slightest contact with the radiating string invariably separates the delicate seed heads from the parent plants, and keeping the string away from the tops of the plants is much more difficult than most people realize. String leaves tell-tale indications that are very easy to recognize.

10. Alternatively, Genuine CFs appear very quickly, regardless of the complexity of the design and they usually, but not always appear in the dead of night. Fake CFs are created during the daytime, presumably because laying out even a simple design at night is immensely more complicated. Leaving no surrounding footprints or other indications of human travel is even tougher. CFs seem to always occur when the cereal crop is fully or nearly mature. This means CFs tend to occur in canola (rapeseed) fields in April. In June and July, the CFs shift to fields of barley, and wheat and oats bear the brunt of the designs in August. In mid- to late summer, the period of total darkness in southern England is a brief four to six hours. Creating anything but the simplest designs in this time interval is virtually impossible. Fakers

will set up their work during the daytime, usually using several days of preliminary work, and then employing lots of artificial lighting to complete even a single night's work.

Why do fakers even bother working so hard to create inferior CFs? Even a simple human-built CF requires a large amount of time and money. In 1994, five men set out to demonstrate that they could create a perfect and respectable CF. It took them two full days, working in full daylight, to create a simple circular formation. Compare this investment of time and effort to the nearly instantaneous appearance of the better-documented CFs.

In 1996, pilots flying tourists around Stonehenge discovered a CF that appeared within a one hour interval! Pilots regularly circle the famous Neolithic structure with tourists aboard. At 5:15 p.m., a pilot circled Stonehenge and nothing unusual was observed in that flyover. At 6:15, the same pilot followed the same flight path over Stonehenge with a new load of sightseers and observed a glyph composed of 151 perfect circles arranged in a geometric expression known as a 'Julia Set.' This formation appeared within easy sight of a busy highway (A103) yet no one reported any circle-making activity. The researchers consulted the security guard at Stonehenge, who saw nothing out of the ordinary. They also consulted surveyors who estimated that it would take two full days to survey and construct the formation.

Real CFs consistently appear in similarly brief, almost instant intervals of time. Incandescent balls of light and structured crafts are sometimes observed in association with the rapid appearance of genuine CFs. For this reason alone, it seems difficult to argue that the CF phenomenon is *not* extraterrestrial in origin. The only real alternative is that a highly sophisticated ability to alter plants (and etch salt flats in the desert) into elaborate patterns is secretly held and being tested by the military of certain countries. It also becomes evident to investigators like Freddy Silva, Jim Hoagland, and many others, that there is a great deal of money being steered into organized efforts to discredit the crop-formation phenomenon. Why? Obviously, it is because the knowledge that genuine CFs are indeed extraterrestrial in origin is seen as a threat to powerful groups right here on Earth.

1996 Julia Set (lower center) and Stonehenge (top center of photo)

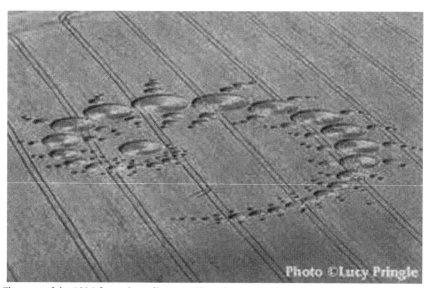

Close up of the 1996 formation adjacent to Stonehenge

In order to substantiate this conclusion, it behooves us to examine a couple of the most fascinating and important CFs ever found. The Mickey Basin geoglyph is unique for its astoundingly perfect geometry, the forbidding location and the impenetrable surface upon which it is inscribed. The CFs of southern

England, on the other hand, are notable for their astoundingly mathematical and geometric complexities, but they are usually found in fields much nearer to towns and roads. In previous times, crop circles were all fairly simple geometric representations. Over time, the size and complexity of genuine CFs has greatly increased. More recently, complex geometric and mathematical theorems are perfectly and precisely manifest in the cereal crops of southern England and elsewhere. But it doesn't end there. Specific messages are ingeniously encoded within certain formations.

Two of the best examples are the remarkable Chilbolton and the Crabwood crop formations. Because of their presumptive messages, these two CFs are often described as the two most important crop formations ever studied.

The Chilbolton Glyph

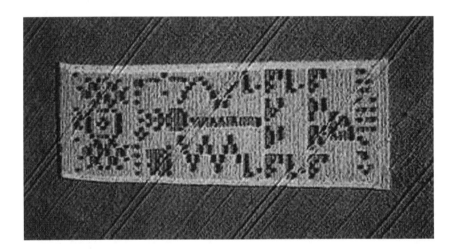

The Chilbolton crop glyph is said to be one of the two most important CFs ever, not only because it contained a definite message, but also because that message, found in a wheat field next to a radio telescope, was a clear and specific reply to a message that was sent *into* space by another radio telescope twenty-five years earlier.

The original message, designed by two famous astronomers, Carl Sagan and Frank Drake, was sent into space using the Arecibo Radio Telescope in Puerto Rico as part of the Search for Extraterrestrial Intelligence (SETI) Program. The message found in the wheat field next to the Chilbolton Radio

Telescope is often called the 'Arecibo reply,' and it has kept crop circle advocates, crop circle skeptics, and the general public scratching their head ever since it appeared in August of 2001.

Veteran crop circle investigators Paul Vigay, Freddy Silva, Lucy Pringle, and Colin Andrews all visited the Chilbolton site within a week of the August 20th appearance of this fascinating formation. Paul Vigay was the first to recognize that this new glyph, which was situated less than a hundred yards from a radio telescope owned by the British Ministry of Defence, bore a striking similarity to the Arecibo message that was beamed into space in 1974. Meanwhile, Lucy Pringle alerted London's *Daily Mail* and three days of intense media attention followed.

Meanwhile, the CF experts were divided: Colin Andrews was suspicious, as was Freddy Silva. Recently, I had the chance to ask Freddy Silva what he thought of the Chilbolton CF and he confided that he had reason to doubt it. Paul Vigay also inspected the site for indications of authenticity and came away undecided. Still, he observed that the creation of such a detailed glyph within the constraints of a few hours darkness is extremely impressive, irrespective of its origin.

When I learned that Carl Sagan was being treated for bone cancer, I encouraged my students, who had watched his *Cosmos* series in class, to write him and reflect on the impact of his presentation. One year after this reply was received, in December of 1996, Carl Sagan died. As a career astronomy teacher, I have closely followed the career of Carl Sagan, and I was aware of the SETI message from its inception in 1974. Yet, like most others outside of Great Britain, my first exposure to the crop circle phenomenon came from a photo of a crop formation used on the album cover of a 1990 Led Zeppelin release entitled "Remasters." It featured a photo of the July, 1990 CF found at Alton Barnes. Interestingly, the release of this album in November of 1990 coincided with the dust-up over the discovery of the Mickey Basin glyph in Oregon, also in the fall of 1990. Being an Oregon resident, I was aware of the media attention being given to the Mickey Basin glyph, and I accepted the official story that it was created by a self-described outdoor artist named Bill Witherspoon and his hand-drawn plow.

Having also followed the controversy surrounding the Chilbolton 'Arecibo reply' for the past thirteen years, I feel more confident than ever that the Arecibo reply is a genuine CF created by ETs. I might qualify my statement by adding that the ETs are perhaps more accurately described as inter-dimensional travelers who have a long, but largely unseen presence here on Earth.

The original Arecibo message was devised by astophysicist Carl Sagan and Dr. Frank Drake, then director of the Arecibo Radio Telescope in Puerto Rico. In 1974, the one thousand foot-diameter telescope had just undergone some renovations that boosted its output. The SETI team was eager to demonstrate its new and improved 20 terawatt (20 trillion watt) capability. On Sagan's encouragement, Dr. Drake devised a binary coded message that could be transmitted toward the stars using a simple collection of 1679 electronic pulses. This number 1679 was chosen for its unique value as the product of two prime numbers, 23 and 73. It was Sagan's thinking that this clue to the interpretation of the message could be deduced by an intelligent group of receiving ETs. If the unique multipes of 1679 were used as axis, the on-off pulses could be configured into a binary-coded rectangular picture that was 23 bits wide by 73 bits high.

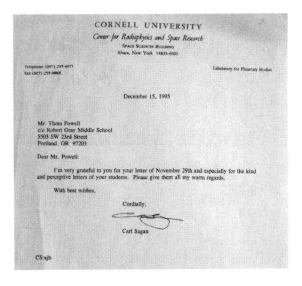

The radio frequency chosen for the transmission, 2380MHz, would also serve as the standard unit of for all measurements provided by the transmission, since one wavelength of that frequency was 12.6 centimeters in length, which is almost exactly five inches.

"Arecibo Reply" glyph (bottom left) "Face" glyph from a week earlier (top left) And Chilbolton Radio Telescope (bottom right).

Drake got busy and designed the message. He later described its unveiling:

> "Carl knew I was constructing this [Arecibo] message, and since he was very interested in it, he volunteered to be a proxy extraterrestrial. So one day we went off to the campus faculty club and had a long lunch while I silently laid out the rough drawing of the message in front of him .... He had a few suggestions for improvements, but the message worked. I felt full of confidence this time as the computers at Arecibo went to work constructing the commands needed to control the radio transmitters."

The plan was to transmit the coded message as part of a ceremonial unveiling of the newly upgraded Arecibo transmitter on November 16th, 1974. It would be directed at M-13, a globular cluster of about 300,000 stars in the constellation Hercules. At light speed, it would take the message 24,000 years to reach M-13, so a reply by conventional means would not be expected to arrive back here on Earth for twice that long: 48,000 years. While this calculation did not bode well for our expectations of receiving a reply any time soon, it was a great gimmick for rolling out the improved capabilities of the Arecibo Radio Transmitter. The 1679 pulses, binary coded into ones and zeros are seen below.

```
0000001010101000000000000010100000101000000010010001000100010010110010101010101
0101010010010000000000000000000000000000000000000111000000000000000000011010000
00000000000000000110100000010000010101000000000000000000000000011111000000000000
000000000000000000000011000011100011000011000100000000000000011001000011010001100010
100001101011110111110111110111110000000000000000000000000000100000000000000000001
000000000000000000000000000000001000000000000000001111100000000000000000011111100000000
0000000000000000110000110000111000110000100000001000000000100001101000001100011110
011010111110111110111111011110000000000000000000000000000001000000011000000000010000
000000011000000000000000100000110000000000111110000011000000111110000000000011
00000000000000010000000010000000001000001000000011000000001000000011000011000000100
0000000011000100001100000000000000000110011000000000000011000100001100000000110
00011000000100000000100000010000001000000010000000100000001000000000011000000000
00001000100000000001000000010000010000000000000000010000000100000000000000000100000111
11000000000000010000101110100101101100000001001110010011111111011100001110000010
11100000000001010000011101100100000010100000011111100100000010100000110000001000
00110110000000000000000000000000000000000011100000100000000000000011101010001001
0101010100111000000000101010100000000000000000101000000000000000011111100000000000
00000111111111000000000000011100000001110000000001100000000000011000000011010000
00000101000001100110000000011001100001000100101000001010001000010001001000100100
10000000010001010001000000000000010000000000000001000000000010000000001000000000000
00100101000000000000111100111111010010011110000
```

Several years later, Sagan would explain the content of the message as follows:

> The decoded message forms a kind of pictogram that says something like this: 'Here is how we count from one to ten. Here are five atoms that we think are interesting or important: hydrogen, carbon, nitrogen, oxygen and phosphorus. Here are some ways to put these atoms together that we think interesting or important - the molecules thymine, adenine, guanine and cytosine, and a chain composed of alternating sugars and phosphates.
>
> These molecular building blocks are put together to form a long molecule of DNA comprising about four billion links in the chain. The molecule is a double helix. In some way this molecule is important for the clumsy looking creature at the center of the message. That creature is 14 radio wavelengths or 5 feet 9.5 inches tall. There are about four billion of these creatures on the third plant from our star. There are nine planets altogether, four big ones toward the outside and one little one at the extremity.
>
> This message is brought to you courtesy of a radio telescope 2,430 wavelengths or 1,004 feet in diameter.
>
> Yours truly."

On the next page, the pictorial message has been changed from zeroes and ones to pixels so as to improve the contrast and readability of the image. The first of the pixilated views (at left, below) shows precisely the same configuration of block images as the original picture made of ones and zeroes. The second of the two side-by-side pixilated images is a mirror image. The mirror-image view becomes important because that is technically NOT the message that was sent into space, but that mirror-image is the image that is usually displayed in textbooks, including Sagan's own books and articles on the subject. The "How to read the 'Arecibo reply'" graphic (below) is also a reverse image of the message that appeared in a wheat field next to the Chilbolton radio telescope in 2001.

When discussing his findings at Chilbolton, Paul Vigay puzzled over the fact that all the textbook images he studied were reversed when compared to the actual message that was transmitted in binary form. Perhaps most importantly, the original image, not the mirror image that usually appears in publications, is the configuration that was imaged in wheat in the glyph that was found next to the Chilbolton radio telescope on August 20, 2001.

The Arecibo message arranged in 23 x 73 binary format (right).

```
00000010101010000000000
00101000001010000000100
10001000100010010110010
10101010101010100100100
00000000000000000000000
00000000000011000000000
00000000001101000000000
00000000001101000000000
00000000010101000000000
00000000011111000000000
00000000000000000000000
11000011100011000011000
10000000000000110010000
11010001100011000011010
11111011111011111011111
00000000000000000000000
00010000000000000000010
00000000000000000000000
00010000000000000000001
11111000000000000011111
00000000000000000000000
11000011000011100011000
10000000100000000010000
11010000110001110011010
11111011111011111011111
00000000000000000000000
00010000001100000000010
00000000011000000000000
00010000001100000000001
11111000001100000011111
00000000001100000000000
00100000001000000000100
00010000001100000001000
00001100001100000010000
00000011000100001100000
00000000001100110000000
00000011000100001100000
00011100001100000010000
00010000001000000001000
00100000001100000000100
01000000001100000000100
01000000000100000001000
00100000001000000010000
00010000000000001100000
00001100000000110000000
00100011101011000000000
00100000000000000000000
00100000111110000000000
00100010111011010011011
00000010011100100111111
10111000011100000110111
00000000010100000111011
00100000010100000111111
00100000011000000110000
00100000110110000000000
00000000000000000000000
00111000001000000000000
00111010100010101010101
00111000000000101010100
00000000000000101000000
00000000111110000000000
00000111111111100000000
00001110000000111000000
00011000000000001100000
00110100000000010110000
01100110000000110011000
01000101000001010001000
01000100100010010001000
00000100010100010000000
00001000001000010000000
00001000000000010000000
00000010010100000000000
01111001111101001111000
```

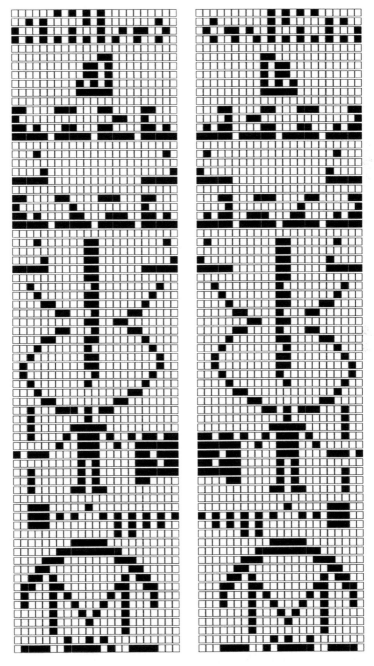

Coded pulses changed to b/w pixel
grid exactly as transmitted, 11/1974

Reverse image that appears in
most texts, including Sagan's

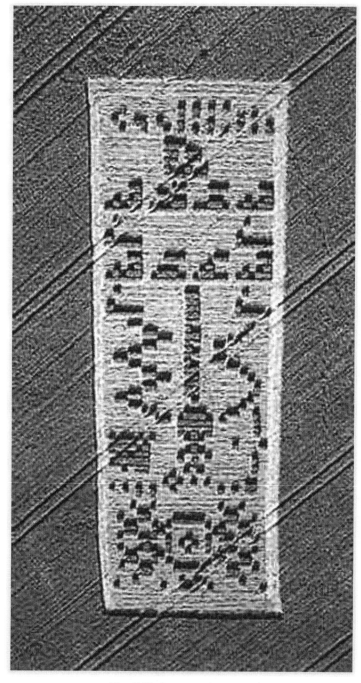

The Chilbolton crop formation

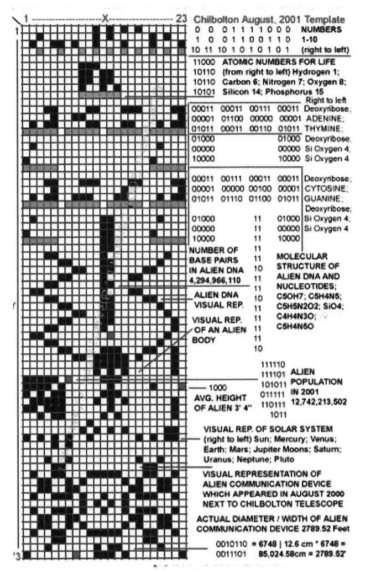

The Chilbolton 'Arecibo reply' glyph andhow to read the 'Arecibo reply'

Several interesting differences appear in the crop formation known as the 'Arecibo reply.' Starting at the top, the number 14 appears in the elements essential for life, indicating that silicon is an important element for life. Indeed, the importance of silicon to life on Earth is something that may have been overlooked by the preparers of the original Arecibo message. This raises the possibility that the Arecibo reply is as much a correction of the errors that were transmitted in the original Arecibo message.

The idea that this crop formation was hoaxed does not stand up to careful scrutiny. The image in the wheat is extremely complex, involving hundreds of square corners, which are much more difficult to achieve in crops than smoothly curving lines. This glyph would have to be practiced in another wheat field somewhere, probably more than once, in order to execute it perfectly. The only ordinary way of accomplishing such a highly structured, angular picture is to lay out an enormous string grid with pre-determined marks on the strings, which would be used to guide the flattening of the wheat. All of this would have to happen in a four hour window of total darkness. Flood lights would presumably be necessary, and the manager of the observatory reported nothing out of the ordinary on the night of August 19-20 when the glyph appeared. This would have taken many hours, perhaps days; an amount of time that hoaxers simply did not have. The usual issues persist: how did hoaxers bend the wheat without creasing any stems or breaking off any of the seed heads. Paul Vigay was among the first to visit the formation personally, and he found the formation to be impressive. Freddy Silva was another of the 'first responders.' He told me he found a laser-sighting device in the glyph. Freddy told me he also had a report of lights being seen in the field that night. He remains generally skeptical of the authenticity of this particular glyph.

It is easy for me to imagine a scenario in which the glyph is authentic despite the presence of a laser-pointer. The radio telescope that is a literal stone's throw from the glyph was operated by the British Ministry of Defense, until it was converted (we are told) to a weather radar station. It was built in 1965 for the official purpose of studying the atmospheric effects on radio waves from space. This is complete baloney. Radio telescopes built in 1965 were built for only one purpose: intercepting signals from NATO's principal adversary, the Soviet Union. The first radio telescope, the horn antenna built in New Jersey by Bell Labs, under the direction of Robert Wilson and Arno Penzias was also built in 1965. It was built to test the idea of intercepting Soviet satellite transmissions. (The serendipitous discovery of three-degree background radiation when Wilson and Penzias first began using the horn antenna eventually earned them the Nobel Prize in Physics.)

The proximity of the Chilbolton radio telescope, an aging piece of Cold War spy gear, to the Arecibo reply glyph is no coincidence. The Arecibo reply is aligned in such a way that it literally points directly at the Chilbolton dish telescope (see photo). The complexity of this glyph is such that it is well beyond the scope of tavern chums Doug Bower and Dave Chorley, even though it appeared in their home county of Hampshire. It has been observed by Richard Hoagland and others that whoever created the Chilbolton glyph must possess what he describes as 'hyper-dimensional physics' technology. Both Hoagland and Vigay suggest that this technology may be in government hands, making the Arecibo Reply a bit of a black project of Britain's Ministry of Defence.

Personally, I don't give MoD that much credit. If they were in possession of such a potentially useful secret technology, why advertise it? At the very least, they could be expected to take their experimentation a little further from home when testing it. On the other hand, if MoD conducts an ongoing campaign to throw off the crop circle investigators and discredit the phenomenon, (and Freddy Silva has documented that fact) then the easiest way to discredit the Arecibo reply (also known as the Chilbolton crop formation) would be to contaminate the site with a piece of technology that would raise the suspicions. Since the glyph was literally in the backyard of their own installation, MoD operatives would be perfectly positioned to do precisely that: go out there and toss a laser-level on the ground for the crop circle detectives to 'discover.' Contamination of the Chilbolton CF by MoD would be a foregone conclusion.

The further creation of a 'witness' who was willing to claim seeing flood lights in the field would be similarly expected, even as no indication could be found of where these lights were situated, how they were powered, or how the field was even accessed without leaving traces of any human ingress or egress. Even the existence of lights (which was by no means demonstrated) would not make creation of such a complex glyph possible within the context of a single night.

Beyond the insurmountable practical problems with the creation of the Arecibo reply, the intellectual achievements manifest in the message, once it is decoded, gives one pause. The information presented, when contrasted with the original Arecibo message, begins to look like a correction; an attempt to educate us as to the true nature of our solar system, as opposed to our slightly flawed understanding of space and our solar system as it was manifest in the original Arecibo message that was prepared by Sagan and Drake.

Of course, anyone who is skeptical of the veracity of the Arecibo reply, such as Seth Shostak, current director of the SETI program, is quick to point out that the reply appeared far too soon. The message was directed at a star cluster 24,000 light years away, yet the answer appeared only twenty-seven years after it was sent.

Really, Seth? Is this simple fact the 'deal breaker' for any argument that the Chilbolton message is genuine. Why am I shocked that the director of SETI, Dr. Shostak, cannot grasp the possibility that advanced extraterrestrials are able to circumvent galactic speed limits? Did this esteemed scientist miss the memo on the possibility of 'Einstein-Rosen bridges'? (for more info, see Zoo Hypothesis, Chapter 8.)

I may be advocating some paranormal ideas in this book, but the idea that extraterrestrials are completely aware of our science, technology, and culture is not one of the more radical ideas I am advocating. I once had dinner with Dr. Shostak on the occasion of his visit to Portland. He ridiculed the fairly ordinary concept of ET existence at dinner, and again spoke disdainfully of the concept in his prepared remarks that evening at the Oregon Museum of Science and Industry, so I guess I am not surprised by his lack of imagination.

In any case, a line-by-line examination of the Arecibo reply opens up a very interesting can of worms. It seems to speak of a keen awareness of many scientific ideas that may have been mis-expressed in the original Arecibo message that was concocted in 1974.

Upon careful study, several changes to the Arecibo Message appear in the CF known Chilbolton 'Arecibo reply.' Here they are:

1. An element with the atomic number 14 (Silicon) was added to the list of elements deemed essential for life. Does this mean the ET's are silicon (instead of carbon) based life forms, or is it telling us that silicon is more important to our own existence than we originally supposed? Even since 1974, when the original Arecibo message was prepared, a greater understanding has been gained of the specific role of silicon in our chemistry. For example, without silicon, our bones would be too weak to withstand the pull of Earth's gravity. Silicon *should* be on the list of elements necessary for terrestrial life, but it was left off. Is our thinking being corrected?

2. The Arecibo reply did not include the same silicon atom in the chemical structure of the sugars and bases that make up their/our

DNA. This suggests that silicon is no more important to their chemical structure than our own. Silicon may not be an important part of their DNA or ours, even though it *is* important in other chemical compounds that are necessary for life.

3. The pictorial representation of the DNA strand on the Arecibo reply appears to show a third strand. Does extraterrestrial DNA consist of three strands as opposed to our familiar two strands? Or, are we being told how genetic manipulation and duplication is really carried out, by attaching a temporary third strand to the familiar double-helix DNA structure. Perhaps the ETs are showing us how our own DNA copies itself and can be artificially manipulated.

4. The vertical bar that extends down the center of both messages encodes the number of base pairs in our DNA. Strangely, Sagan encoded the number 4.2944 billion base pairs in the human genome, even though the most prominent geneticists at the time, Watson and Crick (the discoverers of DNA) were estimating *one billion* base pairs (circa 1974). As the human genome has been sequenced since then, the estimates of the actual number of base pairs in our DNA has steadily risen. Yet, the most current estimates for the number of base pairs in the human genome is still somewhere between 3.0 and 3.2 billion base pairs. That number has not meaningfully changed in the last ten years. If anything, the most current estimates have gone down a bit from 3.2 to 3.0 billion. It must, however, be said that sequencing is not the best way of accurately counting base pairs. Large parts of the human genome appear to be redundant, so certain segments of this huge molecule are reduced to *estimates* of the number of base pairs, especially when sequencing the redundant portions of the human DNA molecule. That said, the 'Arecibo reply' clearly specifies that there are 4.2949 billion base pairs in whoever's DNA is being referred to, whether it is ours or theirs. That's 500,000 base pairs more than the already too-large number that Sagan provided to Frank Drake when preparing the message, and *that* number was vastly greater than the number that was considered 'textbook' in 1974. Yet, when describing the Arecibo transmission in his writings, Sagan repeated this strangely too-high number again and again.

Given the fact that Sagan was a valued source of information for some of the most secretive government departments, it seems that

Sagan knew more than he was letting on. It is probable that Sagan was privy to some sensitive information, up to and including alien autopsy information that may or may not have been obtained as a consequence of the proverbial Roswell crash site. Not only does the Arecibo reply seem to validate Sagan's radical estimate of the number of base pairs in our DNA, it even corrects in an unlikely direction (*upward*).

5. The simple drawing of the human form on the Arecibo message of 1974 was replaced with the almost cliché representation of the same small bodied, big headed ET that we are told was procured at the Roswell crash site. The height of this classic 'Grey' alien is given as something between three and four feet.

6. The population estimate for our planet in 1974, namely 4.2 billion, is replaced with a number in excess of 21 billion. Is this the planet from which the ETs originated, or are there more intelligent inhabitants of our own solar system than we realize? Are some of the 'lower' life forms on our Earth actually worthy of inclusion in our estimates, or do inter-dimensional beings occupy our world in much higher numbers than we realize? Is it possible that the subterranean occupants of our world are as numerous as us surface-dwelling occupants, as was postulated in the previous chapter?

7. In the original transmission, the third rock from the sun is raised to indicate Earth's place in the solar system. The 'reply' instead raises three of the sun's satellites. The similarities to our own solar system are otherwise striking. It again appears to be referring to our own solar system, although we cannot be certain. If it is our solar system, then the ETs omitted Pluto, knowing we would eventually disqualify it as a planet, which was done by the International Astronomical Union (I.A.U.) in August of 2006. Mars is also raised, indicating it is seen as habitable in the ET view, as is (or was) the asteroid belt, which is postulated by some to have once been a planet prior to its unfortunate destruction.

8. And finally, the simple representation of the Arecibo dish is replaced by a stylized portrayal of a device that is presumably an equivalent of a radio-telescope, or perhaps a device they are suggesting we could use to improve our transmitting and receiving of messages. Curiously, the identical image was depicted in wheat in the same field next to the Chilbolton radio telescope in the previous year.

The Chilbolton crop formation displays not only a fairly complex and detailed image, but it appeared too suddenly, too perfectly, and too closely to a Ministry of Defence installation to be the work of loosely-organized hoaxers. The ingenuity of the glyph and the scientific insights that it expresses gives us *so* much to wonder about that it just does not fit into the pattern of hoaxed crop formations.

It not only seems to convey a keen understanding of our earth-based science paradigm, but also an awareness of the limits and even misunderstandings of our 70's-era science. In the thirteen years since its discovery, no one has come forward to claim credit for creating the 'Arecibo reply'(Chilbolton CF), nor has anyone ever presented a coherent scheme for the creation of such a complex glyph. For all of the above reasons, I'm willing to call the Chilbolton glyph the real thing: not just a crop formation that could not have been faked, but one with a profound message for all humanity. It is the message contained within it that makes the Chilbolton glyph so profound. It is all about communication. It is not only an acknowledgement of our own first attempt to communicate using light-speed radio transmission in 1974, but it is also a considered response, albeit a somewhat cryptic one. The Chilbolton glyph is indeed one of the most profound of all crop circles, as it is rightfully described by crop circle investigators. But there is one more crop formation that may be even more profound, and that is the Crabwood Glyph that appeared the following year.

The Crabwood Glyph

On July 19, 1952, the U.S. military detected radar blips of unknown origin over Washington D.C. Calculated speeds ranged between 100 and 7200 miles an hour. F-94 fighter jets were scrambled, but as soon as they closed on the location, the UFOs vanished. When the jet fighters returned to base, the mysterious lights over the U.S. Capitol returned. On July 26th of that same year, the same objects were again detected over Washington D.C. Again, F-94s were scrambled and again the UFOs vanished, only to return when the fighter jets left the area. The fighter jets played cat and mouse with the UFOs, and at one point, one of the fighter pilots was heard to say, "They've surrounded my plane. What should I do?"

Newspapers carried descriptions of the encounters as well as a photograph of a cluster of aerial lights over the U.S. Capitol building. Eager to assuage the intense public concern, a Major Samford of the USAF was quoted as attributing the events to bad weather *and* temperature inversion. Apparently two explanations, even conflicting ones, are more convincing than one (inversions only occur during calm weather). What is the relevance of these curious events to the Crabwood glyph? It appears that the Crabwood glyph actually references these menacing events in the encoded message it contains!

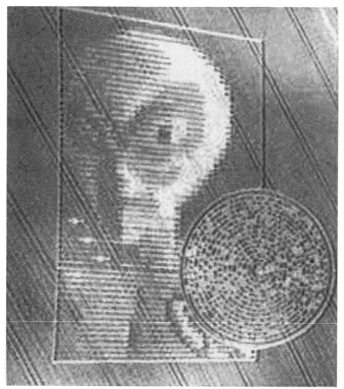

The Crabwood crop formation of 2002

If the 'Arecibo reply' is all about communication, the Crabwood glyph takes the communication theme to a whole new level. It also has few doubts as to its authenticity. The Crabwood glyph profoundly references very significant historical events, it carries multiple, and ingeniously designed codes and it is, for all these reasons, the most profound and significant crop formation of all time.

The Crabwood glyph appeared on August 15th, one year after the Chilbolton glyph and only 8 ½ miles distant. The uniquely detailed formation was first inspected by renowned investigator Lucy Pringle two days after it was noticed at Vale Farm. The farm is owned by Mike Burge, a farmer who grows wheat as a highly valuable seed crop. Unlike many farmers who feel cursed by the appearance of crop formations, Mr. Burge and his son were very interested in the formation and they were unusually accommodating of the crop circle investigators who descended upon his farm in the days following its discovery.

The Crabwood area's human history is positively ancient. Roman coins and pottery shards have been recovered from the immediate area that date back to 80 A.D. Flint fragments from the area suggest the area has been continuously occupied since the Iron Age some 12,000 years ago. Freddy Silva has observed that crop formations often occur in similarly historic, even sacred locations. He further postulates that ley lines with the Earth's greater umbrella of magnetic fields, as well as ground water concentrations, correlate highly with crop formation occurrences. Silva cites these elements as reasons why southern England is such a hotbed of crop formations. Lucy Pringle adds that 90% of CFs are found where the Yorkshire Aquifer moves through deposits of chalk bedrock.

When Lucy Pringle personally visited the Crabwood formation, she observed all the elements of a genuine glyph: Stems all bent at the base, singed stems, but otherwise undamaged stems, and plants that were still growing. The flattened crops were delicately swirled around the standing tufts, with no damage at all to any seed heads and no broken stalks at all. Unlike most crop glyphs, the *standing* wheat formed the image of a face, whereas the flattened wheat almost always formed the basis of the previous crop images. Pringle stated that she had only seen this pattern once before, and that was the Chilbolton face next to the 'Arecibo reply' at Crabwood.

The Crabwood CF was constructed from fifty two lines of imaging, just as old television sets used in the 1950's and '60's. The details of the face were done in a 'half-tone' dot structure, like newspaper photographs. The whole formation was oriented at a perpendicular angle to a pair of very nearby communication antennas owned by Verizon wireless, just as the Chilbolton glyph was placed in close proximity to a radio telescope. Once again, the theme of this impressively-detailed glyph seemed to be 'communication,' maybe even focusing on the 1950's-era televised disinformation.

It was Lucy Pringle's view that no known man-made energy was capable of producing such a formation in the crop. It was also perfectly obvious that the face being portrayed was that of an extraterrestrial. Of this point, there just cannot be any doubt. Three stars appeared near the shoulder of the ET face. Could they be some sort of indication of rank? Was this the face of the crop formation's author?

Upon inspecting the crop formation, Lucy Pringle observed that not a single seed head was missing or even damaged. No rope or string could have been used to lay out this formation or tell-tale damage to the crop would be utterly evident. The half-tone, pixilated image was positively ingenious and almost unprecedented.

Lucy Pringle shared an aerial photo of the formation with computer expert Paul Vigay, who immediately recognized the disc as containing a binary-coded series of digits that could be decoded by translating the message into decimal equivalents, then comparing them to the 128 characters used in the computer language known as ASCII (American Standard Code for Information Interchange). Working as a team, Vigay and Eltjo Hasselhoff were able to translate the coded message precisely as follows:

"Beware the bearers of FALSE gifts & their BROKEN PROMISES. Much PAIN but still time. EEULEVE. [Damaged word?] There is GOOD out there. We OPpose DECEPTION. Conduit CLOSING (BELL SOUND)."

On the one hand, Lucy Pringle, as well as Vigay and Hasselhoff were astounded to see that the coded message implied complete understanding of human computer coding in general, and the ASCII computer language in particular. It was evident to Paul Vigay that the familiarity with Earth-based communication systems and the overall intelligence implied by the images was much higher than they had previously witnessed in their study of CFs.

Yet, the content of the message was a little disappointing to Lucy Pringle. It just wasn't a message that seemed profound enough to originate from an entity of such a presumably high intellect, especially in light of the remarkable sophistication of the crop formation and the obvious understanding of the ASCII computer language. It was however, Pringle's deep suspicion that there was somehow more to the message than first appeared.

I must say the exact same thought occurred to me. On first appraisal, the almost random use of upper case (capital) letters seemed to be something other than poor language skills. It had to be yet another code, I thought, but after staring at it for quite some time, I could make no sense of it. Fortunately, the world contains people much smarter than I, and one of those people is Dr. Horace Drew of Sydney, Australia. Dr. Drew was able to decipher *two* coded messages in addition to the literal message that was binary-coded in ASCII.

Seventeenth century genius Francis Bacon was among the first to observe that the apparent fit of the edges of adjacent continents pointed to a time when the continents were once joined. We now call this idea, 'plate tectonics.' Francis Bacon is also suspected of being the true author of all the brilliant plays that are wrongly attributed to the relatively uneducated actor named William Shakespeare. Francis Bacon was also the inventor of stegenography; that is, the hiding of one message inside another.

For a few years after its discovery, the full meaning of the Crabwood glyph was unrecognized. This finally changed in 2006 when, in an attempt to decipher a hidden meaning in the glyph, Dr. Horace Drew suspected that he was seeing an example of Francis Bacon's stegenography. Dr. Drew suspected that there was a coded message hidden in the false capitalization of the Crabwood disc, and maybe even more than one. In a stroke of brilliant simplicity, Dr. Drew converted the upper and lower case letters to the same binary code as was manifest in the ASCII-encoded message. The second code emerged as Dr. Drew attempted to resolve the damaged word "EEULEVE", which he ultimately achieved by employing a simple substitution.

There were fifty-two examples of false capitalization in the message that Dr. Drew insightfully converted to zeros and ones. Upper case letters became zeroes and lower case letters were ones. Each zero and one then stood for a series of eight digits in the ASCII binary computer language. That yielded a five-by-five binary code:

11110 11001 10010 11011 11010

Dr. Drew searched other character assignments from the present and the past (such as ASCII, Baudot, CCITT2, and others) but found no clear code. So he converted the five base-2 number groups to base-10 and got:

30-25-14-27-26

It had been noticed by Dr. Drew that crop formations favored Mayan themes and even Mayan numerologies. This set of numbers derived from the false capitalization reminded Dr. Drew of another recent crop formation that he had studied at Wayland Smithy in 2005. In that situation, a series of relevant dates was derived by converting the coded number in the crop formation to base-16, as is used in the Mayans' 52-year Sun-Venus calendar.

Using the same mathematical process that seemed to yield relevant dates in the Wayland Smithy glyph, Dr. Drew divided each of the five numbers by descending multiples of 32, then added up the decimal fractions to yield the decimal fraction: 0.962367, which he multiplied by the number of days (18,980) in the 32-year Mayan Sun-Venus calendar. He took the product of this multiplication (18,265.7) and divided it by the number of days in our year (365.25) to get 50.1 years, which he observed to be the precise number of years (50.1) since the previously mentioned extraterrestrial fly-over of Washington on July 19 and 28, 1952.

While this is a rather convoluted set of mathematical manipulations that is not at all obvious, it did have a precedent in at least one other crop formation. This reassured Dr. Drew that his calculations were indeed appropriate. To bolster the view that he was applying a mathematical process that was intended by the creators of the false-capitalization code, Dr. Drew observed that there were 52 examples of false capitalization, fifty of which were contained in wholly capitalized words and 2 that were contained in partially capitalized words. With the number 52 emerging from multiple attempts to make sense of the false-capitalization puzzle, he felt confident that the hint was being given to apply the 52-year Mayan Sun-Venus calendar to the coded message.

Yet another code seemed to be hidden in the fact that extra digits appeared in the spiraling ASCII binary code. The same series of extra digits that was needed to make the original word "EEULEVE" into "BELIEVE" appeared at other intervals that were always multiples of twelve. This led Dr. Drew to derive a series of potentially relevant dates:

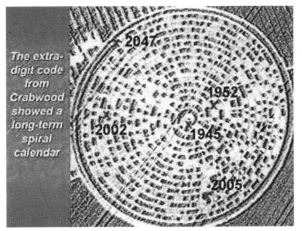

Table 1. The spiral disc from Crabwood 2002 contained yet another "extra digit" code

Location in spiral	ASCII digits= months	Extra digits	Inferred date	Significant event
0	start spiral	-----	August 6, 1945	Hiroshima
1	(12) = 1 year	(01)	August 15, 1946	Define time scale
2	9 x 8 = 72 = 6 years	(0)	July 28, 1952	"greys" over Washington
3	**75 x 8 = 600 = 50 years**	(1)	August 15, 2002	Crabwood crop picture
4	4.5 x 8 = 36 = 3 years	(0101)	August 15, 2005	other important crop pictures
5	63 x 8 = 504 = 42 years	(0)	August 15, 2047	greenhouse, other?
6	end spiral	-----	-----	-----

Dr. Drew and others have concluded, and I wholeheartedly agree, that the Crabwood crop formation of 2002 is a message to humanity that seems to reference certain important historical events that bear great relevance to our past, present, and future relationship with extraterrestrial civilizations.

Meanwhile, what about the face? Is the ominous alien face shown in the Crabwood glyph the face of the crop formation's author? Dr. Drew does not think so. Rather, the face in the Crabwood glyph is more likely the leader of the 'Greys.' Dr. Drew sees other clues in the glyph that suggest that the creator of the Crabwood CF was Quetzalcoatl, an alien visitor and god who was well-known to the Mayans. Quetzalcoatl is described as a very tall, blonde, bearded deity and teacher who often represented himself as a feathered serpent. Indeed, the image of a feathered serpent is seen in several crop formations in the recent past, and the image once again appears in the Crabwood glyph, right next to the ASCII disc.

Arrow points to the signature of the artist

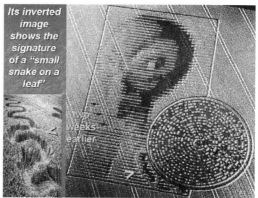

In reverse color it may be more plainly seen

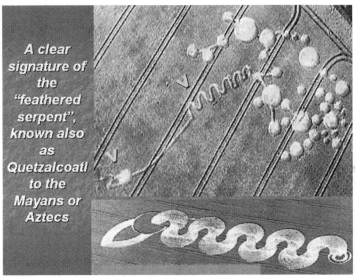

A clear signature of the "feathered serpent", known also as Quetzalcoatl to the Mayans or Aztecs

Here are other glyphs that appear to show not only the "feathered serpent" that the Mayans called Quetzalcoatl (bottom photo) , but also the location of Quetzalcoatl's native star, a faint star in the constellation Hercules.

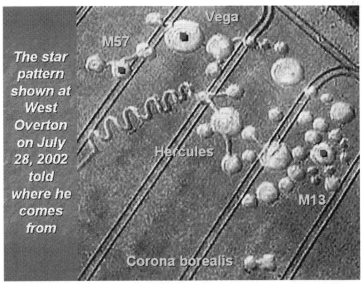

The star pattern shown at West Overton on July 28, 2002 told where he comes from

Here we see indications that Quetzalcoatl, the feathered serpent, originates from a faint star near epsilon-Hercules. Note also the proximity of this star to M-13, the globular cluster that Carl Sagan decided to the target with the Arecibo message. Note also that Vega, the first extra-solar planetary system ever discovered in 1998 is also proximitous to these other significant astronomical objects. Vega also happens to be the fictional point of origin of the extraterrestrials in Carl Sagan's 1985 novel, *Contact.*

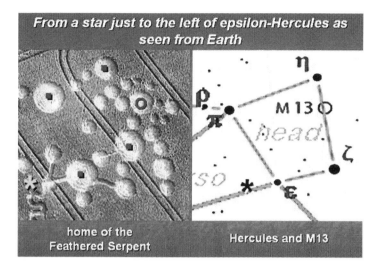

From a star just to the left of epsilon-Hercules as seen from Earth

home of the Feathered Serpent

Hercules and M13

First Contact:

In order to understand what the Crabwood glyph is attempting to convey to humanity, it is necessary to delve more deeply into the events that transpired beginning in July of 1952, when alarming and repeated UFO sightings occurred over Washington D.C.

The UFO phenomenon as we know it today stormed into the public consciousness for the first time right after World War II. Private pilot Kenneth Arnold sighted nine "flying saucers" as he called them, while flying over Mount Rainer on June 24, 1947. The publicity given to Arnold's sighting initiated a flood of similar reports in the ensuing years. Why were we suddenly of so much interest to ETs? Some even wondered at the time whether it was because we recently detonated the first and second atom bombs over wartime Japan in August of 1945. It was only a few, but there were those who speculated that our first detonations of thermo-nuclear devices were indeed events of great concern to extraterrestrial civilizations, and that these same events were the reason for the sudden appearance of all these UFOs.

If there was any truth to this speculation, then an event of even greater concern would have been the imminent development of the enormously more destructive hydrogen bomb which was being actively developed in 1952. The first successful detonation of a hydrogen bomb, code-named "Iron Mike," would ultimately occur on Eniwetok Atoll in the Marshall Islands, on November 1st, 1952. A few months prior to this infamous event, the waves of UFOs were being sighted over the U.S. Capitol and much-ballyhooed in the news media.

No ETs presented themselves for human inspection in conjunction with these initial sightings over the nation's capital. Rather their presumed craft were seen simply hovering over Washington D.C. possibly as a show of force, or possibly with the plan of following-up with a more direct meeting in the near future. In retrospect, it is easier to see that the post-World War II course of human events had taken a disturbing turn. Extremely destructive military technologies were now in the hands of humanity for the first time. In light of this fact, the benevolent ETs, particularly the 'Nordic' variety (whom the Mayans collectively referred to as Quetzalcoatl), decided that they could remain in the shadows no longer. A frank and honest discussion between human and extraterrestrial leaders *had* to occur. The ETs had an enduring interest in the evolution of humanity that dated back at least as far as Biblical times.

The meeting, precipitated by the demonstrations of our newly acquired nuclear capability, finally happened on February 20th, 1954, when President Dwight Eisenhower had his proverbial 'First Contact' meeting with at least one delegation of extraterrestrials.

While many may view the suggestion of such a meeting as fanciful at best and ridiculous fiction at least, the alleged events that surround this potentially historic event have been carefully researched and corroborated by several competent researchers, most notably by Dr. Michael E. Salla, Ph.D. In a paper published on the www.exopolitics.org website and elsewhere, Dr. Salla does a thorough job of documenting this historic, yet officially unverified set of events. The whole matter has been shrouded in secrecy for decades but discussed in print and on the electronic media to the point of becoming a mainstay of UFO folklore. Michael Salla also gathered and published the specifics on a number of individuals who have had the opportunity to view the secret documents that discuss details of not just one but *multiple* meetings between President Eisenhower and one kind of extraterrestrial or another.

As is given to happen when people who harbor huge secrets are faced with their own impending death, holders of big government secrets sometimes decide that they cannot, in good conscience, take their momentous secrets with them to their respective graves. One of the individuals who 'spilled the beans' toward the end of his life was decorated military and government figure Phillip Corso, a career soldier who served on President Eisenhower's National Security Council from 1953-1956. During his military career, Corso managed the relocation of European Jews to Israel after World War II, and he headed the investigation of missing P.O.W.s following the Korean War. He published his tell-all memoirs in the book, *The Day After Roswell* (Pocket Press, 1998) a year before his death. There are other sources that Michael Salla identifies who corroborate the same events that Corso describes as surrounding the 'First Contact' summit.

Dr. Salla's full report can be viewed by simply 'Googling': "Dr. Salla/1954 Meeting With Extraterrestrials". Essentially, Dr. Salla builds a compelling case that, on the night of February 20, 1954, while 'on vacation' in Palm Springs, California, President Eisenhower went suddenly and mysteriously missing. Eisenhower and a select entourage were spirited off to Muroc Field (now known as Edwards Air Force Base) for a prearranged, first-ever meeting with extraterrestrials. Later, by way of explaining the President's sudden absence, a cover story was concocted that the President needed emergency dental surgery to repair a broken a tooth that he sustained while eating fried chicken (!)

Ostensibly, Eisenhower met with some very human-looking extraterrestrials; the ones that are commonly described as tall, blonde, and Swedish-looking. Interestingly, this is the same description offered by the Mayans when describing Quetzalcoatl, as well as the Sumerians and many other ancient cultures who describe god-like entities that had profound influence on their respective civilizations.

Eisenhower did not attend this meeting alone. He was accompanied by a few military personnel and four elderly representatives of the religious, economic, spiritual, and newspaper communities; specifically Roman Catholic Cardinal James Macintyre of the Los Angeles archdiocese, reporter Franklin Allen of the Hearst Newspaper Group, Economist Edwin Nourse of the Brookings Institute and mystic/clairvoyant Gerald Light.

According to Salla, Gerald Light was the first to "spill the beans" of the secret meeting in a letter he sent to Meade Layne two months after the alleged meeting. In his defense, it was Light's understanding that a public announcement of the meeting was imminent. (Obviously, the military keepers of this 'big secret' had other plans.) Another whistleblower identified by Salla was William Cooper, a Naval Intelligence Commander who had access to classified documents. He described Project Sigma which first detected multiple approaching alien spacecraft on radar in 1953, followed by Project Plato, which, using binary computer language, established the contact and set up the meeting attended by Eisenhower and others at Muroc Field (Edwards AFB) in February of 1954.

At the meeting, the human attendees were first dazzled by the advanced spacecraft as well as the magical mental and physical capabilities of the ET delegation. At the meeting, Eisenhower requested that we be provided with some of these advanced capabilities that we could then use to prevail over our current Cold War arch-enemy, the Soviet Union, whom Eisenhower described as hell-bent on world domination. Having recently saved the world from fascism, the United States, at least temporarily, held the moral 'high ground'. This was presumably part of the reason why the ETs were dealing with the U.S. to the exclusion of other nations. The other reason was, of course, the recent demonstrations of our newly-acquired nuclear capability.

In any event, Eisenhower's request was rebuffed. He was informed by Quetzalcoatl (or whoever), in no uncertain terms, that we were doing an abysmal job of managing our currently held weaponry, and that we were essentially on the road to ruin. We were polluting the Earth, and recklessly depleting its natural resources at an alarming rate. In short, we just were not living in harmony with the planet and the ETs were offering to assist us with our spiritual enlightenment, which was seriously lacking. All we had to do was dismantle our nuclear arsenal. To sweeten the deal, the benevolent 'Nordics' offered to give us the secret to cheap energy, and to help rid us of the untrustworthy race of 'Grey' ETs that lurked in the shadows. (Notice: The relationship with the ETs has suddenly become very political, with each ET faction being openly disdainful of the competing ET factions. It is as though we are witnessing the emergence of extraterrestrial politics!) We are also witnessing the dawn of the 'environmental movement' as well as the birth of the New Age sensibilities that really began to find favor with at least some of humanity in the 1980s. (Ya gotta love this!)

Meanwhile, back at Muroc, "Ike", being a military man as well as a politician, politely but firmly explained that this was not a workable deal. We were currently engaged in a Cold War with a megalomaniacal adversary, and now we were faced with an additional threat in the form of potential alien invasion. We were obviously in no position to unilaterally lay down our most potent weapons systems. Eisenhower's point here is well taken, and it even seems a bit naïve on the part of the ETs to presume that Eisenhower himself even held enough power within the much larger governmental structure to enact such a dramatic step as full nuclear disarmament. Additionally, Eisenhower argued, cheap or free energy would only serve to destabilize our economy. (It won't help, but go ahead and cry over this missed opportunity the next time you pay four dollars per gallon for gasoline.) The meeting went on into the wee hours of February 21st, before it ended with no deal being struck.

Others who corroborated the view that this dramatic "First Contact" meeting did indeed take place include retired Marine Corps Sgt. Charles Suggs whose father, Navy Commander Charles Suggs (1909-1987) accompanied Eisenhower to the First Contact meeting, as well as test pilot and CIA contract pilot John Lear, son of Lear Jet inventor William Lear.

Another whistleblower, Robert Dean, who served at the Supreme Headquarters Allied Powers Europe, had access to classified documents while serving under the Supreme Allied Commander of Europe. Documents that Dean claimed to have seen described four different races of ETs, one being the Greys, and another being a very human group that looked just like us. Another group was very tall (up to eight feet or more), very pale, humanoid, and no hair. The final group was reptilian, vertical pupils in the eyes, and scaly skin. According to Dean, these were the four alien races that were known to exist as of 1964. Since that time, I might add a fifth variety of ET has been repeatedly claimed, and that is the big, hair covered 'wookies' that we also call the 'sasquatch.'

In any event, as Dr. Salla concluded from his extensive research, that the 'First Contact' meeting was a bust. Not only had no agreement been reached, but things were about to take a turn for the worse. Later that same year, in November of 1954, a *second* meeting with an ET delegation took place. This time it was at Holloman AFB in New Mexico, and this time it was with the menacing 'Greys' that the 'Nordics' had warned us not to trust. The Greys described themselves as originating from a red star in the constellation Orion that we know as Betelgeuse. The Greys announced that they too wanted to strike a political deal. The deal was that we would be given some advanced technology and in return, the Greys would be permitted to conduct *limited* experiments on cattle *and* human beings. To Eisenhower, this seemed like a pretty good deal, though it was stipulated by 'our side' that these human experimental subjects were to be in all cases returned unharmed, with their brains wiped clean of all memory of any trauma. Further, a list of all the abducted humans was to be dutifully provided to the U.S. government.

The Greys couldn't say "yes" fast enough. They added one final stipulation that was completely agreeable to the American military: the entire deal must remain forever a secret. The deal was struck, and a treaty was supposedly signed by the President, making the U.S. the exclusive beneficiary of this 'deal.' In hindsight, we can plainly see that the cost of this cool new technology would be borne by the portion of the U.S. citizenry that was 'sold down the [galactic] river' for purposes of experimentation. Perhaps, Eisenhower had already been desensitized to this idea, in light of his military background. Ike had personally seen the remains of much more horrifying atrocities that Nazis perpetrated upon humans in the name of experimentation during the war. By comparison, this abduction and experimentation probably did not seem too serious.

In reflecting upon this diplomatic disaster, Phillip Corso observed that, from a purely military point of view, Eisenhower's agreement with the Greys was more of a negotiated surrender than a treaty, per se. We are even told that Eisenhower felt a bit cornered by the Greys at the time, to the point of uttering words to the effect that, "You're so powerful, how can we even stop you?"

To this, the members of the Grey delegation ostensibly replied, "You can't."

According to another whistleblower, Phillip Schneider, who worked on numerous black projects and subterranean bases for the U.S. military, the eventual treaty that was signed with the Greys was called the 1954 Greada Treaty, and it, of course, was never ratified by Congress (as the U.S. Constitution requires). Not so surprisingly, Dr. Salla's sources assert that, as early as 1955, it began to emerge that we had indeed been deceived by the Greys, just as the benevolent but naïve 'Nordics' had warned. The advanced technology we had been given, whatever it was, did not work as promised. Further, according to our own intelligence sources, human abductions were taking place far in excess of the 'limited number' that was agreed upon. Still worse, some of the abductees were not being returned as promised, *and* (not surprisingly) no list of abductees was ever provided to our government by the Greys.

Now it is Eisenhower's turn to appear tremendously naïve. Did he really expect that he would be provided with lists of names, neatly typed out on a piece of paper? Were the ETs supposed to deliver the names by U.S. mail? Did Eisenhower, then, provide them with a stack of those special envelopes that say "No postage necessary if mailed within the United States," or did he just set them up with a free roll of postage stamps? As comedians like to say, "Don't get me started…"

Despite there being enough inherent absurdity in the whole situation to fuel a season's worth of situation comedy sketches, the whistleblowers are dead serious about their description of the events as they understood them. Phillip Corso characterized our 'treaty' with the Greys as a negotiated surrender. In hindsight, we were tricked into entering into a treaty with an untrustworthy ET element. In his 1997 *The Day after Roswell* memoirs, (pg. 292) he wrote:

"We had negotiated a kind of surrender with them [the Greys] as long as we couldn't fight them. They dictated the terms because they knew what we most feared was disclosure."

Yet, there are inconsistencies within Dr. Salla's sources. They do not agree on where the Greys originate, Zeta Reticuli or Betelgeuse. Salla suggests that there may be a close relationship between differing races of Greys. Some sources said the second meeting with the Greys took place at a base in Florida. Salla feels that Holloman AFB in New Mexico was the true location.

Are all the sources unearthed by Michael Salla *lying* about these 'First Contact' meetings and the Greada Treaty? Less than one year later in October of 1955, General Douglas MacArthur offered an ominous warning in a speech he delivered:

"The nations of the world will have to unite, for the next war will be an interplanetary war. The nations of the world must someday make a common front against attack by people from other planets." MacArthur kept his remarks free of specifics but he seems to have known much more than he was letting on. Why else would the Supreme Commander of the Pacific Fleet in World War II raise the specter of imminent world conflict with extraterrestrials? Even Eisenhower, upon retiring from public life, vaguely warned in a speech against the dangers that a too-powerful industrial-military complex posed to our civil liberties. He was referring to the same vast organization that now insists that the whole ET/UFO topic is off limits for official discussion, and has no validity whatsoever. Countless researchers allege, and sometimes are able to document, that there is an active campaign to confuse, discredit, and deny that there is any validity to extraterrestrials. Military and intelligence agencies on both sides of the Atlantic actively discredit whistleblowers and witnesses to extraterrestrial events. Yet, the veneer of 'plausible deniability' has begun to rot and fall away. As exoplanets by the hundreds are discovered by the penetrating eyes of the Kepler space telescope, the notion that we are sole heirs to the whole of the galaxy becomes increasingly absurd. The individuals within the government and military who hold these dramatic secrets eventually retire and die. They are sometimes replaced by a new breed that are not nearly as invested in 'protecting' the public from profound secrets that they we are somehow "not prepared to know." With time, society becomes increasingly mature in its view of our place in the cosmos. A steady diet of TV shows about ancient aliens, government cover-ups, and human abductions inoculates us against any future conflict that we will ostensibly feel when it is finally revealed that the Earth is, at the same time, a gas station, a science fair, and a tourist attraction for multiple extraterrestrial civilizations.

After the disastrous 1954 Greada Treaty was signed by Ike and the Greys, Quetzalcoatl faded into the shadows.

Yet, true to his Mayan reputation as the self-effacing trickster, Quetzalcoatl would return in the 1980s to taunt our maturing global sensibilities through an annual summer ritual of creating profoundly artistic images in English cereal crops. And that brings us back to a consideration of that which is often described by crop circle devotees as the most profound of a crop formations, the Crabwood glyph of July, 2002.

Almost to the day, on the fifty year-anniversary of that first, ominous appearance of UFOs over Washington D.C. in 1952, Lucy Pringle and others discover a glyph which Paul Vigay, Eltjo Hasselhoff, and Horace Drew then collectively decoded. And, maybe not surprisingly, it portrays, we are told, the very leader of the Greys who coerced Ike into making a bad deal, but the only real deal that Ike felt he had available to him. The rendition of the Grey leader is suitably ominous in tone, and also cleverly portrayed in a pixilated, fifty-two line image as was portrayed by all televised media of the 1950s. And the message in the disc, while not overly profound as Lucy Pringle immediately observed, seemed to reference that infamous, if disputed, 'First Contact' summit:

"Beware the bearers of FALSE gifts & their BROKEN PROMISES. Much PAIN but still time. BELIEVE.There is GOOD out there. We OPpose DECEPTION. Conduit CLOSING (BELL SOUND)."

Further, the dates encoded in the false capitalization represents second and third codes that Dr. Drew astutely decoded. His interpretation will also be disputed, but it seemed to reference matters of intra-galactic concern: the emergence of nuclear weapons, the appearance of ETs in 1952, the deceptive practices of the Greys, and the generally politicized nature of dealings with extraterrestrial entities. The 'conduit closing' seems to be a reference to a portal-like means of either viewing terrestrial matters from afar, or even physically traversing the impossibly huge distance that separate our world from the other civilizations that exist within the galaxy or beyond it.

Pure and simple, the Crabwood crop formation is a reference to the bungled 'First Contact' treaty. Without congressional ratification, it may not be utterly valid, but it really doesn't matter since nobody seems to be adhering to the elements of the treaty, anyway.

It has been suggested by some CF investigators like Richard Hoagland that the Crabwood glyph was not the work of ETs, but rather forces with the military of England or U.S. More than one CF investigator suspects that the military is in possession of something that Hoagland calls 'hyper-dimensional technology.' While this is indeed a possibility, I feel that the coded messages contained within the Crabwood glyph effectively discount this possibility. I cannot imagine that the military masterminds behind such an advanced technology would be so foolish as to craft a coded message that invited the crop circle investigators to solve it, nor would they use the message to reference an event that they have made extraordinary efforts to keep secret for fifty years. If and when the crop circle investigators did solve the codes within the Crabwood glyph, it would serve to remind the world of the bungled negotiation that resulted from the 'First Contact' meeting.

Mind you, I do not bear "Ike" Eisenhower any ill will for 'giving away the store' at this meeting, or making a bad deal with the wrong group of ETs. He and his contemporaries in the American and British militaries did indeed save the world from a future of tyranny and fascism. More than that, they did a great deal toward rendering the concept of world war obsolete. No one will ever again play a global game of 'Risk' like Hitler did. Nuclear weapons have arguably kept an uneasy peace, although there have been enough close calls for the ETs to be justifiably concerned about the fate of our nuclear-armed humanity. As much as the advanced weaponry, it is the essentially Christian ethic of NATO countries in general and the United States in particular that has kept the peace on a world level since World War II. The whole of the NATO alliance has demonstrated a commitment to the live-and-let-live principles that are espoused in both Christianity and the Mayan teachings as espoused by Quetzalcoatl. The benevolent Nordics are justified in putting their faith in the NATO countries that prevailed in World War II, if that is what they are doing.

Let us also look at the cultural significance of the entities that presented themselves for human inspection at the 'First Contact' meetings. Their superhuman capabilities would certainly have elevated them to the position of deities in the mind of any previous human era. One of the most troubling aspects of the whole ET phenomenon is that it blurs the distinction between God and aliens. The idea that extraterrestrials have had a big influence on human theology is not new. *Chariots of the Gods* author Erik Von Daniken articulated the idea in his 1968 book which was dismissed by many as pseudoscience. Others accused Von Daniken of plagiarizing earlier authors such as Robert Charroux, who published a total of five non-fiction books on the 'ancient astronauts' theme in the 1960s and 1970s. Even earlier, Brinsley LePoer Trench published a book on the subject in 1960 and Morris K. Jessop predated that with *UFOs and the Bible,* published in 1956. H.P. Lovecraft alluded to the same idea in a fictional short story, "The Call of Cthulhu", published in 1928, and again in a novella, *At the Mountains of Madness,* in 1931.

The whole idea that deities are extraterrestrials will probably always be dismissed as pseudoscience because it cannot ever be proven, and because it is seen by many as a heretical challenge to traditional human theologies, particularly the Judeo-Christian paradigm. Frankly, I never understood why this idea threatens established theologies. A careful analysis of the whole 'ancient aliens' concept may even *provide* validation of some principles of the Judeo-Christian theology. For example, the duality of good and evil, and the conflict between the competing the entities (namely 'the Greys' and 'the Nordics') mirrors the conflict between the Holy Trinity and the evil forces of Satan. Further, the distinctly Christian view that God sent his son, Jesus, to enlighten humanity and elevate their moral and ethical position is very consistent with the theologies of other cultures, most notably the Mayans, the Sumerians, and the Egyptians, all of whom speak of a very tall, very blonde teacher and 'moral compass' who lived within their respective civilizations for a very long time. If there is an analogous figure in Judeo-Christian theology to the Mayan deity Quetzalcoatl, it would have to be Jesus. The ethics and moral principles of Quetzalcoatl are virtually identical to Jesus' New Testament teachings. In multiple respects, Quetzalcoatl and Jesus are cut from the same cloth, so much so that it seems fair to at least wonder (however pseudo-scientifically) if these entities didn't originate from the same distant extraterrestrial civilization.

The analysis of crop formations also pseudo-scientifically suggests a fairly precise point of origin for this benevolent civilization, that being the small star near epsilon-Hercules that is identified by Dr. Horace Drew as the likely home of Quetzalcoatl. These respective Deities, Jesus and Quetzalcoatl, are indeed so similar that it seems possible that either they were the same Deity manifesting itself in separate cultures, or that Jesus and Quetzalcoatl were separate entities that were dispatched by the same civilization, like so many necktie-wearing Mormons riding bicycles through wormholes, on separate missions to rectify the ethical deficiencies in our emerging terrestrial civilizations.

There is at least one reassuring idea that falls out of this almost humorous suggestion. Quetzalcoatl, as described in the few pieces of Mayan literature that survived Spanish destruction, was the equivalent of the tall, blonde race of extraterrestrials sometimes called the Nordics. This could be a cause for great reassurance among people who needed to think of Jesus as a Caucasian. If Jesus was dispatched from the same realm as Quetzalcoatl, then Jesus would indeed have been a white guy. In fact, he would have been a blonde, and probably a very tall one. Amusingly, this would serve to validate all the 1950's era portraits of Jesus that I grew up around: the long-haired benevolent white guy. The revisionist thinking that Jesus was Arabic as a consequence of his place of birth can now be challenged with the admittedly pseudoscientific suggestion that Jesus and Quetzalcoatl originated from the same culture of benevolent extraterrestrials whom Eisenhower rebuffed in the First Contact meeting of 1954.

If Eisenhower attended this meeting with a contingent of wise men that included a Catholic bishop, I would expect that each of the attendees Ike invited would have been given the opportunity to ask at least one question of the ETs in attendance. I can think of no more salient question for Cardinal Macintyre to have asked than, "Was Jesus one of you?" Maybe someday we will find out if the question was asked and what the answer was, but I doubt it. Maybe, also, Ike requested a way to summons the Nordics in the future if he wanted to reopen negotiations at some future date. Doesn't every diplomatic initiative between countries include an effort to establish a "hot line"; that is a means for future communication, especially in emergencies? If this was done at the First Contact meeting, and if Quetzalcoatl and Jesus are contemporaries, then, at risk of oversimplifying, might not Ike essentially have asked for Jesus' phone number? Again, I suspect we will never know.

What may be most important of all is to take a look at the still bigger picture of how the ET phenomenon has changed and evolved over time. Mechanical spacecraft, Kenneth Arnold's flying saucers, were replaced by the benevolent 'space brothers' of the late 1940's and early 1950's. That evolved into the more sinister view of 'alien invaders' on the heels of MacArthur's warning. From there, the sinister abductee phenomenon took hold of a defenseless humanity. Then, the spurned 'space brothers' return in the 1980's with an agenda that seems to center upon on communication. And, upon analysis of that communication, as it is regularly posted in the cereal crops of the English countryside, the message seems to be a combination of education (about higher truths) and invitations to spiritually mature.

Meanwhile, we face a backlash; a resistance on the part of power centers in our own civilization, who wish to suppress any public knowledge of the existence of the highly politicized ET communities. The ETs know this and they know that things change on Earth very slowly. It is often said that, past a certain age, old people never really change their views. But as they die, they take their outdated ideas with them. Only then are they ultimately replaced by newer, more mature, more open-minded ideas. Similarly, it is said that all scientists should retire from science by age 65 because, after that, even good scientists become incapable of formulating, or even just remaining open to, any new ideas.

In order to witness the maturing of humanity, one just has to wait for the old attitudes and ideas to die, then be replaced by new thought and new ethical standards that will carry humanity forward toward a more enlightened view of the cosmos and of our place in it.

We can only hope that the forces that oppose a transformation of human ethics and spirituality will die, leaving room for the newer ideas to take root. As the Crabwood glyph both promises and warns, there is "much pain, but still time."

Meanwhile, the forces that oppose official disclose of ET contact can be expected to push back against the rising tide, no matter how futile their efforts become. Some of the courageous investigators of crop formations have died under mysterious circumstances. Paul Vigay was found dead at the age of 44, floating in the ocean off Portsmouth, on the night he broke up with his girlfriend in February of 2009. It was assumed to be suicide. No note was ever found and the case was never thoroughly investigated by English police. Lucy Pringle confided to me personally that she does NOT believe Paul Vigay was the victim of foul play. Paul took his own life, and Lucy feels his family has suffered enough.

Phillip Schneider, one of the whistleblowers whom Michael Salla relied upon for information about the 'First Contact' events, was also found dead in his Wilsonville, Oregon apartment under mysterious circumstances in January of 1996. A piece of rubber hose was wrapped around his neck.

It's possible he, too, committed suicide, but Schneider did previously express concern for his personal safety. He described numerous instances in which he was followed by ominous vans or sedans that tried to force his car off the road. Chillingly, Wilsonville is twenty miles from my home.

Am I concerned about my personal safety? Maybe I should be but I guess I have decided I don't really care anymore. Living or dead, one's life has to mean something, and the honest presentation of the most significant event in modern human history is worth any risk or any punishment I may endure for the 'crime' of discussing illegitimately-held national secrets. With or without my help, the secrets are already out. Figuratively speaking, *that* train has already left the station. The internet has taken care of that. The resistance will eventually die away and the younger, more open, more enlightened view will eventually take hold. It even appears that this agenda is being actively, if not quietly and patiently pursued by Quetzalcoatl, the 'Nordic'; our spurned 'space brother.'

I suppose the need I feel to advocate for this message also stems from the respect I feel for the perceptive and courageous work of the UFO and crop circle investigators that I have had the pleasure of contacting in the preparation of this essay. Lucy Pringle, the late Paul Vigay, Michael Salla, Freddy Silva, Colin Andrews, Horace Drew, Richard Hoagland, and many others have already done so much to force the expansion of the collective human consciousness. My life is, by comparison, a reasonable sacrifice if it can help these brave pioneers to place this profound revelation before humanity. Thanks to the work of these brilliant individuals living and dead, the transformation of which I speak is slowly, but inexorably, taking place right before our eyes.

"That one always bothered me," Lucy said of the Crabwood formation. "What you've written there…it makes sense," she said, after reading this chapter.

The one who deserves the credit, is Horace Drew. Dr. Drew cracked the code, hidden within another code, which ultimately rendered the Crabwood crop formation as the most profound crop formation of all time. Embracing the message of the Crabwood glyph will make all of humanity wiser. It will open the door to ultimate understanding of our place in the cosmos.

Crabwood of August 15, 2002 marked a 50-year anniversary of when the greys flew over Washington

"Beware the bearers of false gifts and their broken promises."

Quetzalcoatl

Chapter Eleven: Unification

The first time I ever heard a bigfoot researcher claim that he was being spied upon, I thought it was the most egotistical, self-important idea anyone could suggest. Why on earth would anyone in government give a hang about the activities of an amateur bigfoot enthusiast? Imagine my surprise then, when I unexpectedly discovered evidence that I was being spied upon.

It began with the publicity that the Skookum expedition gained, beginning in late September of 2000. Lots of media attention was given to the Skookum Cast (see Chapter 1) and I was asked to do a few presentations for the benefit of local organizations. As a supplementary visual, I made a display of photographs I shot on the expedition. I mounted the photos on one of those tri-fold boards that are used to display science fair experiments. I included some excellent illustrations by artist Pete Travers that depicted the presumed posture of the creature that left the impression in the mud at Skookum Meadow.

When I wasn't using the poster, I stashed it in my house between the wall and the back of the piano. One day, in December of 2000, I reached for the display board and it wasn't there! I was baffled. It took a lot of thinking and a lot of searching before I eventually became convinced that the board had indeed mysteriously disappeared. Once I was absolutely certain that the Skookum Cast display board had been stolen, I opened up the file drawer at my desk where stuff related to the sasquatch subject was kept. That's when I knew for certain that something suspicious had happened.

A Ziploc baggie containing a tuft of hair given to me by bigfoot eyewitness Rocky Bounds was also missing. It was impossible to accept the suggestion that I had somehow misplaced both of these items.

As baffling as all this was, I was also left with the inescapable conclusion that there was absolutely nothing I could do about it. I had no choice but to go on about my life. It still seemed like an egocentric thought that some sort of surveillance was taking place, so I never even brought it up in conversations with my colleagues in the dubious field of bigfoot research.

I put the whole mysterious episode out of my mind until December of 2001, when Allen and April Hoyt informed me that they had a telephone repairman come to their house to investigate problems they were having with their phone connection. To the great surprise of the repairman, he discovered evidence that the Hoyts' phone line had been 'tapped' (surreptitiously accessed) in two places. It was quite a surprise for the repairman. He was actually a bit shook up.

Trying to be skeptical, the Hoyts asked the repairman if it might be someone accessing their phone line for the purpose of making free long-distance calls.

"No way," insisted the repairman. "This was neat and it had been concealed. Besides, the calls would still show up on your bill."

There were no unauthorized charges on the bill. The repairman insisted he had never seen anything like it before. The evidence was incontrovertible.

Knowing that I had things disappear from my house a year earlier made it much easier to accept the Hoyt's claim of eavesdropping. Had I not had some personal precedent, I would have been much more skeptical of the Hoyt's story of wiretapping.

I even remarked to the Hoyts that, "If your phone line is tapped, mine must be, too. We're always talking on the phone about the camera experiments."

Surely, the Hoyts were a little surprised that I was so matter-of-fact about the whole affair. To them, it was a disturbing idea to think that they were being spied upon. They asked me if it might be the BFRO spying on them. I laughed.

"I don't think they're anywhere near that sophisticated," I insisted. "Nor do I think it's any other organization of bigfoot researchers. That would be giving the bigfoot research community way too much credit. I think it has to be either government or private industry, or both."

It may not be a coincidence that this second incident happened shortly after the "USA Patriot Act" was signed into law by George Bush in October of 2001.

"USA PATRIOT Act" is a backronym that stands for "Uniting and Strengthening America by Providing Appropriate Tools Required to Intercept and Obstruct Terrorism Act of 2001." Among other constitutionally dubious provisions, the Patriot Act gave law enforcement officers the power to search a home or business without the owner's consent or knowledge. It also gave the FBI the power to search computer, telephone, or financial records without a court order. All of this was done, of course, in response to the terrorist attacks on New York City in September of 2001. Surely this had no relevance to a bunch of home-grown, amateur sleuths who were forming organizations to investigate UFOs, bigfoot, ghosts, or the myriad other phenomena that may or may not inhabit the Goblin Universe. Paranormal researchers may be a quirky bunch, but they're not terrorists. The question, of course, is whether the Patriot Act was being misused to gain information on ancillary issues that might be of concern to certain folks or groups whose main concern was maintaining some financial or political advantage.

After the completion of my first book in 2003, I got a little publicity and even got some very positive reviews, but the books were not really flying off the shelves. Still, I bought a box full of books from the publisher and tried to make a few bucks selling signed copies. In the days before *Paypal*, people would send me a hand-written letter requesting a signed copy, complete with a personal check.

One such envelope happened to be lying on my desk when something about it caught my eye. It happened to be a letter from a local researcher who I knew very well. Leann McCoy lived in southeast Portland only fifteen miles from my house. She was a regular at Ray Crowe's Western Bigfoot Society monthly meetings. I picked up the envelope and studied it carefully. The edge of the envelope, next to the return address had been sliced open and resealed. I reached for the file of other envelopes I had received recently from people requesting copies. I had a letter from Judy Green, a Seattle-area researcher whom I also knew through internet communications. I was stunned. Her envelope had been sliced open on the same side and very neatly resealed with nearly invisible tape. Lane Guyot of Minnesota wrote me a letter detailing typographic errors he found while reading his copy of *The Locals*. That letter had been opened on the same end of the envelope as the others, but this time it had been resealed with glue. I now had three envelopes that bore unmistakable evidence of having been carefully and surreptitiously opened and resealed.

An epidemic of methamphetamine use in the early 2000s precipitated a whole host of crime and violence in rural Clackamas County. My neighbors occasionally reported stolen mail. Law enforcement and the postal service were warning that 'tweakers' and other criminal elements were stealing mail from unsecured rural mail boxes in search of cash, checks, or credit cards that could be easily converted to illicit income. I had not known of mail being stolen from my box, but I was certainly aware of the possibility.

We just made a point of getting the mail out of the box as quickly as possible after it was delivered, as did all the neighbors. The fact that there were a dozen mailboxes all clustered together on our string meant that diligent neighbors served as a bit of a natural deterrent.

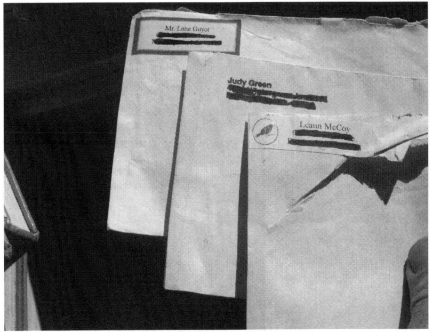

A close up of the tape used to reseal one of the letters. Note: the tape covers the return address label, indicating it was done after the letter was addressed. Three letters that bear evidence of being surreptitiously opened and resealed. The top two were resealed with 'invisible tape,' the bottom one was resealed with glue. All three letters were received between December 1st, 2003 and January 30, 2004

In hopes of resolving the mystery of the resealed envelopes, I happened to talk to one of my neighbors. Marv could see the string of mailboxes from his living room window. I was able to determine that, on the day Leann's letter arrived, the carrier had delivered the mail less than two hours before I came home from work. More significantly, Marv agreed that tweakers would never steal the mail, open it, reseal it, and put it back in the mail box. Tweakers fill a trash bag full of stolen mail, search it on a side road, take the valuable items, and then chuck the whole bag of opened mail into the nearest roadside ditch.

Leann's letter, complete with a check for $25, was intact. So was Mary Green's. Those checks would be the first things to go if tweakers were the culprit.

I took the letter to Leann's house and showed it to her. She confirmed that she had not opened and resealed the end of the letter, but she definitely agreed that that was exactly what happened. I e-mailed Mary Green and asked her if she might have opened and resealed her letter requesting a book. Definitely not. I looked over other mail that had arrived at the same time. No bills or other mail bore evidence of being opened; only the two envelopes, which were both addressed by hand.

The logical conclusion was inescapable: my mail had been searched with post office cooperation, then resealed and routed on to my mailbox. I watched my mail for a while. During that time, a few more hand-addressed requests for books arrived (with checks inside). They had not been opened. After a while I stopped checking, mostly because I also stopped caring. As far as I could tell, a total of three letters were searched.

In October of 2006 I was asked to do a presentation on bigfoot to the Portland chapter of MUFON. While they were setting up the meeting room, I happened to ask the local chapter director, Keith Rowell, whether they ever encountered reports of eavesdropping.

"Oh, sure," he replied.

"Might it be fallout from the Patriot Act?" I asked.

"It's been happening for years," he replied. "It didn't start with the Patriot Act."

"How do you deal with it?" I asked.

"What can you do? Nothing. So, you just ignore it. It eventually stops. We think they eventually get bored with us, so we try our best to be boring. But we also be sure our taxes are paid," he quipped.

Then Keith added another thought that surprised me: "We assume it's government, but we don't know. It might not be. There is another possibility that we have to consider, especially in the UFO game: the creatures themselves are doing some watching. It's similar to the government monitoring, but it originates from the degree of intelligence that exists behind the phenomenon. Basically, it's the 'men in black' phenomenon. This probably creates some confusion in the literature. It's not always easy to tell whether the monitoring results from the MIBs or real government agents/operatives."

Later, as I drove home and reflected on the entire evening, Keith's words replayed in my head. I suddenly remembered where I had heard them before. John Keel warned in his seminal volume, *The Mothman Prophecies,* that as you study the elements of Colin Wilson's Goblin Universe, they study you.

"Wow," I thought. "The Goblin Universe is a weird place, indeed."

On the positive side, at least some of the same ideas were surfacing from multiple sources. Patterns were beginning to emerge, and paranormal research is all about patterns.

I think Keith Rowell is exactly right. Eventually they get bored. You just have to wait it out. In my own experience, exactly three items of personal mail were searched. The situation never recurred, but who uses 'snail mail' anymore? E-mail is so easy to monitor that we could all be wire-tapped 24/7. One would never know.

It does seem that, if *I* noticed I was being 'monitored,' the effort must have been a pretty clumsy. I wasn't even watching for it but I noticed it. This thought leads me to suspect that the monitoring of paranormal researchers is being done by trainees. Spooks who aspire to more important work must first prove themselves on domestic targets. If one can't spy on some UFO or bigfoot researcher without being detected, his handlers certainly aren't going to turn him loose in the world of international espionage.

In July 2013, the cable TV show *Finding Bigfoot* came to town. They filmed an episode utilizing locations in Washington and Oregon. I spent a day helping as a production assistant. As they were concluding the location shooting, the producers found that they needed a few specific shots that would help clarify the story line. They were pretty generic shots of things like Cliff and Bobo setting up their tent. Since their permits to film in the nearby national forest had expired, they called me and asked if they could use the woods on my property to film the remaining handful of shots.

I had a previous commitment to take some friends on a river float that day. Cliff, on the other hand, had been out many times. He knew my property well.

"I'm busy, but you don't need me," I told producer Sean Mantooth. "Cliff can show you out. He knows the way. Your only problem will be keeping our gregarious golden retriever, and maybe a couple goats, out of your shot. Tie them up if you need to. Anyway, make yourselves at home. The gate will be closed to keep the dog in, but I'll leave it unlocked."

Inwardly, I thought to myself, "This should be interesting. Whenever these TV crews show up, something weird always happens."

My humble woods seem to have a unique attraction. I've hosted quite a few TV and film crews over the years, not to mention lots of paranormal researchers who just want to visit, and maybe enjoy a campfire. Between the springs, the lush foliage, and the deep shade created by a thick canopy of mature cedars and maples, that patch of woods has a very palpable mystique.

On two separate occasions I had visits from sensitives. I asked them to use their unique skill to get a feel for the paranormal 'potential' of the place. One of them, Bob Faust, has a reputation for being able to connect with whatever entities may be skulking about in the paranormal shadows. The other one, Tish Paquette, is actually a professional 'sensitive' who reads people's 'chakras' and things like that.

Naturally, I was most interested in any possible bigfoot presence. After lots of meditating and concentrating in the woods, Bob offered his considered assessment: "I don't know about bigfoot, but you have *ghosts* on this property...two of 'em. I'm seeing a young male, who was about twenty-years-old when he died."

"About five years ago, a twenty-year-old guy died in a single car wreck a short distance from my driveway," I offered. "Maybe that was what you're getting."

"I guess so," Bob agreed.

A year later, Tish Paquette got a nearly identical impression: "Maybe a bigfoot, definitely two ghosts."

I never thought much about it, nor did I personally experience any indications of ghosts. I did know that odd things sometimes happened, especially when people with paranormal interests came out for a visit.

It was this thought, not bigfoot, that was in the back of my mind when Sean Mantooth wanted to bring the *Finding Bigfoot* crew out to shoot a few scenes. I didn't want to be a paranormal buzz-kill so I didn't say anything except, "Fine."

I do remember thinking, "Something's gonna happen."

I was floating the river on a bright, sunny day when the crew arrived, did their shooting, and left. I never saw them. After my river trip, I was putting the boats away when Sean called. He thanked me for the use of my location and reported that shooting was very successful. In fact, they liked the location so much that they wanted to come back at sunset to get some night-time shots.

"My buddy Kirk is bringing his boss out for a picnic tonight but we'll be on the lawn. You can do whatever you want in the woods."

The *Finding Bigfoot* crew returned, did their taping, then joined us for a late-evening picnic on the lawn. We memorialized the event with a few photos (below).

Kirk Sigurdson and Renae Holland.

Matt and Renae hassling my goats

Finding Bigfoot cast, crew, and guests.

It was a memorable evening of revelry on a balmy summer night. The crew didn't stay very late. The following day would be filled with tying up loose ends as the crew prepared to leave town.

Late the next morning, I got a call from one of the assistant producers. There was a problem. The video tape that contained most of the day's work was missing. This assistant producer, who was responsible for managing the tapes, was in a panic. She wanted to know if I would look around the property, especially the woods where all the filming had been done. I kept her on the line as I walked the trails. She described the places where she thought the tape might have been lost. I did my best to cover the spots she recollected. I saw no sign of any errant video cassette.

To the whole TV crew, it was obviously a very important item. It was the net result of the whole crew's full day of work. I anticipated that they would not be satisfied with my search, so while I still had her on the line, I suggested to the assistant producer that she might want to come out and look around herself. I had some commitments that day, but if she wanted to send someone, or even a few people out to take a look around, they were certainly free to do so.

Sure enough, when I returned home later that day, there was Tyler Bounds, a friend and fellow BFRO investigator, who was now working as a location manager for the *Finding Bigfoot* team. As I pulled up, Tyler was just coming out of the woods, followed by Wilson, the exuberant golden retriever. It was a pleasure to see Tyler again. The circumstances of this visit did not leave time for reliving old times, but I couldn't help making a few jokes. After all, we had the world's first videotape abduction mystery; a videotape CE-4, if you will.

Together, we walked all the trails one more time. We searched the areas where vehicles had been parked with particular care. Still no luck. In our attempts to cover all the bases, we even discussed the possibility that it was lost somewhere inside the house, perhaps while someone was using the bathroom. Tyler sheepishly asked if he might look *inside* the house. I had no problem with that at all. We looked in the bathrooms. We lifted up the sofa cushions. We looked upstairs and downstairs.

As we walked past my desk, Tyler was studying the surroundings very carefully. I pulled open a desk drawer to reveal a pile of video cassettes of the same size as the missing one. Tyler's eyes widened. He reached out his hand, then paused and looked at me.

"Go ahead, Tyler. The guv-mint probably searched this drawer once. BFRO may as well do the same," I joked.

"I can see that these are all home video tapes. They have red bands on them. They are the same size as the missing one, but professional tapes have a gold band." In the name of thoroughness, Tyler half-heartedly rummaged through the stack of tapes. He knew what he was looking for and he knew it wasn't there.

I opened all the desk drawers, which surprised him a bit.

"Wow, Thom. I feel weird doing this, but I really appreciate your openness."

"Not a problem," I assured him. "I just want you to know that I have no desire to come between you and this tape. If I found it, I would have turned it over to you in a New York minute. It is of absolutely no value to me, but I know it represents a lot of work. Reshooting those scenes is a hassle you're hoping to avoid."

"You got that right," Tyler agreed.

To this day, the tape has never been found. The crew ended up reshooting the scenes at a park in Portland near the hotel where they were staying. I was told the woman who was responsible for managing the tapes would probably get fired. The whole matter was completely baffling to the crew.

To me, it was just another in the string of bizarre events that occurs in the paranormal nexus that *is* my property. I guess I should have warned them before they came out to do their filming. I doubt they would have believed me.

No matter. I now have a new claim to fame: I live in the only house in the world that has been searched by representatives of the U.S. Government *and* the Bigfoot Field Research Organization!

At least the BFRO asked if they could search the place. If the government had asked, I would have let them look around, too. I realize they weren't looking for any particular item. They wanted information. They wanted to know how much I knew. I still don't understand why they didn't just ask. If they had, I would have told them anything they wanted to know.

When it comes to paranormal research, I've never understood people's need for secrecy. My policy has always been one of complete honesty and openness. I will tell anyone, in or out of government, everything that I think I know. It is my only chance of verifying my observations, conclusions, and suspicions about what's really going on in the Goblin Universe.

So, as we get to the end of this book, I will freely share everything else I think I know. I invite interested readers to dispute my conclusion and share their own. It's the only way we're going to make any progress. Recall a statement I made in the introduction of this book. Alfred Wegener said that only through open and honest sharing among various scientific [and paranormal] disciplines do we stand any chance of making real progress in the quest to understand what is really going on in Colin Wilson's Goblin Universe.

Here are my conclusions. No one has to search my house or my computer to get them. Take 'em or leave 'em:

The bigfoot phenomenon does indeed appear to be just one star in a constellation of paranormal phenomena. It may be the most accessible element of the Goblin Universe since it is terrestrially based, as are we. But it also appears to me that there is actually a little more to it than that. The bigfoot phenomenon does seem to emanate from within the Earth, exactly as Jim Brandon speculated in *The Rebirth of Pan*. But unlike Brandon's view that the living Earth Mother *creates* the bigfoot spirit phenomenon to notify us that our lifestyle is out of balance, I feel that the bigfoot largely reside within the Earth in the vast complex of subterranean enclaves that are tangible, physical installations. They were constructed a long time ago by a consortium of extraterrestrial species who still use them.

The tailings of this vast construction project can be found throughout the Earth's surface. They manifest themselves in the mysterious Mima mounds, the so-called Indian mounds, and the Neolithic mounds of Europe and elsewhere. Such mounds are now observed in countless locations on every continent. Based on the efforts to determine the ages of some of these mounds, I suspect that at least some subterranean complexes were constructed between 15,000 years before present (b.p.) and 7000 years b.p. There is one beneath Mt. Shasta or very near it, as well as around other Cascade strato-volcanoes like Rainier and Mt. Adams. The Yakama Indians have known this for a long time. There's one in Ohio or Pennsylvania, one in the Four Corners region of the American southwest, one in southern England, and probably a whole bunch of other places around the globe.

Many of the modifications that were made to planet Earth were performed on the backs of the sasquatch. The sasquatch are a product of genetic manipulation by extraterrestrial civilizations. The sasquatch were installed on the virgin Earth, essentially to perform the 'heavy lifting' that was necessary to adapt the Earth to suit the ambitions of these extraterrestrial entities. Not to make us humans sound any better than the sasquatch, for we too represent a genetic manipulation that was installed on Earth, just as a gardener plants a crop in the freshly tilled spring garden.

Recall the nineteenth century words of Charles Fort: "The Earth is a farm." To that I add, "And we are the crop."

Abductees are being routinely taken as a source of genetic material, which leaves the planet for some uncertain world or worlds. Mercifully, most, but not all abductees are returned to their blissfully unaware existence once their genetic material is harvested. Some are not. The same abductees are accessed again and again. The abductee thing may even extend across generations. Why wouldn't it? If one finds a source of good genetic material, why walk away from it?

One wonders whether the ones who are not returned remain alive and aware of their surroundings and whether it is pleasant or not. Any transition must be a traumatic one, to say the very least, but it does not make sense that humans would be held in miserable isolation in some distant alien zoo. We don't like seeing animals looking miserable in zoos. We want to see them looking happy, doing natural animal things like reproducing and raising young. Remember Miri's impression of her ET handlers. They regard us, almost disdainfully, as wildlife; slightly germy wildlife.

Meanwhile, the sasquatch tend the farm, generally keeping an eye on things, watching for pests, and reporting problems to the owners of the agricultural business. The garden needs occasional weeding and thinning or the crop gets out of control. Not only was the subterranean realm built on the backs of the sasquatch, but they are also the custodians of the biome.

Not all the sasquatch kowtow to the proverbial 'alien agenda.' Some may go rogue, especially in their later years, and take up permanent residence in the forests and mountains of the Earth's surface. Other sasquatch that retain their access to the vast subterranean enclaves do indeed kowtow to an agenda that is not of their own choosing.

The subterranean realm has many access points: lava caves like the ones in Big Lava Beds, limestone caves in many parts of the world, and submerged access points like the famous one in the Santa Catalina Channel. It is possible that portals and worm holes serve as gravity tunnels that connect us to other worlds or other dimensions, but it is equally possible that they simply connect the surface to the underground realm. People like Larry Kelm who entered a portal and lived to tell about it describe a place of diffuse, indirect light. Hopi legend describes the Third Realm, the subterranean world, as a place that is illuminated in precisely the same way. The Ancestral Puebloan kivas may be nothing more than connections to this Third (subterranean) Realm. Once the Anasazi earned their figurative construction merit badges by constructing the great pueblo complexes, they returned to the Third Realm to resume supervision of the real construction project, which is Earth's underground realm. The Earth *is* alive, as Jim Brandon speculates, but rather than being a single living entity, it teems with inner life like an ant hill or gopher colony. The Mima Mounds were built by a type of 'gophers' after all. These gophers happen to be very intelligent and very mobile, and the actual dens, logically, were a lot farther from the tailings, and a lot bigger, than anyone supposes.

People who have witnessed multiple ET entities on presumed spacecraft also report sometimes seeing sasquatches aboard the same crafts. One such eyewitness even stated that she saw a sasquatch sitting in a chair, casually reading a human newspaper. It is certainly an amusing, if unverifiable concept. They keep up on human activities by scrutinizing our media. (Maybe that's where it goes when my newspaper disappears from the paper box.) In any event, whenever the sasquatch are observed to be interacting with other extraterrestrial species, the sasquatch do not ever seem to have any kind of supervisory role. Rather, they are seen as the subservient ones; the underlings and the laborers.

Clairvoyant New Agers sometimes say sasquatch claim responsibility for the Neolithic structures that dot the European landscape. Americans are generally unaware of how many Stonehenge-like structures, mostly smaller but still impressive, are found throughout the European landscape. And it does not end there. Impossibly ambitious prehistoric temples and pyramids on almost every continent bear silent witness to the enduring efforts of some sort of beings who appear to possess superhuman strength.

When the sasquatch are accidentally witnessed in North America, it is often in some of the continent's most scenic locations. Could the sasquatch be given time on the terrestrial surface to enjoy the sights before they have to resume their arduous subterranean chores? I think so. Perhaps, after a lifetime of servitude, they are given freedom to venture around the surface during retirement. Perhaps the surface is also a place to raise the young before they come of age.

Whether or not the sasquatch inhabit the subterranean world, there can be no real doubt that such a place does indeed exist. Virtually all Native American cultures tell of such a place, and most see it as their place of origin. They may not be able to show verifiable proof of such a place, but the citizens of these cultures were not stupid, either. I suspect that their oral histories and mythologies are based on fact, not imagination. The consistencies are just too numerous and the logic is just too compelling.

Recognition of this profound concept also serves to unify the various paranormal events that are too often seen as somehow separate from each other. The subterranean realm is the not just a single meeting point or clubhouse for extraterrestrials, but rather a complex of enclaves that may entail entire villages or even cities.

Shows that discuss UFO sightings and ancient aliens positively abound these days on cable TV. They often assert that ETs visited Earth in ancient times and will someday return. When they do return, it is asserted, the greatest impact it is likely to have on humanity is that their reappearance on the scene will greatly destabilize religious views throughout the world. It is supposed that religious organizations throughout the world will become obsolete.

I seriously doubt that is accurate. Indeed, I think the *opposite* is actually much closer to the truth. But first, it must be observed that, in order to return, something would have to have left, and the ETs, once they arrived, never really left. They do a pretty good job of staying out of sight most of the time, but they are still very much here. There most certainly are more than a few ETs that are living among humanity and that is one of the not-so-closely held secrets that multiple governments know.

ETs stay out of sight as Enrico Fermi's zoo hypothesis suggests, but if they ever decide to manifest themselves more overtly, one of their first orders of business will be to endorse the teachings and principles of multiple world religions. The only religions that have anything to fear from a wider recognition of ET presence are the institutions constructed by charlatans or by those who profit from cults of personality. The true and moral teachings of Buddha, Allah, Yahweh, Vishnu, Jehovah, Jesus, Quetzalcoatl, and others will be validated as the direction that humanity must continue to pursue.

Religion will be the conduit, as it always has been, through which we will be afforded greater access to, and dialogue with our creators. It appears that there is indeed more than one entity that presides over human affairs. There is even a degree of conflict between competing entities, as The Bible has always held. In this sense, exopolitics do underlie not only extraterrestrial, but spiritual affairs. Any way you slice it, politics matter, even in the Goblin Universe.

Perhaps the best thing about teaching eighth graders is having the opportunity to witness the moment when children first acquire adult sensibilities. It's as if they are escaping a mental cage and allowed to experience the intellectual world they inhabit for the first time. Suddenly, they know how to talk, think, act, and joke with adults on an adult level. It becomes possible to treat at least some eighth grader as colleagues, not subordinates.

World recognition of the ET presence that already surrounds us will have the same transformational effect on humanity at large. This will serve to elevate our sense of accountability for the way we treat each other and our precious planet. We will have a new and greater understanding of who God really is, and what God expects of us. Like the suddenly more mature eighth-graders, we may be afforded the opportunity to dialogue with God on something closer to a collegial level. What a concept!

I'm pretty sure that, when this happens, Quetzalcoatl will invoke and embrace the concepts that have been espoused by humanity's true and moral religions. Religions, not government, will be the conduit though which we will be afforded the opportunity to dialogue with, our Creator or creators. The only thing that will change is the way we define God. The concept of a spirit entity may change into something or someone more tangible and more physical in form, but every bit as moral and spiritual as ever.

Until this happens, we will soldier on as blissfully unaware and slightly germy wildlife. Some of us will keep pushing the envelope of human awareness. I know I will. Others will deny it, resist it, and struggle to maintain the *status quo* that appears to serve and sustain their perceived advantage. As the kids say these days, "Haters gonna hate."

I will offer one final piece of intel that I have acquired in my years of paranormal research. As one probes the Goblin Universe in the search of better understanding, it is possible to get in way over your head. Field researchers like Toby Johnson, Kirk Sigurdson, Larry Kelm, and others have occasionally been confronted by an entity or entities that did not seem to have their best interests at heart. Such people sometimes report that they were being pushed in a direction that would result in their immediate demise. In those situations, the only important thing to know is how to get the *hell* out of there, and according to people who have been there, here is how you do it:

Say loudly and with conviction, that *you know Jesus*, that you are friends with Jesus and that he protects you. Invoking other deities like Jehovah, Vishnu, or Allah may also work, but I am told, by people who claim to have been in situations of supreme and palpable dread, the name of 'Jesus' works best. If you use that name and use it with conviction, the danger will suddenly cease. Apparently, the demonic presence will be forced into retreat by nothing more than a little well-timed name dropping, as long as you drop the right name.

From a purely scientific point of view, I cannot say why this is so, but if the situation is dangerous enough, it doesn't really matter *why*. The only thing that matters is that it works, and according to those who claim to have been in such situations, using the name 'Jesus' will definitely help you get your ass out of there in one piece.

This last chapter is essentially a set of unverifiable conclusions and some daring predictions. If they are ever going to be verified, it will only happen if we someday get to meet some ETs and ask them what they know that we do not. If that ever happens, will someone please bring up these predictions and let me know what is said about them?

In a nutshell, it is my abiding suspicion that the most, maybe all of the various paranormal mysteries that we confront are somehow intertwined. If there is any truth to unification of paranormal phenomena, the ETs ought to know about it. Time will tell.

Spooks working for certain governments, particularly the United States and Great Britain, did in the recent past, engage in misinformation campaigns intended to 'take down' the ET topic in general, and the crop circle phenomenon in particular. They really believed that the whole phenomenon would eventually go away. If they just kept up the disinformation long enough they would succeed, and the push for disclosure of truth would also go away.

It didn't. Crop formations not only didn't go away, but they became more numerous and more complex. Crop formation research proliferated. It became increasingly apparent to those who studied them that genuine CFs are indeed extraterrestrial in origin. It now appears that, through crop formations, UFO sightings, and other phenomena, we are on a path toward eventual acknowledgement and even interaction with the extraterrestrials who probably guide terrestrial matters from the dimensional shadows.

Meanwhile, the admirable efforts of mostly British crop circle investigators like Lucy Pringle (and many others) deserve our support. We owe these people a debt of gratitude. They continue to scrutinize crop formations with trained eyes, verifying genuine CFs and making efforts to decode the profound messages that are embedded in them. The importance of this work cannot be overstated. Humanity is being led toward a greater awareness of the guiding extraterrestrial presence here on Earth. We are headed toward a more mature cultural view of the extraterrestrial phenomenon and it will clarify and support existing human theology.

Efforts within government to conceal these facts have failed, and they are largely dissolving away. They tried but they lost. They lost because the pursuit of honesty and truth has been relentless. That truth is that we are being led toward an elevation in human awareness and a greater awareness of our place in the galactic community. Answers are coming but not from science. The answers to the most important questions are just beyond the edges of science.

Appendices

Appendix 1:

Drawing the line on offensive place names

Published on August 16, 2010 at Oregonlive.com

By Thom Powell

The Oregonian's story on the removal of offensive place names was interesting and accurate -- mostly. A few additions: The modern-day movement to change offensive place names began with an Oprah Winfrey show in 1992. A guest on her show declared that use of "squaw" as a place name was offensive. The Oregonian's story explained that the word was derived from an Algonquian name for "woman." More accurately, the translation is said to be something on the order of "female reproductive parts."

Algonquian as a tribal language was spoken only in the northeast corner of the U.S. and Canada. Three quarters of the continent's tribes did not recognize the word at all, much less regard it as something offensive. Nineteenth century linguists may have incorrectly translated the word as a more general reference to female Indians. Being easy to pronounce and remember, it was then carried across the continent in the minds of explorers, trappers and settlers who were completely unaware of any implied insult associated with the term.

They were a hardy bunch, but the early settlers were not always literate, and they definitely weren't politically correct. They doubtless used disparaging terms for females of all races, including their own. Yet, "squaw" was not meant to demean or offend when it was assigned to plants (squawberry, squawroot), places (Squawback Ridge, Squaw Butte), and people, male or female. Interestingly, a white man who took an Indian bride was a "squawman."

Consciousness-raising began with a 1992 episode of the daytime talk show "Oprah." Guest and Native American activist Suzan Harjo appealed for change to demeaning names used by professional sports teams (think: Washington, Cleveland and Atlanta) even though such names are intended to convey generally positive images of warrior-like fierceness.

In any case, Harjo bolstered her position by invoking other linguistic insults such as use of the word "squaw." Not being an expert in Algonquian herself (she is Cheyenne), Harjo cited a 1972 book, "Literature of the American Indian," in which the authors raised the dubious claim that the word referenced female genetalia in the Naraganset dialect of the Algonquian Nation.

In truth, it is not at all clear which of several words has been anglicized into "squaw," but "eskwaw," "esqua" and "ojiskw" are all possibilities. Other Algonquian tribes used "squa." By the way, the Algonquian term for white settlers was "wasichu." How would that do as a team name? Anyone want tickets to see the Washington Wasichu play?

In any event, leave it to explorers and settlers to phoeneticize and simplify tricky pronunciations, then carry them westward, but the story probably doesn't end there. No Indian in western North America ever named a place using Algonquian terms, but white explorers and settlers may have.

Why places such as the remote Squaw Butte in Clackamas County would be so named is less clear. Did an explorer see a female Indian there? That's possible, but I doubt it. My own research suggests that another Indian term in use more locally may have been confused and simplified into the handier term "squaw."

Squaw Butte sits within the lands once occupied by the Clackamas band of the Chinook Indians. Nearby, the Kwakiutl Indians of the

Pacific coast used the term Tsonoqua. This term, also spelled "Tsonokwa," translates into "a wild, very hairy female being with big feet."

Another put down? I don't think so. Rather, it's a reference to a female "sesquac" or sasquatch, as we call them today. The "tsonoqua" was a female bigfoot, and while the concept of the sasquatch or bigfoot is much ridiculed in modern society, the Indians in virtually all parts of North America had terms to describe these elusive and mysterious beings. As it turns out, Squaw Butte lies in a remote location in the Mount Hood National Forest where the legend of the sasquatch persists to the present.

Pioneering research on this point, done by Molalla resident Frank Kaneaster, even identifies Squaw Butte as being at the center of a cluster of modern sasquatch sightings. My own research bolsters Kaneaster's dubious data set with two more sightings by local hunters who emphatically claim that a sasquatch is what they saw while hunting the flanks of Squaw Mountain.

When one examines the places in Oregon alone that bear (or once did) the name "Squaw", they all bear an interesting similarity: They are remote, even by today's standards, and so were even more remote in the days of early wasichu (white) settlement. They are surrounded by other place names that hearken of the mysterious wild beings: Devil's Ridge, Devil's Lake, Skookum Lake, Tarzan Springs, Skookum Meadow, Diablo Mountain and more.

Virtually all North American tribes embrace the wildman or sasquatch phenomenon. They uniformly regard these beings not as animals but people, member of a mysterious but very real tribe. And if the sasquatch, or skookums, exists then there are females, for which one of the local terms was Tsonoqua. This is a more likely origin for the word "squaw" when referencing remote geographical places in the Pacific Northwest that were actually named by the Indians, not the wasichu.

I guess it doesn't matter anymore. The Forest Service has removed the name from the creek and its parent butte. It is now known as Tumala Creek and Tumala Butte, which, in the Klamath dialect, means either "wild plum" or "cold water," depending on which translation one accepts. A strange choice considering the Klamath Indians didn't live around here, and the name "Tumalo" is already prominent in central Oregon. It's also kind of a boring name. I mean, "Coldwater Creek"? "Wild Plum Butte"? C'mon, guys, is that the best you could do? If we're going to change the name, how about reverting to "Tsonoqua"? It's probably the original name for the place, and laugh if you will, but the place does have a history of reported sasquatch encounters to back it up. The Indians don't laugh, but they don't discuss their feelings on the subject with the wasichu either. They know all too well our tendency to label unfamiliar beings as animals, then use that as an excuse to shoot them.

Tsonoqua may be an old name, but it is not as easy to spell or pronounce as is "squaw." The nice thing about "Tsonoqua" is that if some of the locals don't like it, they can just slur it, and it will sound like the traditional wasichu name. That's probably the way Squaw Butte got its name in the first place. Now, if I could just get on "Oprah," I know I could change people's minds.

Thom Powell lives in rural Clackamas County and teaches sciences at Robert Gray Middle School in Portland. He is the author of "The Locals: A Contemporary Investigation of the Bigfoot/Sasquatch Phenomenon."

Appendix 2: Beckjord

Erik Beckjord, America's most enigmatic bigfoot researcher, died of prostate cancer in 2008. During the three decades that he was involved in the field of bigfoot research, he was an irritant; a fly in the ointment, to those who pursued the subject seriously. His website was hyper-critical and shrill in tone. In my days as a BFRO curator, Matt Moneymaker advised me not to interact with him or respond to his tireless attempts to engage others in argument and circular debate. He would phone-call at inconvenient times, and even call peoples' place of employment just to rebuke a person's interest in the bigfoot topic for the benefit of their employer! His tactics definitely crossed the line into the realm of harassment.

After publication of *The Locals* in February of 2003, he called frequently. Even my kids knew who Erik Beckjord was. If I wasn't home, he would engage my daughter in conversation, asking her where she went to school, where I worked, and so forth.

On one such unsolicited, late night phone call, Erik demanded to know why I used so many of *his* thoughts and ideas without giving him any credit in print. I decided I'd been polite long enough. This time, I took the bull by the horns.

"You don't have a job, Erik, but you keep up your campaign of irritation. You do your best to trivialize the whole bigfoot topic and annoy everybody in the research community. I know you get money from an outside source. Before I answer any more of your questions, why don't you answer one simple question: Who funds you?"

"I can't tell you. They want to remain anonymous," was his predictable reply. "They don't want their name dragged through the mud."

"Well, isn't it ironic that this person asked you, of all people, to protect their good name? You've made a career out of flinging mud on people's names. Ask Paul Freeman. Ask Loren Coleman. Ask Henry Franzoni. Ask Bobbie Short. I'll be honest with you, Erik. You do such a good job of making bigfoot researchers look bad that a lot of us up here [in Oregon] think you're paid by some entity in government or industry to 'take down' bigfoot research."

"Nope," he replied. "It's just a person who wants to remain anonymous. It could be the Sultan of Brunei. He just doesn't want his name out there."

"Did it ever occur to you that, if you *were* being paid by some alphabet soup agency like CIA or NSA that they wouldn't tell you who they really were? They don't work that way, Erik. You know that. And, if they wanted to screw up the whole bigfoot research effort, they wouldn't put a 'mole' in there, because there's an easier way. All they need to do is identify the guy who is causing the most commotion and chaos already. Then they fund his efforts. I think that's exactly what's going on.

"I don't believe for a minute," I continued, "that they'd tell you who is *really* covering your expenses. Some spook printed up a business card and told you he was a rich philanthropist and that he thinks you're a groovy dude. After he's stroked your ego a bit, you get handed a check, drawn on a Cayman Islands bank, no doubt. Then you're put to work fighting whatever proxy war they want fought. In this case, your job is to maintain the internecine squabble in the bigfoot research community. And, they picked the perfect person because, like nobody else, you do a great job of keeping everybody at loggerheads. You make sure no agreement, and therefore no progress, ever happens. You know, Erik, if you *aren't* paid by the government to take the bigfoot subject down, you *should* be. I hope you're not working for free, 'cuz you're definitely giving somebody their money's worth."

Long silence.

Usually, a conversation with Beckjord ends when you decide to hang up. This was the first and only time Erik ended the conversation.

"I gotta go," Erik declared, flatly.

That was February of 2004 and it was the last time I ever spoke with Beckjord. Strangely, a month later, 3/4/2004, a review of *The Locals* was posted on Amazon.com by none other than Erik Beckjord. It's still there.

Shortly thereafter, Beckjord ceased to be such a presence in the bigfoot sub-culture. In 2008, he died.

He liked to talk about his high IQ and the fact that he was a member of MENSA. I will concur that, despite his mercurial personality, he was a bright guy. He told me in 2003 that he too was working on a book. I don't think it was ever completed.

At this point, I bear Erik no ill will. His unique perspectives have been preserved in this document that he first circulated in 2005.

Rest in peace, Erik Beckjord

Beckjord's BIGFOOT RESEARCH MAXIMS AND GUIDELINES

1) Understand that this is a weird being that does not follow our rules.
2) Screams and yells do not mean danger, no matter how close. (We had two, fifty ft on each side, scream at once.)
3) The creatures never harm anyone, ever, in all of history.
4) Rocks thrown do not hit you.
5) Knocks on walls do not mean harm.
6) Bf will usually run away, not towards you.
7) There are no "bluff charges"... these are not gorillas.
8) No physical trap will work. These are not bears and not beavers.
9) Most camera traps do not work, usually.
10) You can't go to bigfoot, bigfoot must come to you - my quote: 1976.
11) You must be in good bigfoot areas, however.
12) Best results will happen around your camp.
13) Try recorded baby cryings, and bigfoot yells on a big speaker.
14) Leave dogs at home. They may be hurt.
15) Bring kids and women.
16) Make lots of noise, like rock and roll.
17) Cook lots, with fried foods.
18) Leave extra packsacks out with food in them, tied up at tops.
19) Do not bring guns.
20) Do not bring guns
21) Do not bring guns --for ANY reason. If you are afraid of the 1/2 % chance of cougar attack, then go home.
22) Leave a tape recorder running 24/7. Bring lots of tape.
23) If you are really, really, really brave, sleep away from main camp and let yourself be kidnapped. So far, kidnappees, five, have survived, and returned.
24) Do not expect much from night vision or thermal cameras. Try it, but there may be no results.
25) Spend time in camp inside tents, napping. In pairs, let one be awake, other asleep. BF may walk thru the camp.
26) If you see bf closely, do not run - they are faster than you. Be calm, and watch.
27) Do not let kids go off alone.
28) Take lots of "random" photos, day and night. BF often shows up in them later. (We got 17!) Steve Williams got a good one, also. Was watching his wife and kids.
29) Do not expect to see and photograph one. Of course, it might happen.
30) Avoid digital still cameras. USE 35MM FILM.
31) Take digital video, or, even better, 16mm film camera like Patterson's.

32) If enough crew, have one with color still film, another with b&w still film, another with B&W infrared film, another with tape recorder and one with film or video camera.

33) Try wood knocking.

34) Beware of ruffled grouse -- they sound like wood knocking.

35) Rarely, a bf has come up to campfire and sat down (very rare). Stay still, and make mental notes.

36) Even more rarely, a female bf has come up to a male human, "in heat". (Ultra rare-). If you accept, assume doggie style and have an experience no one today has ever had. No cigarette after. Lol!

37) Set out trade items -- whole fish, tobacco, chocolate, bananas, apples, fruit, dead deer. See what they leave. Maybe firewood.

38) There will be no Jane Goodall interaction.

39) There will be no sit-down-and-talk interaction. (prove me wrong).

40) You can't tame them.

41) You can't capture them.

42) You can't kill them....ever ---- (prove me wrong -- well .. don't even try....you'll usually freeze up and not fire)

43) Bring sacrificial rabbits. Put out in cages.

44) Maybe a goat or two. Bring horse trailer for that.

44a) Sounds you may hear of owls, or birds, or other animals... may be BF making them.

44b) However, BF is not the Blair Witch. Relax.

44c) You may smell smells that seem to come after you...this is BF. projecting smells.

44d) You may get paralyzed in your sleeping bag and cannot get up to look out. BF is doing this. It will pass.

44e) Strange "people" may come into your camp ... even little girls with hypnotic eyes. This may be Bigfoot in a shape-shifting mode. Don't grab them. Do not touch. Be friendly, offer food. Try for a pic. Maybe ask them if they are from another world, or such. They will be weird or dingy. Never get demanding or nasty. Do not turn your back-or they may disappear, in 1/2 second. The Lord of the Rings is real.......Gandalf is everywhere.

45) To locate BF, sit in bars, make friends, pass out business cards with your HOTLINE NUMBER ON IT.

46) Integrate in to the community in a town near a good area. Get folks to trust you. Say you are NOT armed. Bring photos and tapes of bigfoot to show. Lecture to them at a set place and time. (Town Hall).

47) Meet the cops. Know them.

48) One person in each village KNOWS EVERYBODY. Find that person.

49) Meet the mailman. Go on local TV. Go on local radio. Give out your number

50) Also preachers.

51) Live there a month if possible. Rent a cabin. Or rent one and come back weekly.

52) Do not go about in ATVs at night. Let April Williams do that. :-)

53) Go out in snow... as soon as it stops. Cruise the back roads, look for tracks. Bring snowmobiles on a trailer if you can. Bring snowshoes. Bring parkas,etc. Thermos of hot coffee. Food.

54) If you follow tracks (Brian!) videotape them as you go, from start, or videotape your leader from behind him/her.

55) Measure snow trax, and also take stills. Measure stride as well.

56) Talk to camera, make commentary.

57) IF YOU FIND TRACKS 'ENDING" be sure to videotape that carefully. Show there are no tracks further and no trees to jump into, nor rocks to jump onto. MAKE VIDEO AND STILLS. VIDEOTAPE THE WITNESSES AND TAKE STILLS OF WITNESSES. Because the backward bfers will challenge you and call you a liar. (Brian!) Get names on videotape. Full names, and interview each one.

58) Ditto for where tracks "start" with no previous tracks or entry to a milling-about zone.

59) If Todd Neiss shows up, videotape him and then give him a beer, ask him to chill.

60) Report everything to the Bigfoot Investigation Project (aka SRP) 415-289-6666.

61) EXPECT TO SPEND MONEY. Bigfoot research is never free. We've spent over $60,000 (at least) over the years.

62) Your wife may leave you. Are you ready for that?

63) Do not expect to get rich from this.

More ---T.B.A.

" Due to too much spam, I am asking friends and contacts to send email to me at rudy@stealthaccess.net --- thank you.

About the author

Edges of Science is Thom Powell's third book. Previously he published *The Locals: An Investigation of the Bigfoot Phenomenon,* in 2003. That book quietly revolutionized the field of bigfoot research, pioneering the concepts of habituation, aversion to cameras, human levels of intelligence, and other ideas that had not been published up to that point. These same ideas now reside in the mainstream of thought on this still-mysterious subject.

Thom published the novel *Shady Neighbors* in 2011. In that story, a rural-living family notices a series of strange occurrences that leads them to embrace the idea that they have some mysterious neighbors who share their concern about imminent changes to their rural landscape. The discoveries Thom wrote about in *The Locals* become plot elements in this light-hearted story sprinkled with autobiographical elements.

Thom grew up in Shaker Heights, Ohio. He was very active in scouting and earned his Eagle Scout rank in 1971. He graduated from Ohio State University in 1979. He was a whitewater guide for many years, beginning in West Virginia in the 1970s, then migrating to the western rivers of Idaho, Oregon, and California, in the 1980s. Thom remains an avid whitewater boater and fisherman, raising his family along the Clackamas River in western Oregon. Thom was the first to bring a revolutionary kind of stunt kayak, known as the squirt boat, to the western U.S. in 1985, as a consequence of his friendship with kayaking genius James E. (Jimmy) Snyder during his years in West Virginia.

Thom has taught Earth/Space Science for the past thirty years at Robert Gray Middle School in the Hillsdale neighborhood of southwest Portland, Oregon. He is well known in that community as an enthusiastic and dedicated science teacher who has inspired many of his former students to pursue science careers.

Index

379

Notes

Made in the USA
Middletown, DE
10 March 2019